Documents of the Lewis and Clark Expedition

Documents of the Lewis and Clark Expedition

C. BRÍD NICHOLSON

Eyewitness to History

An Imprint of ABC-CLIO, LLC
Santa Barbara, California • Denver, Colorado

Copyright © 2019 by ABC-CLIO, LLC

Library of Congress Cataloging-in-Publication Data

Names: Nicholson, C. Bríd, author.
Title: Documents of the Lewis and Clark Expedition / C. Bríd Nicholson.
Description: 1st edition. | Santa Barbara, California : ABC-CLIO, [2019] |
    Series: Eyewitness to history | Includes bibliographical references and index.
Identifiers: LCCN 2018030408 (print) | LCCN 2018031097 (ebook) |
    ISBN 9781440854569 (ebook) | ISBN 9781440854552 (alk. paper)
Subjects: LCSH: Lewis and Clark Expedition (1804–1806)—Sources. | Lewis,
    Meriwether, 1774-1809—Sources. | Clark, William, 1770-1838—Sources. |
    West (U.S.)—Discovery and exploration—Sources.
Classification: LCC F592.7 (ebook) | LCC F592.7 .N47 2019 (print) | DDC
    917.804/2—dc23
LC record available at https://lccn.loc.gov/2018030408

ISBN: 978-1-4408-5455-2 (print)
       978-1-4408-5456-9 (ebook)

23 22 21 20 19   1 2 3 4 5

This book is also available as an eBook.

ABC-CLIO
An Imprint of ABC-CLIO, LLC

ABC-CLIO, LLC
130 Cremona Drive, P.O. Box 1911
Santa Barbara, California 93116–1911
www.abc-clio.com

This book is printed on acid-free paper ∞

Manufactured in the United States of America

Contents

Preface

In 1804, Meriwether Lewis and William Clark set out on an expedition that did not just change America, it changed the world. They explored and documented an area of the North American continent that was previously unmapped. Twenty-five years after their return, a quarter of the population of the United States lived west of the Appalachian Mountains. Lewis and Clark made that change possible.

Each of the documents included in this documentary history was chosen with one primary purpose: to bring each reader, each historian, old and young, beginner and advanced, closer to the people who went on this expedition, and to the events that happened. There are literally hundreds, if not thousands, of books and documents available on the Lewis and Clark expedition, but this book is designed to help the reader to know more about the people who went west, to find out how they felt, what they did, how they prepared, and what life was like for them afterward. This set of documents differs from previous editions, as it attempts to give insight into a greater variety of people who were part of the expedition. To achieve this, this book uses longer excerpts than other books to allow for a fuller picture. Edited documents give a different picture and often do not tell the whole story. I have sometimes used different accounts from different journals to describe the same day, or the same event. These differing texts—sometimes between Lewis and Clark, more often between the officers and enlisted men—expand our knowledge, bringing us closer not only to the success of the trip, but also to the fears and near-failures. Equally important, this book also contextualizes the trip within the personal and political history of Thomas Jefferson, third president of the United States, the man who long envisioned such an adventure. Vital to this story are the previous failed attempts, the Louisiana Purchase, the background economic issues of the new United States as it attempted to expand in order to survive, and the security of the new republic. I have provided this historical context to help the readers get a greater understanding of the events, the era, and the people.

So while Meriwether Lewis, William Clark, and Thomas Jefferson are necessarily in the forefront of this story and are found in the vast majority of the documents, other members of the expedition and others whose lives were impacted by it need to be recognized and remembered. Had Lewis and Clark's original party tried to make this trip by themselves, not only would they have failed, but the chances are that all would have died. It was only with the help of the Native American population—in particular Sacagawea, as well as other Native Americans—that their voyage succeeded. Often forgotten and overlooked but fundamental to the success of the trip was the local knowledge and the language skills of the mostly

French Canadian fur trappers. These men, who were mostly outcasts from society, living outside the social norms, proved crucial.

There was another person on this trip whose life has not generally been studied enough: York, the African American slave owned by William Clark. York went on this journey, was given a gun, and regularly explored freely by himself. He was crucial at times when speaking to and dealing with the Native population. His care for Charles Floyd when Floyd was dying was commented on and was appreciated by the men of the Corps. He was treated as an equal on this trip, and so before the party left Fort Mandan, he, like everyone else, sent letters and gifts home to his family. When the group reached the Pacific Ocean and took a vote about where they would spend the winter, York voted like everyone else. His vote counted equally.

Yet, tragically, when York arrived back east with Clark, his life as a slave resumed. His life was harsh, and he and his family were treated particularly cruelly. Clark had York flogged on numerous occasions, and he even sold York's wife to another slave owner. Despite York's pleading, Clark refused to sell him to the same person.

This book will allow the reader to travel with the Lewis and Clark party through the West, from the initial planning stages to the organizing of food and medical supplies to the harsh discipline imposed on some of the men to the crossing of the Continental Divide to the Pacific Ocean and back again to St. Louis to home. It will also allow the reader to see just how complicated life became in particular for Meriwether Lewis when he returned home.

This was a unique moment in time, based on respect, learning, and science. All too soon, that would change. This is the story of an adventure and of a group of people who trusted in each other enough for them to find a way from the East Coast to the West Coast and back again. Together, they opened up the American West to the world.

Evaluating and Interpreting Primary Documents

In historiography, which is the study of the writing of history and the employment of historical methods, a primary source is a document, recording, artifact, work of art or literature, or other information resource that was created at or near the time being studied, usually by someone with direct, personal knowledge of the particular past events, persons, or topics being described. Primary sources are original sources of information about the past, unlike secondary sources, which are works later historians create from a study, citation, and evaluation of primary sources. A modern text of American history, like Stephen Ambrose's *Undaunted Courage*; a modern biography, like Danisi and Johnson's *Meriwether Lewis*; or a modern television series, like PBS's *Lewis and Clark: The Journey of the Corps of Discovery* may all be helpful in explaining the journey of Lewis and Clark in the nineteenth century to contemporary readers and viewers, but they are all *secondary* descriptions and depictions based on firsthand experiences and recollections recorded and preserved in the primary documents of the period.

Primary documents—as illustrated by the document selections included in *Documents of the Lewis and Clark Expedition*—come in many forms and types, including letters, journals, polemics, speeches, literary works, and public records and documents. All these types of sources were written by a particular person at a particular time in a particular place for a particular reason. Some were written with no expectation that they would ever be read by anyone other than the original recipient; others were written for publication or at least with an eye to wider distribution. Some were meant to inform, some to persuade, some to entertain, and some to obfuscate. Each exhibits the political, religious, class, ethnic, or personal biases of their creators, whether those attitudes were consciously or unconsciously expressed. Some are the product of poor memories, bad information, or outright deception, but all are authentic voices of someone alive at the time, and all can add at least a little to the information we have of an otherwise-irrecoverable past age or person. Nonetheless, historians must carefully evaluate and test all primary sources to determine how much weight and credibility each should be given.

How to Read Primary Documents

When evaluating a primary source, historians ask the following questions:

1. Who wrote or produced it? What is known about this person's life or career?
2. When was the source written or produced? What date? How close or far was that date from the date of the events described?

3. Where was it produced? What country, what region, what locality?

4. How was the source written or produced? What form did it originally take? Was it based upon any preexisting material? Does the source survive in its original form?

5. Why was the source written or produced? What was its creator trying to do, and for whom?

6. For whom was the source written or produced? Who was its audience, and why? What do we know about the audience?

7. What is the evidential value of its contents? How credible is it?

Readers of the document selections contained in this volume should apply these same questions to the selections they read or study.

When analyzing a primary document, scholars also seek to identify the key-words and phrases used by the author and try to understand what the author meant by those terms. They also try to summarize the main thesis of the source to understand what point the author was trying to make. Once the author's thesis is understood, historians evaluate the evidence the author provided to support that argument and try to identify any assumptions the author made in crafting those arguments. Historians also examine the source within the context of its time period by asking if the document is similar to others from the same period, how widely it was circulated, or what tone, problems, or ideas it shares with other documents of the period. Scholars also seek to determine if the author agrees or disagrees with other contemporary authors on the same subject and whether the source supports what they already know or have learned about the subject from other sources.

Primary sources offer modern readers and researchers the actual words of people who lived through a particular event. Secondary sources, like textbooks, offer an interpretation of a historical person or event by someone who did not know the person or witness the period. Reading primary sources allows us to evaluate the interpretations of historians for ourselves and to draw our own conclusions about a past personage or events. Asking the questions listed earlier will help users of this volume better understand and interpret the documents provided here. Because of unfamiliar and archaic language or terminology, or very different modes of expression or styles of writing, some primary sources can be difficult to read and hard to understand.

However, an important part of the process of reading and using historical sources is determining what the documents can tell about the past and deciding whether one agrees with the interpretation offered, both by the author of the original source and by later creators of secondary works based on the original document. By using primary sources, modern readers become aware that all history is based on sources that are themselves interpretations of events rooted in the interpreter's own opinions and biases. This awareness allows modern students to recognize the subjective nature of history. Thus, reading primary sources provides modern readers with the tools and evidence needed to make informed statements about the world of the past and of the present.

Note on Texts

When presenting the primary texts, an editorial choice was made to leave the spelling and grammar as it was originally written. This may, at times, make it a little more difficult for today's reader, but it does give the reader insight into the people and the time. The author has not corrected Jefferson's failure to use capital letters when beginning a sentence, nor has the author attempted to correct William Clark's 19 spelling variations of the word mosquito, nor his 27 variations of the spelling of Toussaint Charbonneau.

While Lewis and Clark had more formal education than many others in the Corps of Discovery, Clark's formal education ended when he was 13 years old. Even if he had continued his education, there was no standard orthography at the time; there was no set way to write or spell, so words were written as they sounded regionally. The result is a somewhat creative and certainly inconsistent use of spelling and grammar.

Historical Introduction

At 4 p.m., on Monday, May 14, 1804, Second Lieutenant William Clark and a group of men (no one is sure of exactly how many) left Camp Dubois, in southern Illinois. It took them two days to travel 24 miles by boat and reach St. Charles, Missouri. At St. Charles, they met up with the expedition coleader, Captain Meriwether Lewis, and from there, the whole group, known to posterity as "the Corps of Discovery," traveled together to St. Louis, Missouri. Then on Monday, May 21, at 3:30 p.m., the Corps left St. Louis to the cheers of hundreds of people gathered on the banks of the river. They would only manage to travel four miles that first day, a sign of just how slow and long this journey was going to be.

The Corps were going into the unknown. They were attempting the dangerous, perhaps even the impossible. The group was setting out to map land and gather encyclopedic knowledge of animals and plants. They were going to make contact with the Native peoples and announce to them that they were now governed by Thomas Jefferson, third president of the United States. However, what they sought most of all was a passage through the northwest area of the American continent, a commercial trade route, between the eastern and western coasts of the United States. Meriwether Lewis had been personally selected by Thomas Jefferson to lead the trip, and Lewis had in turn asked his friend and former army colleague William Clark to be part of the expedition. Both men had accepted the task knowing the probable risks and the very real possibility that neither they nor anyone else would return.

The journey would take 863 days (2 years, 4 months, and 10 days). During that time, most people, including President Thomas Jefferson, had presumed them all dead. Remarkably, only one of the original group of 33, Sergeant Charles Floyd, actually died, and he most likely died after his appendix burst. At its largest, the Corps would at one time expand to 59 people, including York, an African American slave owned by William Clark, as well as Sacagawea, a Native American woman, and her infant son Jean Baptiste Charbonneau, born during the expedition.

In one sense, the trip would turn out to be a failure. They never did discover the Northwest Passage. It did not exist.

After 1 year, 5 months, and 25 days, the group reached the Pacific Ocean. The return would be quicker, and once back, they were treated to a hero's welcome everywhere from St. Louis to the White House. They had returned with maps, animals, drawings, and reports of meetings with Native Americans. They had survived grizzly bears, huge mosquitoes, harsh winters, and the Rockies. They had gathered previously unknown animals, including prairie dogs, woodrats, mule deer, species of fox, jack rabbits, and types of catfish, and brought them back east for the first time. They had mapped out and named mountains, rivers, and streams. They had, in a sense, made America.

Why an Expedition?

On July 4, 1803, President Thomas Jefferson announced that the United States had just bought 825,000 square miles from the French emperor, Napoleon Bonaparte. The cost was $15 million, or less than 3 cents per acre. The Louisiana Purchase was perhaps the best land deal ever made. It doubled the size of the United States, adding all or part of 15 modern states: Arkansas, Colorado, Iowa, Kansas, Louisiana, Minnesota, Missouri, Montana, Nebraska, New Mexico, Oklahoma, North Dakota, South Dakota, Texas, and Wyoming. This vast new addition needed to be thoroughly mapped and explored. It needed careful observers to collect and record previously unknown plants and animals. It needed a summary of the Native nations who lived there, and it needed contact to be established between the president of the United States and these nations. Its rivers, streams, and mountains needed to be noted and named. But most of all Thomas Jefferson wanted to find the Northwest Passage.

The Northwest Passage would provide a navigable water route between the Missouri River and the Pacific Ocean, one that Jefferson and many others at the time believed existed. Having waterborne access to the Pacific from the East Coast of the United States would mean a more direct trade route to and from Asia. Such a route would mean greater wealth for America.

Ever since he was a boy growing up in Virginia, Jefferson had been fascinated by the West. His father, Peter Jefferson, had been a landowner, surveyor, and map-maker who documented previously uncharted parts of North Carolina and Virginia. After his father died in 1757, two of the most important people in Jefferson's life, Dr. Thomas Walker and Reverend James Maury, were both interested in science and exploration. With these three influences in his life it is no surprise that Jefferson spent much of his youth exploring Virginia, studying the Native peoples and reading everything he could about science, in particular geology and paleontology. Even during his time in college at William and Mary in Williamsburg, Virginia, from March 1760 to April 1762, Jefferson continued these studies along with classes in philosophy and math.

After graduation, Jefferson returned to his family home in Monticello, where he continued these scientific pursuits and began collecting all sorts of historical artifacts such as arrowheads, axes, and pottery, which he studied in great detail. He also had a collection of plants and animals. Later, he added mammoth bones, tusks, and huge numbers of fossils to this collection. Jefferson was also always expanding his library. It is estimated that Jefferson owned somewhere between 9,000 and 10,000 books during his lifetime. In 1815, Congress bought Jefferson's library at the time for $23,950. It contained 6,700 books.

From 1784 to 1789, Jefferson lived in Paris, France, as a representative of the Congress of the United States. His job was to negotiate trade agreements between France and the new United States. When living in Paris, Jefferson used the information he had gathered about the West when he argued with Count Georges-Louis Leclerc Buffon (1707–1788), one of the most influential thinkers of the French Enlightenment. Buffon argued that animals in America were frail when compared to those in Europe and that any animal or plant imported from Europe would degenerate quickly. Buffon insisted that much of America was swamp and that the country was still drying out from a biblical flood. Buffon's theory on weak American animals and life, which he included in his popular encyclopedic, 36-volume book, *Histoire Naturelle* (*Natural History*), was accepted as science and promoted as fact at the time.

Jefferson was determined to prove Buffon wrong and went to all sorts of lengths to get Buffon to change his mind, including importing a seven-foot-tall moose to Paris. While Jefferson did not succeed in changing his mind, these debates with Buffon made Jefferson more determined than ever to gather all the information he could about the American West.

Jefferson's interest in the West was never wholly scientific, nor was it ever simply an intellectual or philosophical debate. It was always practical and political. His interest was primarily about the safety of the new United States—but it was also about finding new trade routes. Great Britain, France, and Spain all had significant territory in North America in the days of the early republic, and there was a very real fear that any one of these European empires could begin a war with the United States in order to gain more territory. The young United States could not afford another war, but if one were to happen, detailed knowledge of the terrain would be vital. Finally, but significantly for Jefferson, the West was also an area ripe for U.S. expansion—a territory where people could travel from the East and where new American communities could grow. There was space in the West, and the more people lived there, the wealthier and safer they and the country would be.

Jefferson's multilayered fascination with the West included the idea that it could provide a vital way to travel from the Atlantic to the Pacific Ocean. Jefferson's reading and study had led him to believe there was a Northwest Passage, a direct water route between the eastern and western parts of the country. This river route, he believed, would allow trade and travel to occur throughout the year, as it was far enough south that the harsh northern winters would not impact navigation. For Jefferson, the Missouri River was key. Jefferson and many others believed that the Missouri, or a tributary thereof, led directly to the Pacific Ocean. The problem was that there was no map of the river west from St. Louis. Once this route could be mapped, trade between the United States and Asia would be vastly accelerated. In 1800, the only way from the eastern United States to Asia involved a sea route south around the tip of Argentina and Chile at Tierra Del Fuego, and then north, across the Pacific. This journey took at least six months, which meant a year traveling there and back. It was expensive, it was dangerous, and it was difficult. A water route across the continent would be safer, quicker, and far more economical, as it was hoped such a Northwest Passage would cut this time at least in half.

Jefferson had made a number of attempts to confirm and map such a route. In 1783, Jefferson tried to persuade General George Rogers Clark, older brother of William Clark, to lead an expedition that would travel from Missouri to California. Clark turned him down on the grounds that such a trip would take years to complete, time he could ill afford away from his businesses. The following year, Jefferson was part of a group that funded John Ledyard's audacious attempt to sail to the West Coast of North America from Russia and then walk from his arrival on the American West Coast back to the East Coast! Ledyard did manage to get as far as Russia, but while in Siberia the Russian police became suspicious that he was spying on the fur trade. He was expelled, and the adventure ended in failure. Nine years later, in 1793 Jefferson, through the American Philosophical Society, backed yet another trip, this time led by the French explorer Andre Michaux. Michaux's instructions were similar to those later given to Lewis and Clark. Like Ledyard's aborted attempt, this trip also came to a sudden stop when Michaux was accused of being a spy for the French against the United States. In July 1793, Michaux had started west, but by the time he reached the Mississippi, rumors of him spying for France against the Spanish had reached the American Philosophical Society. Jefferson, who was anxious that the Spanish would not see this trip as anything other than scientific and exploratory, canceled the expedition in spring 1784 and demanded the French government recall Michaux.

What all of these failures had shown Jefferson was that in order for an expedition to succeed, it would need a leader with extraordinary qualifications. He would have to be physically fit to endure the adventure, scientifically educated, and politically astute. Ideally then, the best candidate would have a military background, as this was a key to strong organization and leadership. The leader of this trip had to be known in Washington circles and yet also have a background in the wilderness. The person Jefferson settled on was his personal secretary, fellow Virginian and Army Captain Meriwether Lewis.

On January 18, 1803, with the Louisiana Purchase details still secret and not yet signed, Jefferson, following the advice of Albert Gatlin, his secretary of the Treasury, sent a confidential request to Congress asking for funds for an expedition west, to explore the vast area that would soon become part of the United States. As Jefferson's personal secretary, Meriwether Lewis had been working secretly on the trip since the summer of 1802. The budget for the trip was $2,500, which included food, medical supplies, a keelboat, and $696 for gifts for Native Americans. Once Congress approved the money, Jefferson gave specific written instructions to Lewis on June 20, 1803. His mission was as follows: (1) to explore the Missouri River and to chart a course to the Pacific Ocean; (2) to map the areas en route, making note of rivers and mountains; (3) to make contact with the Native Americans, find out about their life, family, and homes, and do this in a diplomatic way; (4) to make notes about all plants, animals, minerals encountered; and (5) to keep accurate journals and notes.

With his instructions clear and the budget approved, Meriwether Lewis began the process of gathering men and supplies for the trip.

Meriwether Lewis

Meriwether Lewis was born in Virginia on August 18, 1774, the first son and second child born to William and Lucy Meriwether Lewis. When his father died of pneumonia at the age of 43, Lucy was 27, and Lewis was 5. Soon afterward, his mother remarried a second cousin, John Marks, a retired army captain. When Lewis was about 10 years old, Marks moved the family to Oglethorpe County, Georgia. It was in Georgia, on his stepfather's large plantation, that the young Lewis learned how to hunt and was taught some basic skills in using herbs as medicine by his mother. It was here, too, that he first showed his interest in nature and where he had his first interaction with the local Native American population. John and Lucy Marks had two more children while in Georgia: a son, John Hastings Marks, born in 1785, and a daughter, Mary Garland Marks, born in 1788. Around the age of 13, Meriwether Lewis returned to Virginia to receive a formal education. However, in 1791, he returned to Georgia to help his mother and younger siblings return to Virginia. John Marks had died suddenly, and Lucy made the decision to return the family to Virginia, where they all worked hard to make the farm land pay.

In 1791, Alexander Hamilton, the Treasury secretary, imposed a tax on whiskey, in an attempt to ease the national debt caused by the American Revolution. It was an unpopular decision. Farmers were furious and rioted, as they felt they would have no way to make a profit from selling their grain. President Washington asked for men to join the militias and help quell this "Whiskey Rebellion," and so in 1794, Meriwether Lewis, perhaps tired of life on the farm, joined the 13,000 forces made up of men from Virginia, Pennsylvania, New Jersey, and Maryland. Lewis enjoyed his life in the army. He was quickly promoted to ensign (equivalent to second lieutenant in today's military), and though he was eligible for a discharge the following year, he chose instead to be transferred to the regular army.

While he enjoyed his adventures in the army, his political opinions about the happenings in Washington almost got him into trouble. On November 6, 1795, Ensign Meriwether Lewis was charged with "conduct unbecoming an officer." It was charged that while intoxicated, he had challenged a more senior officer, Lieutenant Joseph Elliot, to a duel. The drunken argument was over politics: Lewis was supporter of Jefferson and a Republican, while Elliot was a Federalist. A challenge to duel was a serious offense. Duels were banned by General Anthony Wayne, after at least six officers had been killed because of them in the preceding years. Frankly there were far too few officers, and the army could not afford deaths because of duels. Lewis denied the charge and mounted his own defense. Lewis's intelligence, organization, and verbal skills showed. His questioning and arguments won out, and six days later, he was found not guilty on all counts. To avoid any more possible run-ins with Elliot, Lewis was transferred to the Chosen Rifle Company commanded by William Clark.

In March 1801, Thomas Jefferson became the third president of the United States. Jefferson was a neighbor, sometime mentor, and friend to Meriwether Lewis. Both were Virginians, whose family homes were 10 miles apart. When Jefferson was in France for four years, it was Lewis's uncle Nicholas Lewis who managed his estate and affairs. Just two days after his election, Jefferson wrote to Lewis and asked him to come to Washington to be his personal secretary. Meriwether Lewis's personal and political credentials were well suited for the job. He was related to George Washington through marriage and had fought for Washington in the Whiskey Rebellion. He was a Republican, rather than a Federalist; he was intelligent and loyal; and this opportunity came a great time for him. Jefferson promised that Lewis would maintain his rank and that the new position would offer him the possibility of getting to know and learn from the people who were shaping the new country. Lewis happily accepted the position.

Jefferson had two other reasons for choosing Meriwether Lewis. Jefferson wanted to know as much as possible about the army and its officers, and he wanted someone who knew the West. There had been a bitter election fought in 1800, and the Republicans who had won were committed to reducing the size of the army. One of Lewis's first jobs was to go through a roster of all officers and note who were deemed capable and who were Republicans or Federalists. After Lewis finished this first task, his second was to begin the organization of an expedition to go west.

Six-foot-tall, healthy, and in good physical condition, Lewis had the necessary military expertise and experience for such a trip. But Jefferson knew that for the trip to succeed, Lewis would need further specialized education to learn how to survive in the wilderness, to navigate there and back, as well as enough scientific knowledge to collect, process, and preserve what they found. In early 1803, Lewis's education began. His first teacher was Jefferson himself—and Jefferson's vast library of history, science, map-making, and geography books. Here at this early stage, Jefferson impressed upon Lewis the importance of keeping a daily scientific journal.

Jefferson then had Lewis schooled by a variety of teachers: Albert Gallatin, who was secretary of the Treasury, taught Lewis about maps; Andrew Elliot, one of the best surveyors in the country, taught Lewis how to navigate using the stars. Lewis learned about geography from Robert Patterson, an ex-soldier who was brilliant at physics and was Eliot's teacher. Dr. Benjamin Smith Barton, a member of the American Philosophical Society, taught him botany, while Dr. Caspar Wistar, a medical doctor, taught him about fossils.

From the outset, it was clear that one of the most important jobs on the voyage was going to be that of a physician—a medical doctor, or at the very least someone with medical knowledge, who could tend to the expedition's members. Accidents and injuries were bound to happen on such a trip, so a doctor was vital. Initially, Jefferson and Lewis had considered asking Dr. Benjamin Rush to be part of the trip. Considered to be the best medical doctor in America at the time, Rush was a firm believer in the American Revolution and had been one of the signatories of the Declaration of Independence. Educated at the College of New Jersey (now

Princeton) and the University of Edinburgh, Rush was professor of medicine at the University of Pennsylvania when Jefferson asked him to be part of the group to educate Lewis. Like many people of his day, Rush believed that bloodletting was one of the most important aspects of medicine and explained to Lewis how to do this effectively. He also supplied Lewis with his famous pills, sometimes known as "Thunderbolts," which were made up of some chamomile and jalap, as well as mercury and alcohol. These pills acted as purgative, which Rush insisted cleansed the body of toxins. Though Rush was willing to join the expedition, Lewis decided that with the knowledge and medicines supplied by Rush and the knowledge of plants and herbs he had learned from his mother, he himself would be able to look after any medical situation that arose.

William Clark

Though Meriwether Lewis was strong and capable, it was clear that he would need a co-captain's help in leading the expedition. There was a huge amount of work that had to be done: mapping, collecting animals and plants, finding routes, making political allies across America, and ensuring discipline was maintained. A coleader was needed on the trip who could be counted on to pay attention to detail and also to write accurate daily journals. Lewis turned to his former army colleague and friend, William Clark. Clark, like Lewis and Jefferson, was born in Virginia. Also like Lewis's, Clark's family had strong military connections, with five of his brothers having fought in the Revolutionary War. Initially Jefferson had asked William Clark's older brother, George, to consider a trip west. George Clark refused the offer but did suggest that his younger brother William, who at the time was only 18 years old, would be capable of such a trip.

In 1785, the Clark family moved to Kentucky, settling in "Mulberry Hill," a plantation near Louisville. It was here that Clark's older brothers taught him crucial survival skills that he would later use on the expedition. William Clark served with the militia beginning in 1789 and then with the U.S. Army, where in 1795 he met Meriwether Lewis. In 1796, Clark resigned his commission due to ill health and returned to Kentucky to manage the family's plantation. Though Lewis and Clark served together only for six months, Clark impressed Lewis so much that when he needed a coleader for the trip, he asked Clark, who immediately accepted.

The Journey

The original plan for the journey was to leave St. Louis in August 1804, upriver in the winter, then cross the country to the Pacific in the spring, and return to east in the summer of 1805. The first part of the plan was a success: The Corps left St. Louis in 1804, but almost immediately there were problems. They spent the summer and fall paddling upstream against a strong current. Their main boat was a 55-foot keelboat made specifically in Pittsburgh for shallow river travel and was capable of carrying heavy amounts of supplies. But because it was so heavy, it was impossible to row against the current. Consequently, the boat had to be manually dragged upstream most days by men pulling it by ropes from each side. Their progress was extremely slow, traveling only 12 to 15 miles on a good day, and leaving the men absolutely exhausted. If the daytime physical work was tough, there was little nighttime rest for anyone. Mosquitoes in huge numbers attacked the men. They moved camps, tried different insect repellents, and used the smoke from the fire to try and ward off the bugs, but it was useless. The number and size of the bites caused such pain that the men were in constant discomfort, making sleep almost impossible.

Each man chosen for the trip had a skill that was needed: hunting, carpentry, and frontier skills, such as tracking animals, building shelters, and making clothes. The entire Corps was made up of soldiers, each with his military rank: Lewis and Clark were officers; Lewis a captain, and while Clark was considered a co-captain during the trip, his rank actually was second lieutenant. This fact was never known by the men. There were originally three sergeants, namely Charles Floyd, John Ordway, and Nathaniel Pryor (Patrick Gass was later promoted to the rank of sergeant when Charles Floyd died) and one corporal Richard Warfington. (John Robertson may have been a corporal at one stage, as he was referred to as both a corporal and a private. He was sent back to St. Louis in June 1804, so it is possible that he was demoted and dismissed then.) All the other men were privates.

The harshness of the bugs and the rough terrain was matched only by the discipline imposed by Lewis and Clark. As all members of the Corps were soldiers, the expedition was carried out as a military operation. Any violations of the code of conduct were therefore punishable under military law. Even before they had left St. Louis, there had been a court-martial: in March 1804, when Private John Collins was found guilty of a variety of charges, including speaking back to an officer, he was sentenced to 50 lashes. Soon after they left St. Louis, on May 17, 1804, there was another incident in which a number of men were charged with being absent without leave (AWOL) and answering their officers. They were each sentenced to 25 to 50 lashes. Lewis and Clark deemed this insistence on rigorous military discipline necessary to ensure that the expedition succeeded. In August 1804, Moses Reed pled guilty to desertion, while in October 1804, John Newman was found guilty of mutinous acts. They were both sent back to St. Louis with the keelboat in spring 1805.

By October 1804, the Corps had reached North Dakota. With winter coming, they built a fort, called Fort Mandan, about 12 miles from present-day Washburn, North Dakota, at the banks of the Missouri River. There they spent the winter with the native Mandan and Hidatsa nations, establishing the type of relationship that Jefferson had instructed them: talking to Native populations, learning about them, and gathering scientific as well as socioeconomic information. The rest of their time that winter was also spent preparing for travel the following spring, since it was this next part of the journey that was largely into unknown and totally unmapped territory. They were in contact with fur traders who knew the area well, and through conversations with the Native Americans, Lewis and Clark were able to put together a basic map that they hoped would guide them as they began the next part of the journey.

During this time of conversation, trade, and eating meals with various Native groups, one of the most important members of the Corps to emerge was York, William Clark's personal slave who accompanied him. York was a skilled hunter, who often went out on hunting expeditions. Also as the Native groups had never seen an African American before, they were fascinated by him and his color, thinking he had some magical powers.

It was also this winter, on November 11, 1804, that the Canadian fur trapper and trader, Toussaint Charbonneau, along with his two wives, Otter Woman and the pregnant Sacagawea, arrived at Fort Mandan.

Sacagawea and York

Two of the most important people on the expedition along with Lewis and Clark were Sacagawea, a Lemhi Shoshone woman, and York, an African American slave. The roles of Sacagawea and York were both political and practical, as each one negotiated with various Native nations and each at different times saved the expedition.

Without Sacagawea, it is probable that Lewis and Clark and their whole expedition would have died. Her knowledge of the territory and her ability to communicate in a variety of languages made her an invaluable companion. It was her brother, Cameahwait, chief of the Shoshones, who supplied the expedition with horses as a gift of gratitude for the safe return of his sister. These horses made the trip over the Rocky Mountains possible. Without the horses, all members of the Corps would have died in the winter snow or been forced to return never having seen the Pacific.

Sacagawea was most likely born near the present-day city of Salmon in central Idaho. She, along with other women, was kidnapped by the Hidatsa Nation, in about 1800, when she was 12 years old. All the kidnapped Shoshone women were brought to a Hidatsa site near present-day Washburn, North Dakota, over 800 miles away. The Hidatsa then sold her and another Shoshone woman called "Otter Woman" to Toussaint Charbonneau, a French Canadian fur trader. Both women were declared his wives. In November 1804, the Corps arrived at the Mandan village, in North Dakota, where the Corps, who were joined by Sacagawea and Charbonneau, stayed for the winter. On February 11, 1805, Sacagawea, nicknamed "Janey" by Clark, gave birth to her son Jean-Baptiste. When the Corps left Fort Mandan on April 7, 1805, Sacagawea, Toussaint Charbonneau, and her almost two-month-old son, nicknamed "Pompy" or "Little Pomp" by Clark, went with them.

Touissaint Charbonneau and Sacagawea were employed as interpreters between the expedition and the Shoshones, but this interpretation was not a simple process, as neither Sacagawea nor Charbonneau spoke English, and only Sacagawea spoke Shoshone. This meant that Sacagawea listened to the Shoshone, then translated into Hidatsa, which was understood by Charbonneau, who then duly translated into French, which was understood and spoken by Corps member Francois Labiche, who in turn translated from French into English for Lewis and Clark. Any response by Lewis and Clark had to be then translated from English into French, then into Hidatsa, and finally into Shoshone.

While Sacagawea's practical role in the expedition, like that of her husband, was that of translator and interpreter, it was her emotional calm that was impressive very early on the trip. On May 4, 1805, as the Corps headed upriver against a particularly strong current, the boat capsized, and some of their supplies went overboard and started floating away. It was Sacagawea who calmly gathered the supplies from the water, impressing Lewis and Clark so much that they named the river the "Sacagawea River" after her.

York was William Clark's personal slave who accompanied the Corps. Clark inherited York after the death of his father, John. York was born in Virginia, where his parents, brother, and sister were all slaves owned by the Clark family. At 14, York became William Clark's personal slave, and when Clark agreed to go on the expedition, York went with him. While our knowledge of York is limited, we do know that he was married, as at one stage on the trip, he along with Clark and others sent letters and parcels home to family, and in his case his wife. York was the only member of the expedition who was married, as a requirement for being a member was being single. As York was not recruited but was instead (probably) required to go on the voyage, the rules were not applied to him. Clark completely trusted York, who was given a gun, allowed to explore alone, and was granted the freedom to mix with the Native Americans.

They Proceeded On—The Voyage Resumes

With winter over and the snow finally melting, it was time to begin the journey into the unknown. On April 7, 1805, under the command of Corporal Richard Warfington, Privates John Boley and John Dame and the French Canadian boatman Baptiste Deschamps, along with John Newman and Moses Reed, who had been dismissed after their court-martial, were sent back to St. Louis with the keelboat, boxes of samples of minerals, skins, skeletons, various animals, including four live magpies and a prairie dog, and a map of what they had thus far surveyed, along with letters to family members and to President Jefferson. The remainder of the party—joined by Toussaint Charbonneau; Sacagawea; two-month-old Jean-Baptiste; Pierre Dorion, a trapper and interpreter; George Drouillard, a scout and map-maker; Jean Baptiste Le Page, a fur-trapper hired to take the place of John Newman; and York, along with Seaman the dog—set out to go west in eight boats: six dugout canoes and two small sailboats called pirogues. Lewis wrote in his journal that they were about to go 2,000 miles into the country where few had ever traveled; he also commented that this was the happiest day of his life.

By the end of April 1804, they had reached Montana, where they saw herds of wild buffalo. They experienced the ferocity of a grizzly bear and killed one. Though they had been told about grizzly bears by the Native Americans, they did not believe such an animal existed. As they traveled, they named rivers, streams, and mountains after friends and family. They noted and charted each. They drew pictures of birds and various animals.

In late July, as they continued west, Sacagawea began to recognize the area, as she was getting closer to what was her childhood home. On August 8, she specifically identified Beaverhead Rock, close to Dillon, Montana, as being the area from which she had been kidnapped as a child years ago. But time was running out. The expedition party needed to make contact quickly with the Shoshones in order to get horses to get over the Rocky Mountains, and they needed to do this before the snow began.

On August 9, Lewis along with George Drouillard, Hugh McNeal, and John Shields left the main party in an attempt to find the Shoshones. The group traveled along the Jefferson River and followed a trail toward Beaverhead Rock. On August 12, the group reached Lemhi Pass, the area between modern-day Montana and Idaho. Here, as Lewis looked around him, he saw a snow-covered mountain range in the West. They had discovered the source of the Missouri River. This crossing was the first recorded crossing of the Continental Divide by Americans.

The Continental Divide is the division that separates rivers so that each system flows into a different ocean. Here, Lewis realized that the Missouri did not continue west. There was a huge mountain range that had to be overcome for any trade route to be established. They needed to get over this range and then search out another river going west.

This discovery by Lewis, six days before his 31st birthday, was a moment of amazing success, and yet this same discovery confirmed that there was no continuous waterway between east and west. The Northwest Passage that Jefferson had hoped to find did not exist. But the Corps still needed to continue to the Pacific, map the route, and return home.

On August 11, the group saw a Shoshone man for the first time. But he was afraid of the group and rode away. Lewis was about to give up hope of ever finding the Shoshones when the next day they came across a group of women, who brought them to the main camp where they met Chief Cameahwai. While waiting for Clark and the main party to catch up with them, Lewis offered gifts and greetings brought from President Jefferson and spoke with the chief about where they were going. He asked about specific landmarks to help them on their journey. Clark and the others arrived three days later. Sacagawea was asked to join the group meeting in a tent so that she could help translate the conversation between Lewis and Chief Cameahwai more easily. After entering the tent, Sacagawea looked up and recognized her brother, the chief. Bursting into tears, she embraced him. Over conversations she and her brother had over the next few days, she learned that except for two of her brothers all her family were dead. This meeting of brother and sister was to be of paramount importance, as it was through Sacagawea that Lewis and Clark were able to obtain horses that were vital for the group to get through the Rocky Mountains. The group was also given a guide named Old Toby, who was to help them get as far as another Native group the Nez Perce.

Well-fed and rested, the party set off on August 31, 1805, with 29 horses. They traveled daily until September 9, when they stopped for two days at an area since named Travelers Rest, one mile south of Lolo, Montana. They were to camp here again on their return journey as well. Then they began to cross the Bitterroot

Mountains, situated in Idaho and Montana. It took them 11 brutal days to cross the mountain range. Snow had begun to fall. Food was in short supply.

On September 20, 1805, arriving on the other side of the range, cold and hungry, they were helped once again by a woman, Watkuweis, an older member of the Nez Perce. Like Sacagawea, she had been kidnapped as a young girl but had been helped in her return to her family by a group of Canadian fur trappers. She urged the other members of her tribe to help the expedition. The Nez Perce agreed. Here again the Corps were fed and allowed to rest. Here they were shown crucial skills that would help them survive and explore. This time they were shown how to make canoes. Using their new canoes, the Corps continued their journey on October 6, following the Clearwater and Snake Rivers, from modern Idaho into Oregon. They traveled quickly and reached the Columbia River on October 10, 1805.

On October 18, William Clark saw Mount Hood, about 50 miles southeast of modern-day Portland, Oregon. He was delighted. Recognizing Mount Hood, Clark knew the Pacific Ocean was near. It took them a further three weeks to see the Pacific Ocean.

The Vote

On November 15, 1805, the Corps of Discovery finally reached the Pacific Ocean. They had achieved the seemingly impossible. Yet they had also failed. They had proved that there was no Northwest Passage. But on November 15, the group had a much more pressing issue: the coming winter. A decision had to be made about where to spend the next few months safely. Amazingly, Lewis and Clark took a vote. These men who had run the expedition with strict military discipline now allowed each member of the Corps to weigh in equally on this decision. The verdict was for the whole group to move to the southern shore of the Columbia River. There they built Fort Clatsop, a basic structure. In one room, Lewis, Clark, Charbonneau, Sacagawea, and Little Jean Baptiste slept, while the rest of the men slept in the other room. This building would keep everyone safe for the winter and where they would remain until March 22, 1806, when they began the journey east to St. Louis.

Both Sacagawea and York participated in voting on November 24, 1805. Both were given an equal vote to everyone else present, all white men. Slavery would not be abolished until some 60 years in the future. It would take the passing of the Fifteenth Amendment in 1869 before African American men were allowed to register to vote and the passing of the Nineteenth Amendment in 1920 before women were allowed to vote. It took until 1924 before Native Americans were granted U.S. citizenship, with some states banning Native Americans from voting until 1957. The expedition of Lewis and Clark at this moment not only mapped the United States geographically but at this moment mapped its social and political future as well.

On March 22, 1806, the Corps began the journey home. They arrived in St. Louis on September 23—just six months later. Though the return journey was much faster, they still had to contend with the formidable terrain: mountains had to be recrossed, rivers had to be traversed, and food had to be hunted and eaten.

President Thomas Jefferson wrote to them of his "unspeakable joy" on hearing that they had returned safely. He, like everyone else, had presumed them dead. After a dinner in St. Louis, Lewis and Clark set out separately to Washington, D.C., as both men wanted first to visit family as well. Lewis reached Washington in December, and while the official celebrations were delayed to see if Clark would join them, the celebrations then went ahead without him. He arrived later and stayed seven weeks as both men attended event after event in their honor. Both men were given new positions by Jefferson: Lewis was made governor of Upper Louisiana, and Clark was made brigadier general of the militia and Indian agent for the Upper Louisiana Territory.

Keeping a Journal

The most amazing historical sources for this trip are all the journals, not just those of Meriwether Lewis and William Clark, but also those written by Sergeant Charles Floyd, Sergeant Patrick Gass, Sergeant John Ordway, and Private Johnny White-house. Sergeant Nathaniel Pryor and Private Robert Frazer also kept journals, but both of these have been lost. Privates Frazer and Whitehouse wrote voluntarily, as only the sergeants and captains were ordered to write a journal. Taken together, these journals give us an account of each day of the expedition, providing a remarkable, and almost unique, collection of primary sources. Sergeant Ordway kept the most complete records of the group, recording entries for each of the 863 days. Clark was almost as good, missing only February 3–12, 1805, when he was on a hunting trip, though he did fill in this gap on his return.

It was Thomas Jefferson who insisted that such detailed records needed to be kept. In his June 20, 1803, letter to Lewis, he specified his instructions:

> Your observations are to be taken with great pains & accuracy, to be entered distinctly & intelligibly for others, as well as yourself, to comprehend all the elements necessary, with the aid of the usual tables, to fix the latitude and longitude of the places at which they were taken, and are to be rendered to the war office for the purpose of having the calculations made concurrently by proper persons within the US. several copies of these as well as of your other notes should be made at leisure times, & put into the care of the most trust-worthy of your attendants, to guard by multiplying them against the accidental losses to which they will be exposed. A further guard would be that one these copies be on the paper of the birch, as less liable to injury from damp than common paper.

Jefferson is clear here: he demanded that records with a scientific exactness be kept, that copies of these records be made, and that the records and journals be sent back east whenever possible. He also wanted as many details as possible to be added to these records whenever possible. Interestingly, Jefferson also issued a security reminder, asking them to put "into cypher (code) whatever might do injury if betrayed." Security and science were of paramount importance. Despite Jefferson's instructions and the volume of documents that are available, historians have questions about why there are so many missing entries in the journals. One of the biggest questions comes from the gap in the journals of Meriwether Lewis. There are three major times when Lewis's journals have little or nothing written: May 24, 1804–April 7, 1805 (there are a few entries for February 3–12, 1805), August 27, 1805–December 31, 1805 (again a few entries from September 18–22 and November 29–December1), and only 10 from August 13, 1806–August 24, 1806.

The gap that is easiest explained is the last one: Lewis had been accidentally shot and was lying down in the canoe as the group headed back toward St. Louis. Understandably, he did not write. But the other two have caused much debate and conjecture. Did he write in his journal at the time? If so, where are these entries? If he did not write for an extended period of time, why not?

The first gap, May 24, 1804–April 7, 1805, is the one that causes most questions, as this is the time period that covers the trip from St. Louis, through the first winter, until the group left Fort Mandan. This is by any stretch of the imagination one of the most important parts of the journey. Yet we have no information from Lewis. Adding to the mystery is the fact that tiny pieces of a journal written by Lewis do exist on sheets of paper, but these are not written in chronological order. Some historians, such as Donald Jackson, have proposed that in May 1805 some papers were soaked and destroyed. Other historians, including Reuben Gold Thwaites, have suggested that the journals were stolen when Lewis died. Both of these theories argue for the case that Lewis did keep journals but they were lost. Others who say he kept a journal point to the fact that various papers belonging to Lewis and Clark have been found recently and that perhaps these missing journals will be found some day.

Others have argued that Lewis did not keep a journal during this "missing" time. They point to an incident on July 14, 1804, when notes were damaged and destroyed after the keelboat almost capsized. William Clark wrote that he used the notes from the journals of the sergeants to re-create his own journal. But why would Clark use the sergeants' journals if Lewis's had been available? Surely, if Lewis had kept a journal, Clark would have used Lewis's notes to re-create his own. We may never know if Lewis kept or did not keep a journal during these times.

Copies of the journals, notebooks, and various other notes are available online and in many sources today. The originals of most of the Lewis, Clark, and Ordway journals are kept at the American Philosophical Society in Philadelphia. There are some parts of Williams Clark's journals at the Missouri Historical Society and in the Beinecke Library at Yale. Sergeant Floyd's journals can be found at the Newberry Historical Society at Wisconsin, while those of Private Whitehouse are at the Newberry Library at the University of Chicago. The original journals of Sergeant Patrick Gass have never been found, though there is a published version of them available online and in many libraries.

Accomplishments

As the Corps of Discovery began to get closer to St. Louis, Lewis began to write a report to President Jefferson describing what they had seen and achieved on the voyage. Lewis also explained to him that the Corps had both succeeded and failed with the Northwest Passage: they had found a route across the Rockies, but the hoped-for waterway from east to west did not exist.

Despite this disappointment, the truth is that the Lewis and Clark expedition accomplished the almost impossible, as they had traveled from St. Louis to the West Coast of the United States and created invaluable maps along the way. They collected and described nearly 200 species of plants new to science, as well as a hundred new animal species.

They had met with, talked to, and traded with 48 different Native American nations. It was entirely thanks to the knowledge shared by these nations that the Corps were able to find a route over the Rockies.

Lewis and Clark had mapped the new United States. They found a route that made trade between the East and the West possible. Soon after their journey, hundreds of thousands of settlers would move into the new territory, just as Jefferson had hoped. Meriwether Lewis and William Clark had made America, had noted its size, its people, its flora and fauna. Most of all they noted greatness was found in cooperation and respect.

Chronology

February 6, 1732	George Washington is born at Pope's Creek Plantation, Westmoreland County, Virginia.
1743	American Philosophical Society is founded by Benjamin Franklin.
April 13, 1743	Thomas Jefferson is born in Virginia.
March 8, 1746	Andre Michaux is born in France.
November 27, 1746	Robert Livingston is born in New York City.
March 16, 1751	James Madison is born in Virginia.
November 1751	John Ledyard is born in Connecticut.
November 19, 1752	George Rogers Clark is born in Virginia.
August 17, 1757	Peter Jefferson (Thomas Jefferson's father) dies.
September 6, 1757	Marquis de Lafayette is born in Auvergne, France.
April 28, 1758	James Monroe is born in Virginia.
August 15, 1761	Napoleon Bonaparte is born in Corsica.
March 20, 1767	Toussaint Charbonneau is born in Quebec, Canada.
May 18, 1768	Jefferson begins to build Monticello, his home in Albemarle County, Virginia.
1770	York is born in Virginia to parents, Old York and Rose.
August 1, 1770	William Clark is born in Virginia.
August 18, 1774	Meriwether Lewis is born in Virginia.
March 23, 1775	Patrick Henry delivers "Give Me Liberty or Give Me Death" speech at Second Virginia Convention.
July 4, 1776	Congress accepts Declaration of Independence.
July 31, 1777	Marquis de Lafayette is commissioned a major general in the army.
September 11, 1777	At the Battle of Brandywine the Marquis de Lafayette is injured.
1779	Marquis de Lafayette's only son Georges Washington Louis de Lafayette is born.
December 4, 1783	Jefferson asks General George Rogers Clark to lead an expedition to explore the American West.
1784–1789	Thomas Jefferson lives in France.

May 7, 1784	Thomas Jefferson is appointed U.S. minister based in Paris.
December 1786	John Ledyard leaves London heading to the American West Coast via Russia.
February 1788	John Ledyard is arrested in Russia under the orders of Catherine the Great (1729–1796), and he was expelled as he was suspected of being a spy.
May 1788	Sacagawea is born near Salmon, Idaho.
January 10, 1789	John Ledyard dies in Cairo, Egypt.
April 30, 1789	George Washington takes the oath of office, administered by Robert Livingston at Federal Hall in New York City, and becomes the first president of the United States.
1789–1799	The French Revolution takes place.
1791–1794	The Whiskey Rebellion takes place.
1792	Jefferson proposes to the American Philosophical Society that an adventurer explore the continent.
1793	Merriweather Lewis joins the Frontier Army and serves six years in Ohio and Tennessee.
January 21, 1793	Louis XVI, king of France, is executed by guillotine.
January 28, 1793	Jefferson gives Andre Michaux instructions about his trip west.
March 4, 1793	George Washington's second inaugural takes place, this time in Philadelphia, Pennsylvania.
October 16, 1793	Marie Antoinette, Louis XVI's wife, is executed by guillotine.
1797–1815	Jefferson is president of the American Philosophical Society.
December 14, 1799	George Washington dies at Mount Vernon, Virginia.
1800	Sacagawea is kidnapped by the Hidatsa Nation.
October 1800	Spain gives up Louisiana to Napoleon via the Treaty of Ildefenso.
March 1801	Jefferson appoints Robert Livingston U.S. minister (ambassador) to France.
March 4, 1801	Thomas Jefferson becomes third president of the United States.
March 6, 1801	Thomas Jefferson asks Lewis to be his personal secretary.
January 1802	Napoleon aims to retake Haiti.
November 13, 1802	Andre Michaux dies in Madagascar.
January 1803	Jefferson appoints James Monroe "Envoy Extraordinary" to France to join Robert Livingston in negotiations.
January 18, 1803	Thomas Jefferson writes a secret letter to Congress requesting $2,500 to fund an expedition to explore the Missouri River to the western shores. Funding is approved on February 28.
Spring 1803	Jefferson asks Lewis to lead an expedition to explore the West and find a route to the Pacific Ocean.

February 28, 1803	Jefferson writes a letter to Dr. Benjamin Rush notifying him of Lewis's travel to Philadelphia and asks him to help prepare Lewis for the trip west.
April 1803	Merriweather Lewis continues his education learning from some of best teachers of the time. He also ordered supplies for the trip while in Philadelphia.
April 27, 1803	Jefferson sends Lewis specific instructions for the upcoming expedition. These instructions are very similar to those he gave years earlier to Andre Michaux.
April 30, 1803	Monroe and Livingston successfully negotiate the Louisiana Purchase, adding 827,000 square miles to the United States.
May 14, 1803	Lewis writes to Jefferson from Philadelphia. He informs Jefferson of the navigation instruments that mathematician Robert Patterson and astronomer and surveyor Andrew Ellicott have recommended for the expedition.
June 19, 1803	Lewis writes a letter to William Clark requesting him to co-command the expedition with him.
July–August 1803	Lewis spends over a month in Pittsburgh supervising the construction of a 55-foot keelboat. During this time, Lewis buys Seaman, his Newfoundland dog for $20.
July 4, 1803	The Louisiana Purchase is announced.
July 5, 1803	Merriweather Lewis leaves Washington, D.C., for Pittsburgh, where the boat is being built.
July 6, 1803	Lewis goes to Harpers Ferry, in present-day West Virginia, to collect many of the supplies that had been delivered there.
July 18, 1803	William Clark accepts Lewis's request to join the expedition as coleader.
October 14, 1803	Lewis arrives in Clarkesville, where he reunites with Clark. Nine of Clark's men from Kentucky and Clark's slave, York, become part of the party.
October 20, 1803	The Senate ratifies the Louisiana Purchase Treaty by a vote of 24–7.
November 30, 1803	Louisiana is officially transferred from Spanish to French control.
December 8–9, 1803	Lewis and Clark spend the winter months of 1803 and early 1804 at Camp Dubois, Illinois, located on the east bank of the Mississippi River. The two recruit more men to their expedition, bringing their numbers to over 40. Food and supplies are continually gathered during this time.
December 20, 1803	Louisiana is transferred from French to the United States.
March 29, 1804	John Colter, Robert Frazer, and John Shields are court-martialed. No reason is recorded. No punishment is given.
May 14, 1804	The expedition begins.

May 17, 1804	William Werner, Hugh Hall, and John Collins are court-martialed for being absent without leave. Collins is also charged with behaving in an unbecoming manner. Werner and Hall, who both pled guilty, are each sentenced to 25 lashes, but the sentence is suspended due to previous good behavior. However, Collins who pled guilty to the first charge but not guilty to the second is sentenced to and receives 50 lashes. This punishment is given in public that evening.
May 25, 1804	Expedition passes La Charrette, about 60 miles from St. Louis, which is considered the beginning of the unknown.
June 12, 1804	Isaac White, and perhaps John Robertson, and Ebenezer Tuttle are sent back to St. Louis with a party of fur traders. While the reasons for this are not clear, Robertson, at one stage, is referred to as a corporal and another as a private, so it is possible that he was demoted and that they were all dismissed from the Corps.
June 29, 1804	John Collins is court-martialed once again; this time he is charged with getting drunk at his post. He is sentenced to 50 lashes.
May 21–July 31, 1804	Clark largely spends time making maps and charting the proper course. Lewis often goes ashore and uses his scientific knowledge on land, studying rock formations, soil, animals, and plants.
July 4, 1804	First recorded Fourth of July celebration west of the Mississippi occurs. A cannon is fired, and Independence Creek is named in celebration.
July 12, 1804	Alexander Willard is court-martialed for lying down and sleeping while on duty. He is sentenced to 100 lashes. This was commonly done over four nights with 25 lashes being administered each time so as to avoid infection or death.
August 13, 1804	Lewis and Clark hold council with a group of Oto and Missouri chiefs. They distribute gifts and peace medals. Lewis delivers a speech encouraging trade and peace on the plains.
August 18, 1804	Moses Reed is court-martialed for desertion. He is discharged from the expedition and sentenced to run the gauntlet.
August 20, 1804	Corps member sergeant Charles Floyd dies of what was probably a burst appendix. He is the only member of the expedition to die.
August 22, 1804	Lewis and Clark allow the men to select a leader to replace Sergeant Floyd's position: Patrick Gass from West Virginia is chosen.
August 30, 1804	Lewis and Clark hold council with the Yankton Sioux (located in modern-day South Dakota). Trade and peace are primarily discussed. Clark makes a speech, and gifts are distributed.

	The Yankton accept an invitation to send a delegation to Washington, D.C., where trade could be discussed with Thomas Jefferson.
September 7, 1804	The Corps see a prairie dog; it is the first recorded sighting of the animal.
October 13, 1804	John Newman is court-martialed for mutinous words. He is sentenced to work as a laborer, and in the spring, he is sent back to St. Louis with the keelboat.
October 26, 1804	The Corps arrive at the Mandan villages (near that of modern-day North Dakota). There are two Mandan villages and three others comprising the Hidatsa and Arahami tribes.
November 2–3, 1804	Lewis and Clark find a place to set up for the winter. They select a place on the east bank of the Missouri and build a structure that they call Fort Mandan.
November 4, 1804	French Canadian trapper, Toussaint Charbonneau joins the Corps as an interpreter. His wife, Sacagawea, who had been kidnapped by the Hidatsas about five years ago, accompanies him.
December 17, 1804	Clark records the temperature as being 45 degrees below zero.
December 17, 1804	Corps member Hugh Heney makes sketches of the country between the Missouri and the Mississippi Rivers, while a member of the Mandan Nation makes a map of the land to the west.
December 24, 1804	Fort Mandan is finished, and the men move in for the winter.
February 10, 1805	Thomas Howard is court-martialed for climbing over the fence, instead of entering through the gate. He is sentenced to 50 lashes, but the verdict is set aside.
February 11, 1805	Sacagawea gives birth to her son Jean Baptiste Charbonneau at Fort Mandan. He is nicknamed "Pompy" or "Little Pomp" by William Clark.
April 7, 1805	Lewis and Clark send the keelboat back down the Missouri River with a shipment for President Jefferson under the command of Corporal Richard Warfington. Moses Reed and John Newman, who had been expelled from the Corps, are sent back to St. Louis at this time. It is probable that Baptiste Deschamps also returned to St. Louis then. The rest of the Corps (consisting of Lewis, Clark, 27 soldiers, York, Charbonneau, Sacagawea, and her infant son) depart Fort Mandan.
April 13, 1805	One of the boats used to navigate nearly capsizes in an accident. While many were unnerved by the incident, tracks of the legendary white bear (grizzly) are spotted along with buffalo.

April 29, 1805	Lewis kills a never-seen-before grizzly bear. They had not believed that such an animal existed though they had been told about the bear from the local peoples.
Early to mid-May 1805	As the crew enters Valley county, Montana, they see large herds of buffalo, wolves, antelope, elk, and deer.
May 19, 1805	Seaman is injured.
May 20, 1805	Lewis and Clark name a river after Sacagawea.
May 26, 1805	Lewis sees the Rockies for the first time.
May 26, 1805	The Corps enter Fergus County, Montana (just two miles below the mouth of Windsor Creek). Lewis sees the Rocky Mountains for the very first time.
May 29, 1805	Clark names a river the Judith, after his cousin whom he hopes to marry on his return.
June 2, 1805	The expedition comes to a fork in the river, and they spend time scouting which direction they should go. Lewis and Clark both think the south fork is the correct route, while the rest of the party think it's the north fork. They go south and name the other fork Marias, after Lewis's cousin.
June 13, 1805	Lewis and Clark are proven correct in their decision after Lewis discovers the Great Falls of the Missouri while scouting ahead with a small group.
June 17, 1805	The Corps find a way to navigate around the Great Falls.
June 29, 1805	A dangerous hailstorm catches Lewis, Clark, Sacagawea, and Charbonneau away from shelter. A washout nearly drowns the group, when Clark loses a compass and other belongings. Some men along the portage route are also wounded in the process.
July 4, 1805	Fourth of July is celebrated for a second time in the West. Once again, the men are given extra whiskey.
July 30, 1805	Sacagawea begins to recognize the area as where she lived as a child before she was kidnapped.
August 8, 1805	Sacagawea recognizes Beaverhead Rock, which is close to her home.
August 12, 1805	The journals, papers, and animals sent by Lewis and Clark arrive in Washington, D.C., to President Jefferson.
August 12, 1805	Lewis crosses the Continental Divide and realizes there is no river route from east to west.
August 13, 1805	Lewis meets with Shoshones, and their chief Cameahwait.
August 17, 1805	Clark catches up with Lewis. Sacagawea reunites with her brother, Chief Cameahwait, and meets a woman who was kidnapped the same time she was.
September 11, 1805	The Corps begin their trek into the Bitterroot Mountains, helped by their Shoshone guide, Old Toby.

Late September to early October 1805	The Nez Perce assist the Corps in constructing canoes.
October 1805	The Corps make significant progress as they travel down the Columbia River.
November 3–8, 1805	On November 3, the Corps camp out on Diamond Island. On November 7, they camp on Pillar Rock. Clark makes the first note about seeing the Pacific Ocean (although they were still 20 miles away).
November 15–17, 1805	Lewis and the Corps finally reach and view the Pacific Ocean. Preparations to explore the coast throughout the winter and spring are made.
November 18–23, 1805	Lewis and Clark take turns leading Corps members throughout the coast to familiarize themselves. The areas of Haley's Bay, Cape Disappointment, and the northern coast are explored. They interact mainly with three Native nations: the Chinnook (who lived in the lower country), Chiltz (who largely resided on the sea coast), and the Clatsop (who were known for largely residing on the other side of the Columbia).
November 24, 1805	Lewis and Clark allow the Corps members to vote on where they would like to reside for the winter season. Every member of the group participates (including Sacagawea and York). Ultimately, Fort Clatsop (south of the Columbia River) is built for the winter. The Corps spend their remaining time on the Pacific coast here, prior to their return voyage home.
December 1805	The month is largely spent preparing for the coming winter. The discovery of elk on this coast comes as a large surprise to most of the Corps.
December 25, 1805	Lewis and Clark celebrate Christmas by handing out the last of the tobacco supplies and handkerchiefs.
January 1, 1806	Lewis notes in his journal that nothing of note is happening. This and the comments about the rain summarize the boredom and frustration the whole group felt.
January 4, 1806	In the U.S. capital, Thomas Jefferson meets with a delegation of Native chiefs (the Osages, Missouris, Kanzas, Ottos, Panis, Ayowas, and Siouxmeet), thanking them for the help they gave to Lewis and Clark.
January 8, 1806	In modern-day Ecola State Park, Oregon, Clark and company see the skeleton of a whale washed up onshore.
March 23, 1806	The Corps leave Fort Clatsop and begin the voyage home. The fort is given to Clatsop chief Coboway.
April 10–20, 1806	On April 10, the crew goes by the Great Rapids of the Columbia, and on April 18, they reach the Great Falls of the Columbia. On April 20, the expedition switches from canoes to horses to traverse the Rocky Mountains.

April 11, 1806	A group of Native Americans steals Seaman, Lewis's dog, which was quickly returned. Lewis was so furious after his dog was stolen, that he threatened to raze the village if this ever happened again.
April 27, 1806	Chief Yelleppit of the Walla Wallas invites the Corps to stay in his village, offering them food and horses in the process. A map is drawn of the confluence of the Columbia and Snake Rivers. The camp is in Benton County, Oregon.
April 28, 1806	The Corps leave modern-day Oregon.
May 5, 1806	The Corps leave modern-day Washington and cross into modern-day Idaho.
May 9, 1806	Near modern-day Orofino, Idaho, the Nez Perce bring 21 horses to the Corps.
May 10–mid June 1806	The Corps remain there, waiting over a month for the snow to melt.
June 29, 1806	The Corps cross Lolo Pass from Idaho into modern-day Montana.
July 3, 1806	Lewis and Clark split the party into two separate groups to look for more favorable passage over the Rocky Mountains. Lewis follows the Missouri eastward. Clark follows the Yellowstone to its junction with the Missouri.
Early to late July 1806	The split parties continue to navigate through their respective areas. The Continental Divide is crossed by both parties between July 6 and 7.
July 1806	Seaman's Creek is named after Lewis's dog Seaman.
July 25, 1806	Clark names a rock pillar on the Yellowstone River "Pompey's Tower" after Sacagawea's son. Clark carves his own name into the rock, leaving the only physical historical marker of the expedition that remains today.
July 27, 1806	Lewis camps in Blackfeet Native territory the day prior. They camp with a group of eight Blackfeet hunters they encountered. On July 27, the Blackfeet steal rifles from Corps members Drouillard and Lewis. Joseph Field wakes up and struggles with one of the hunters and stabs the man to death. In the chaos, Lewis shoots and potentially kills a second hunter. These are the only documented violent deaths on the expedition.
August 11, 1806	Private Cruzatte accidentally shoots Lewis while they are hunting elk.
August 12, 1806	Lewis and Clark's groups reunite.
August 14, 1806	The Corps reach the Mandan village again.
August 16, 1806	Corps member John Colter is allowed to leave the group to join two white trappers from Illinois (Joseph Dickson and Forest Hancock).

August 17, 1806	Sacagawea, Pompey, and Charbonneau leave the Corps.
August 20, 1806	The Corps make great progress toward St. Louis.
September 17, 1806	Across from Brunswick, Missouri, the Corps meet Captain John McClallen. He tells them that he presumed they were dead.
September 23, 1806	The Corps of Discovery finally reach St. Louis. Lewis writes to Jefferson detailing his successful mission of getting through the country to the Pacific Ocean.
October 20, 1806	Jefferson receives Lewis's letter that the expedition made it to the Pacific Ocean and that they have returned. Jefferson writes of his "unspeakable joy."
December 2, 1806	Jefferson makes a statement to Congress stating that the Lewis and Cark expedition was a success.
1807	Patrick Gass publishes his journals and coins the phrase "Corps of Discovery."
January 14, 1807	A dinner is held in Washington, D.C., to honor Lewis and Clark. (Clark did not arrive in time.)
February 4, 1807	Richard Bates is appointed secretary of Louisiana.
February 28, 1807	Jefferson nominates Lewis to be the governor of Upper Louisiana.
March 9, 1807	Clark is appointed agent for Indian affairs of Louisiana.
1808	Gass's journal is successfully published in London by John Budd. (It had been published in America the previous year.)
January 5, 1808	William Clark is married to Julia Hancock.
1809–1810	Frederick Bates becomes acting governor of Louisiana Territory.
January 10, 1809	William Clark's first child and son, Meriwether Lewis Clark, is born.
February 24, 1809	Lewis and Clark sign an agreement with the Missouri Fur Company.
March 4, 1809	James Madison becomes fourth president of the United States.
August 16, 1809	Thomas Jefferson writes what will turn out to be his last letter to Meriwether Lewis. Jefferson asks when the journals will be published, as he has already promised copies to people.
September 4, 1809	Meriwether Lewis leaves St. Louis for Washington, D.C.
September 11, 1809	Lewis writes his will, leaving everything to his mother, and he writes a (now-lost) letter to William Clark.
September 16, 1809	Lewis writes to President James Madison explaining why he will now go to Washington by land.
Fall 1809	Sacagawea, Charbonneau, and Pompey visit St. Louis. Clark had desired to tutor Pompey, while Charbonneau was given land to farm for the opportunity.
October 10, 1809	Lewis arrives at Grinders Inn.

October 11, 1809	Lewis dies at Grinders Inn.
October 18, 1809	Major James Neely writes to Thomas Jefferson stating that Lewis had committed suicide.
November 26, 1809	Jefferson writes to James Madison stating that Madison as president should have Lewis's papers and journals.
April 30, 1812	Louisiana becomes the 18th state of the United States.
December 1812	Sacagawea dies at Fort Manuel. Clark gets custody of Jean Baptiste (Pompey), along with her daughter Lisette.
February 26, 1813	Robert Livingston dies.
July 1, 1813	William Clark becomes the fourth governor of the Missouri Territory.
August 13, 1813	Jefferson writes to Paul Allen, who was publishing the Lewis and Clark journals. Jefferson provides biographical information on his late friend, Merriweather Lewis.
1814	The journals of Lewis and Clark are published.
1815	Jefferson sells his library of 6,500 books to Congress for $23,950.
February 13, 1818	George Rogers Clark dies.
Summer 1820	William Clark's wife Julia dies.
1821	William Clark marries Harriet Kinnerly Radford.
May 5, 1821	Napoleon died on the Island of St. Helena, over a thousand miles west of Angola, Africa. He had been banished from France in 1815.
November 15, 1824	Frederick Bates becomes the second governor of Missouri.
July 4, 1826	Thomas Jefferson dies.
July 4, 1831	James Monroe dies.
May 20, 1834	Marquis de Lafayette dies in Paris, France.
July 14, 1834	Edmond-Charles Genet dies in East Greenbush, New York.
June 28, 1836	James Madison dies.
September 8, 1837	Lucy Marks (Meriwether Lewis's mother) dies.
September 1, 1838	William Clark dies.
1843	Toussaint Charbonneau dies.
May 16, 1866	Jean Baptiste Charbonneau dies.
April 2, 1870	Patrick Gass, the last member of the Corps of Discovery, dies.

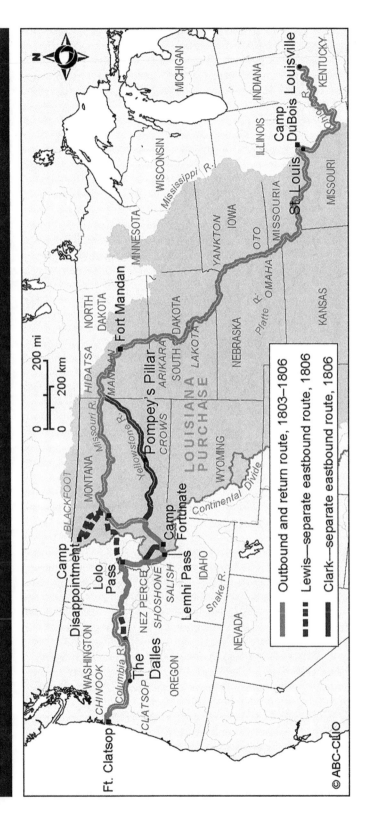
LEWIS AND CLARK EXPEDITION

Acknowledgments

Many years ago, Stephen Ambrose walked into an undergraduate classroom in Dublin, Ireland, and began teaching a class on the American presidency. One particular afternoon, he spoke about Thomas Jefferson, Meriwether Lewis, and William Clark and how the three of them banded together to carry out one of the most amazing feats of all time: traveling to, exploring, and surviving the American West. He described the route, the trails, the mosquitoes, and the bears. I was fascinated then and have remained in awe of their accomplishments ever since. So when many years later Mark Lender called me and said that Michael Millman was looking for someone to write about Lewis and Clark, I was delighted and excited at the chance to put this book together.

Michael has been patient with me as I gathered and wrote, and so he is the first person I would like to thank here. I would like also to thank Mark Lender, who took a chance on hiring a newly minted PhD all those years ago. My colleagues in the Department of History at Kean—Frank Argote-Freyre, Christopher Bellitto, Frank Esposito, Sue Gronewold, Elizabeth Hyde, Dennis Klein, Xurong Kong, Jonathan Mercantini, Abigail Perkiss, Brian Regal, and Frank Wetta—are the best a person could ask for, and I am grateful that we work so well together. Mrs. Mary Woubneh, as has been pointed out many times, runs the show and organizes us all every semester; thank you Mary. Two Kean students, Christian Mills and Keven Swidzinski, helped me gather together a bibliography and a timeline. Others at Kean to whom I am grateful include Susan Gannon and Christina Leedy. The Kean Foundation has provided me grants that have allowed me to write, and I am truly grateful. My mother Kathleen and my brother Shay are always supportive. I want to thank my "frousins" Cristin, Christianna, and Teresa, who have helped me in so many ways. I am lucky to have many friends who have helped in all sorts of different ways, each unique, each important. So thank you, Bob, Dave, Grace, Joe, Kevin, Mary, Pam, Patti, Paula, Susan, and Theresa.

Mark and Emma are amazing. They allowed me to write and made me write. Emma also helped find art work for the cover and helped me find books and articles in libraries. It is to Mark and Emma (and Beethoven) I dedicate this book. I also dedicate it to the memory of my father, Sean Nicholson, who was my first and best teacher of history.

Mark, Emma, and I have found Lewis, Clark, Sacagawea, and York in museums from Washington, D.C., to Texas. May our adventures continue, and may our love of life, smiles, and laughter last forever.

Chapter 1

Thomas Jefferson and the American West

Introduction

Thomas Jefferson loved the idea of the American West. He spent considerable time reading about, thinking about, and wondering about the West. He gathered in his library books about the possible peoples and animals who lived there. For Jefferson, the West held the promise of American expansionism: it was a place for Americans to move to, live in, and farm. Those who farmed and defended their farms would then help defend America. The West was a vital part of the creation and expansion of America. From his father, Thomas Jefferson understood the importance of map-making, and so he would try four different times to organize exploratory expeditions into the American West. The first three attempts all ended in failure.

On December 4, 1783, Jefferson, who had been appointed as a Virginia delegate to the Confederation Congress, wrote a letter to General George Rogers Clark (1752–1818), when he made his first attempt to organize an expedition to the West. In that letter to Clark, Jefferson, always the collector, thanked Clark for the seeds and shells he had received and then told Clark that he would be happy to have the bones and teeth of all buffalos and mammoths that Clark could find. Jefferson was convinced that the West was filled with fossils and bones of antediluvian beasts, but he also wondered if some of these animals were not in fact extinct. In the same letter, he also informed Clark that there was an expedition being organized in England to travel to the American West. The British expedition was being organized for supposedly scientific reasons, but Jefferson was suspicious. He expressed his fears that such a scientific exploration easily could become a military takeover of the area, and so Jefferson wanted to have the area mapped in case war broke out. With Clark's military background, experience, and previous military successes, Jefferson asked Clark if he would consider leading an expedition. Clark replied on February 8, 1784. He turned Jefferson down, explaining that he simply could not financially afford such a trip. However, Clark did advise Jefferson as to how such a trip might be organized. This advice would later form the basis of the 1804 expedition, which was co-commanded by George Rogers Clark's younger brother, William Clark.

George Clark advised Jefferson that any exploratory party should be as small as possible, so as not to alarm the Native population. He also recommended that the group should seek to learn about the animals, the plants, and the people of the West, rather than seek to take over land. The expedition should seek to engage with and listen to the local population. This way, Clark insisted, they would bring with them a message of peace from the government of the United States. Later in another letter in 1802, George Clark specifically suggested his younger brother William would be the ideal person to take part in such a trip.

Three years later, while in Paris first as part of a trade negotiations team, Jefferson joined with a group, which included Benjamin Franklin, that attempted to send the American explorer John Ledyard from Russia to America via the Bering Straits. From there, the plan was that Ledyard would travel overland to Virginia. This audacious plan almost worked. Ledyard left London in December 1786 and reached St. Petersburg, Russia's second-largest city, in March 1787. A few months later, in June 1787, Ledyard set off from St. Petersburg in a horse-drawn coach. He reached the Siberian city of Yakutsk in September. It was here that his journey came to an abrupt end when the Russian police arrested him under suspicion of spying. Up until his arrest, Ledyard's journals describe the people and places along his route. His respect for, and interest in, the groups of people he met was obvious. While this journey was yet again a failure for Jefferson, he would use something from this trip for the Lewis and Clark expedition: the idea of keeping detailed journals about who and what were encountered en route.

Jefferson's third attempt to organize a trip to explore the West began in 1793 when Jefferson tried to get other members of the American Philosophical Society to finance the French botanist and explorer Andre Michaux (1746–1802) to find the shortest way from the eastern United States to the Pacific Ocean. This trip failed soon after it began, as Michaux's spying for France became known.

In 1801, Thomas Jefferson became the third president of the United States. The same year, France acquired Louisiana from Spain through the secret Treaty of San Ildefonso. With the port of New Orleans now under the control of France, Napoleon Bonaparte intended to expand France's empire and promote trade between Europe, America, and the islands of the Caribbean. Key to Napoleon's plan for renewed expansion was the French-controlled island of Saint Dominque, which had been taken from France in a revolt beginning in 1791. Despite the fact that the treaty was a secret, rumors of it had reached Washington, D.C. Jefferson feared it could mean that France would attempt a takeover of land in America, which would mean another war for the United States, one that the United States could not afford.

To try to find out more about the treaty and to see just what France was thinking, Jefferson dispatched Robert Livingston (1746–1813), a member of the Committee of Five who had drafted the Declaration of Independence, to Paris to negotiate with Napoleon's Foreign Minister Charles-Maurice de Talleyrand (1754–1838). Jefferson instructed Livingston to attempt to purchase New Orleans and west Florida for $10 million. This area along the Gulf of Mexico and the mouth of the Mississippi River was key to controlling trade not only in the Caribbean islands but also within North America. Livingston's attempts at negotiation were met with French resistance. In April 1803, Jefferson sent James Monroe (1758–1831) to help.

Livingston was a skilled diplomat. During the negotiations, he carefully suggested that the United States would soon reach an agreement with the British.

The French knew the British could take New Orleans by force if they wanted to. But Livingston was not expecting the French response. The French offered to sell for $15 million the whole 828,000 square miles of the Louisiana Territory to the United States. The two agreed quickly to the offer. The treaty was dated April 30, 1803, and signed by Livingston and Monroe on May 2. When he was told about the agreement, Jefferson was in a bit of a dilemma as the U.S. Constitution did not allow him to purchase land. Jefferson decided to forge ahead with the purchase and not wait for a constitutional amendment. The treaty was announced on July 4, 1803, and was ratified by the Senate on October 20, by a vote of 24 to 7.

The Louisiana Purchase was probably the best land deal ever. The United States bought 828,000,000 square miles from France for $15 million, adding part or all of 15 present-day states to the United States. This new area extended the United States west from the Mississippi River to the Rocky Mountains and added the area from the Gulf of Mexico up to the Canadian border, doubling the size of the United States.

Now the territory had to be explored and mapped. The person chosen to lead the trip was Jefferson's secretary and fellow-Virginian Meriwether Lewis. His co-captain was William Clark, younger brother of George Roger Clark.

Document 1

LETTER FROM THOMAS JEFFERSON TO GENERAL GEORGE ROGERS CLARK (DECEMBER 4, 1783)

Introduction: Shells, Seeds, and a Mammoth, and a Transcontinental Trip

George Rogers Clark (1752–1818) was born in Charlottesville, Virginia, the second of ten children born to John and Ann Rogers Clark. Trained to be a surveyor, he made trips to western Virginia and Kentucky, claiming land there for himself and his family. By 1774 he was a captain in the local militia. During the Revolutionary War, he became a national hero for his success in the Northeast. After the war, Clark was financially broke, as he had taken personal responsibility for much of the cost of the campaigns he fought. He later wrote his memoirs in an attempt to make some money, but he struggled financially for the rest of his life.

In December 1783, when Clark and Jefferson were exchanging letters, Clark was still in severe financial debt. He was constantly traveling and always in contact with Thomas Jefferson, sending him specimens of animals and bones he came across. Jefferson was always part scientist, part paleontologist, as well as a political statesman concerned for the new United States. Jefferson knew that peace was vital if the country was to survive and have a chance to thrive economically.

In order to survive, the new country's military had to have as much knowledge as possible, and so Jefferson wanted the West to be explored. With his military and surveyor background, as well as his practical knowledge of the Native people, Clark would be ideal for such an expedition. The Treaty of Paris, which formally ended the Revolutionary War between the United States and Great Britain, was not yet ratified, and so the security of the United States was not guaranteed. In the following letter, Jefferson expresses his concern about an alleged scientific expedition by the British. Jefferson was suspicious of Britain's motives and feared that it was interested in further "colonizing" the continent. Ironically, while the British were planning an extensive expedition to North America, Jefferson was not sure the new United States had enough money to finance an expedition of its own.

While Jefferson's interest was in part political, it was also always partly personal. Jefferson wanted Clark to continue to gather bones and remnants of animals for him as Clark traveled. In particular, what Jefferson was anxious for Clark to find were bones of a mammoth anywhere in the West. Jefferson believed that these animals might still exist.

To George Rogers Clark

Annapolis Dec. 4. 1783.

DEAR SIR

I received here about a week ago your obliging letter of Oct. 12. 1783. with the shells and seeds for which I return you many thanks. You are also so kind as to keep alive the hope of getting for me as many of the different species of bones, teeth and tusks of the Mammoth as can now be found. This will be most acceptable. Pittsburgh and Philadelphia or Winchester will be the surest channel of conveyance. I find they have subscribed a very large sum of money in England for exploring the country from the Missisipi to California. They pretend it is only to promote knolege. I am afraid they have thoughts of colonising into that quarter. Some of us have been talking here in a feeble way of making the attempt to search that country. But I doubt whether we have enough of that kind of spirit to raise the money. How would you like to lead such a party? Tho I am afraid our prospect is not worth asking the question. The definitive treaty of peace is at length arrived. It is not altered from the preliminaries. The cession of the territory West of Ohio to the United states has been at length accepted by Congress with some small alterations of the conditions. We are in daily expectation of receiving it with the final approbation of Virginia. Congress have been lately agitated by questions where they should fix their residence. They first resolved on Trentown. The Southern states however contrived to get a vote that they would give half their time to Georgetown at the Falls of Patowmac. Still we consider the matter as undecided between the Delaware and Patowmac. We urge the latter as the only point of union which can cement us to our Western friends when they shall be formed into separate states. I shall always be happy to hear from you and am with very particular esteem Dr. Sir Your friend & humble servt.,

TH: JEFFERSON

Source: "Thomas Jefferson to George Rogers Clark, 4 December 1783," in Jameson, J. Franklin, ed. *The American Historical Review*, Volume III, October 1897 to July 1898. New York: The Macmillan Company, 1898, 673.

Further Reading

Ambrose, Stephen. *Undaunted Courage*. Urbana: University of Chicago Press, 1991.

Ellis, Joseph. *American Sphinx: The Character of Thomas Jefferson*. New York: Vintage Books, 1998.

Harris, Matthew, and Jay H. Buckley, eds. *Zebulon Pike, Thomas Jefferson and the Opening of the American West*. Norman: University of Oklahoma Press, 2012.

Harrison, Lowell. *George Roger Clark and the War in the West*. Lexington: University of Kentucky Press, 2001.

McCullough, David. *1776*. New York: Simon and Schuster, 2016.

Nester, William. *George Clark: I Glory in War*. Norman: University of Oklahoma Press, 2012.

Thom, James Alexander. *Long Knife*. New York: Ballantine Books, 1994.

U.S. Department of the Interior. *George Rogers Clark and the Winning of the Old Northwest*. Create Space, 2016.

Document 2

LETTER FROM GENERAL GEORGE ROGERS CLARK TO THOMAS JEFFERSON (FEBRUARY 8, 1784)

Introduction: Looking Forward: A Refusal and Advice for the Future

A soldier and surveyor, George Rogers Clark was also someone who had been in constant contact with many of the Native American nations throughout his career. While he had taken part in wars with many Native nations, he had also been involved in treaties. He was exactly the sort of man that Jefferson needed: someone with the political ability to deal peacefully with various groups.

On December 4, 1783, Jefferson wrote to Clark asking him to consider leading a trip west to explore and map the land. On February 1784, Clark replied to Jefferson and gently refused his request, citing financial considerations.

Despite the fact that he declined to lead such an expedition, Clark outlined in his response to Jefferson a blueprint for any trip west. Clark explained in great detail just how such a trip should be set up and how the people on the trip should deal with the Native population. Surprisingly, for the time, Clark's suggestions were based on the need to respect the languages and cultures of the Native people.

Clark begins by telling Jefferson that one of the most important aspects of the expedition was the size the expedition: that the expedition party should be as small as possible, for a large group would be taken as a sign of war. Second, Clark suggests that any group that goes should be aware of the importance of knowing and understanding languages and customs. Clark stresses the distinctiveness of each nation and advises Jefferson that the group sent by him needs to be aware of the history of these different peoples. Clark recommends that the people who go will need specific education beforehand to avoid any mistake that could result in a war. Even at this early stage of Western history, Clark suggests to Jefferson the long-term idea of appointing a superintendent of Indian affairs in the West.

Jefferson would later educate Meriwether Lewis in just such a manner as Clark described. A decade after this correspondence, Lewis and George Rogers Clark's younger brother William would travel west and respectfully talk to and listen to the various Native American nations.

Richmond Feby. 8th 1784

Sᴿ

Your favour of the 4th Decr. last came Safe to hand. I should have given you an answer Sooner but some part of the subject required serious attention in a person in my cituation. It gives me pleasure to suppose you my friend originating from the Idea I have of your Sentiments. The Bones you wish for will undoubtedly be sent to you without some misfortune should happen me as I am now divesting myself of a trust that I have long Suffered in and hope in future to have pleasure in private connections. Your proposition respecting a tour to the west and North west of the Continent would be Extreamly agreable to me could I afford it but I have late discovered that I knew nothing of the lucrative policy of the world Supposing my duty required every attention and sacrifice to the Publick Interest but must now look forward for future Support. Should Congress resolve to have the western Country Explored I should take pleasure in lending all the aid in my power as an Individual it is what I think we ought to do. But pardon me when I inform you that I think our Ideas of this Business is generally wrong. Large parties will never answer the purpose. They will allarm the Indian Nations they pass through. Three or four young Men well qualified for the Task might perhaps compleat your wishes at a very Trifling Expence a tolerable subsistance on their return might procure them. They must learn the Language of the distant Nations they pass through, the Geography of their Country, antient Speech or Tradition, passing as men tracing the steps of our four Fathers wishing to know from whence we came. This would require four or five years, an Expence worthey the attention of Congress, from the Nature of things I should suppose that you would require a general superintendant of Indian affairs to the westward as the greatest body of those people live in that quarter I should have no objections in serving them. I shall set out for the Falls of Ohio in a few Days whare I expect to reside perhaps for Life. Letters that you might think of Honouring me with might be sent by the way of Pittsburgh. Such favours will be always gratefully receiv'd. I am Sr with Respect your obedt. Servt,

G R Cʟᴀʀᴋ

Source: "To Thomas Jefferson from George Rogers Clark, 8 February 1784." *Founders Online,* National Archives. Available at: http://founders.archives.gov/documents/Jefferson/01-15-02-0587.

Further Reading

Ambrose, Stephen. *Undaunted Courage.* Urbana: University of Chicago Press, 1991.
Ellis, Joseph. *American Sphinx: The Character of Thomas Jefferson.* New York: Vintage Books, 1998.

Harris, Matthew, and Jay H. Buckley, eds. *Zebulon Pike, Thomas Jefferson and the Opening of the American West*. Norman: University of Oklahoma Press, 2012.

Harrison, Lowell. *George Roger Clark and the War in the West*. Lexington: University of Kentucky Press, 2001.

McCullough, David. *1776*. New York: Simon and Schuster, 20016

Nester, William. *George Clark: I Glory in War*. Norman: University of Oklahoma Press, 2012.

Thom, James Alexander. *Long Knife*. New York: Ballantine Books, 1994.

U.S. Department of the Interior. *George Rogers Clark and the Winning of the Old NorthWest*. Create Space, 2016.

Document 3

LETTER FROM THOMAS JEFFERSON TO MARQUIS DE LAFAYETTE (FEBRUARY 9, 1786)

Introduction: John Ledyard: His Journey to the West Coast via Russia

Finally by 1786, Jefferson had found someone who could go west: John Ledyard (1751–1789). John Ledyard was born in Groton, Connecticut, the first child of Abigail and Captain John Ledyard, a sea captain. Ledyard showed his adventuring spirit when he was young; in 1773, he left Dartmouth College without permission in a canoe, traveling the 130 miles to his grandfather's farm. Ledyard became part of Dartmouth history forever, and his "escape" is remembered each year by the Ledyard Canoe Club. Ledyard soon after began a series of voyages while employed as a seaman, which took him from America to Europe to the Caribbean.

In 1775, Ledyard joined the British Navy and was a member of Captain James's Cook's third and final voyage, which he would later describe in his book: A Journal of Captain Cook's Last Voyage. After he returned to England, still in the British Navy, he was ordered on a ship to go to Long Island. Ledyard, who did not wish to fight against his fellow Americans in the Revolutionary War, arrived at Long Island and then promptly deserted.

In 1784, Ledyard returned to Europe and soon became interested in a trip organized by Thomas Jefferson. Jefferson wanted someone to explore and map a route across America. Ledyard came up with a unique way to do this: his suggestion was for him to travel to the East Coast of America via the West Coast. The plan was for him to travel to Russia, sail across the Pacific Ocean to the Nootka Sound, part of present-day Vancouver Island, British Columbia, Canada. From there, the plan was for Ledyard to walk across America to the East Coast of the United States.

On February 9, 1789, Jefferson wrote a letter of introduction for Ledyard to the Marquis de Lafayette (1757–1834) to secure his political and financial support. Lafayette, a wealthy French nobleman, had fought in the American Revolutionary War. His parents died before he was 13 years old, leaving him an orphan—but very rich. He arrived in America at 19 years old, ready to fight the British, partly as a revenge, as his father had been killed fighting them in the Seven Years' War. He was commissioned major general by the Continental Congress on July 31, 1771, and his reputation as a brave soldier was made as he was wounded at the Battle of Brandywine on September 11, 1777, and stayed at Valley Forge in the winter of 1777–1778.

Lafayette duly gave Ledyard the necessary introductions and support. With his backing, Ledyard began well, leaving Paris and traveling as far as Siberia. However, in Siberia he was arrested, as he was suspected of being a spy, was duly deported to Poland, and was warned not to return. Jefferson's second attempt at an expedition to the West had failed.

To Lafayette

Paris Feb. 9. 1786.

Dear Sir

The Mr. John Ledyard, who proposes to undertake the journey through the Northern parts of Asia and America, is a citizen of Connecticut, one of the united states of America. He accompanied Capt. Cook in his last voiage to the North-western parts of America, and rendered himself useful to that officer, on some occasions, by a spirit of enterprize which has distinguished his whole life. He has genius, an education better than the common, and a talent for useful and interesting observation. I believe him to be an honest man, and a man of truth. To all this he adds just as much singularity of character, and of that particular kind too, as was necessary to make him undertake the journey he proposes. Should he get safe through it, I think he will give an interesting account of what he shall have seen.

I have the honour to be with sentiments of sincere esteem and respect Dear Sir Your most obedient and most humble servant.

Th: Jefferson

Source: "From Thomas Jefferson to Lafayette, 9 February 1786," in Randolph, Thomas Jefferson, ed. *Memoirs, Correspondence, and Miscellanies, from the Papers of Thomas Jefferson.* Volume 1. Charlottesville: F. Carr, and Co., 1829, 444.

Further Reading

Bernier, Oliver. *Lafayette: Hero of Two Worlds.* New York: Dutton Adult, 1993.

Clary, David. *Adopted Son: Washington, Lafayette and the Friendship That Saved the Revolution.* New York: Bantam, 2007.

Ellis, Joseph. *Founding Brothers: The Revolutionary Generation.* New York: Vintage Books, 2002.

Gaines, James. *For Liberty ad Glory: Washington, Lafayette, and Their Revolutions.* New York: Norton, 2007.

Gifford, Bill. *In Search of the First American Explorer.* New York: Harcourt, 2007.

Gray, Edward. *The Making of John Ledyard: Empire and Ambition in the Life of an Early American Traveler.* New Haven, CT: Yale University Press, 2017.

Holbrook, Sabra. *Lafayette: Man in the Middle.* New York: Atheneum Books, 1977.

Kramer, Lloyd. *Lafayette in Two Worlds: Public Cultures and Personal Identities in an Age of Revolution.* Chapel Hill: North Carolina Press, 1996.

Leepson, Marc. *Lafayette: Lessons in Leadership from an Idealist General.* New York: St. Martin's Press, 2011.

Unger, Harlow. *Lafette.* Hoboken, NJ: Wiley, 2003.

Zug, James. *American Traveler: The Life and Adventures of John Ledyard, The Man Who Dreamed of Walking the World.* New York: Basic Books, 2004.

Document 4

LETTER FROM THOMAS JEFFERSON TO RICHARD CLAIBORNE (AUGUST 7, 1787)

Introduction: The Case for Germans to Settle in the West

One of the many reasons as to why Jefferson wanted the West mapped was so that Americans, and in particular new immigrants to America, could settle there. People were therefore needed in the West, but who would go and begin a new life there? Who would want to go?

Even at the beginning of the nineteenth century, immigration was already a difficult, even contentious topic. Those who did not speak English as a first language were seen as less than American, or even un-American.

In his following 1787 letter to Richard Claiborne, Jefferson outlined his plans that the people who would settle the West would be non-English speakers. Of all the groups arriving to the United States at the time, Jefferson thought that the new German-speaking immigrants would be best suited to the West.

Thus while the West was about security for Jefferson, it was also about expansion. The West provided wide open land that was as yet unclaimed. For Jefferson, farmers were the basis of a society, as farmers would not easily give up land, and so was a naturally strong defense. The idea of "Manifest Destiny"—the notion that the United States was destined by God to expand its boundaries—would not become part of American culture and politics until 1845. But here in 1787, more than a half century earlier, Jefferson saw the West and its expansion as a vital part of expanding America and its agrarian culture for the sake of safety and security.

Richard Claiborne (1755–1819) was a fellow Virginian and friend of Washington and Jefferson. Claiborne would later serve as secretary for New Orleans Territory and was appointed a territorial judge by Jefferson in 1808.

To Richard Claiborne

Paris Aug. 8. 1787.

Sir

I am of opinion that American tenants for Western lands could not be procured, and if they could, they would be very unsure. The best as far as I have been able to judge are foreigners who do not speak the language. Unable to communicate with the people of the country they confine themselves to their farms and their families, compare their present state to what it was in Europe, and find great reason to be contented.

Of all foreigners I should prefer Germans. They are the easiest got, the best for their landlord, and do best for themselves. The deed in which you were interested having been sent to me the other day to be authenticated, I took the inclosed note of it's particulars for you. I am with much esteem Sir Your most obedient & most humble servt.,

Tн: Jefferson

Source: "From Thomas Jefferson to Richard Claiborne, 8 August 1787," in Washington, H. A., ed. *The Works of Thomas Jefferson.* Volume II. New York: Townsend Mac Coun., 1884, 235.

Further Reading

Aron, Stephen. *The American West: A Very Short Introduction.* Oxford: Oxford University Press, 2015.

Blackhawk, Ned. *Violence over Land: Indians and Empires in the Early American West.* Cambridge, MA: Harvard University Press, 1998.

Brown, Dee. *The American West.* New York: Touchstone, 1995.

Carlson, Paul. *The Plains Indians.* Austin, TX: A & M University, 1998.

Fenster, Julie. *Jefferson's America: The President, the Purchase, and the Explorers Who Transformed a Nation.* New York: Crown, 2016.

Richter, Daniel. *Facing East from Indian Country: A Native History of Early America.* Cambridge, MA: Harvard University Press, 1993.

Stephanson, Anders. *Manifest Destiny: American Expansion and the Empire of the Right.* New York: Hill and Wang, 1996.

Taylor, Alan. *American Revolutions: A Continental History, 1750–1804.* New York: Norton, 2017.

Document 5

LETTER FROM THOMAS JEFFERSON TO GEORGE WASHINGTON (JANUARY 22, 1793)

Introduction: Requesting Support for Andre Michaux

In 1793, Jefferson was once again planning an expedition west and had found someone who was willing and able to explore: Andre Michaux (1746–1802). Michaux was a French botanist and explorer. His father was a farmer who worked for the royal family. By the age of 20, he too was working for King Louis XVI and in 1782 was sent by Queen Marie Antoinette (1755–1793) to Persia, modern-day Iran, to collect seeds and plants for a new garden in France. He returned to France with a huge collection of seeds and plants and was appointed "King's Botanist." King Louis XVI sent him to the United States in order to see what plants and seeds could be used by the French to help restore forests in France.

Michaux arrived in the United States in 1785, delighted with everything he found. He spent time in the United States and Canada, traveling along the East Coast collecting plants and various seeds, even setting up gardens in New Jersey. He also bought property

in Charleston, South Carolina, where he began to create a garden. Michaux was also an explorer and enjoyed adventure. He traveled into areas of the Cherokee Nation, in modern-day Virginia and North and South Carolina.

In 1792, Michaux approached Jefferson and the American Philosophical Society with the proposal that he would explore the Missouri River and a possible route west. The American Philosophical Society was founded in 1743 by Benjamin Franklin for what he described as "promoting useful knowledge." Its primary purpose was to give a place where natural sciences could be discussed and studied in the Americas. Its members wanted America to improve industrially and agriculturally so that the economy would grow, and the idea of an exploratory trip west appealed to them.

Jefferson in the letter that follows tells George Washington about Michaux. Washington, who became president of the United States in 1789, had always believed that expansion of the United States was a primary factor in its security. The potential knowledge that a trip west would supply could be vital to not just the long-term expansion of the United States but its short-term and even immediate survival.

To George Washington

Jan. 22. 1793.

Th: Jefferson has the honor to inclose to the President the subscription paper he has prepared for enabling the Philosophical society to send Mr. Michaux on the mission through the country between the Missisipi and South sea, and he will have that of waiting on him tomorrow morning on the subject.

Source: "From Thomas Jefferson to George Washington, 22 January 1793," *Founders Online,* National Archives. Available at: http://founders.archives.gov/documents/Jefferson/01-25-02-0090.

Further Reading

Calloway, Colin. *The Indian World of George Washington: The First President, the First Americans, and the Birth of the Nation.* Oxford: Oxford University Press, 2018.

Chernow, Ron. *Washington: A Life.* New York: Penguin Books, 2011.

Ellis, Joseph. *His Excellency: George Washington.* New York: Vintage Reprint, 2005.

Ellis, Joseph. *The Quartet: Orchestrating the Second American Revolution, 1783–1789.* New York: Vintage Reprint, 2016.

Flexner, James Thomas. *Washington: The Indispensable Man.* New York: Back Bay Books, 1994.

McCracken Peck, Robert, Patricia Tyson Stroud, and Rosamond Purcell. *A Glorious Enterprise: The Academy of Natural Sciences of Philadelphia and the Making of American Science.* Philadelphia: University of Pennsylvania Press, 2012.

Rhodehamel, John. *George Washington: The Wonder of the Age.* New Haven, CT: Yale University Press, 2017.

Savage, Henry and Elizabeth Savage. *Andre and Francois Michaux.* Charlottesville: University of Virginia Press, 1996.

Stark, Peter. *Young Washington: How Wilderness and War Forged America's Founding Father.* New York: Ecco Press, 2018.

Document 6

LETTER FROM GEORGE WASHINGTON TO THOMAS JEFFERSON (JANUARY 22, 1793)

Introduction: Washington's Response and Support for the Expedition Led by Michaux

George Washington (1732–1799) was born in Westmoreland County, Virginia, the son of Augustine Washington and Mary Ball Washington. Raised in Virginia, he grew up to be a surveyor, soldier, and the first president of the United States. In 1748, aged 16, Washington with George William Fairfax surveyed the Virginian frontier. At age 17, Washington was appointed country surveyor for Culpeper County, Virginia.

Washington's military ability was established during the French Indian War, 1754–1763. His experience in the war taught him that military battles were fought successfully only if tactics could be matched to the territory where they were fighting. Exact knowledge of the geography of an area was vital in war.

By the time the Revolutionary War was won, Washington was the leader of the new country. But his military successes had helped shape his political opinions. Washington's keen interest in Michaux's trip can be seen in the fact that he replied to Jefferson's letter the day it arrived. He too was anxious for the project to go ahead, and he also offered to back the project financially. Washington's support was key for any expedition. Washington was the country's political leader, and with his support, others would quickly join. Jefferson was eventually able to raise $870.

To Thomas Jefferson

Philadelphia 22d Jan. 1793

DEAR SIR,

Nothing occurs to me as necessary to be added to the enclosed project.

If the Subscription is not confined to the members of the Philosophical Society I would readily add my mite to the means for encouraging Mr Michaud's undertaking—and do authorize you to place me among, & upon a footing with the respectable sums which may be Subscribed. I am always Yours.

GO: WASHINGTON

Source: "From George Washington to Thomas Jefferson, 22 January 1793," *Founders Online,* National Archives. Available at: http://founders.archives.gov/documents/ Washington/05-12-02-0016. Originally printed in *The Papers of George Washington,* Presidential Series, Volume 12, *16 January 1793–31 May 1793,* ed. Christine Sternberg Patrick and John C. Pinheiro. Charlottesville: University of Virginia Press, 2005, 39–40.

Further Reading

Calloway, Colin. *The Indian World of George Washington: The First President, the First Americans, and the Birth of the Nation.* Oxford: Oxford University Press, 2018.

Chernow, Ron. *Washington: A Life.* New York: Penguin Books, 2011.

Ellis, Joseph. *His Excellency: George Washington.* New York: Vintage Reprint, 2005.

Ellis, Joseph. *The Quartet: Orchestrating the Second American Revolution, 1783–1789.* New York: Vintage Reprint, 2016.

Flexner, James Thomas. *Washington: The Indispensable Man.* New York: Back Bay Books, 1994.

Peterson, Merrill. *Thomas Jefferson and the New Nation: A Biography.* Oxford University Press, 2013.

Rhodehamel, John. *George Washington: The Wonder of the Age.* New Haven, CT: Yale University Press, 2017.

Savage, Henry. *Andre and Francois Michaux.* University of Virginia Press, 1996.

Stark, Peter. Young *Washington: How Wilderness and War Forged America's Founding Father.* New York: Ecco Press, 2018.

Document 7

AMERICAN PHILOSOPHICAL SOCIETY'S INSTRUCTIONS TO ANDRE MICHAUX (JANUARY 23, 1793)

Introduction: Finding the Shortest Route between the United States and the Pacific Ocean

On April 19, 1793, the American Philosophical Society agreed to financially back Andre Michaux's trip west. On April 30, Jefferson wrote to Michaux with specific instructions for the journey. It is practically these same instructions that Jefferson would later give to Lewis and Clark when they headed west.

The most important and primary goal of this trip was to find the quickest and easiest route between the eastern United States and the Pacific Ocean. Michaux was told to explore the Missouri River all the way to the Pacific Ocean; map the route; and make notes about rivers, animals, vegetables, plants, and soil. Jefferson instructed him to note who lived in these various areas, their language and culture, and how economic interactions, in particular the buying and selling of goods, between the various Native nations occur. Jefferson was clear about a particular thing—Michaux's relations with the Native Americans had to remain friendly.

Of special note are the instructions given by Jefferson regarding the care he wanted taken with Michaux's journals. When he reached the Pacific Ocean, Michaux was to make contact with Europeans there and give them copies of his notes so that they could bring these copies back to the East Coast by boat.

Once back in Philadelphia, Michaux was told he would be expected to return to the Philosophical Society and give a detailed talk about his travels and answer all and any questions the members of the society might have. Jefferson was always clear that scientific knowledge should be shared.

But these elaborate plans for Michaux's trip fell apart quickly when Michaux was discovered of acting as a spy for France.

[ca. 30 Apr. 1793]

To Mr. Andrew Michaud.

Sundry persons having subscribed certain sums of money for your encouragement to explore the country along the Missouri, and thence Westwardly to the Pacific ocean, having submitted the plan of the enterprize to the direction of the American Philosophical society, and the Society having accepted of the trust, they proceed to give you the following instructions.

They observe to you that the chief objects of your journey are to find the shortest and most convenient route of communication between the US. and the Pacific ocean, within the temperate latitudes, and to learn such particulars as can be obtained of the country through which it passes, it's productions, inhabitants and other interesting circumstances.

As a channel of communication between these states and the Pacific ocean, the Missouri, so far as it extends, presents itself under circumstances of unquestioned preference. It has therefore been declared as a fundamental object of the subscription, (not to be dispensed with) that this river shall be considered and explored as a part of the communication sought for. To the neighborhood of this river therefore, that is to say to the town of Kaskaskia, the society will procure you a conveyance in company with the Indians of that town now in Philadelphia.

From thence you will cross the Missisipi and pass by land to the nearest part of the Missouri above the Spanish settlements, that you may avoid the risk of being stopped.

You will then pursue such of the largest streams of that river, as shall lead by the shortest way, and the lowest latitudes to the Pacific ocean.

When, pursuing these streams, you shall find yourself at the point from whence you may get by the shortest and most convenient route to some principal river of the Pacific ocean, you are to proceed to such river, and pursue it's course to the ocean. It would seem by the latest maps as if a river called Oregan interlocked with the Missouri for a considerable distance, and entered the Pacific ocean, not far Southward of Nootka sound. But the Society are aware that these maps are not to be trusted so far as to be the ground of any positive instruction to you. They therefore only mention the fact, leaving to yourself to verify it, or to follow such other as you shall find to be the real truth.

You will, in the course of your journey, take notice of the country you pass through, it's general face, soil, rivers, mountains, it's productions animal, vegetable, and mineral so far as they may be new to us and may also be useful or very curious; the latitude of places or materials for calculating it by such simple methods as your situation may admit you to practice, the names, numbers, and dwellings of the inhabitants, and such particularities as you can learn of their history, connection with each other, languages, manners, state of society and of the arts and commerce among them.

Under the head of Animal history, that of the Mammoth is particularly recommended to your enquiries. As it is also to learn whether the Lama, or Paca of Peru is found in those parts of this continent, or how far North they come.

The method of preserving your observations is left to yourself, according to the means which shall be in your power. It is only suggested that the noting them on the skin might be best for such as are most important, and that further details may be committed to the bark of the paper birch, a substance which may not excite suspicions among the Indians, and little liable to injury from wet, or other common accidents. By the means of the same substance you may perhaps find opportunities, from time to time, of communicating to the society information of your progress, and of the particulars you shall have noted.

When you shall have reached the Pacific ocean, if you find yourself within convenient distance of any settlement of Europeans, go to them, commit to writing a narrative of your journey and observations and take the best measures you can for conveying it by duplicates or triplicates thence to the society by sea.

Return by the same, or such other route, as you shall think likely to fulfill with most satisfaction and certainty the objects of your mission; furnishing yourself with the best proofs the nature of the case will admit of the reality and extent of your progress. Whether this shall be by certificates from Europeans settled on the Western coast of America, or by what other means, must depend on circumstances.

Ignorance of the country thro' which you are to pass and confidence in your judgment, zeal, and discretion, prevent the society from attempting more minute instructions, and even from exacting rigorous observance of those already given, except indeed what is the first of all objects, that you seek for and pursue that route which shall form the shortest and most convenient communication between the higher parts of the Missouri and the Pacific ocean.

It is strongly recommended to you to expose yourself in no case to unnecessary dangers, whether such as might affect your health or your personal safety: and to consider this not merely as your personal concern, but as the injunction of Science in general which expects it's enlargement from your enquiries, and of the inhabitants of the US. in particular, to whom your Report will open new feilds and subjects of Commerce, Intercourse, and Observation.

If you reach the Pacific ocean and return, the Society assign to you all the benefits of the subscription beforementioned. If you reach the waters only which run into that ocean, the society reserve to themselves the apportionment of the reward according to the conditions expressed in the subscription.

They will expect you to return to the city of Philadelphia to give in to them a full narrative of your journey and observations, and to answer the enquiries they shall make of you, still reserving to yourself the benefits arising from the publication of them.

Source: "American Philosophical Society's Instructions to André Michaux, [ca. 30 April 1793]," in Thwaites, Reuben Gold, ed. *Original Journals of the Lewis and Clark Expedition, 1804–1806*. Volume 7. New York: Dodd, Mead & Company, 1905, 202–204.

Further Reading

Ambrose, Stephen. *Undaunted Courage*. Urbana: University of Chicago Press, 1991.

Bedini, Silvio. *Jefferson and Science*. Chapel Hill: University of North Carolina Press, 2002.

Bedini, Silvio. *Thomas Jefferson: Statesman of Science*. New York: Macmillan, 1990.

Cerami, Charles. *Jefferson's Great Gamble: The Remarkable Story of Jefferson, Napoleon and the Men behind the Louisiana Purchase*. New York: Source Books, 2004.

Fenster, Julie. *Jefferson's America: The President, the Purchase, and the Explorers Who Transformed a Nation*. New York: Crown, 2016.

Issacson, Walter. *Benjamin Franklin: An American Life*. New York: Simon and Schuster, 2004.

Peterson, Merrill. *Thomas Jefferson and the New Nation: A Biography*. Oxford University Press, 2013.

Savage, Henry. *Andre and Francois Michaux*. Charlottesville: University of Virginia Press, 1996.

Document 8

THOMAS JEFFERSON TO MERIWETHER LEWIS (FEBRUARY 23, 1801)

Introduction: Personal Secretary and One of My Family

When Thomas Jefferson became president on March 4, 1801, he needed a personal secretary. Just 11 days before his inauguration, Jefferson asked Captain Meriwether Lewis to fill this position. Jefferson had known the Lewis family from Virginia since his childhood. Meriwether Lewis's uncle, Nicholas Lewis, had looked after Jefferson's plantation, Monticello, while Jefferson was in France, and two of Jefferson's siblings married into the Lewis family: his sister Lucy Jefferson married Charles Lewis, while his brother Randolph Jefferson married Anne Lewis.

Though the pay was not good, only $500 a year, Jefferson assured Meriwether Lewis that Lewis would keep his rank and right to promotion. Jefferson also assured Lewis that he would be treated like one of his family. Lewis accepted the position and soon was working closely with Jefferson on many projects.

Washington Feb. 23. 1801.

Dear Sir

The appointment to the Presidency of the US. has rendered it necessary for me to have a private secretary, and in selecting one I have thought it important to respect not only his capacity to aid in the private concerns of the houshold, but also to contribute to the mass of information which it is interesting for the administration to acquire. your knolege of the Western country, of the army and of all it's interests & relations has rendered it desireable for public as well as private purposes that you should be engaged in that office. in point of profit it has little to offer: the salary being only 500. D. which would scarcely be more than an equivalent for your pay & rations, which you would be obliged to relinquish while withdrawn from active service, but retaining your rank & right to rise. but it would be an easier office, would make you know & be known to characters of influence in the affairs of our country, and give you the advantage of their you would of course save also the expence of subsistence & lodging as you would be one of my family. if these or any other views which your own reflections may suggest should present the office of my private secretary as worthy of acceptance you will make me happy in accepting it. it has been sollicited by several, who will have no answer till I hear from you. should you accept, it would be necessary that you should wind up whatever affairs you are engaged in as expeditiously as your own & the public interest will admit, & repair to this place: and that immediately on reciept of this you inform me by letter of your determinations. it would also be necessary that you wait on Genl Wilkinson & obtain his approbation, & his aid in making such arrangements as may render your absence as little injurious to the service as may be. I write to him on this subject.

Accept assurances of the esteem of Dear Sir Your friend & servt.

TH: JEFFERSON

Source: "From Thomas Jefferson to Meriwether Lewis, 23 February 1801," *Founders Online,* National Archives. Available at: http://founders.archives.gov/documents/Jefferson/01-33-02-0048.

Further Reading

Aberbach, Alan David. *In Search of an American Identity: Samuel Latham Mitchell, Jeffersonian Nationalist.* New York: Peter Lang, 1988.

Ambrose, Stephen. *Undaunted Courage.* Urbana: University of Chicago Press, 1991.

Danisi, Thomas C. and Robert Moore. *Uncovering the Truth about Meriwether Lewis.* New York: Prometheus Book, 2001.

Dillon, Richard. *Meriwether Lewis: A Biography.* New York: Coward-McCann, 1965.

Fenster, Julie. *Jefferson's America: The President, the Purchase, and the Explorers Who Transformed a Nation.* New York: Crown, 2016.

Harris, Matthew and Jay H. Buckley, eds. *Zebulon Pike, Thomas Jefferson and the Opening of the American West.* Norman: University of Oklahoma Press, 2012.

Stroud, Patricia. *Bitterroot: The Life and Death of Meriwether Lewis.* Philadelphia: University of Pennsylvania Press, 2018.

Document 9

LETTER FROM THOMAS JEFFERSON TO GENERAL JAMES WILKINSON (FEBRUARY 23, 1801)

Introduction: Jefferson Asks for Permission for Lewis to Work for Him

On the same day that Jefferson wrote to Meriwether Lewis asking him to become his personal secretary, he wrote to General James Wilkinson (1757–1825), senior officer of the army (modern-day chief of staff), not only asking him to allow Lewis to come work for him in the White House, but also requesting that Lewis maintain his rank and right to promotion.

In that letter, Jefferson explains that Lewis is an ideal choice as Jefferson feels he needs someone who knows the western area of the country and someone who is a soldier. Jefferson also points out that another reason for this choice is that Lewis is also from Virginia and so Jefferson knows him well.

To James Wilkinson

Washington Feb. 23. 1801.

Dear General

I take the liberty of asking the protection of your cover for a letter to Lieutt. Meriwether Lewis, not knowing where he may be. in selecting a private secretary, I have thought it would be advantageous to take one who possessing a knolege of the Western country, of the army & it's situation, might sometimes aid us with informations of detail, which we may not otherwise possess. a personal acquaintance with him, arising from his being of my neighborhood, has induced me to select him, if his presence can be dispensed with, without injury to the service: for tho' the public ought justly to be relieved from the charge of pay and rations while absent from his post, yet I should propose that he might retain his rank & right to rise. I have him to wait on you and to recieve your pleasure on this subject, and I would sollicit such arrangements from you as might enable him to wind up whatever affairs he is engaged in as speedily as the public, & his own, interest would permit, without injury to either. should he not be with you, I will ask the favor of you to avail your of the best conveyance of this which may occur.

I pray you to accept assurances of high consideration & regard Dear Genl. Your most obedt. & most humble servt

Th: Jefferson

Source: "From Thomas Jefferson to James Wilkinson, 23 February 1801," *Founders Online,* National Archives. Available at: https://founders.archives.gov/documents/Jefferson/01-33-02-0053.

Further Reading

Aberbach, Alan David. *In Search of An American Identity: Samuel Latham Mitchell, Jeffersonian Nationalist.* New York: Peter Lang, 1988.

Danisi, Thomas C., and Robert Moore. *Uncovering the Truth about Meriwether Lewis.* New York: Prometheus Book, 2001.

Dillon, Richard. *Meriwether Lewis: A Biography.* New York: Coward-McCann, 1965.

Fenster, Julie. *Jefferson's America: The President, the Purchase, and the Explorers Who Transformed a Nation.* New York: Crown, 2016.

Meacham, John. *Thomas Jefferson: The Art of Power.* New York: Random House, 2013.

Peterson, Merrill. *Thomas Jefferson and the New Nation: A Biography*. Oxford: Oxford University Press, 2013.

Stroud, Patricia. *Bitterroot: The Life and Death of Meriwether Lewi*. Philadelphia: University of Pennsylvania Press 2018.

Document 10

LETTER FROM MERIWETHER LEWIS TO THOMAS JEFFERSON (MARCH 10, 1801)

Introduction: Lewis Accepts Jefferson's Offer

Two weeks after Jefferson offered Lewis the position of personal secretary, Lewis accepted. Lewis is obviously overcome by the opportunity to work directly for Jefferson and to serve his new country and explains his delay in replying. He is anxious to begin working for Jefferson and explains that he will go to Washington, D.C., as soon as he can.

Pittsburgh, March 10th. 1801.

DEAR SIR,

Not untill two late on friday last to answer by that days mail, did I receive your much esteemed favour of the 23rd. Ult, in it you have thought proper so far to honour me with your confidence, as to express a wish that I should accept the place of your private Secretary; I most cordially acquiesce, and with pleasure accept the office, nor were further motives necessary to induce my complyance, than that you Sir should conceive that in the discharge of the duties of that office, I could be servicable to my country, or ucefull to youreself: permit me here Sir to do further justice to my feelings, by expressing the lively sensibility with which I received this mark of your confidence and esteem.

I did not reach this place on my return from D,Etroit, untill late on the night of the 5th. inst., five days after the departure of Genl. Wilkinson, my report therefore on the subject of your letter was immediately made to Colo Hamtramck, the commanding Officer at this place; since which, not a moment has been lost in making the necessary arrangments in order to get forward to the City of Washington with all possible despatch: rest assured I shall not relax in my exertions.

Receive I pray you Sir, the most undesembled assureances of the attatchment and friendship of.

Your most obedient, & Very Humble Servt,

MERIWETHER LEWIS.

Source: "To Thomas Jefferson from Meriwether Lewis, 10 March 1801," *Founders Online,* National Archives. Available at:http://founders.archives.gov/documents/Jefferson/01-33-02-0196.

Further Reading

Aberbach, Alan David. *In Search of an American Identity: Samuel Latham Mitchell, Jeffersonian Nationalist.* New York: Peter Lang, 1988.

Ambrose, Stephen. *Undaunted Courage.* Urbana: University of Chicago Press, 1991.

Danisi, Thomas C. and Robert Moore. *Uncovering the Truth about Meriwether Lewis.* New York: Prometheus Book, 2001.

Dillon, Richard. *Meriwether Lewis: A Biography.* New York: Coward-McCann, 1965.

Fenster, Julie. *Jefferson's America: The President, the Purchase, and the Explorers Who Transformed a Nation.* New York: Crown, 2016.

Gutzman, Kevin. *Thomas Jefferson- Revolutionary: A Radical's Struggle to Remake America.* New York: St Martin's Press, 2017.

Harris, Matthew and Jay H. Buckley, eds. *Zebulon Pike, Thomas Jefferson and the Opening of the American West.* Norman: University of Oklahoma Press, 2012.

Peterson, Merrill, *Thomas Jefferson and the new Nation: A Biography.* Oxford: Oxford University Press, 2013.

Stroud, Patricia. *Bitterroot: The Life and Death of Meriwether Lewis.* Philadelphia: University of Pennsylvania Press, 2018.

Document 11

LETTER FROM THOMAS JEFFERSON TO ROBERT LIVINGSTON (APRIL 18, 1802)

Introduction: Difficult and Dangerous Negotiations

Robert Livingston (1746–1813) was born in New York to one of the most prominent families in the colonies. He graduated from Kings College, New York (now called Columbia University) and afterward began to study law.

In June 1776, Livingston was a member of the Committee of Five (along with John Adams, Benjamin Franklin, Thomas Jefferson, and Roger Sherman) that drafted the Declaration of Independence. He was recalled by his state before he could sign it, but his cousin, Philip Livingston, did so on his behalf. After the Articles of Confederation were adopted on March 1, 1781, Livingston was appointed secretary of foreign affairs (now called secretary of state), and he served in this position until 1783, when he was appointed chancellor (judge) of New York. On April 30, 1789, Robert Livingston administered the presidential oath to George Washington on the second floor balcony of Federal Hall, New York City, when Washington became the first president of the United States.

When Jefferson became president in March 1801, he appointed Livingston to be the U.S. minister (Ambassador) to France. Livingston had after all shown himself to be a clever diplomat and shrewd politician, and it was going to take huge skill to persuade the French to sell New Orleans and the territory around it to the new United States.

In January 1803, Jefferson asked James Monroe to join Livingston to help with the negotiations. Monroe, who previously served in France as ambassador, was seen to be sympathetic to the French, and Jefferson hoped Monroe could help Livingston.

This letter to Livingston was given to him by Jefferson's friend Pierre Samuel du Pont de Nemours (1739–1817). Du Pont was an economist and writer who immigrated to the United States during the French Revolution, and was a close friend of Jefferson.

The political dangers of the time can be understood best by noting that the letter begins by Jefferson explaining to Livingston the need to use the cypher code. This was high-stakes politics, and Jefferson was concerned that Spain or France could yet start a war. Jefferson refers to a previous letter sent by James Madison acting in his role as secretary of state, who had noted that France had been slow in fulfilling the terms of the Convention of 1800 (Treaty of Mortefontaine), which had ended the Quasi War. This made the Americans even more nervous and suspicious about the French, but it also made Jefferson more determined to buy New Orleans and West Florida. Commercially and economically this area around New Orleans was vital to the United States.

Jefferson here also writes about the rumor that had been circulating: that the French, having put down a rebellion in St. Domingo (Haiti), were now sending troops to New Orleans. Jefferson writes that even if this is true, it will not happen quickly, so that Livingston still has time to get the deal done.

A favorable and a confidential opportunity offering by Mr. Dupont de Nemours, who is revisiting his native country, gives me an opportunity of sending you a cypher to be used between us, which will give you some trouble to understand, but, once understood, is the easiest to use, the most indecypherable, and varied by a new key with the greatest facility of any one I have ever known. I am in hopes the explanation inclosed will be sufficient.

Let our key of letters be 6.5.1.2.7.9.8.4.3 | 9.2.3.1.7.8.5.4.6 | 3.1.4.2.8.5.7.6.9.
& the key of lines be 9.4.7.6.1.8.5.2.3 | 2.1.8.9.6.5.7.3.4 | 7.6.9.3.1.2.4.5.8.

and lest we should happen to lose our key or be absent from it, it is so formed as to be kept in the memory and put upon paper at pleasure; being produced1 by writing our names & residences at full length, each of which containing 27. letters is divided into 3. parts of 9 letters each;2 each of the 9. letters is then numbered according to the place it would hold if the 9 were arranged alphabetically. thus.

6. 5. 1. 2. 7. 9. 8. 4. 3. | 9. 2. 3. 1. 7. 8. 5. 4. 6. | 3. 1. 4. 2. 8. 5. 7. 6. 9.
r o b e r t r l i | v i n g s t o n o | f c l e r m o n t
9. 4. 7. 6. 1. 8. 5. 2. 3. | 2. 1. 8. 9. 6. 5. 7. 3. 4. | 7. 6. 9. 3. 1. 2. 4. 5. 8.
t h o m a s j e f | f e r s o n o f m | o n t i c e l l o
robertrli alphabetically arranged would be
1. 2. 3. 4. 5. 6. 7. 8. 9.
b e i l o r r r t

the numbers over the letters being then arranged as the letters to which they belong stand in our names, we can always construct our key. but why a cypher between us, when official things go naturally to the Secretary of state, and things not political need no cypher? 1. matters of a public nature, and proper to go on our records, should go to the Secretary of state. 2. matters of a public nature not proper to be placed on our records may still go to the Secretary of state, headed by the word "private." but. 3. there may be matters merely personal to ourselves, and which require the cover of a cypher more than those of any other character. this last purpose, and others which we cannot foresee may render it convenient & advantageous to have at hand a mask for whatever may need it. but writing by mr Dupont, I need use no cypher. I require from him to put this into your own & no other hand, let the delay occasioned by that be what it will.

The cession of Louisiana & the Floridas by Spain to France works most sorely on the US. on this subject the Secretary of state has written to you fully. yet I cannot forbear recurring to it personally, so deep is the impression it makes in my mind. it compleatly reverses all the political relations of the US. and will form a new epoch in our political course. of all nations of any consideration France is the one which hitherto has offered the fewest points on which we could have any conflict of right, and the most points of a communion of interests. from these causes we have ever looked to her as our *natural friend*, as one with which we never could have an occasion of difference. her growth therefore we viewed as our own, her misfortunes ours. there is on the globe one single spot, the possessor of which is our natural & habitual enemy. it is New Orleans, through which the produce of three eighths of our territory must pass to market, and from it's fertility it will ere long yield more than half of our whole produce and contain more than half our inhabitants. France placing herself in that door assumes to us the attitude of defiance. Spain might have retained it quietly for years. her pacific dispositions, her feeble state, would induce her to increase our facilities there, so that her possession of the place would be hardly felt by us, and it would not perhaps be very long before some circumstance might arise which might make the cession of it to us the price of something of more worth to her. not so can it ever be in the hands of France. the impetuosity of her temper, the energy & restlessness of her character, placed in a point of eternal friction with us, and our character, which though quiet, & loving peace & the pursuit of wealth, is high minded, despising wealth in competition with insult or injury, enterprizing & energetic as any nation on earth, these circumstances render it impossible that France and the US. can continue long friends when they meet in so irritable a position. they as well as we must be blind if they do not see this; and we must be very improvident if we do not begin to make arrangements on that hypothesis. the day that France takes possession of N. Orleans fixes the sentence which is to restrain her forever within her low water mark. it seals the union of two nations who in conjunction can maintain exclusive possession of the ocean. from that moment we must marry ourselves to the British fleet & nation. we must turn all our attentions to a maritime force, for which our resources place us on very high ground: and having formed and cemented together a power which may render reinforcement of her settlements here impossible to France, make the first cannon which shall be fired in Europe the signal for tearing up any settlement she may have made, and for holding the two continents of America in sequestration for the common purposes of the United British & American nations. this is not a state of things we seek or desire. it is one which this measure, if adopted by France, forces on us, as necessarily as any other cause, by the laws of nature, brings on it's necessary effect. it is not from a fear of France that we deprecate this measure proposed by her. for however greater her force is than ours compared in the abstract, it is nothing in comparison of ours when to be exerted on our soil. but it is from a sincere love of peace, and a firm persuasion that bound to France by the interests and the strong sympathies still existing in the minds of our citizens, and holding relative positions which ensure their continuance we are secure of a long course of peace. whereas the change of friends, which will be rendered necessary if France changes that position, embarks us necessarily as a belligerent power in the first war of Europe. in that case France will have held possession of New Orleans during the interval of a peace, long or short, at the end of which it will be wrested from her. will this shortlived possession have been an equivalent to her for the transfer of such a weight into the scale of her enemy? will not the amalgamation of a young, thriving, nation continue to that enemy the health & force which are at present so evidently on the decline? and will a few years possession of N. Orleans add equally to the strength of France? she may say she needs Louisiana for the supply of her West Indies. she does not need it in time of peace, and in war she could not depend on them because they would be so easily intercepted. I should suppose that all these considerations might in some proper form be brought into view of the government of France. tho' stated by us, it ought not to give offence; because we do not bring them forward as a menace, but as consequences not controulable by us, but inevitable from the course of things. we mention them not as things which we desire by any means, but as things we deprecate; and we beseech a friend to look forward and to prevent them for our common interests.

If France considers Louisiana however as indispensable for her views she might perhaps be willing to look about for arrangements which might reconcile it to our interests. if any thing could do this it would be the ceding to us the island of New Orleans and the Floridas. this would certainly in a great degree remove the causes of jarring & irritation between us, and perhaps for such a length of time as might produce other means of making the measure permanently conciliatory to our interests & friendships. it would at any rate relieve us from the necessity of taking immediate measures for countervailing such an operation by arrangements in another quarter. but still we should consider N. Orleans & the Floridas as no equivalent for the risk of a quarrel with France produced by her vicinage.— I have no doubt you have urged these considerations on every proper occasion with the government where you are. they are such as must have effect if you can find the means of producing thorough reflection on them by that government. the idea here is that the troops sent to St. Domingo, were to proceed to Louisiana after finishing their work in that island. if this were the arrangement, it will give you time to return again & again to the charge. for the conquest of St. Domingo will not be a short work. it will take considerable time and wear down a great number of souldiers. every eye in the US. is now fixed on this affair of Louisiana. perhaps nothing since the revolutionary war has produced more uneasy sensations through the body of the nation. notwithstanding temporary bickerings have taken place with France, she has still a strong hold on the affections of our citizens generally.—I have thought it not amiss, by way of supplement to the letters of the Secretary of state, to write you this private one to impress you with the importance we affix to this transaction. I pray you to cherish Dupont. he has the best dispositions for the continuance of friendship between the two nations, and perhaps you may be able to make a good use of him. accept assurances of my affectionate esteem & high consideration.

TH: JEFFERSON

Source: "From Thomas Jefferson to Robert R. Livingston, 18 April 1802," in *State Papers and Correspondence Bearing upon the Purchase of the Territory of Louisiana.* Washington, DC: Government Printing Office, 1903, 15–18.

Further Reading

Brecher, Frank. *Negotiating the Louisiana Purchase: Robert Livingston's Mission to France, 1801–1804.* New York: McFarland and Company, 2006.

Cerami, Charles. *Jefferson's Great Gamble: The Remarkable Story of Jefferson, Napoleon and the Men behind the Louisiana Purchase.* New York: Source Books, 2004.

Dangerfield, George. *Chancellor Robert R. Livingston of New York, 1746–1813.* New York: Harcourt Brace and Company, 1960.

Feldman, Noah. *The Three Lives of James Madison: Genius, Partisan, President.* New York: Random House, 2017.

Fenster, Julie. *Jefferson's America: The President, the Purchase, and the Explorers Who Transformed a Nation.* New York: Crown, 2016.

Gutzman, Kevin. *Thomas Jefferson—Revolutionary: A Radical's Struggle to Remake America.* New York: St Martin's Press, 2017.

Kukla, Jon. *A Wilderness So Immense: The Louisiana Purchase and the Destiny of America.* New York: Anchor, 2004.

Meacham, John. *Thomas Jefferson: The Art of Power.* New York: Random House, 2013.

Merrell, James H. *Into the American Woods: Negotiators on the Pennsylvania Frontier.* New York: W.W. Norton, 1999.

Peterson, Merrill. *Thomas Jefferson and the New Nation: A Biography.* Oxford University Press, 2013.

Document 12

LETTER FROM GENERAL GEORGE ROGERS CLARK TO THOMAS JEFFERSON (DECEMBER 12, 1802)

Introduction: Clark Recommends His Younger Brother William

George Clark wrote to Jefferson in December 1802. The West was becoming more important as the United States was still recovering economically from both the Revolutionary War and Whiskey Rebellion. It was the unmapped land that needed much more attention to be paid in order to secure the safety and security of the United States. In this letter Clark writes to Jefferson and explains the need to construct forts, in particular those that need to be built near rivers which in turn were the primary waterways and supply routes for the country. Protection of the country meant control and knowledge of water routes. These all linked to commerce, trade, and the survival of the new country.

Though George Clark may not have been in a position to help his nation at this point in his life, he was hopeful that his younger brother William would be considered by Jefferson for any position in government, but in particular in dealing with the West.

Falls of Ohio 12th. December 1802

SIR

I latterly had the pleasure of the perruseal of a letter from the Secretary of War to my brother on the Subject of the post of Fort Jefferson on the Mississippi. his Answer to that letter completely discribed the place—A Military post & Tradeing Town there, must be Obvious to every man of Observation that is acquainted with the Geography of the Countrey—I was the more pleased as I had Contemplated the importance of that spot from my earliest acquaintance with the Western Countrey.

When I was ordered fix the garrison at or near the mouth of the Ohio in the year 1780 I lay three weeks in the point, and explored the banks of the river and Countrey before I fixed on the spot to build a Fort—and if my Instructions had not have been to place the Garrison South of the Ohio I certainly should have raised a Fortress in the point. I marked the ground the annual inundations flooded, it is about *five* feet, and from that to *seven* feet is the depth of the water that Covers this butifull Tract of bottom, which may be raised for a City of any Size, by the earth thrown out of the Canals, cut through the City and those Canals may be kept pure by turning the Cash River throgh them—I thus drew the plan and have been improveing on it frequently to the present time—what caused me to view this ground with more attention was that the Spanish shore opposit so high that a small expence, would free two or three hundred Acres of Land.

This circumstance induced me to think that it would be necessary for us, at least to have a fortress in this point as a Key to the enterance of the Ohio—Those were my Ideas while on the ground I segest to you, Sir, if worthey your attention, any further information, and the best perhaps that can be Obtained of that Country, may be got from my brother William, who is now settled at Clarksville in the Indiana Territory—I have long since laid asside all Idea of Public affairs, by bad fortune, and ill health I have become incapable of persueing those enterpriseing & active persuits which I have been fond of from my youth—but I will with the greatest pleasure give my bro: William every information in my power, on this, or any other point which may be of Service to your Administration. he is well quallified almost for any business—If it should be in your power to Confur on him any post of Honor and profit, in this Countrey in which we live, it will exceedingly gratify me—I seem to have a right to expect such a gratification when asked for—but what will greatly highten it is, that I am sure it gives you pleasure to have it in your power to do me a service.

With the greatest assureance of your prosperity I have the honor to be your ever sincere

G R CLARK

NB Mr. Hurst the gentleman whome will hand you this letter is a young Lawyer from Vincennes, a Man of integrity and a good republican whom I beg leave to recommend to you.

GRC

Source: "To Thomas Jefferson from George Rogers Clark, 12 December 1802," *Founders Online,* National Archives. Available at: http://founders.archives.gov/documents/Jefferson/01-39-02-0130.

Further Reading

Brown, Dee. *The American West*. New York: Touchstone, 1995.

Danisi, Thomas C. and Robert Moore. *Uncovering the Truth about Meriwether Lewis*. New York: Prometheus Book, 2001.

Dillon, Richard. *Meriwether Lewis: A Biography*. New York: Coward-McCann, 1965.

Harrison, Lowell. *George Roger Clark and the War in the West*. Lexington: University of Kentucky Press, 2001.

Kukla, Jon. *A Wilderness So immense: The Louisiana Purchase and the Destiny of America*. Anchor Books, 2004.

Nester, William. *George Clark: I Glory in War*. University of Oklahoma Press, 2012.

U.S. Department of the Interior. *George Rogers Clark and the Winning of the Old Northwest*. Create Space, 2016.

Chapter 2

Preparation for the Expedition West

This expedition was going into unknown and uncharted areas of the western North American continent. To have any chance of success, as many details as possible needed to be thought about, and organized beforehand. The expedition's leaders had to be picked carefully, and the people who accompanied them had to be chosen with equal care. This was a purposefully small expedition, as had been suggested years earlier by General George Rogers Clark, as the failure of a few could lead to disaster for all. Thomas Jefferson's choice of Meriwether Lewis as expedition leader was the first step. Jefferson knew Lewis, professionally and personally. While at the White House he saw Lewis at work and saw how Lewis coped with the strain and the politics of Washington, D.C. He saw Lewis was capable of making decisions, and initiating, and carrying out various difficult projects. Jefferson was convinced that Lewis was capable of leading this type of expedition. Equally important there would be no accusations of spying this time. The Lewis family were American heroes.

With the leader now in place, financial support was needed to make this expedition a reality. On the advice of Albert Gatlin, on January 18, 1803, Jefferson made a secret request to Congress for $2,500. Although certain Federalist members of Congress were not totally convinced about the need for such an expedition, they had just said yes to purchasing the Louisiana Territory from France. Another $2,000 to map it did not seem extreme. Then the question became who else was going to go? How would these people be chosen?

From the beginning it was agreed that everyone who went had to have military experience. While the expedition itself was not a formal military operation, it was to be organized and conducted in a disciplined military manner. The logistics of organizing the necessary supplies—the boats, the clothes, weapons, tents, and medicines—had to be carefully considered—each inch of space and ounce of weight was significant. Then there was the issue of training. How do you train people for the unknown? How do you prepare people to go to a place where no one has been?

The choice of William Clark was as equally important as the selection of Lewis. If Jefferson had faith in Lewis, then Lewis's trust in Clark was total. Congress, however, was a different story. When Congress was asked to promote Clark to the rank of captain, it refused. So while Lewis and Clark co-captained the trip with equal responsibility, Clark's actual army rank on this adventure was a lieutenant. (It was not until January 17, 2001, that Clark was posthumously promoted to the rank of captain. President Bill Clinton, on one of his last days on office, promoted

Clark to the rank of captain, effective March 26, 1804. President Clinton also promoted Sacagawea and York to the honorary rank of sergeants.) Clark's inferior rank was never revealed to other members of the expedition throughout the journey.

William Clark's primary task was to recruit the men to make up the expedition. The basic requirement for those who volunteered was that each man had to be healthy and single, and skilled in hunting and frontier survival. Clark spent the winter of 1803–1804 training with these men at Camp Dubois in Indiana Territory, leaving on May 14, 1804, to meet with Lewis at St. Charles, Missouri.

While Clark was training and preparing the men, Lewis was gathering as much information as he could about the West and how to conduct such a journey, from some of the best minds in the country. Initially, Jefferson opened up his vast library to Lewis, giving him certain books to read. One of the books that Lewis brought on the expedition was Antoine Simon Le Page du Pratz's *History of Louisiana* (1753). This book is most likely the source of Jefferson's idea that a river connected the eastern and western parts of North America. Du Pratz's book includes an account of a journey supposedly made by Moncacht-Apé, a member of the Yazoo Nation from the Mississippi Delta area. Moncacht-Apé allegedly traveled west in the 1750s along the Mississippi River to present-day Montana, and from there via a river to the Pacific Ocean. The story has long been doubted by historians, and one of the many reasons for historians to be dubious is that the Rocky Mountains are not mentioned in the book. But the book was popular, and certainly known by Jefferson, and brought on the trip by Lewis so they, like many at this time, believed that the West Coast was only a (very long) river boat ride away.

To aid with Lewis's preparation, Jefferson asked some of his friends from the American Philosophical Society to help prepare him. Among his teachers then were Benjamin Rush and Caspar Winstar, two of the top physicians of the time; Benjamin Smith Barton, a botanist; Robert Patterson, a surveyor and mathematician; and the astronomer Andrew Ellicott. Each of these men gave Lewis information vital to the success of the expedition. Of particular importance was Lewis's education on map-making and surveying. Those maps would be most useful to the army if war broke out. Maps would also make it possible for people to farm the West.

At the same time as Lewis was receiving this important education, he was also responsible for getting the equipment and supplies ready for the trip. While in Philadelphia, Lewis ordered supplies such as medicine (Rush's famous Thunderbolt Pills), uniforms, tobacco, tools of various kinds, tents, gun powder, and guns, as well as various gifts for the Native population.

One of the most important preparations for the expedition was the keelboat, which was built in Pittsburgh in the summer of 1803. The construction of the boat took much longer than Lewis had hoped. It was not until August 31, 1803, that Lewis began his journey with the boat to rendezvous with Clark. The boat was heavy and large: it was 55 feet in length, and 8 feet wide in its center. It had one 32-foot mast, and 22 oars. Its draft was three feet. The keelboat could carry a considerable amount of supplies. While the boat's design made it excellent when going downstream in sufficient water, it was difficult, if not impossible, to sail the boat upstream in shallow water.

With the boat built, the supplies bought, and the men trained, Lewis, Clark, and the Corps of Discovery were ready to set out on their journey.

Document 13

Meriwether Lewis: Estimated Costs of Missouri River Expedition (January 1803)

Introduction: The Financial Cost of Adventure

Before January 1803, Lewis prepared an estimate for Jefferson of the cost of an expedition west. The highest cost item in Lewis's $2,500 budget was $695 for "Indian Presents," while medicine was estimated to cost $55. Boats were expected to cost $430. While $2,500 does not seem like a lot of money, Jefferson was warned by Albert Gatlin that there could be some opposition from the Federalist members of Congress, so it was decided to make this request in secret.

.—

Mathematical Instruments	$217.–
Arms & Accoutrements extraordinary	81.–
Camp Ecquipage	255.–
Medecine & packing	55.–
Means of transportation	430.–
Indian presents	696.–
Provisions extraordinary	224.–
Materials for making up the various articles into portable packs	55.–
For the pay of hunters guides & Interpreters	300.–
In silver coin to defray the expences of the party from Nashville to the last white settlement on the Missisourie	100.–
Contingencies	87.–
Total	$2,500.–

Source: Wheeler, Olin Dunbar. *The Trail of Lewis and Clark, 1804–1904.* Volume 1. New York: G. P. Putnam's Sons, 1904, 33.

Further Reading

Brecher, Frank. *Negotiating the Louisiana Purchase: Robert Livingston's Mission to France, 1801–1804.* New York: McFarland and Company, 2006.

Dangerfield, George. *Chancellor Robert R. Livingston of New York, 1746–1813.* New York: Harcourt Brace and Company, 1960.

Ellis, Joseph. *American Sphinx: The Character of Thomas Jefferson*. New York: Vintage Books, 1998.

Fenster, Julie. *Jefferson's America: The President, the Purchase, and the Explorers Who Transformed a Nation*. New York: Crown, 2016.

Gutzman, Kevin. *Thomas Jefferson—Revolutionary: A Radical's Struggle to Remake America*. New York: St. Martin's Press, 2017.

Kukla, Jon. *A Wilderness So Immense: The Louisiana Purchase and the Destiny of America*. New York: Anchor, 2004.

Meacham, John. *Thomas Jefferson: The Art of Power*. New York: Random House, 2013.

Peterson, Merrill. *Thomas Jefferson and the new Nation: A Biography*. Oxford University Press, 2013.

Document 14

JEFFERSON'S SECRET MESSAGE TO CONGRESS (JANUARY 18, 1803)

Introduction: Commerce, Rivers, and Native Americans

Jefferson in this message to Congress does not ask for any specific amount of money until the very end of the message. Instead in the opening paragraph he concentrates on continuing a policy for the sake of the "public good." He writes about the peaceful attitude of the Native Americans and about how commercial success would benefit all. He writes about what he believes is the need to create a nation based on agriculture and farming. He writes of the Native American population, also giving up their nomadic lifestyle and also settling and raising stock.

As he gets to the end of this message Jefferson states that Congress should want to create this land, to explore this land, to develop this land, and help commerce to improve. It is only then that Jefferson asks for the money: "two thousand five hundred dollars."

Jefferson had decided to keep this request secret, and therefore not part of the annual budget, after listening to the advice of his secretary of the Treasury Albert Gallatin (1761–1849). The reason for the secrecy was that the area being explored at the time of this request was still outside the borders of the United States and could involve a variety of questions—legal, constitutional, and political. To avoid these complications, secrecy was key.

Congress took the notion of secrecy seriously to impose "an injunction of Secrecy" order on itself. This rule allows for Congress to debate and vote in secret; therefore this request for money was referred to as the "act for extending external commence of the United States." Both the House and Senate voted on and passed the act on February 22, 1803, allowing the expedition to go ahead.

January 18, 1803

Gentlemen of the Senate, and of the House of Representatives:

As the continuance of the act for establishing trading houses with the Indian tribes will be under the consideration of the Legislature at its present session,

I think it my duty to communicate the views which have guided me in the execution of that act, in order that you may decide on the policy of continuing it, in the present or any other form, or discontinue it altogether, if that shall, on the whole, seem most for the public good.

The Indian tribes residing within the limits of the United States, have, for a considerable time, been growing more and more uneasy at the constant diminution of the territory they occupy, although effected by their own voluntary sales: and the policy has long been gaining strength with them, of refusing absolutely all further sale, on any conditions; insomuch that, at this time, it hazards their friendship, and excites dangerous jealousies and perturbations in their minds to make any overture for the purchase of the smallest portions of their land. A very few tribes only are not yet obstinately in these dispositions. In order peaceably to counteract this policy of theirs, and to provide an extension of territory which the rapid increase of our numbers will call for, two measures are deemed expedient. First: to encourage them to abandon hunting, to apply to the raising stock, to agriculture and domestic manufacture, and thereby prove to themselves that less land and labor will maintain them in this, better than in their former mode of living. The extensive forests necessary in the hunting life, will then become useless, and they will see advantage in exchanging them for the means of improving their farms, and of increasing their domestic comforts. Secondly: to multiply trading houses among them, and place within their reach those things which will contribute more to their domestic comfort, than the possession of extensive, but uncultivated wilds. Experience and reflection will develop to them the wisdom of exchanging what they can spare and we want, for what we can spare and they want. In leading them to agriculture, to manufactures, and civilization; in bringing together their and our settlements, and in preparing them ultimately to participate in the benefits of our governments, I trust and believe we are acting for their greatest good. At these trading houses we have pursued the principles of the act of Congress, which directs that the commerce shall be carried on liberally, and requires only that the capital stock shall not be diminished. We consequently undersell private traders, foreign and domestic, drive them from the competition; and thus, with the good will of the Indians, rid ourselves of a description of men who are constantly endeavoring to excite in the Indian mind suspicions, fears, and irritations towards us. A letter now enclosed, shows the effect of our competition on the operations of the traders, while the Indians, perceiving the advantage of purchasing from us, are soliciting generally, our establishment of trading houses among them. In one quarter this is particularly interesting. The Legislature, reflecting on the late occurrences on the Mississippi, must be sensible how desirable it is to possess a respectable breadth of country on that river, from our Southern limit to the Illinois at least; so that we may present as firm a front on that as on our Eastern border. We possess what is below the Yazoo, and can probably acquire a certain breadth from the Illinois and Wabash to the Ohio; but between the Ohio and Yazoo, the country all belongs to the Chickasaws, the most friendly tribe within our limits, but the most decided against the alienation of lands. The portion of their country most important for us is exactly that which they do not inhabit. Their settlements are not on the Mississippi, but in the interior country. They have lately shown a desire to become agricultural; and this leads to the desire of buying implements and comforts. In the strengthening and gratifying of these wants, I see the only prospect of planting on the Mississippi itself, the means of its own safety. Duty has required me to submit these views to the judgment of the Legislature; but as their disclosure might embarrass and defeat their effect, they are committed to the special confidence of the two Houses.

While the extension of the public commerce among the Indian tribes, may deprive of that source of profit such of our citizens as are engaged in it, it might be worthy the attention of Congress, in their care of individual as well as of the general interest, to point, in another direction, the enterprise of these citizens, as profitably for themselves, and more usefully for the public. The river Missouri, and the Indians inhabiting it, are not as well known as is rendered desirable by their connexion with the Mississippi, and consequently with us. It is, however, understood, that the country on that river is inhabited by numerous tribes, who furnish great supplies of furs and peltry to the trade of another nation, carried on in a high latitude, through an infinite number of portages and lakes, shut up by ice through a long season. The commerce on that line could bear no competition with that of the Missouri, traversing a moderate climate, offering according to the best accounts, a continued navigation from its source, and possibly with a single portage, from the Western Ocean, and finding to the Atlantic a choice of channels through the Illinois or Wabash, the lakes and Hudson, through the Ohio and Susquehanna, or Potomac or James rivers, and through the Tennessee and Savannah, rivers. An intelligent officer, with ten or twelve chosen men, fit for the enterprise, and willing to undertake it, taken from our posts, where they may be spared without inconvenience, might explore the whole line, even to the Western Ocean, have conferences with the natives on the subject of commercial intercourse, get admission among them for our traders, as others are admitted, agree on convenient deposits for an interchange of articles, and return with the information acquired, in the course of two summers. Their arms and accoutrements, some instruments of observation, and light and cheap presents for the Indians, would be all the apparatus they could carry, and with an expectation of a soldier's portion of land on their return, would constitute the whole expense. Their pay would be going on, whether here or there. While other civilized nations have encountered great expense to enlarge the boundaries of knowledge by undertaking voyages of discovery, and for other literary purposes, in various parts and directions, our nation seems to owe to the same object, as well as to its own interests, to explore this, the only line of easy communication across the continent, and so directly traversing our own part of it. The interests of commerce place the principal object within the constitutional powers and care of Congress, and that it should incidentally advance the geographical knowledge of our own continent, cannot be but an additional gratification. The nation claiming the territory, regarding this as a literary pursuit, which is in the habit of permitting within its dominions, would not be disposed to view it with jealousy, even if the expiring state of its interests there did not render it a matter of indifference. The appropriation of two thousand five hundred dollars, "for the purpose of extending the external commerce of the United

States," while understood and considered by the Executive as giving the legislative sanction, would cover the undertaking from notice, and prevent the obstructions which interested individuals might otherwise previously prepare in its way.

Source: President Thomas Jefferson's confidential message to Congress concerning relations with the Indians, January, 18, 1803; Record Group 233, Records of the United States House of Representatives, HR 7A-D1; National Archives.

Further Reading

Brecher, Frank. *Negotiating the Louisiana Purchase: Robert Livingston's Mission to France, 1801–1804.* New York: McFarland and Company, 2006.

Dangerfield, George. *Chancellor Robert R. Livingston of New York, 1746–1813.* New York: Harcourt Brace and Company, 1960.

Ellis, Joseph. *American Sphinx: The Character of Thomas Jefferson.* New York: Vintage Books, 1998.

Fenster, Julie. *Jefferson's America: The President, the Purchase, and the Explorers Who Transformed a Nation.* New York: Crown, 2016.

Gutzman, Kevin. *Thomas Jefferson—Revolutionary: A Radical's Struggle to Remake America.* New York: St. Martin's Press, 2017.

Kukla, Jon. *A Wilderness So Immense: The Louisiana Purchase and the Destiny of America.* New York: Anchor, 2004.

Meacham, John. *Thomas Jefferson: The Art of Power.* New York: Random House, 2013.

Peterson, Merrill. *Thomas Jefferson and the New Nation: A Biography.* Oxford University Press, 2013.

Document 15

LETTER FROM MERIWETHER LEWIS TO THOMAS JEFFERSON (APRIL 20, 1803)

Introduction: Report to Jefferson on the Preparations up to This Point

In this letter to Jefferson, Lewis explains everything he has done so far in terms of preparation for the trip: He has written to John Conner from Indiana Territory, offering him $300 to work as an interpreter. He had also tried to contact Robert McClelland, and John Hamilton, by sending letters to them through Captain Findley, who was probably James Findley. Mc Clelland and Hamilton were both difficult to contact as they both lived in the western part of the country with little contact with the East. Mc Clelland had previously worked as a scout for the army, while Hamilton has been an interpreter. These skills were going to be vital for the expedition, so understandably Lewis was anxious to contact them to persuade them to go on the expedition. Conner would turn down the offer, claiming that $300 was way too little and demanded payment of $5,000.

Lewis here also explains the supplies he was ordering, which included rifles, toma-hawks, and knives, and he gives the first report on his invention: the iron boat. Here he describes this 60-foot boat, which was to be light and strong, so it could be stored easily and carried on the trip. Despite the delays, Lewis was still optimistic that all the deadlines would be met.

Lancaster Apl. 20th. 1803.

SIR,

With a view to forward as much as possible the preparations which must nec-essarily be made in the Western country previous to my final departure, as also to prevent the delay, which would attatch to their being made after my arrival in that quarter, I have taken the following measures, which I hope will meet your appro-bation; they appear to me to be as complete as my present view of the subject will admit my making them, and I trust the result will prove as favorable as wished for.—

I have writen triplicates to Mr. John Conner accepting his services as an Inter-preter; he is the young man I recollect mentioning to you as having proffered his services to accompany me: to him I have communicated the real extent and ob-jects of my mission, but with strict injunctions to secresy. He is directed to bring with him two Indians, provided he can engage such as perfectly answer the de-scription given him. I have informed him of the Military posts at which I shall touch on the Ohio and Mississippi rivers, and the probable time of my arrival at each, leaving it discretionary with himself to meet me at either: in these letters are inclosed triplicates, addressed to the Commandants of those posts, recommend-ing Mr. Conner to their good offices, and requesting for him every aid in their power to bestow, should he be in want of assistance to enable him to get forward in due time. The circumstance of Mr. Conner's residence being at the Delleware Town on White river, and distant of course from any post office, induced me to give these letters different conveyances, which I did by inclosing them by different mails to three gentlemen of my acquaintance in that country, two of whom, Capts. Mc,Clelland & Hamilton, live within twenty seven miles of the town; they are re-quested, and I am confident will find the means of conveying the letters to him; the other with a similar request was inclosed to Capt. Findley of Cincinnatti, in whose exertions tho' more distant, I have equal confidence.—

I have also written to Majr. Mac Rea, the Commandant of South West Point, and to several officers of my acquaintance who constitute that garrison, stating to them that my destination was up the Mississippi for the purpose of accomplishing the objects, which we agreed on as most proper to be declared publicly: the qualifi-cations of the men are mentioned, and they are requested to look out in time for such volunteers as will answer that description; the inducements for those per-sons engaging in this service were also stated. The garrison of South West Point must form my first resourse for the scelection of my party, which I shall afterwards change as circumstances may seem to recommend; and with a view to this change, I have written in a similar manner to the officers commanding the posts of Mas-sac, Kaskaskais and Illinois, the posts at which I shall touch previous to ascending the Missourie, and subsequent to my departure from S.W. Point. the men in every instance are to be engaged conditionally, or subject to my approval or otherwise.—

I have also written to Dr. Dickson, at Nashville, and requested him to contract in my behalf with some confidential boat-builder at that place, to prepare a boat for me as soon as possible, and to purchase a large light wooden canoe: for this purpose I inclosed the Dr. 50. Dollars, which sum I did not concieve equal by any means to the purchase of the two vessels, but supposed it sufficient for the purchase of the canoe, and to answer also as a small advance to the boat-builder: a discription of these vessels was given. The objects of my mission are stated to him as beforementioned to the several officers.—

I have also written to Genl. Irwine of Philadelphia, requesting that he will have in a state of prepareation some articles which are necessary for me, and which will be most difficult to obtain, or may take the greates length of time in their prepareation.—

My detention at Harper's Ferry was unavoidable for one month, a period much greater than could reasonably have been calculated on; my greatest difficulty was the frame of the canoe, which could not be completed without my personal attention to such portion of it as would enable the workmen to understand the design perfectly; other inducements seemed with equal force to urge my waiting the issue of a full experiment, arising as well from a wish to incur no expence unnecessarily, as from an unwillingness to risk any calculation on the advantages of this canoe in which hereafter I might possibly be deceived; experiment was necessary also to determine it's dementions: I therefore resolved to give it a fair trial, and accordingly prepared two sections of it with the same materials, of which they must of necessity be composed when completed for servise on my voyage; they were of two disciptions, the one curved, or in the shape necessary for the stem and stern, the other simicilindrical, or in the form of those sections which constitute the body of the canoe. The experiment and it's result wer as follow.

Dementions.

Curved Section.	F.	I.	*Simicilindrical Section.*	F.	I.
Length of Keel from junction of section to commencement of curve	1.	2	Length of Keel	4.	6
			ditto Beam	4.	10
			Debth of Hole	2.	2
Length of curve	4.	5	Note—The curve of the body		
Width of broad end	4.	10	of the canoe was formed by		
Debth of Do. Do.	2.	2	a suspended cord.—		

Weight of the materials.

Curved Section	lbs.	*Simicilindrical Section*	
Iron	22.	Iron	22
Hide	25	Hide	30
Wood	10	Wood	12
Bark	21	Bark	25
Total	78	Total	89

Competent to a Burthen of 850. lbs. Burthen of 920. lbs.

Necessary to be transported by land.

> Iron and Hide of Curved Section 47.
> Iron and Hide of Simicilindrical do. 52.= 99. lbs.
> Burthen of Curved Section 850.
> Do.   Do. Simicilindrical 920.= 1,770. lbs.

Thus the weight of this vessel competent to the burthen of 1,770 lbs. amounts to no more than 99 lbs.—the bark and wood, when it becomes necessary to transport the vessel to any considerable distance, may be discarded; as those articles are reaidily obtained for the purposes of this canoe, at all seasons of the year, and in every quarter of the country, which is tolerably furnished with forest trees. When these sections were united they appeared to acquire an additional strength and firmness, and I am confident that in cases of emergency they would be competent to 150 lbs. more than the burthen already stated.—Altho' the weight of the articles employed in the construction of a canoe on this plan, have considerably exceeded the estimate I had previously made, yet they do not weigh more than those which form a bark canoe of equal dementions, and in my opinion is much preferable to it in many respects; it is much stronger, will carry it's burthen with equal ease, and greater security; and when the Bark and wood are discarded, will be much lighter, and can be transported with more safety and ease. I was induced from the result of this experiment to direct the iron frame of the canoe to be completed.—

My Rifles, Tomahawks & knives are preparing at Harper's Ferry, and are already in a state of forwardness that leaves me little doubt of their being in readiness in due time.—

I arrived at this place yesterday, called on Mr. Ellicot, and have this day commenced, under his direction, my observations &c, to perfect myself in the use and application of the instruments. Mr. Ellicot is extreemly friendly and attentive, and I am confident is disposed to render me every aid in his power: he thinks it will be necessary I should remain here ten or twelve days.—

Being fully impressed with the necessity of seting out as early as possible, you may rest assured that not a moment shall be lost in making the necessary preperations. I still think it practicable to reach the mouth of the Missourie by the 1st. of August.—

I am Sir, with much esteem and regard Your Most Obt. Servt.

MERIWETHER LEWIS.

Source: "To Thomas Jefferson from Meriwether Lewis, 20 April 1803," *Founders Online*. National Archives. Available at: http://founders.archives.gov/documents/Jefferson/01-40-02-0175.

Further Reading

Brecher, Frank. *Negotiating the Louisiana Purchase: Robert Livingston's Mission to France, 1801–1804.* New York: McFarland and Company, 2006.

Dangerfield, George. *Chancellor Robert R. Livingston of New York, 1746–1813*. New York: Harcourt Brace and Company, 1960.

Ellis, Joseph. *American Sphinx: The Character of Thomas Jefferson*. New York: Vintage Books, 1998.

Fenster, Julie. *Jefferson's America: The President, the Purchase, and the Explorers Who Transformed a Nation*. New York: Crown, 2016.

Gutzman, Kevin. *Thomas Jefferson—Revolutionary: A Radical's Struggle to Remake America*. New York: St. Martin's Press, 2017.

Kukla, Jon. *A Wilderness So Immense: The Louisiana Purchase and the Destiny of America*. New York: Anchor, 2004.

Meacham, John. *Thomas Jefferson: The Art of Power*. New York: Random House, 2013.

Peterson, Merrill. *Thomas Jefferson and the New Nation: A Biography*. Oxford: Oxford University Press, 2013.

Document 16

LETTER FROM DR. BENJAMIN RUSH TO THOMAS JEFFERSON CONTAINING HIS INSTRUCTIONS TO MERIWETHER LEWIS (JUNE 11, 1803)

Introduction: For the Preservation of Health during the Expedition to the Pacific

Benjamin Rush (1746–1813) was born in Northwest Philadelphia, Pennsylvania, to John Rush and Susanna Hall Harvey. In 1759, Rush attended the College of New Jersey (now called Princeton University) and graduated from there in 1760. On his return to Philadelphia, Rush began to work with physicians, and in 1766, Rush went to the University of Edinburgh, in Scotland, one of the top medical schools in the world, to formally study medicine.

He returned to Philadelphia in 1769, where he began to practice medicine. He was also appointed professor of medicine at the College of Philadelphia. Benjamin Rush also published the first text book on chemistry in America in 1770. In 1776, Rush signed the Declaration of Independence, as representative of Pennsylvania to the Continental Congress. After the Revolutionary War, Rush combined medicine and politics: he was a doctor at Pennsylvania hospital, while he was also treasurer at the U.S. mint.

Though Rush was not going on the expedition, his expertise was needed, and as per the request made by Jefferson in this letter, Rush is giving instructions to Lewis explaining how to attend to basic medical issues relating to health. The existing letter is a copy made by Jefferson. Lewis was with Jefferson in Washington on June 19, when the letter arrived. Lewis left on July 5 and probably took the letter with him. The original has not been found yet.

Some of the more interesting suggestions for Lewis were the notion of fasting and purging. One of the medicines sent in hundreds for the trip was Rush's "Thunderbolt Pills." The pill was a purgative that was given as a cure for just about everything. It was made up of the mineral calomel, a compound of mercury, and jalap resin (made from the Jalap root plant). Rush warns Lewis that one of the most important symptoms to be aware of was "costiveness" (constipation). Should anyone feel this, he or she should immediately take one of the Thunderbolt Pills.

Another medicine that Lewis brought was sulfuric acid (acid of vitriol), which can cause death and burning in its unadulterated form, but which Rush recommends in moderation mixed with sweetened water as a "wholesome drink" with meals.

Rush also warns Lewis about the danger of "spirits" (alcohol). Rush insisted that any alcohol consumed should be done in tablespoons and heavily diluted; otherwise tiredness would only get worse.

Philadelphia June 11th. 1803.

DEAR SIR,

I have endeavoured to fulfil your Wishes by furnishing Mr Lewis with some inquiries relative to the natural history of the Indians. The enclosed letter contains a few short directions for the preservation of his health, As well as the health of the persons Under his Command.

His mission is truly interesting. I shall wait with great solicitude for its issue. Mr. Lewis appears admirably qualified for it. May its Advantages prove no less honourable to your Administration, than to the interests of Science!

The enclosed letter from Mr Sumpter contains some new Views of the present military arrangements of France & Great Britain. You need not return it.

From Dear Sir yours very respectfully & sincerely

BENJN: RUSH
June 11. 1803.

Dr. Rush to Capt. Lewis. for preserving his health.

1. when you feel the least indisposition, do not attempt to overcome it by labour [sic] or marching. *rest* in a horizontal posture.—also fasting and diluting drinks for a day or two will generally prevent an attack of fever. to these preventatives of disease may be added a gentle sweat obtained by warm drinks, or gently opening the bowels by means of one, two, or more of the purging pills.

2. Unusual costiveness is often a sign of approaching disease. when you feel it take one or more of the purging pills.

3. want of appetite is likewise a sign of approaching indisposition. it should be obviated by the same remedy.

4. in difficult & laborious enterprizes & marches, *eating sparingly* will enable you to bear them with less fatigue & less danger to your health.

5. flannel should be worn constantly next to the skin, especially in wet weather.

6. the less spirit you use the better. after being *wetted* or *much* fatigued, or *long* exposed to the night air, it should be taken in an *undiluted* state. 3 tablespoonfuls taken in this way will be more useful in preventing sickness, than half a pint mixed with water.

7. molasses or sugar & water with a few drops of the acid of vitriol will make a pleasant & wholesome [sic] drink with your meals.

8. after having had your feet much chilled, it will be useful to wash them with a little spirit.

9. washing the feet every morning in *cold* water, will conduce very much to fortify
   them against the action of cold.

10. after long marches, or much fatigue from any cause, you will be more refreshed
    by *lying down* in a horizontal posture for two hours, than by resting a much longer
    time in any other position of the body.

11. shoes made without heels, by affording *equal* action to all the muscles of the legs,
    will enable you to march with less fatigue, than shoes made in the ordinary way.

Source: "Rush's Directions to Meriwether Lewis for Preserving Health, 11
June 1803," *Founders Online.* National Archives. Available at: http://founders
.archives.gov/documents/Jefferson/01-40-02-0396-0002.

Further Reading

Butterfield, Lyman H., ed. *Letters of Benjamin Rush, 1793–1813.* 2 vols. Princeton, NJ:
    Princeton University Press, 1951.
Duffi, Jacalyn. *History of Medicine: A Scandalously Short Introduction.* University of Toronto
    Press, 1999.
Duffy, John. *Epidemics in Colonial America.* Baton Rouge: Louisiana State University, 1971.
Nuland, Sherwin. *Doctors: The Biography of Medicine.* New York: Vintage Books, 1995.
Rush, Benjamin. *An Account of the Bilious Remitting Yellow Fever.* Philadelphia, PA: Thomas
    Dobson, 1794.
Valencius, Conevery Bolton. *The Health of the Country: I-low American Settlers Understood
    Themselves and Their Land.* New York: Basic Books, 2002.
Worth, Estes J. and Billy G. Smith, eds. *A Melancholy Scene of Devastation: The Public Response
    to the 1793 Philadelphia Yellow Fever Epidemic.* Canton, Mass: Watson Publications, 1997.
Zarrow, Sheila. *Friendship and Healing: The Dreams of John Adams and Benjamin Rush.* New
    York: Chiron Publications, 2010.

Document 17

SUPPLIES ORDERED BY MERIWETHER LEWIS FOR THE EXPEDITION (SPRING 1803)

Introduction: Clothes, Shoes, Blankets, Weapons, and Gifts

*In the spring of 1803, Meriwether Lewis traveled to Philadelphia, Pennsylvania, to pre-
pare for the journey west. After he consulted with his various teachers, he gave Israel
Whelan (1752–1806) and General William Irvine (1741–1804) long lists of needed*

supplies, which included mathematical instruments and camp supplies, such as blankets, pots, pans and plates, guns, ammunition, medical supplies, diaries, journals, paper, and clothing.

Israel Whelan, purveyor of public supplies, had gotten notice from the War Office to help Lewis obtain everything he needed, with a $1,000 advance. Whelan bought over 200 different items from different suppliers in the Philadelphia area.

As superintendent of the Schuylkill Arsenal in Philadelphia, General William Irvine was responsible for providing clothing, blankets, tents, knives, and knapsacks.

As the amount of supplies grew to nearly 3,500 pounds, the question arose: how all of these materials were going to be transported from Philadelphia to Pittsburgh, where the keelboat was being built. Lewis hired William Linard, who supplied Conestoga wagons with a team of 10 horses to get the supplies to Pittsburgh. These large, heavy covered wagons were capable of carrying up to six tons. After the Lewis and Clark expedition, these wagons would become a common sight as people began to move west.

- surveyor's compass
- hand compass
- quadrants
- telescope
- thermometers
- 2 sextants
- set of plotting instruments
- chronometer
- Magnets
- Tables
- Lamps
- Brass Kettles
- Sauce pan
- Table spoons
- flannel shirts
- coats
- frocks
- shoes
- woolen pants
- blankets
- knapsacks
- stockings
- Thread
- Cloth

- 15 prototype Model 1803 muzzle-loading .54 caliber rifles
- Knives
- 125 Muskets
- 500 rifle flints
- 420 pounds of sheet lead for bullets
- 176 pounds of gunpowder packed in 52 lead canisters
- 1 long-barreled rifle that fired its bullet with compressed air, rather than by flint, spark and powder
- 15 Shot pouches
- Knives
- Tomhawks
- 50 doz. Bilious Pills of B. Rush
- Tinctures
- ½ lb. Jalap
- 4 oz. Calomel
- 4 lbs. Cinnamon
- 2 lbs. Cloves
- 2 lbs. Nutmeg
- Tourniquet
- P. Soup
- Blankets
- 100 Quills
- Writing Paper
- Ink Stands
- Ink Powder

Source: "A Memorandum of Articles in Readiness" for the Voyage, 1803. Held at the Beinecke Library, Yale University.

Further Reading

Botkin, Daniel. *Our Natural History, The Lessons of Lewis and Clark*. Oxford University Press, 2004.

Chuinard, Eldon G. *Only One Man Died: The Medical Aspects of the Lewis and Clark Expedition*. Glendale, CA: Arthur Clark Company, 1980.

Cutright, Paul Russell. "Contributions of Philadelphia to Lewis and Clark History." *We Proceeded On*, special issue, July 1982.

Duffy, John. *Epidemics in Colonial America*. Louisiana State University, 1971.

Josephy, Alvin M. *Lewis and Clark through Indian Eyes: None Indian Writers on the Legacy of the Expedition*. New York: Vintage Press, 2007.

Ronda, James P. *Lewis and Clark among the Indians*. Lincoln: University of Nebraska Press, 1984.

Russel, Carl. "The Guns of the Lewis and Clark Expedition." *North Dakota History*, vol. 27 (Winter 1960).

Slaughter, Thomas P. *Exploring Lewis and Clark: Reflections on Men and Wilderness*. New York: Vintage Press, 2004.

Document 18

LETTER FROM THOMAS JEFFERSON TO MERIWETHER LEWIS (JUNE 20, 1803)

Introduction: Instructions for the Expedition West

Jefferson was extremely clear that much of this journey was to be spent talking to and listening to the Native American population. Jefferson once again had taken the early advice of General George Rogers Clark here and made it clear that that he (Jefferson) was sending a purposeful small group of people so that this expedition would neither be considered an act of aggressive nor even ever thought of as an act of war. Jefferson wanted detailed information about the nations who lived in the West, but these instructions were set up so that respect would be given. This was not about war or takeover of land but about science and cooperation. Jefferson believed that the Native population could be persuaded to farm the land and to live with the people from the East who would move there and also farm, but for this to happen, this trip, which was the vital beginning of the process, had to be peaceful in every way.

Science was also vital here. Jefferson demanded that details of weather, rivers, streams, mountains, plants, and animals were kept. This would be part of any maps that would be made, but it was also new information. Jefferson was aware that accepted and promoted science of the time thought that American nature was physically weak and unable to cope and was less than European animals. The only way that such science could be refuted was with many accurate detailed observations.

To aid these observations, Jefferson demanded that at least two journals be kept—presumably the two were to be kept by the expedition leaders: Meriwether Lewis and William Clark. Later Lewis and Clark ordered that each of the sergeants also keep journals in order to help with this, and two privates would voluntarily keep journals as well. Just as Jefferson had done with Andre Michaux, he asked that these journals and any and all papers get sent back east when possible and then when the group got to the Pacific that copies would be sent back by ship to ensure that these documents would be kept safe.

This was a military-style operation with Lewis in command, and military rank, order, and discipline was expected. But because of this, Jefferson also stated that he had informed Great Britain, France, and Spain that this group was going west, not as a military hostile takeover of the area, but as a scientific exploration. Another war on the North American continent was a real possibility as Britain, France, and Spain all had troops on the North American continent. Britain, France, and Spain were nineteenth-century superpowers, but the United States was not. So Jefferson needed to ensure that the actions of this group would not be mistaken for an act of war.

As this was a venture into the unknown, death was a real possibility. In this letter, Jefferson asks Lewis to name his successor in case of anything happening to him, and then Jefferson promises land to each person who returns.

Jefferson, realizing how difficult and dangerous this trip was, offers his prayers and hopes.

Jefferson's instructions were clear in that this journey was about science and learning and not about war nor the violent takeover of land. So while the expedition had the outward appearance of a military operation with Lewis in command, and military rank and discipline was expected, everyone of the journey was meant to listen to and appreciate the Native American peoples and cultures. They were to learn about, and share with.

To ensure that this would be educational not only for the people on the expedition but for generations to come, Jefferson was insistent that journals were to be kept and that copies were to be sent back east at every opportunity.

Finally, Jefferson, realizing how difficult and dangerous this trip was, offers his prayers and hopes.

To Meriwether Lewis esq. Capt. of the 1st. regimt, of Infantry of the US. of A.

Your situation as Secretary of the President of the US. has made you acquainted with the objects of my confidential message of Jan. 18. 1803 to the legislature; you have seen the act they passed, which they expressed in general terms, was meant to sanction these objects, and you are appointed to carry them into execution.

Instruments for ascertaining by celestial observations, the geography of the country through which you will pass, have been already provided. Light articles for barter and presents among the Indians, arms for your attendants, say from 10. to 12. men, boats, tents, & other travelling apparatus with ammunition, medicine, surgical instruments and provisions you will have prepared with such aids as the Secretary at War can yield in his department; & from him also you will recieve authority to engage among our troops, by voluntary agreement, the number of attendants above mentioned, over whom you, as their commanding officer, are invested with all the powers the laws give in such a case.

As your movements while within the limits of the US. will be better directed by occasional communications, adapted to circumstances as they arise, they will not be noticed here. What follows will respect your proceedings after your departure from the United States.

Your mission has been communicated to the ministers here from France, Spain & Great Britain, and through them to their governments; & such assurances given them as to it's objects as we trust will satisfy them. The country of Lousiana having been ceded by Spain to France, and possession by this time probably given, the passport you have from the minister of France, the representative of the present sovereign of the country, will be a protection against with all its subjects, & that from the minister of England will entitle you to the friendly aid of any traders of that allegiance with whom you may happen to meet.

The object of your mission is to explore the Missouri river, & such principal stream of it as by it's course and communication with the waters of the Pacific ocean whether the Columbia, Oregon, Colorado or any other river may offer the most direct & practicable water communication across this continent for the purposes of commerce.

Beginning at the mouth of the Missouri, you will take careful observations of latitude & longitude at all remarkable points on the river, & especially at the mouth of rivers, at rapids, at islands, & other places & objects distinguished by such durable natural marks & characters of a durable nature kind as that they may with certainty be recognized hereafter. The course of the river between these points of observation may be supplied by the compass, the log-line & by time, corrected by the observations themselves. The variations of the compass too, in different places should be noticed.

The interesting points of the portage between the heads of the Missouri, & of the water offering the best communication with the Pacific ocean, should also be fixed by observation, & the course of that water to the ocean, in the same manner as that of the Missouri.

Your observations are to be taken with great pains & accuracy, to be entered distinctly & intelligibly for others, as well as yourself, to comprehend all the elements necessary, with the aid of the usual tables, to fix the latitude and longitude of the places at which they were taken, and are to be rendered to the war office for the purpose of having the calculations made concurrently by proper persons within the US. several copies of these as well as of your other notes should be made at leisure times, & put into the care of the most trust-worthy of your attendants, to guard by multiplying them against the accidental losses to which they will be exposed. A further guard would be that one these copies be on the paper of the birch, as less liable to injury from damp than common paper.

The commerce which may be carried on with the people inhabiting the line your will pursue, renders a knolege of those people important. You will therefore endeavour to make yourself acquainted with as far as a diligent pursuit of your journey shall admit, with the names of the nations & their numbers;

the extent & limits of their possessions; their relations with other tribes of nations;

their language, traditions, monuments;

their ordinary occupations in agriculture, fishing, hunting, war, arts & the implements for these;

their food, clothing, & domestic accomodations;

the diseases prevalent among them, & the remedies they use;

moral & physical circumstances which distinguish them from the tribes we know;

peculiarities in their laws, customs & dispositions;

and articles of commerce they may need or furnish & to what extent.

And considering the interest which every nation has in extending & strengthening the authority of reason & justice among the people around them, it will be useful to acquire what knolege you can of the state of morality, religion, & information among them; as it may better enable those who may endeavor to civilize & instruct them, to adapt their measures to the existing notions & practices of those on whom they are to operate.

Other objects worthy of notice will be

the soil & face of the country it's growth & vegetable productions, especially those not of the US.

the animals of the country generally, & especially those not known in the US.

the remains & accounts of any which may be deemed rare or extinct;

the mineral productions of every kind; but more particularly metals; limestone, pit-coal, & salt-petre; salines & mineral waters, noting the temperature of the last & such circumstances as may indicate their character;

volcanic appearances;

climate, as characterized by the thermometer, by the proportion of rainy, cloudy, & clear days, by lightening, hail, snow, ice, by the access & recess of frost, by the winds prevailing at different seasons, the dates at which particular plants put forth or lose their flower, or leaf, times of appearance of particular birds, reptiles or insects.

Altho' your route will be along the channel of the Missouri, yet you will endeavor to inform yourself, by enquiry, of the character & extent of the country watered by it's branches & especially on it's Southern side, the North river or Rio Bravo which runs into the gulph of Mexico, and the North river, or Rio colorado which runs into the gulph of California, are understood to be the principal streams heading opposite to the waters of the Missouri, and running Southwardly. Whether the dividing grounds between the Missouri & them are mountains or flat lands, what are their distance from the Missouri, the character of the intermediate country, & the people inhabiting it, are worthy of particular enquiry. The Northern waters of the Missouri are less to be enquired after, because they have been ascertained to a considerable degree, & are still in a course of ascertainment by English traders, and travellers. But if you can learn any thing certain of the most Northern source of the Missisipi, & of it's position relatively to the lake of the woods, it will be interesting to us.

Two copies of your notes at least & as many more as leisure will admit, should be made & confided to the care of the most trusty individuals of your attendants. Some account too of the path of the Canadian traders from the Missisipi, at the mouth of the Ouisconsing to where it strikes the Missouri, & of the soil and rivers in its traverses course, is desirable.

In all your intercourse with the natives, treat them in the most friendly & conciliatory manner which their own conduct will admit; allay all jealousies as to the object of your journey, satisfy them of it's innocence, make them acquainted with the position, extent character, peaceable & commercial dispositions of the US. of our wish to be neighborly, friendly, & useful to them, & of our dispositions to a commercial intercourse with them; confer with them on the points most convenient as mutual emporiums, and the articles of most desireable interchange for them & us. If a few of their influential chiefs within practicable distance, wish to visit us, arrange such a visit with them, and furnish them with authority to call on our officers, on their entering the US. to have them conveyed to this place at the public expence. If any of them should wish to have some of their young people brought up with us, & taught such arts as may be useful to them, we will recieve, instruct & take care of them. Such a mission whether of influential chiefs or of young people would give some security to your own party. Carry with you some matter of the kinepox; inform those of them with whom you may be, of it's efficacy as a preservative from the smallpox; & instruct & encourage them in the use of it. This may be especially done wherever you winter.

As it is impossible for us to foresee in what manner you will be recieved by those people, whether with hospitality or hostility, so is it impossible to prescribe th exact degree of preserverance with which you are to pursue your journey. We value too much the lives of citizens to offer them to probable destruction. Your numbers will be sufficient to secure you against the unauthorised opposition of individuals or of small parties: but if a superior force authorised, or not authorised by a nation, should be arrayed against your further passage, and inflexibly determined to arrest it, you must decline it's farther pursuit, and return. In the loss of yourselves, we should lose also the information you will have acquired. By returning safely with that, you may enable us to renew the essay with better calculated means. To your own discretion therefore must be left the degree of danger you risk, and the point at which you should decline, only saying we wish you to err on the side of your safety, and to bring back your party safe even if it be with less information.

As far up the Missouri as the white settlements extend, an intercourse will probably be found to exist between them & the Spanish posts of St. Louis opposite Cahokia, or Ste. Genevieve opposite Kaskaskia. From still further up the river, the traders may furnish a conveyance for letters. Beyond that, you may perhaps be able to engage Indians to bring letters for the government to Cahokia or Kaskaskia, on promising that they shall there recieve such special compensation as you shall have stipulated with them. Avail yourself of these means to communicate to us, at seasonable intervals, a copy of your journal, notes & observations, of every kind, putting into cypher whatever might do injury if betrayed.

Should you reach the Pacific ocean inform yourself of the circumstances which may decide whether the furs of those parts may not be collected as advantageously at the head of the Missouri (convenient as is supposed to the waters of the Colorado & Oregan or Columbia) as at Nootka sound, or any other point of that coast; and that trade be consequently conducted through the Missouri & U.S. more beneficially than by the circumnavigation now practised.

On your arrival on that coast endeavor to learn if there by any port within your reach frequented by the sea-vessels of any nation, & to send two of your trusty people back by sea, in such way as shall appear practicable, with a copy of your notes: and should you be of opinion that the return of your party by the way they went will be eminently dangerous, then ship the whole, & return by sea, by the way either of cape Horn, or the cape of good Hope, as you shall be able. As you will be without money, clothes or provisions, you must endeavor to use the credit of the U.S. to obtain them, for which purpose open letters of credit shall be furnished you, authorising you to draw upon the Executive of the U.S. or any of it's officers, in any part of the world, on which draughts can be disposed of, & to apply with our recommendations to the Consuls, agents, merchants, or citizens of any nation with which we have intercourse, assuring them, in our name, that any aids they may furnish you, shall be honorably repaid, and on demand. Our consuls Thomas Hewes at Batavia in Java, Wm. Buchanan in the Isles of France & Bourbon & John Elmslie at the Cape of good Hope will be able to supply your necessities by draughts on us.

Should you find it safe to return by the way you go, after sending two of your party round by sea, or with your whole party, if no conveyance by sea can be found, do so; making such observations on your return, as may serve to supply, correct or confirm those made on your outward journey.

On re-entering the U.S. and reaching a place of safety, discharge any of your attendants who may desire & deserve it, procuring for them immediate paiment of all arrears of pay & cloathing which may have incurred since their departure, and assure them that they shall be recommended to the liberality of the legislature for the grant of a souldier's portion of land each, as proposed in my message to Congress; & repair yourself with your papers to the seat of government to which I have only to add my sincere prayer for your safe return.

To provide, on the accident of your death, against anarchy, dispersion, & the consequent danger to your party, and total failure of the enterprize, you are hereby authorized, by any instrument signed & written in your own hand, to name the person among them who shall succeed to the command on your decease, and by like instruments to change the nomination from time to time as further experience of the characters accompanying you shall point out superior fitness: and all the powers and authorities given to yourself are, in the event of your death, transferred to, & vested in the successor so named, with further power to him, and his successors in like manner to name each his successor, who, on the death of his predecessor, shall be invested with all the powers & authorities given to yourself.

Given under my hand at the city of Washington this 20th day of June 1803.* . . . Th. J. Pr. U.S. of A.

Source: "Instructions for Meriwether Lewis, 20 June 1803." Library of Congress.

Further Reading

Ambrose, Stephen. *Undaunted Courage*. Urbana: University of Chicago Press, 1991.

Bedini, Silvio. *Thomas Jefferson: Statesman of Science*. New York: Macmillan, 1990.

Brown, Dee. *The American West*. New York: Touchstone, 1995.

Dillon, Richard. *Meriwether Lewis: A Biography*. New York: Coward-McCann, 1965.

Fenster, Julie. *Jefferson's America: The President, the Purchase, and the Explorers Who Transformed a Nation*. New York: Crown, 2016.

Harris, Matthew and Jay H. Buckley, ed. *Zebulon Pike, Thomas Jefferson and the Opening of the American West*. Norman: University of Oklahoma Press, 2012.

Harrison, Lowell. *George Roger Clark and the War in the West*. Lexington: University of Kentucky Press, 2001.

Kukla, Jon. *A Wilderness So Immense: The Louisiana Purchase and the Destiny of America*. New York: Anchor, 2004.

Richter, Daniel K. *Facing East from Indian Country: A Native History of Early America*. Cambridge, MA: Harvard University Press, 2001.

Document 19

LETTER FROM WILLIAM CLARK TO MERIWETHER LEWIS (JULY 18, 1803)

Introduction: Clark Agrees to Go on the Expedition to the Pacific

On June 19, 1803, Lewis wrote to his friend and former army colleague William Clark, and asked him to co-captain an expedition to the Pacific. Clark wrote back the day after he received the letter that he was delighted to accept the offer. Clark realizes the dangers and difficulties that a trip will involve but is excited about the possibilities and the adventure. He agrees to Lewis's plans and sets out finding people who will be part of the trip.

Here Clark tells Lewis that he will accept the "Credentials." This was the offer that Clark would also be given the equal rank to Lewis of captain. In March 1804, however, Henry Dearborn wrote to Lewis stating that Clark's rank would be a lieutenant. This fact was kept secret from the men during the trip, and Clark was referred to always as Captain Clark.

CLARKSVILLE JULY 18TH. 1803

DEAR LEWIS

I received by yesterdays Mail, your letter of the 19th. ulto: The Contents of which I recived with much pleasure—The enterprise &a. is Such as I have long anticipated and am much pleased With—and as my Situation in life will admit of my absence the length of time necessary to accomplish Such an undertakeing I will chearfully join you in an 'official Charrector' as mentioned in your letter, and partake of the dangers, difficulties, and fatigues, and I anticipate the honors & rewards of the result of Such an enterprise, Should we be successful in accomplishing it. This is an under takeing fraited with many difeculties, but My friend I do assure you that no man lives Whith Whome I would perfur to under take Such a Trip &c. as your Self, and I shall arrange My Matters as well as I can against your Arrival here.

It may be necessary that you inform the President of My acceding to the proposals, so that I may be furnishd with such Credentials as the nature of the Toure may require—Which I Suppose had best be fowarded to Louisville. The Objects of this Plan of Government, are Great and Worthey of that great Charecetor the Main-Spring of its Action—The Means with which we are furnished to carry it into effect, I think may be Sufficintly liberal—The plan of operation, as laid down by you (with a Small addition as to the out fit) I highly approve of.

I shall indeaver to engage (temporally) a few men, such as will best answer our purpose, holding out the Idea as stated in your letter—The subject of which has been Mentioned in Louisville several weeks agoe.

Pray write to me by every post after recving this letter, I shall be exceedingly anxious to here from you.

With every sincerity & frendship

WM. CLARK

Source: "William Clark to Meriwether Lewis, 18 July 1803," in Thwaites, Reuben Gold, ed. *Original Journals of the Lewis and Clark Expedition, 1804–1806.* Volume 7. New York: Dodd, Mead & Company, 1905, 259.

Further Reading

Ambrose, Stephen. *Undaunted Courage.* Urbana: University of Chicago Press, 1991.
Blumberg, Rhoda. *The Incredible Journey of Lewis and Clark.* New York: Scholastic, 1993.
Brown, Dee. *The American West.* New York: Touchstone, 1995.
Buckley, Jay H. *William Clark: Indian Diplomat.* University of Oklahoma Press, 2008.
Foley, William. *Wilderness Journey: The Life of William Clark.* University of Missouri, 2004.
Holmberg, James. *Dear Brother: Letters of William Clark to Jonathan Clark.* New Haven, CT: Yale University Press, 2002.

Document 20

LETTER FROM MERIWETHER LEWIS TO THOMAS JEFFERSON (JULY 22, 1803)

Introduction: Expedition Vessels

The primary means of transport initially used by the expedition were two small boats called the red and white pirogues and a very large 55-foot keelboat. The red pirogue as described by Lewis and Clark was a 41-foot boat designed to carry nine tons of supplies and eight people, while the white pirogue carried six people and contained the most valuable equipment, including the instruments.

There was a fourth boat carried by the expedition as well. This was the collapsible "iron boat" designed by Lewis. Lewis had the boat built at Harpers' Ferry, West Virginia. It had a collapsible frame that was stored on the main keelboat. Lewis referred to this as his favorite boat, as it was after all the one he invented. The idea behind it was when the volume of water in the river decreased, they would use the iron frame as a basis for a new boat. They did carry this frame with them and made a boat in June 1805. The experiment turned out to be a failure: first, the boat took much longer to make than Lewis had originally thought (it took two weeks as opposed to hours), and second, it floated for a very short time and sank, as it proved too heavy for the river system and was not waterproof. Lewis buried the frame, and though he dug it up on the return journey, there is no more mention of it anywhere.

This main keelboat (sometimes referred to as a barge or just boat in the journals) was a single-mast, 55-foot boat with 22 foot oars, capable of holding 22 people, and 12 tons of supplies. It even had a cabin for the captains. It had been ordered in Pittsburgh early in the summer of 1803, and Lewis thought it would be ready by July, before the river levels dropped off and travel became much more difficult. In 1803, the river levels were actually to be at a record low level. On July 22, 1803, however, Lewis was frustrated. As he writes to Jefferson from Pittsburgh, he recounts that he had made an order for a keelboat and it was taking much longer than he was promised. As the river level was low, every day was causing problems as the whole expedition needed to begin west long before the winter. The supplies had arrived, and he was ready, but the boat was not.

More frustration was to happen as the keelboat would not be ready until August 31, delaying Lewis and the whole expedition.

Pittsburgh July 22nd. 1803.

Dear Sir,

Yours of the 11th. & 15th. Inst. were duly recieved, the former on the 18th. inst., the latter on this day. For my pocketbook I thank you: the dirk could not well come by post, nor is it of any moment to me, the knives that were made at Harper's ferry will answer my purposes equally as well and perhaps better; it can therefore be taken care of untill my return: the bridle is of no consequence at all. After the reciept of this letter I think it will be best to direct to me at Louisville Kentuckey.—

The person who contracted to build my boat engaged to have it in readiness by the 20th. inst.; in this however he has failed; he pleads his having been disappointed in procuring timber, but says he has now supplyed himself with the necessary materials, and that she shall be completed by the last of this month; however in this I am by no means sanguine, nor do I believe from the progress he makes that she will be ready before the 5th. of August; I visit him every day, and endeavour by every means in my power to hasten the completion of the work: I have prevailed on him to engage more hands, and he tells me that two others will join him in the morning, if so, he may probably finish the boat by the time he mentioned: I shall embark immediately the boat is in readiness, there being no other consideration which at this moment detains me.—

The Waggon from Harper's ferry arrived today, bringing every thing with which she was charged in good order.

The party of recruits that were ordered from Carlisle to this place with a view to descend the river with me, have arrived with the exception of one, who deserted on the march, his place however can be readily supplyed from the recruits at this place enlisted by Lieut. Hook.

The current of the Ohio is extreemly low and continues to decline, this may impede my progress but shall not prevent my proceeding, being determined to get forward though I should not be able to make a greater distance than a mile pr. day.—

I am with the most sincere regard Your Obt. Servt.

Meriwether Lewis.

Source: "To Thomas Jefferson from Meriwether Lewis, 22 July 1803," in Thwaites, Reuben Gold, ed. *Original Journals of the Lewis and Clark Expedition, 1804–1806.* Volume 7. New York: Dodd, Mead & Company, 1905, 260–261.

Further Reading

Dunbar-Ortiz, Roxanne. *An Indigenous Peoples' History of the United States*. Beacon Press, reprint, 2015.

Fenn, Elizabeth. *Encounters at the Heart of the World: A History of the Mandan People*. Hill and Wang, reprint, 2015.

Hine, Robert V. and John Mack Faragher. *The American West: A New Interpretive History*. New Haven, CT: Yale University Press, 2000.

Husner, Verne. *On the River with Lewis and Clark*. Austin, TX: A & M Press, 2004.

Merrell, James H. *Into the American Woods: Negotiators on the Pennsylvania Frontier*. New York: W.W. Norton, 1999.

Rogers, Ann. *Lewis and Clark in Missouri*. University of Missouri, 2002.

Russel, Carl. "The Guns of the Lewis and Clark Expedition." *North Dakota History*, vol. 27 (Winter 1960).

Document 21

GIFTS FOR THE NATIVE AMERICAN POPULATION (SPRING 1803)

Introduction: Items Brought on Expedition

Meriwether Lewis estimated the cost of this trip to be $2,500, out of which nearly $700 was to be spent on "Indian Presents." Very little was known about the various indigenous peoples of the West at the time. Some contact had been made through various fur traders, and various military operations had been carried out along the western borders of Pennsylvania, Virginia, and New York. But almost nothing was known about the peoples who lived west of St. Louis.

Jefferson was not interested in a war with the Native Americans. When in 1784 General George Rogers Clark replied to Jefferson's initial request to take an expedition west, he had been clear in his response to Jefferson that for any exploratory trip to be successful, knowledge of the cultures and languages of the Native peoples was of paramount importance. Jefferson seems to have kept this advice in mind.

Indian Presents

12 Pipe Tomahawks
6 ½ lb Strips Sheet Iron
1 p. red flannel 47 ½ yd
11 ps. Handkerchief ass
1 doz Ivory Combs
½ Catty Indn. S. Silk
21 lb Tread ass(orted)
1 ps. Scarlet Cloth 22 yd

5 ½ doz fan
6 Gro[cer]: Binding
2 Cards Beads
4 doz: Butcher Knives
12 doz. Pocket Looking Glass
15 doz. Pewter
8 doz. Burning
2 doz. Nonsopretty
2 doz. Red Striped tapes
72 ps Striped silk ribbon
3 lb red Beads
6 Paper Small Bells
1 box with 100 larger do
73 Beads ass(orted)
3 ½ doz Tinsel Beads ass(orted)
1 # Thread
1 doz: Needle cases
2 /34 doz Lockets
8 ½ [illegible] Red Beads
2 doz: Earrings
8 Brass kettles
12 lb Brass Strips
500 Broaches
72 Rings
2 Corn Mills
15 doz: Scissors
12 lbs Brass Wire
14 lbs Knittings Pins
4600 Needles
2800 Fish Hooks
1 Gro Iron Combs
3 Gro Curtain Rings
2 Gro Thimbles
11 doz knives
10 lbs Brads
8 lbs Red lead
2 lbs. Vermillion
130 Rolls of Tobacco Pigtail
48 Calico Ruffled Shirts
15 blankets
1 Trunks to pac sundry ind
Prests
Grose seat or Mockasin
Awls

Source: National Archives, Record Group 92, Records of the Office of the Quarter-master General, 1774–1985. Available at: https://catalog.archives.gov/id/300353.

Further Reading

Blumberg, Rhoda. *The Incredible Journey of Lewis and Clark*. New York: Scholastic, 1993.

Calloway, Colin G. *One Vast Winter Count: The Native American West before Lewis and Clark*. Lincoln: University of Nebraska Press, 2003.

Dowd, Gregory Evans. *A Spirited Resistance: The North American Indian Struggle for Unity, 1745–1815*. Baltimore, MD: Johns Hopkins University Press, 1992.

Dunbar-Ortiz, Roxanne. *An Indigenous Peoples' History of the United States*. Beacon Press, reprint, 2015.

Merrell, James H. *Into the American Woods: Negotiators on the Pennsylvania Frontier*. New York: W.W. Norton, 1999.

Ostler, Jeffrey. *The Plains Sioux and U.S. Colonialism from Lewis and Clark to Wounded Knee*. Cambridge: Cambridge University Press, 2004.

Richter, Daniel K. *Facing East from Indian Country: A Native History of Early America*. Cambridge, MA: Harvard University Press, 2001.

Saunt, Claudio. *A New Order of Things: Property, Power, and the Transformation of the Creek Indians, 1773–1816*. Cambridge: Cambridge University Press, 1999.

West, Elliot. *The Last Indian War: The Nez Perce Story*. Oxford: Oxford University Press, 2011.

Document 22

LETTER FROM DR. BENJAMIN RUSH TO MERIWETHER LEWIS (MAY 17, 1803)

Introduction: Sample of Questions from Rush about the Native American Nations

As Jefferson had continually made clear, the expedition was part scientific, part anthropological. Lewis and Clark had a long list of questions that they were to ask each group they encountered. Some of these questions were suggested by Dr. Benjamin Rush, who was particularly interested in medical and anthropological issues. But Clark added some questions of his own, as did Caspar Winstar and Benjamin Smith Barton. Jefferson had his own questions, which were included along with yet others posed by members of the American Philosophical Society. One of the people who organized the questions was Jefferson's Attorney General Levi Lincoln (1749–1820). It was Lincoln who strongly pushed Jefferson to include questions about religion, legal issues, punishments, and property. It was also Lincoln who suggested that Lewis and Clark bring some anti-smallpox medicine with them. Lincoln's suggestions were politically based; he was thinking of future commercial and trading agreements. Knowledge was vital to all kinds of expansion, but Lincoln was also aware that the Federalists were opposed to this expedition, but this trip couched in scientific language with exploration and not expansion as its key would be considered differently. Jefferson, recognizing the sound political advice, took Lincoln's suggestions, and so social and scientific questions about the Native population became of huge importance to this trip.

- What is their State of Life as to longevity?
- At what age do both Sexes marry?
- What is the diet of their Children?
- What time do they generally consume in sleep?
- What are their acute diseases?
- What are their chronic diseases?
- Is rheumatism, Pluricy, or bilious fevers known among them? And does the latter ever terminate in vomiting of black matter?
- What is their mode of treating the Small pox particularly?
- Have they any other diseases amongst them, and what are they?
- What are their remedies for their different diseases?
- Is murder common among them and do their Laws punish it by Death?
- Can the crime of murder ever be palliated by pecuniary Considerations?
- What are their principal objects of worship?
- How do they dispose of their dead?
- What species of grain or pulse do they cultivate?
- What are their implements of husbandry, and in what manner do they use them?
- Have they any domestic animals and what are they?
- In what form and of what materials are their Lodges or houses usually built?
- Do more than one family inhabit the same lodge and in such case is the furniture of the lodge considered as the common property of the inhabitants of it?
- How do they peruse and how do they take their game?
- What is the ceremony of declaring war, and making peace; or forming alliances?
- Do women ever accompany them?
- At what season of the year do they usually go to War?
- What are their implements of War, how do they prepare and how do they use them?
- Do they play at any games of risk and what are they?
- Have they any and what are their festivals of feasts?
- Do they ever dance and what is the cermimony [sic] of their dance?
- Have they any music and what are their musical instruments?
- Do they ever dance and what the ceremony of their dance?
- Do they tattoe [sic] their bodys?
- Do they use paints of various colors on their skin?
- What is the ceremony of receiving a Stranger at their village?

Source: "Benjamin Rush to Meriwether Lewis, May 17, 1803," in Thwaites, Reuben Gold, ed. *Original Journals of the Lewis and Clark Expedition, 1804–1806.* Volume 7. New York: Dodd, Mead & Company, 1905, 283–287.

Further Reading

Aron, Stephen. *The American West: A Very Short Introduction.* Oxford: Oxford University Press, 2015.

Bedini, Silvio. *Thomas Jefferson: Statesman of Science.* New York: Macmillan, 1990.

Brown, Dee. *The American West.* New York: Touchstone, 1995.

Buckley, Jay H. *William Clark: Indian Diplomat.* University of Oklahoma Press, 2008.

Calloway, Colin G. *One Vast Winter Count: The Native American West before Lewis and Clark.* Lincoln: University of Nebraska Press, 2003.

Carlson, Paul. *The Plains Indians.* Austin, TX: A & M University, 1998.

Coates, Robert. *Outlaw Years: The History of the Land Pirates of the Natchez Trace.* Pelican Press, 2002.

Daniels, Jonathan. *Devil's Backbone: The Story of the Natchez Trace.* Pelican Press, 1985.

Dunbar-Ortiz, Roxanne. *An Indigenous Peoples' History of the United States.* Beacon Press, reprint, 2015.

Richter, Daniel K. *Facing East from Indian Country: A Native History of Early America.* Cambridge, MA: Harvard University Press, 2001.

Document 23

LETTER FROM MERIWETHER LEWIS TO THOMAS JEFFERSON (SEPTEMBER 8, 1803)

Introduction: Delays and Boat Making

One of the biggest frustrations for Lewis was the length of time it took for the main boat or barge to be made. He bargained, threatened, and cajoled the boat-makers trying to push them along, but he ended up staying there six weeks waiting. Finally, on August 31, it was ready, and Lewis immediately left Pittsburgh, but at this stage, the water level on the Ohio River was extremely low, and so travel was slow. However, on September 8, as he wrote, he was still frustrated as he now had to buy a smaller boat in order to get supplies from the shore to the bigger boat, as the larger boat could not get close enough to shore.

Wheeling, September 8th. 1803.

DEAR SIR,

It was not untill 7 O'Clock on the morning of the 31st. Utmo. that my boat was completed, she was instantly loaded, and at 10. A.M. on the same day I left Pittsburgh, where I had been moste shamefully detained by the unpardonable negligence of my boat-builder. On my arrival at Pittsburgh, my calculation was that the boat would be in readiness by the 5th. of August; this term however elapsed and the boat so far from being finished was only partially planked on one side; in this situation I had determined to abandon the boat, and to purchase two or three perogues and descend the river in them, and depend on purchasing a boat as I descended, there being none to be had at Pittsburgh; from this resolution I was dissuaded first by the representations of the best informed merchants at that place who assured me that the chances were much against my being able to procure a boat below; and secondly by the positive assureances given me by the boat-builder that she should be ready on the last of the then ensuing week, (the 13th.): however a few days after, according to his usual custom he got drunk, quarrelled with his workmen, and several of them left him, nor could they be prevailed on to return: I threatened him with the penalty of his contract, and exacted a promise of greater sobriety in future which, he took care to perform with as little good faith, as he had his previous promises with regard to the boat, continuing to be constantly either drunk or sick.

I spent most of my time with the workmen, alternately presuading and threatening, but neither threats, presuasion or any other means which I could devise were sufficient to procure the completion of the work sooner than the 31st. of August; by which time the water was so low that those who pretended to be acquainted with the navigation of the river declared it impracticable to descend it; however in conformity to my previous determineation I set out, having taken the precaution to send a part of my baggage by a waggon to this place, and also to procure a good pilot. my days journey have averaged about 12 miles, but in some instances, with every exertion I could make was unable to exceed 4½ & 5 miles pr. day. This place is one hundred miles distant from Pittsburgh by way of the river and about sixty five by land—

When the Ohio is in it's present state there are many obstructions to it's navigation, formed by bars of small stones, which in some instances are intermixed with, and partially cover large quntities of drift-wood; these bars frequently extend themselves entirely across the bed of the river, over many of them I found it impossible to pass even with my emty boat, without geting into the water and lifting her over by hand; over others my force was even inadequate to enable me to pass in this manner, and I found myself compelled to hire horses or oxen from the neighbouring farmers and drag her over them; in this way I have passed as many as five of those bars, (or as they are here called *riffles*) in a day, and to unload as many or more times. The river is lower than it has ever been known by the oldest settler in this country. I shall leave this place tomorrow morning, and loose no time in geting on.

I have been compelled to purchase a perogue at this place in order to transport the baggage which was sent by land from Pittsburgh, and also to lighten the boat as much as possible. On many bars the water in the deepest part dose not exceed six inches.—

I have the honour to be with the most perfect regard and sincere attattchment Your Obt. Servt.

MERIWETHER LEWIS.

CAPT. 1ST. US REGT. INFTY.

Source: "To Thomas Jefferson from Meriwether Lewis, 8 September 1803," in Thwaites, Reuben Gold, ed. *Original Journals of the Lewis and Clark Expedition, 1804–1806.* Volume 7. New York: Dodd, Mead & Company, 1905, 269–270.

Further Reading

Brown, Dee. *The American West.* New York: Touchstone, 1995.

Buckley, Jay H. *William Clark: Indian Diplomat.* University of Oklahoma Press, 2008.

Calloway, Colin G. *One Vast Winter Count: The Native American West before Lewis and Clark.* Lincoln: University of Nebraska Press, 2003.

Carlson, Paul. *The Plains Indians.* Austin, TX: A & M University, 1998.

Coates, Robert. *Outlaw Years: The History of The Land Pirates of the Natchez Trace.* Pelican Press, 2002.

Daniels, Jonathan. *Devil's Backbone: The Story of the Natchez Trace.* Pelican Press, 1985.

Dunbar-Ortiz, Roxanne. *An Indigenous Peoples' History of the United States.* Beacon Press, reprint, 2015.

Richter, Daniel K. *Facing East from Indian Country: A Native History of Early America.* Cambridge, MA: Harvard University Press, 2001.

Document 24

LETTER FROM MERIWETHER LEWIS TO THOMAS JEFFERSON (SEPTEMBER 13, 1803)

Introduction: The Problems with the Heavy Barge

The barge built in Pittsburgh, though no one knows exactly where, was made to travel downstream in plenty of water, but the summer of 1803 had been unusually dry, and as the boat was very heavy, supplies that were supposed to last a year were now on board. Lewis wrote to Jefferson from present-day West Virginia and explained that in an act of desperation and frustration, Lewis was forced to hire ox and horses to help drag the boat through the drier sections of the river.

On board my boat opposite Marietta.

September 13th. 1803.

DEAR SIR,

I arrived here at 7. P.M. and shall pursue my journey early tomorrow. This place is one hundred miles distant from Wheeling, from whence in descending the water is reather more abundant than it is between that place and Pittsburgh, insomuch that I have been enabled to get on without the necessity of employing oxen or horses to drag my boat over the ripples except in two instances; tho' I was obliged to cut a passage through four or five bars, and by that means past them: this last operation is much more readily performed than you would imagin; the gravel of which many of these bars are formed, being small and lying in a loose state is readily removed with a spade, or even with a wooden shovel and when set in motion the current drives it a considerable distance before it subsides or again settles at the bottom; in this manner I have cut a passage for my boat of 50 yards in length in the course of an hour; this method however is impracticable when drift-wood or clay in any quantity is intermixed with the gravel; in such cases Horses or oxen are the last resort: I find them the most efficient sailors in the present state of the navigation of this river, altho' they may be considered somewhat clumsey.—

I have the honour to be with much respect Your Obt. Servt.

MERIWETHER LEWIS.

CAPT. 1ST. US. REGT. INFTY.

Source: "To Thomas Jefferson from Meriwether Lewis, 13 September 1803," in Thwaites, Reuben Gold, ed. *Original Journals of the Lewis and Clark Expedition, 1804–1806.* Volume 7. New York: Dodd, Mead & Company, 1905, 271.

Further Reading

Blumberg, Rhoda. *The Incredible Journey of Lewis and Clark.* New York: Scholastic, 1993.

Fenster, Julie. *Jefferson's America: The President, the Purchase, and the Explorers Who Transformed a Nation.* New York: Crown, 2016.

Gutzman, Kevin. *Thomas Jefferson—Revolutionary: A Radical's Struggle to Remake America.* New York: St. Martin's Press, 2017.

Kukla, Jon. *A Wilderness So Immense: The Louisiana Purchase and the Destiny of America.* New York: Anchor, 2004.

Meacham, John. *Thomas Jefferson: The Art of Power.* New York: Random House, 2013.

Peterson, Merrill. *Thomas Jefferson and the New Nation: A Biography.* Oxford: Oxford University Press, 2013.

Chapter 3

The Voyage West

With the preparations at last completed, including having the weapons and a cannon on board, the expedition left Camp Dubois, Illinois, on May 14, 1804. For everyone involved, including Thomas Jefferson in Washington D.C., there was a mixture of excitement and relief. The voyage had finally begun. Those planning the trip believed it would take a year. It would in fact take double that amount of time. But as they began upriver, everyone was optimistic.

While the science and exploratory parts of this trip were important, Meriwether Lewis and William Clark were both aware that strict military discipline was necessary if there was going to be any chance of survival. Orders must be obeyed without question. Three days after the trip began there was a court-martial, the first of seven courts-martial that would happen within the first nine months. Each case would result in severe punishments, which were carried out in public as a way of demonstrating the consequences of a breach of discipline. Moses Reed's court-martial for desertion was the most serious. He was found guilty and was expelled from the Corps. Other lesser infringements were punished with lashes of a whip. The strict punishments got the point across. After these first months, there was no need for any further courts-martial.

This whole journey can be easily divided up into three acts: Act I was the trip up the Missouri River as far as Fort Mandan, where they spent the winter of 1804–1805. Act II covered the voyage from spring 1805 through the following spring, when the Corps successfully crossed the Rocky Mountains and wintered in the Pacific Northwest. Act III was the return trip back to St. Louis.

It was during the first part of the trip, on August 20, 1804, that the only person of the Corps would die: Sergeant Charles Floyd. He died of what was probably a burst appendix. No medical doctor at the time could have saved him, and certainly not Lewis or Clark with their very rudimentary medical knowledge and treatments.

Jefferson had been clear in his instructions that establishing peaceful relations with the Native Americans was paramount on this trip, and with very few exceptions, the Corps succeeded in carrying out his orders. The biggest item in the expedition's budget had been allocated to what was referred to as "Indian Presents." For all Native groups, Lewis and Clark had a prepared speech about Thomas Jefferson, president of the United States, how he was now their ruler, but someone who was willing to meet and talk with them and who had sent them with gifts.

By the time Lewis, Clark, and the Corps reached the Mandan villages in the winter of 1804, and built a fort there, friendly relations were the norm. It was also here this winter that Toussaint Charbonneau, Sacagawea, and Jean Baptiste joined the Corps. Charbonneau was a fur trader, a "mountain man" of sorts, who lived outside the social norm. He took or was given Sacagawea as his wife about a year before he met the Corps. A member of the Shoshone Nation, Sacagawea had been kidnapped by the Hidatsa when she was about 12 years old. Like many other Shoshone girls who were kidnapped, she was initially brought from her home in Lemhi, Idaho, to an area over 600 miles away, near modern-day Washburn, North Dakota. It is thought that soon after her arrival she met Toussaint Charbonneau, who took her as his wife, and so she traveled with Charbonneau wherever he went. By the time she reached Fort Mandan, North Dakota, that winter, she was expecting a child. Her son, Jean Baptiste, was born on February 11 1805, and when the Corps began the second part of their journey in April that year, Toussaint Charbonneau, Sacagawea, and a not-yet three-month-old Jean Baptiste accompanied them.

This second part of the journey was physically demanding. Often during this time, the Corps lacked food, and many times people fell sick. Time and time again, the Corps were saved by Native American groups, who shared food and/or their expertise with them. The crossing of the Rocky Mountains, for example, would not have happened without Sacagawea's family and her nation.

By the time the Corps got through the Rockies, they were tired and hungry, and once again they were saved due to the generosity of Native Americans—this time the Nez Perce. The Nez Perce, famous for their breeding of appaloosa horses, had never seen white people before, and they were generous with their supplies and knowledge. They shared their food, mainly fish at that time of the year, and showed the expedition how to make canoes out of trees by burning the trees to create a boat. These canoes were vital as winter was closing in quickly, and these canoes made it possible for the group to travel quickly down the Columbia River to reach the Pacific Ocean.

The expedition spent the winter of 1805–1806 at the Pacific. They were wet, cold, and unhappy. They had, however, achieved the most important target as laid out by President Thomas Jefferson—to find a route from east to west across the American continent.

In the spring, they would retrace their journey back to St. Louis.

Document 25

THEY PROCEEDED ON—THE JOURNEY BEGINS. CAMP DUBOIS, ILLINOIS (MAY 14, 1804)

Introduction: Leaving Camp Dubois

On May 14, 1804, the expedition inspired and created by Thomas Jefferson and led by Meriwether Lewis and William Clark began. Clark (without Lewis) left Camp Dubois, Illinois, and arrived at St. Charles Missouri, where he would wait for Lewis. William Clark had been training the men for a few months, while Meriwether Lewis had been gathering supplies and in the end rather desperately trying to get the barge boat built.

This day Clark organized the men and the three boats: the large keelboat and the two pirogues for their first trip.

Despite all the records available, the exact number of people who left Camp Dubois is not known. There are discrepancies here in the two journals in terms of numbers, and it is not clear if at this stage Clark counted his slave York as a person. We do know the group at this stage included John Ordway (c. 1775– c. 1817), Patrick Gass (1771–1870), Joseph Whitehouse (1775–date unknown), and Charles Floyd (1782–1804), all of whom would keep a diary during the trip. On this first day, they traveled just over four miles, and they reached the point where Clark had said they would wait for Lewis to join them.

The men who had signed on had done so knowing that there were huge risks and real dangers involved. Most had warned their families that there was a real possibility that they would not return. But this day, considered the first day of the voyage, was optimistic, and each of these journals revealed that.

May 14th, 1804

Set out from Camp River a Dubois at 4 oClock P. M. and proceded up the Missouris under Sail to the first Island in the Missouriand Camped on the upper point opposit a Creek on the South Side below a ledge of limestone rock Called Colewater, made 4½ miles, the Party Consisted of 2, Self one frenchman and 22 Men in the Boat of 20 ores, 1 Serjt. & 7 french in a large Perogue, a Corp and 6 Soldiers in a large Perogue. a Cloudy rainey day. wind from the N E. men in high Spirits.

Rained the forepart of the day I determined to go as far as St. Charles a french Village 7 Leags. up the Missourie, and wait at that place untill Capt. Lewis Could finish the business in which he was obliged to attend to at St Louis and join me by Land from that place 24 miles; by this movement I calculated that if any alterations in the loading of the Vestles or other Changes necessary, that they might be made at St. Charles.

I Set out at 4 oClock P. M. in the presence of many of the Neighbouring inhabitents, and proceeded on under a jentle brease up the Missourie to the upper Point of the 1st Island 4 Miles and Camped on the Island which is Situated Close on the right (or Starboard) Side, and opposit the mouth of a Small Creek called Cold water, a heavy rain this after-noon.

Source: Thwaites, Reuben Gold, ed. *Original Journals of the Lewis and Clark Expedition, 1804–1806.* New York: Dodd, Mead & Company, 1905.

May 14th, 1804

A Journal Commenced at River Dubois

Monday May the 14th 1804. Showery day. Capt Clark Set out at 3 oClock P. M. for the western expedition. one Gun fired. a nomber of Citizens see us Start. the party consisted of 3 Sergeants & 38 Good hands, which maned the Batteaux and two pearogues. we Sailed up the Missouri 6 miles & encamped on the N. Side of the River.

Source: The Journals of Captain Meriwether Lewis and Sergeant John Ordway: Kept on the Expedition of Western Exploration, 1803–1806. Madison, WI: The Society, 1916.

May 14, 1804

A Journal commenced at River Dubois—monday may 14th 1804 Showery day Capt Clark Set out at 3 oclock P m for the western expidition the party Consisted of 3 Serguntes and 38 working hands which maned the Batteaw and two Perogues we Sailed up the missouria 6 miles and encamped on the N. side of the River.

Source: Journal of Charles Floyd. Worcester, MA: Charles Hamilton Press, 1894.

On Monday the 14th of May 1804, we left our establishment at the mouth of the river du Bois or Wood river, a small river which falls into the Mississippi, on the east-side, a mile below the Missouri, and having crossed the Mississippi proceeded up the Missouri on our intended voyage of discovery, under the command of Captain Clarke. Captain Lewis was to join us in two or three days on our passage.

The corps consisted of forty-three men part of the regular troops of the United States, and part engaged for this particular enterprize. The expedition was embarked on board a batteau and two periogues. The day was showery and in the evening we encamped on the north bank six miles up the river. Here we had leisure to reflect on our situation, and the nature of our engagements: and, as we had all entered this service as volunteers, to consider how far we stood pledged for the success of an expedition, which the government had projected; and which had been undertaken for the benefit and at the expence of the Union: of course of much interest and high expectation.

The best authenticated accounts informed us, that we were to pass through a country possessed by numerous, powerful and warlike nations of savages, of gigantic stature, fierce, treacherous and cruel; and particularly hostile to white men. And fame had united with tradition in opposing mountains to our course, which human enterprize and exertion would attempt in vain to pass. The determined and resolute character, however, of the corps, and the confidence which pervaded all ranks dispelled every emotion of fear, and anxiety for the present; while a sense of duty, and of the honour, which would attend the completion of the object of the expedition; a wish to gratify the expectations of the government, and of our fellow citizens, with the feelings which novelty and discovery invariably inspire, seemed to insure to us ample support in our future toils, suffering and dangers.

Source: Journals of Patrick Gass. Chicago: A.C. McClurg, 1904.

Monday 14th May 1804. hard Showers of rain. this being the day appointed by Capt. Clark to Set out, a number of the Sitizens of Gotian Settlement came to See us Start. we got in readiness. Capt. Lewis is now at St. Louis but will join us at St. Charls. about 3 Oclock P.M. Capt. Clark and the party consisting of three Sergeants and 38 men who manned the Batteaux and perogues. we fired our Swivel on the bow hoisted Sail and Set out in high Spirits for the western Expedition. we entered the mouth of the Missourie haveing a fair wind Sailed abt. 6 miles and Camped on the North Side.—

1804 Monday May 14th This day being appointed for our departure, from Wood River, a number of the Inhabitants (Americans) from Goshen settlement came to see us start for the Western Ocean; we got in readiness, at 3 o'Clock P.M. Captain William Clark, Three Sergeants and 38 Men, who mann'd the boat, and Two pettiaugers; fired the Swivel from the Bow of the Boat; hoisted Sail, and set out in high spirits, for our intended Western expedition: we entered the mouth of the Mesouri River, having a fair Wind from So East, and Rain; we sailed up the said River about Six Miles, and encamped on the North side of it.—The River Misouri is about one Mile wide, and on the South side of it near its mouth is an Island and its waters are always muddy occasion'd by its banks falling in, the current Runs at about five Miles & a half p hour; the banks are very steep, and the bottom very muddy. Wood River lies in Latitude 38° 54° North & the mouth of the River Mesouri 38° 54 39' North & Longitude 112° 15 West from Greenwich.

Source: Journal of Joseph Whitehouse. New York: Dodd Mead and Company, 1905.

Further Reading

Allen, John Logan. *Passage through the Garden: Lewis and Clark and the Image of the American Northwest.* Urbana: University of Illinois Press, 1975.

Botkin, Daniel. *Our Natural History, The Lessons of Lewis and Clark.* Oxford University Press, 2004.

Buckley, Jay H. *William Clark: Indian Diplomat.* University of Oklahoma Press, 2008.

Danisli, Thomas. *Meriwether Lewis.* Prometheus Books, 2009.

Dillon, Richard. *Meriwether Lewis: A Biography.* New York: Coward-McCann, 1965.

Fenster, Julie. *Jefferson's America: The President, the Purchase, and the Explorers Who Transformed a Nation.* New York: Crown, 2016.

Husner, Verne. *On the River with Lewis and Clark.* Austin, TX: A & M Press, 2004.

Jones, Landon. *William Clark and the Shaping of the West.* Bison Books, 2009.

Document 26

MILITARY DISCIPLINE—COURT-MARTIALS (MAY 17, 1804)

Introduction: Harsh Punishments

After just three days on the river, on Thursday May 17, 1804, Clark ordered a court-martial against three men: William Werner (?–1839), Hugh Hall (1772– ?), and

John Collins (?–1823), who were each charged with going absent without official leave (AWOL). Collins was also charged with "behaving in an unbecoming manner" and disrespecting "the orders of a commanding officer."

Werner and Hall pled guilty to the charge and were sentenced to 25 lashes, but the sentence was suspended. Collins pled guilty to going AWOL, but not guilty to the other charges. He was found guilty of all charges and sentenced to 50 lashes on his back—a punishment that took place that evening in front of the entire membership of the Corps. While this severe corporal punishment might seem harsh today, at the time these were considered the norm under the military code of conduct. It was common practice that the punishments were carried out in public as a reminder to others of what they would face should they disobey a command or a rule.

It should be noted that this was not the first nor would it be the last court-martial that would take place while the group was under the command of Lewis and Clark. When training for the voyage, a court-martial had taken place on March 29, 1804, when William Clark brought charges against John Colter (1775–1812), Robert Frazer (?–1837), and John Shields (1769–1809). All together a total of seven courts-martial were recorded over the first nine months of the trip. The next one was on June 29, 1804, when John Collins was once again charged, this time with being drunk. He was sentenced this time to 50 lashes. On July 12, 1804, Alexander Willard (1778–1865) was charged with lying down and sleeping while on duty, and having been found guilty, he was sentenced to 100 lashes that were broken up into 25 lashes received over 4 days, as was common practice, to ensure death would not result. On August 18, 1804, Moses Reed (dates unknown) was charged with desertion, as he claimed to have left his knife, at a previous camp site, but he instead used this as an excuse, and attempted to leave the group. His sentence was the harsh running of the gauntlet, and he was discharged from the expedition. On October 13, 1804, John Newman (1785–1838) was charged with what amounted to mutinous conduct. He was found guilty and sentenced to 75 lashes, and was discharged from the expedition. He would stay until the spring when the keelboat was sent back to St. Louis with journals, letters, and some members of the expedition. On February 10, 1805, the last court-martial took place; this time Thomas Howard (1779–1814) was charged with climbing over the wall of the fort as opposed to asking for permission to enter. He was found guilty and sentenced to 50 lashes, but the punishment was "set aside," so he never received the punishment.

May 17, 1804

A Sergeant and four men of the Party destined for the Missourri Expidition will convene at 11 oClock to day on the quarter Deck of the Boat, and form themselves into a Court martial to hear and determine (in behalf of the Capt.) the evidences aduced against William Warner & Hugh Hall for being absent last night without leave; contrary to orders;—& John Collins 1st for being absent without leave—2nd for behaveing in an unbecomeing manner at the Ball last night—3rdly for Speaking in a language last night after his return tending to bring into disrespect the orders of the Commanding officer

Signd. W. Clark Comdg.

Detail for Court martial
Segt. John Ordway Prs.
members
R. Fields
R. Windsor
J. Whitehouse
Jo. Potts

The Court convened agreeable to orders on the 17th of May 1804 Sgt. John Ordway P. *members* Joseph Whitehouse Rueben FieldsPotts Richard Windsor after being duly Sworn the Court proceded to the trial of William Warner & Hugh Hall on the following Charges Viz: for being absent without leave last night contrary to orders, to this Charge the Prisoners plead *Guilty.* The Court one of oppinion that the Prionsers Warner & Hall are Both Guilty of being absent from camp without leave it being a breach of the Rules and articles of war and do Sentence them Each to receive twenty-five *lashes* on their naked back, but the Court recommend them from their former Good conduct, to the mercy of the commanding officer.—at the Same court was tried John Collins Charged 1st for being absent without leave—2d. for behaveing in an unbecomming manner at the ball last night 3dly for Speaking in a languguage after his return to camp tending to bring into disrespect the orders of the Commanding officer—The Prisoner Pleads Guilty to the first Charge but not Guilty to the two last chrges.—after mature deliberation & agreeable to the evidence aduced. The Court are of oppinion that the Prisnair is Guilty of all the charges alledged against him it being a breach of the rules & articles of War and do Sentence him to receive fifty lashes on his naked back—The Commanding officer approves of the proceedings & Desicon of the Court *martial and orders* that the punishment of John Collins take place this evening at *Sun Set* in the Presence of the Party.—The punishment ordered to be inflicted on William Warner & Hugh Hall, is remitted under the assurance arriveing from a confidence which the Commanding officer has of the Sincerity of the recommendation from the Court.—after the punishment, Warner Hall & Collins will return to their squads and Duty—
The Court is Disolved.

Source: The Journals of Captain Meriwether Lewis and Sergeant John Ordway: Kept on the Expedition of Western Exploration, 1803–1806. Madison, WI: The Society, 1916.

Further Reading

Ambrose, Stephen E. *Lewis & Clark: Voyage of Discovery.* Washington, DC: National Geographic Society, 1998.

Bergon, Frank, ed. *The Journals of Lewis and Clark.* New York: Penguin Press, 1989.

Blumberg, Rhoda. *The Incredible Journey of Lewis and Clark.* New York: Scholastic, 1993.

Brown, Dee. *The American West.* New York: Touchstone, 1995.

Calloway, Colin G. *One Vast Winter Count: The Native American West before Lewis and Clark.* Lincoln: University of Nebraska Press, 2003.

Cutright, Paul Russell. "The Journal of Captain Meriwether Lewis." *We Proceeded On,* vol. 10, no. 1 (February 1984).

Fisher, John W. *Medical Appendices of the Lewis and Clark Expedition.* Juliaetta, ID: Fisher, 2006.

Jones, Landon Y. *William Clark and the Shaping of the West.* New York: Hill and Wang, 2004.

Document 27

MERIWETHER LEWIS JOINS WITH MAIN GROUP. ST. CHARLES, MISSOURI (MAY 20, 1804)

Introduction: The Corps of Discovery

Meriwether Lewis had been waiting for the main group to meet with him in St Charles, Missouri. While he gives an account of his meetings with various politicians and other people who have come to wish them well, Clark is ensuring that all supplies have now been put on the barge, and that the men are taken care of. Lewis's enthusiasm bubbles in this piece. He describes whom he is meeting with, the weather, the geography of the surrounding area. He comments on the people, their socioeconomic position. Lewis here is doing exactly what Jefferson asked of him—making scientific-style notes.

The morning was fair, and the weather pleasent; at 10 oCk A M. agreably to an appointment of the preceeding day, I was joined by Capt. Stoddard, Lieuts. Milford & Worrell together with Messrs. A. Chouteau, C. Gratiot, and many other respectable inhabitants of St. Louis, who had engaged to accompany me to the Vilage of St. Charles; accordingly at 12 Oclk after bidding an affectionate adieu to my Hostis, that excellent woman the spouse of Mr. Peter Chouteau, and some of my fair friends of St. Louis, we set forward to that village in order to join my friend companion and fellow labourer Capt. William Clark who had previously arrived at that place with the party destined for the discovery of the interior of the continent of North America the first 5 miles of our rout laid through a beatifull high leavel and fertail prarie which incircles the town of St. Louis from N. W. to S. E. the lands through which we then passed are somewhat broken up fertile the plains and woodlands are here indiscriminately interspersed untill you arrive within three miles of the vilage when the woodland commences and continues to the Missouri the latter is extreamly fertile. At half after one P. M. our progress was interrupted the near approach of a violent thunder storm from the N. W. and concluded to take shelter in a little cabbin hard by untill the rain should be over; accordingly we alighted and remained about an hour and a half and regailed ourselves with a could collation which we had taken the precaution to bring with us from St. Louis.

    The clouds continued to follow each other in rapaid succession, insomuch that there was but little prospect of it's ceasing to rain this evening; as I had determined to reach St. Charles this evening and knowing that there was now no time to be lost I set forward in the rain, most of the gentlemen continued with me, we arrived at half after six and joined Capt Clark, found the party in good health and sperits. suped this evening with Charles Tayong a Spanish Ensign & late Commandant of St. Charles at an early hour I retired to rest on board the barge—St. Charles is situated on the North bank of the Missouri 21 Miles above it's junction with the Mississippi, and about the same distance N. W. from St. Louis; it is bisected by one principal street about a mile in length runing nearly parrallel with the river, the plain on which it stands—is narrow tho' sufficiently elivated to secure it against the annual inundations of the river, which usually happen in the month of June, and in the rear it is terminated by a range of small hills, hence the appellation of *petit Cote,* a name by which this vilage is better known to the French inhabitants of the Illinois than that of St. Charles. The Vilage contains a Chappel, one hundred dwelling houses, and about 450 inhabitants; their houses are generally small and but illy constructed; a great majority of the inhabitants are miserably pour, illiterate and when at home excessively lazy, tho' they are polite hospitable and by no means deficient in point of natural genious, they live in a perfect state of harmony among each other; and plase as implicit confidence in the doctrines of their speritual pastor, the Roman Catholic priest, as they yeald passive obedience to the will of their temporal master the commandant. a small garden of vegetables is the usual extent of their cultivation, and this is commonly imposed on the old men and boys; the men in the vigor of life consider the cultivation of the earth a degrading occupation, and in order to gain the necessary subsistence for themselves and families, either undertake hunting voyages on their own account, or engaged themselves as hirelings to such persons as possess sufficient capital to extend their traffic to the natives of the interior parts of the country; on those voyages in either case, they are frequently absent from their families or homes the term of six twelve or eighteen months and alwas subjected to severe and incessant labour, exposed to the ferosity of the lawless savages, the vicissitudes of weather and climate, and dependant on chance or accident alone for food, raiment or relief in the event of malady. These people are principally the decendants of the Canadian French, and it is not an inconsiderable proportian of them that can boast a small dash of the pure blood of the aboriginees of America. On consulting with my friend Capt. C. I found it necessary that we should pospone our departure untill 2 P M. the next day and accordingly gave orders to the party to hold themselves in readiness to depart at that hour.—

Captn. Clark now informed me that having gotten all the stores on board the Barge and perogues on the evening of the 13th of May he determined to leave our winter cantainment at the mouth of River Dubois the next day, and to ascend the Missouri as far as the Vilage of St. Charles, where as it had been previously concerted between us, he was to wait my arrival; this movement while it advanced us a small distance on our rout, would also enable him to determine whether the vessels had been judiciously loaded and if not timely to make the necessary alterations; accordingly at 4 P. M. on Monday the 14th of May 1804, he embarked with the party in the presence of a number of the neighbouring Citizens who had assembled to witness his departure. during the fore part of this day it rained excessively hard. In my last letter to the President dated at St. Louis I mentioned the departure of Capt. Clark from River Dubois on the 15th Inst, which was the day that had been calculated on, but having completed the arrangements a day earlyer he departed on the 14th as before mentioned. On the evening of the 14th the party halted and encamped on the upper point of the first Island which lyes near the Larbord shore, on the same side and nearly opposite the center of this Island a small Creek disimbogues called Couldwater.

The course and distance of this day was West 4 Miles the Wind from N. E.

Source: Thwaites, Reuben Gold, ed. *Original Journals of the Lewis and Clark Expedition, 1804–1806.* Volume 1. New York: Dodd, Mead & Company, 1904, 22–25.

Further Reading

Bergon, Frank, ed. *The Journals of Lewis and Clark.* New York: Penguin Press, 1989.

Duncan, Dayton and Ken Burns. *Lewis and Clark: The Journey of the Corps of Discovery: An Illustrated History.* New York: Alfred A. Knopf, 1997.

Gass, Patrick. *A Journal of the Voyages and Travels of a Corps of Discovery under the Command of Capt. Lewis and Capt. Clark.* Minneapolis, MN: Ross and Haines, 1958.

Holloway, David. *Lewis and Clark and the Crossing of North America.* New York: Saturday Review Press, 1974.

Jones, Landon Y. ed. *The Essential Lewis and Clark.* New York: HarperCollins, 2002.

Merrell, James H. *Into the American Woods: Negotiators on the Pennsylvania Frontier.* New York: W.W. Norton, 1999.

Document 28

LEAVING ST. CHARLES, MISSOURI (MAY 21, 1804)

Introduction: They "Proceeded On"

The Corps "proceeded on." This has become the phrase most associated with this whole voyage as it was used again and again, by each person who wrote a journal. Having met up with Lewis, who was still enjoying his social position by having dinner with various dignitaries, the whole party began its voyage. The weather was already difficult—a sign of things to come—Clark noted the intensity of the rain. But with the cheers of the crowd, the newly formed Corps of Discovery were optimistic about their adventure.

Dine with Mr. Ducete & Set out from St. Charles at three oClock after getting every matter arranged, proceeded on under a jentle Breese, at one mile a Violent rain with Wind from the S. W. we landed at the upper point of the first Island on the Stbd Side & Camped, Soon after it commenced raining & continued the greater part of the night; 3 french men got leave to return to Town, and return early.

25st refured to fig: 2 Left St: Charles May 21st 1804. Steered N. 15° W 1¾ Ms N 52° W to the upper point of the Island and Camped dureing a rain which had been falling half an hour, opposit this Isd. Coms in a Small creek on the St. Sd. and at the head one on the Ld. Side rains powerfully.

All the forepart of the Day Arranging our party and prcureing the different articles necessary for them at this place—Dined with Mr. Ducett and *Set* out at half passed three oClock under three Cheers from the gentlemen on the bank and pro-ceeded on to the head of the Island 3 miles Soon after we Set out to day a hard Wind from the W. S W accompanied with a hard rain, which lasted with Short intervales all night, opposit our Camp a Small creek coms in on the Lbd Side.

Source: Thwaites, Reuben Gold, ed. *Original Journals of the Lewis and Clark Expedition, 1804–1806.* Volume 2. New York: Dodd, Mead & Company, 1904.

Further Reading

Bergon, Frank, ed. *The Journals of Lewis and Clark*. New York: Penguin Press, 1989.

Duncan, Dayton and Ken Burns. *Lewis and Clark: The Journey of the Corps of Discovery: An Illustrated History*. New York: Alfred A. Knopf, 1997.

Gass, Patrick. *A Journal of the Voyages and Travels of a Corps of Discovery under the Command of Capt. Lewis and Capt. Clark*. Minneapolis, MN: Ross and Haines, 1958.

Holloway, David. *Lewis and Clark and the Crossing of North America*. New York: Saturday Review Press, 1974.

Jones, Landon Y., ed. *The Essential Lewis and Clark*. New York: HarperCollins, 2002.

Merrell, James H. *Into the American Woods: Negotiators on the Pennsylvania Frontier*. New York: W.W. Norton, 1999.

Document 29

THE LAST SETTLEMENT. LA CHARRETTE, MISSOURI (MAY 25, 1804)

Introduction: Into the Uncharted

After four days of slow traveling and leaving St. Charles, the expedition had already reached the end of known settlements. Each person noted this in their journal, as each seemed to be aware of the vastness of the journey before them.

Set out early Course West to a Point on Sbd. Side at 2 Miles passd a Willow Isd. in a Bend to the Ldb: a creek called wood rivr Lbd. Side N 57° W. to a pt. on the Sb. Side 3 Miles passed the Mouth of a Creek St. Side Called Le quever, this Same course continued to a Point Ld. Side 2 ½ Miles further. opposit a Isd. on Sd Side Passed a Creek Called R. La freeau at the pt. N 20° W 2 miles To a Small french Village called La Charatt of five families only, in the bend to the Starbord.

Source: Thwaites, Reuben Gold, ed. *Original Journals of the Lewis and Clark Expedition, 1804–1806.* Volume 2. New York: Dodd, Mead & Company, 1904.

Friday may 25th 1804 Set out and Came 4 miles passed a Creek Called Wood River on the South Side the Land is Good & handsom the Soil Rich & high Banks encamped at a French village Called St Johns this is the Last Setelment of whites on this River.

Source: *Journal of Charles Floyd.* Worcester, MA: Charles Hamilton Press, 1894.

Friday 25th. We proceeded three miles and passed a creek on the south side, called Wood river the banks of the river are here high and the land rich: arrived at St. John's, a small French village situated on the north side, and encamped a quarter of a mile above it. This is the last settlement of white people on the river.

Source: *Journals of Patrick Gass.* Chicago: A.C. McClurg, 1904.

Friday May 25th 1804, came 3 miles passed a Creek called wood River on S Side land handsome the Soil Rich &C—high Banks, encamped at a French village N. S. called St John, this is the last Settlement of whites on this River,

Source: *The Journals of Captain Meriwether Lewis and Sergeant John Ordway: Kept on the Expedition of Western Exploration, 1803–1806.* Madison, WI: The Society, 1916.

Further Reading

Bergon, Frank, ed. *The Journals of Lewis and Clark.* New York: Penguin Press, 1989.

Duncan, Dayton and Ken Burns. *Lewis and Clark: The Journey of the Corps of Discovery: An Illustrated History.* New York: Alfred A. Knopf, 1997.

Gass, Patrick. *A Journal of the Voyages and Travels of a Corps of Discovery under the Command of Capt. Lewis and Capt. Clark.* Minneapolis, MN: Ross and Haines, 1958.

Holloway, David. *Lewis and Clark and the Crossing of North America.* New York: Saturday Review Press, 1974.

Jones, Landon Y., ed. *The Essential Lewis and Clark.* New York: HarperCollins, 2002.

Merrell, James H. *Into the American Woods: Negotiators on the Pennsylvania Frontier.* New York: W.W. Norton, 1999.

Document 30

ORGANIZATION INTO THREE SQUADS (MAY 26, 1804)

Introduction: Orders and Organization

As this was a military operation, Lewis organized the men into three squads under a sergeant, and this same organization would continue to the Pacific and back to St. Louis. These groups were billeted together, given duties together, and as the boat went upstream, they worked together in these groups. Lewis also gave the sergeants responsibilities for setting up a series of guards each time the boat stopped, and how each sentry was to relay messages.

Lewis's system meant that each person knew exactly what had to be done each day under each circumstance. Each person knew where they should stand, sit, and be whether in the boat going upstream or when they stopped for the night. While the sergeants were

relieved on some manual labor, they were on the other hand expected to be the main lookout at each stage of the journey.

There is an "X" beside the name of Moses Reed; it is thought this was placed there after he was dismissed from the Corps, while the "F" is thought to mean "French."

The Commanding Officers direct, that the three Squads under the command of Sergts. Floyd Ordway and Pryor heretofore forming two messes each, shall untill further orders constitute three messes only, the same being altered and organized as follows (viz)—

1	*Sergt. Charles Floyd.*
	Privates:
2	Hugh McNeal
3	Patric Gass
4	Reubin Fields
5	John B Thompson
6	John Newman
7	Richard Winsor
+	Francis Rivet &
8	Joseph Fields
9	*Sergt. John Ordway.*
	Privates.
10	William Bratton
11	John Colter
X 12	Moses B. Reed
13	Alexander Willard
14	William Warner
15	Silas Goodrich
16	John Potts &
17	Hugh Hall
18	*Sergt. Nathaniel Pryor.*
	Privates.
19	George Gibson
20	George Shannon
21	John Shields
22	John Collins
23	Joseph Whitehouse
24	Peter Wiser
F 25	Peter Crusat &
F 26	Francis Labuche

The posts and duties of the Sergts. shall be as follows—when the Batteaux is under way, one Sergt. shall be stationed at the helm, one in the center on the rear of the Starboard locker, and one at the bow. *The Sergt. at the helm,* shall steer the boat, and see that the baggage on the quarterdeck is properly arranged and stowed away in the most advantageous manner; to see that no cooking utensels or loos lumber of any kind is left on the deck to obstruct the passage between the burths—he will also attend to the compas when necessary.—

The Sergt at the center will command the guard, manage the sails, see that the men at the oars do their duty; that they come on board at a proper season in the morning, and that the boat gets under way in due time; he will keep a good look-out for the mouths of all rivers, creeks, Islands and other remarkable places and shall immediately report the same to the commanding officers; he will attend to the issues of sperituous liquors; he shall regulate the halting of the batteaux through the day to give the men refreshment, and will also regulate the time of her departure taking care that not more time than is necessary shall be expended at each halt—it shall be his duty also to post a centinel on the bank, near the boat whenever we come too and halt in the course of the day, at the same time he will (acompanied by two his guard) reconnoiter the forrest arround the place of landing to the distance of at least one hundred paces. when we come too for the purpose of encamping at night, the Sergt. of the guard shall post two centinels immediately on our landing; one of whom shal be posted near the boat, and the other at a convenient distance in rear of the encampment; at night the Sergt. must be always present with his guard, and he is positively forbidden to suffer any man of his guard to absent himself on any pretext whatever; he will at each relief through the night, accompanyed by the two men last off their posts, reconnoiter in every direction around the camp to the distance of at least one hundred and fifty paces, and also examine the situation of the boat and perogues, and see that they ly safe and free from the bank—

It shall be the duty of the *sergt. at the bow,* to keep a good look out for all danger which may approach, either of the enimy, or obstructions which may present themselves to [the] passage of the boat; of the first he will notify the Sergt. at the center, who will communicate the information to the commanding officers, and of the second or obstructions to the boat he will notify the Sergt. at the helm; he will also report to the commanding officers through the Sergt. at the center all perogues boats canoes or other craft which he may discover in the river, and all hunting camps or parties of Indians in view of which we may pass. he will at all times be provided with a seting pole and assist the bowsman in poling and managing the bow of the boat. it will be his duty also to give and answer all signals, which may hereafter be established for the government of the perogues and parties on shore.

The Sergts. will on each morning before our departure relieve each other in the following manner—The Sergt. at the helm will parade the new guard, relieve the Sergt. and the old guard, and occupy the middle station in the boat; the Sergt. of the old guard will occupy the station at the bow, and the Sergt. who had been stationed the preceeding day at the bow will place himself at the helm.—The sergts. in addition to those duties are directed each to keep a seperate journal from day today of all passing occurences, and such other observations on the country &c. as shall appear to them worthy of notice—

The Sergts. are relieved and excempt from all labour of making fires, pitching tents or cooking, and will direct and make the men of their several messes perform an equal proportion of those duties.—

Source: Thwaites, Reuben Gold, ed. *Original Journals of the Lewis and Clark Expedition, 1804–1806.* Volume 2. New York: Dodd, Mead & Company, 1904.

Further Reading

Bergon, Frank, ed. *The Journals of Lewis and Clark.* New York: Penguin Press, 1989.

Duncan, Dayton and Ken Burns. *Lewis and Clark: The Journey of the Corps of Discovery: An Illustrated History.* New York: Alfred A. Knopf, 1997.

Gass, Patrick. *A Journal of the Voyages and Travels of a Corps of Discovery under the Command of Capt. Lewis and Capt. Clark.* Minneapolis, MN: Ross and Haines, 1958.

Holloway, David. *Lewis and Clark and the Crossing of North America.* New York: Saturday Review Press, 1974.

Jones, Landon Y., ed. *The Essential Lewis and Clark.* New York: HarperCollins, 2002.

Merrell, James H. *Into the American Woods: Negotiators on the Pennsylvania Frontier.* New York: W.W. Norton, 1999.

Document 31
CARROLL COUNTY, MISSOURI (JUNE 17, 1804)

Introduction: Bugs and Food

The group traveled just one mile between June 16 and 17. The remoteness and beauty of the area is noticeable in the journal entries. There were no other people, but meat was plentiful. The exhaustion from fighting the river current in the boat was at the fore of the mind, and so the men had been eating five to six times a day, and the French Canadian fur trappers complained when they were not eating this often, much to Clark's annoyance. The other issue that at this stage was bothering Clark in particular were the mosquitoes. This was to be a constant complaint for the whole trip.

Cloudy Wind, S. E. Set out early S. 65° W 1 Me. Came too to Make ores, and a Cord for a Toe Rope all this day imployed in getting out Ores, & makeing for the use of the Boat out of a large Cable rope which we have, G Drewyer Came up [with] a Bear & 2 Deer, also a fine horse which he found in the woods, Supposed to have been left by Some war party from the osages, The *Ticks* are numerous and large and have been trousom [troublesome] all the way and the Musquetors are beginning to be verry troublesom, my Cold Continues verry bad the French higherlins Complain for the want of Provisions, Saying they are accustomed to eat 5 & 6 times a day, they are roughly rebuked for their presumption, the Country about abounds in Bear Deer & Elk and the S. S. the lands are well timbered and rich for 22 ms. to a butifull Prarie which risies into hills abt 8 or 9 ms. back—on the L. S a Prarie coms. on the bank which is high and contines back rich & well watered as far.

Source: Thwaites, Reuben Gold, ed. *Original Journals of the Lewis and Clark Expedition, 1804–1806.* Volume 2. New York: Dodd, Mead & Company, 1904.

We Renued our Journey much fetegeued of yesterday's work Came one mil encamped for the purpos of maken ores for ouer Boat and make a rope for the purpos of towen on the North Side of the River ouer hunters Returnd and Killed on Bar one Deer and found a Stray Horse who had Been Lost for sometime nothing Remarkeble to day.

Source: Journal of Charles Floyd. Worcester, MA: Charles Hamilton Press, 1894.

Further Reading

Bergon, Frank, ed. *The Journals of Lewis and Clark.* New York: Penguin Press, 1989.

Duncan, Dayton and Ken Burns. *Lewis and Clark: The Journey of the Corps of Discovery: An Illustrated History.* New York: Alfred A. Knopf, 1997.

Gass, Patrick. *A Journal of the Voyages and Travels of a Corps of Discovery under the Command of Capt. Lewis and Capt. Clark.* Minneapolis, MN: Ross and Haines, 1958.

Holloway, David. *Lewis and Clark and the Crossing of North America.* New York: Saturday Review Press, 1974.

Jones, Landon Y., ed. *The Essential Lewis and Clark.* New York: HarperCollins, 2002.

Merrell, James H. *Into the American Woods: Negotiators on the Pennsylvania Frontier.* New York: W.W. Norton, 1999.

Document 32
PRESENT-DAY ATCHISON, KANSAS (JULY 4, 1804)

Introduction: First Independence Day Celebrated in the West

This was the first recorded celebration of July 4 in the West. There are no journal entries during this time from Meriwether Lewis, but Clark and Floyd both mention in their journal entries that Lewis spent his time on shore walking with Seaman, his Newfoundland dog. From the other journals, it is recorded that the Fourth of July was celebrated by firing the cannon on the keelboat and giving each man an extra ration of whiskey. Independence Creek, near modern-day Atchison, Kansas, was named on this July 4.

Perhaps also because it was July 4th, Clark notes that everyone was allowed to rest. The keelboat worked really well going downstream with a lot of water, but it was heavy, and at this early stage, it was also full of supplies. Both men also took the time to note the beauty of the scenery, and they also note the danger as Joseph Field was bitten by a snake. Clark here mentions meeting the Kaw or Kansa people, a small Native American nation, related to the Osage people. The Kansa people were noted for their distinctive hairstyle of a shaved head, with a single long pony tail.

July 4th Wednesday 1804

Ussered in the day by a discharge of one shot from our Bow piece, proceeded on, passed the mouth of a Bayeau lading from a large Lake on the S. S. which has the apperance of being once the bed of the river & reaches parrelel for Several Miles Came to on the L. S. to refresh ourselves &. Jos: Fields got bit by a Snake, which was quickly doctered with Bark by Cap Lewis. Passed a Creek 12 yds. wide on L. S. comeing out of an extensive Prarie reching within 200 yards of the river, as this Creek has no name, and this being the we Din (on corn) the 4th of July the day of the independance of the U. S. call it 4th of July 1804 Creek, Capt. Lewis walked on Shore above this Creek and discovered a high moun from the top of which he had an extensive view, 3 paths Concentering at the moun Saw great numbers of Goslings to day which Were nearly grown, the before mentioned Lake is clear and Contain great quantities of fish an Gees & Goslings, The great quantity of those fowl in this Lake induce me to Call it the Gosling Lake, a Small Creek & Several Springs run in to the Lake on the East Side from the hills the land on that Side verry good—We came to and camped in the lower edge of a Plain where 2d old Kanzas village formerly Stood, above the mouth of a Creek 20 yds wide this Creek we call Creek Independence as we approached this place the Praree had a most butifull appearance Hills & Valies interspsd with Coops [copses] of Timber gave a pleasing deversity to the Senery. the right fork of Creek Independence Meandering thro: the middle of the Plain a point of high Land near the river givs an allivated Situation. at this place the Kanzas Indians formerley lived. this Town appears to have covd. a large Space, the nation must have been noumerous at the time they lived here, the Cause of their moveing to the Kanzas River, I have never heard, nor Can I learn; war with their neghbors must have reduced this nation and Compelled them to retire to a Situation in the plains better Calculated for their defence and one where they may make use of their horses with good effect, in persueing their enemey, we Closed the [day] by a Discharge from our bow piece, an extra Gill of whiskey.

Source: Thwaites, Reuben Gold, ed. *Original Journals of the Lewis and Clark Expedition, 1804–1806.* Volume 2. New York: Dodd, Mead & Company, 1904.

Wensday July 4th 1804 Set out verry erley this morning passed the mouth of a Beyeu leading from a Lake on the N. Side this Lake is Large and was once the Bead of the River it reaches Parrelel for Several miles Came to on the South Side to Dine rest a Short time a Snake Bit Jo. Fieldes on the Side of the foot which Sweled much apply Barks to passed a Creek on the South Side about 15 yards wide Coming out of an extensive Prarie as the Creek has no name and this Day is the 4th of July we name this Independance a Creek above this Creek the wood Land is about 200 yards Back of these wood is an extensive Praria open and High whigh may be Seen Six or Seven below saw Grat nomber of Goslins to day nearley Grown the Last mentioned prarie I call Jo. Fieldes Snake prarie Capt Lewis walked on Shore we camped at one of the Butifules Praries I ever Saw open and butifulley Divided with Hills and vallies all presenting themselves.

Source: Journals of Charles Floyd. Worcester, MA: Charles Hamilton Press, 1894.

Wednesday July 4th 1804, we Set out Eairly & passed the mouth of the outlet of a large lake which comes in on the north Side. this pond or lake is large & their has been a Great many bever found in it, high land on the South Side & praries, we Delayed a Short time at noon to dine. a Snake bit Jo. Fields on the out Side of his foot, this was under the hills near the praries on the South Side, we passed a Creek on the South Side about 15 yards wide. comes out of the large prarie, and as it has no name & as it is the 4 of July, Capts. name it Independence Creek we fired our Bow piece this morning & one in the evening for Independance of the U. S. we saw a nomber of Goslins half grown to day. we camped in the plans one of the most beautiful places I ever Saw in my life, open and beautifully Diversified with hills & vallies all presenting themselves to the River.

Source: The Journals of Captain Meriwether Lewis and Sergeant John Ordway: Kept on the Expedition of Western Exploration, 1803–1806. Madison, WI: The Society, 1916.

Further Reading

Bergon, Frank, ed. *The Journals of Lewis and Clark*. New York: Penguin Press, 1989.
Duncan, Dayton and Ken Burns. *Lewis and Clark: The Journey of the Corps of Discovery: An Illustrated History*. New York: Alfred A. Knopf, 1997.
Gass, Patrick. *A Journal of the Voyages and Travels of a Corps of Discovery under the Command of Capt. Lewis and Capt. Clark*. Minneapolis, MN: Ross and Haines, 1958.
Holloway, David. *Lewis and Clark and the Crossing of North America*. New York: Saturday Review Press, 1974.
Jones, Landon Y., ed. *The Essential Lewis and Clark*. New York: HarperCollins, 2002.
Merrell, James H. *Into the American Woods: Negotiators on the Pennsylvania Frontier*. New York: W.W. Norton, 1999.

Document 33

ILLNESSES AND CURES: ST JOSEPH, MISSOURI (JULY 7, 1804)

Introduction: Strange Medicine

As expected, Lewis's medical training and skills were soon needed. The expedition team was now close to what is modern-day St. Joseph, Missouri. On July 7, 1804, Robert

Frazer (while Clark does not name him, John Ordway does in his journal entry) suffered what seems to have been heatstroke. He was weak, sick, and probably fainted. He was unable to move or work. Lewis used one of the treatments he had been taught by Benjamin Rush—bloodletting, also known as phlebotomy. Rush was a major proponent of bloodletting, as he believed that tension in the blood vessels was the cause of all diseases. The practice involved using a spring-loaded knife with 12 blades called a "scarificator," which punctured the skin in small, narrow, equal-sized holes usually done in a person's arm. The person was usually bled until he fainted, or until the amount of blood was measured in phlebotomy cups. While this may sound almost barbaric, it was common medical practice at the time. George Washington was bled quite severely just days before his death, and there is still some argument today as to whether the bloodletting was a direct cause of his death.

Amazingly, Frazer recovered, though probably not because of the bloodletting. The technique would be used later in the voyage as well. In January 1805, one of the men was diagnosed with pleurisy, and Clark treated him with "a bleed." That same month, Sacagawea was ill with an unrecorded disease, and once again Clark "bled her."

July 7, 1804

Set out early passed Some Swift water, which obliged us to draw up by roapes, a Sand bare at the point opposit a butifull Prarie on the S. Side Calld. St. Michul, those Praries on the river has verry much the appearence of farms from the river Divided by narrow Strips of wood land, which wood land is Situatd. on the runs leading to the river. passed a Bluff of yellow Clay above the Prarie. Saw a large rat on the bank. Killed a Wolf. at 4 oClock pass a Verry narrow part of the river water Confd. in a bead not more than 200 yards wide at this place the Current runs against the L. Side. no Sand to Confine the Current on the S. S. passed a Small sand Island above the Small Islds. Situated at the points, in low water form a part of the Sand bars makeing out from those points.

Incamped on the S. S. at 7 oClock a Violent Ghust of wind from the N. E. with Some rain, which lasted half an hour G D.informs me that he Saw in a Pond on the S. S. which we passed yesterday; a number of young Swans—one man verry Sick, Struck with the Sun, Capt. Lewis bled him & gave Niter which has revived him much.

Source: Thwaites, Reuben Gold, ed. *Original Journals of the Lewis and Clark Expedition, 1804–1806.* Volume 1. New York: Dodd, Mead & Company, 1904, 68–69.

Saturday July 7th 1804. we Set our eairly passed Swirt waters on the South Side, verry warm morning, passed a beautiful prarie on the North Side which extends back, those praries called St. Michel has much the appearance from the river of farms Divided by narrow Strips of woods those Strips of timber grows along the runs which rise on the hills, & pass to the River, I went on Shore with the Horses in the afternoon In the North Side crossed a Creek 2 miles up in the evening followed down to the mouth, and Camped it being too late to find the boat, the Musquitoes troubled me So that I Could not Sleep, as this Creek is without name & my Descri-being it to my Capt. he named it Ordway Creek. Some of the men in the Boat killed a wolf to day they Camped on the South Side of the Missouris. one man taken Sick (Frasier).

Source: The Journals of Captain Meriwether Lewis and Sergeant John Ordway: Kept on the Expedition of Western Exploration, 1803–1806. Madison, WI: The Society, 1916.

Further Reading

Bergon, Frank, ed. *The Journals of Lewis and Clark*. New York: Penguin Press, 1989.
Brodhead, Michael. "The Military Naturalist: A Lewis and Clark Heritage." *We Proceeded On*, vol. 9, no. 4 (November 1983).
Chuinard, Eldon G. *Only One Man Died: The Medical Aspects of the Lewis and Clark Expedi-tion*. Glendale, CA: Arthur Clark Company, 1980.
Cutright, Paul Russell. "I Gave Him Barks and Saltpeter." *American Heritage: The Magazine of History*, vol. 15 (December 1963): 58–61, 94–101.
Duffi, Jacalyn. *History of Medicine: A Scandalously Short Introduction*. University of Toronto Press, 1999.
Slaughter, Thomas P. *Exploring Lewis and Clark: Reflections on Men and Wilderness*. New York: Vintage Press, 2004.

Document 34

MEETING THE SIOUX AT THE KANSAS–NEBRASKA BORDER (JULY 9, 1804)

Introduction: Fear and Gifts

By July 9, 1804, the expedition had reached a point south of the modern-day Kansas–Nebraska border. Clark reports in his journal that they saw a Sioux party, and so the men were "on their guard." The Sioux had a reputation as being aggressive and forceful, but Jefferson had already clearly instructed his expedition not to start a war with any of the Indigenous peoples. Despite Jefferson's directive, the Corps members knew if they were attacked, it would be necessary to defend themselves. Here they were even wary of the possibility that if the Sioux saw them, they would attack.

As this was a military operation, Lewis and Clark had devised both a scouting and reporting system. The idea was that a small group of the men would scout ahead of the main party in order to lessen the possibility of a surprise attack. Once a potential threat was spotted, then one of the scouts would report back to warn the rest of the group.

July 9, 1804

Sent one man back to the mouth of the River to mark a tree, to let the party on Shore See that the Boat had passed the river, Set out early passed the head of the

Island Situated in the middle of the river a Sand bar at the head, passed the mouth of a Creek or Bayou on the S. S. leading from a large Pond of about three miles in length, at 8 oClock it commenced raining, the wind changed from N E. to S. W. at 6 miles passed the mouth of a Small Creek on the L. S. called Monters Creek, the river at this place is wide with a Sand bar in the Middle, passed a place on the L. S. about 2 miles above the Creek, where Several french men camped two years to hunt—passed a Island on the S S. of the river in a bend, opsd. a high Land on the L. S. wind Shifted to the N. W. in the evining, opsd. this Island, and on the L. S. Loup or *Wolf* River Coms in, this river is about 60 yards Wide, but little water running at the mouth, this river heads with the waters of the Kanzas, and has a perogue navigation Some distance, it abounds with Beaver, Camped opposit the head of the Island on the L. S. Saw a fire on the S. S. Supposedly the four flankers, to be theire, Sent a perogue for them, the Patroon & Bowman of the Perogue French, they returned & informed, that when they approached the fire, it was put out, which caused them to return, this report causd. us to look out Supposeing a pty. of Soux going to war, firierd the *bow piec* to allarm & put on their guard the men on Shore everey thing in readiness for Defence.

Source: Thwaites, Reuben Gold, ed. *Original Journals of the Lewis and Clark Expedition, 1804–1806.* Volume 2. New York: Dodd, Mead & Company, 1904.

Further Reading

Blackhawk, Ned. *Violence over Land: Indians and Empires in the Early American West.* Cambridge, MA: Harvard University Press, 1998.

Buckley, Jay H. *William Clark: Indian Diplomat.* University of Oklahoma Press, 2008.

Calloway, Colin G. *One Vast Winter Count: The Native American West before Lewis and Clark.* Lincoln: University of Nebraska Press, 2003.

Criswell, Elijah. *Lewis and Clark: Linguistic Pioneers.* Columbia: University of Missouri Press, 1940.

Danisli, Thomas. *Meriwether Lewis.* Prometheus Books, 2009.

Dillon, Richard. *Meriwether Lewis: A Biography.* New York: Coward-McCann, 1965.

Dowd, Gregory Evans. *A Spirited Resistance: The North American Indian Struggle for Unity, 1745–1815.* Baltimore, MD: Johns Hopkins University Press, 1992.

Thwaites, Reuben Gold, ed. *Journals of Lewis and Clark.* New York: Dodd, Mead & Company, 1905.

Document 35

NATURE IN NEBRASKA (JULY 30, 1804)

Introduction: Wild Life and Science

By the end of July, the expedition reached north of modern-day Omaha, Nebraska. In the excerpt from his journal that follows, Clark gives us an account of the vegetation observed. He is entranced by the colors and the grass. Clark also recounts that Joseph

Fields (c. 1780–1807) kills a badger. This badger was probably the first animal, which, after it was killed, was skinned and stuffed, so that it could be preserved and sent back east to Jefferson. Clark also gives a detailed description here of how it looks, but more interestingly, he describes what the badger eats and the amount that it eats. This is the precise type of scientific detail that Jefferson wanted.

As well as science, the constant struggle with health and wild life is evident here: Clark notes that everyone is in "high spirits" and also notes that there are no mosquitoes that evening. Mosquitoes had proven to be the bane of the expedition. On March 25, the mosquitoes were "bad" or "very bad." But soon the description of them had changed to "verry troublesom," then "uncommonly troublesome," or even "extreemly troublesome." But this one night, there were none, and though some of the men had "very bad boils," a painful skin condition that was probably due to lack of washing, but with no mosquitoes, spirits were high! They could all relax and sleep.

One of the other interesting notes from July 30 is an account from Meriwether Lewis in which he describes the badger killed by Fields. A second point worth noting is that Clark mentions here that Floyd has a bad cold. This was the beginning of Floyd's illness that would result in his death.

July 30, 1804

Set out early & proceeded on West 3¾ mes. passd. one pt. to the L. S and one to the S. S. to a Clear open Prarie on the L. S. which is on a rise of about 70 feet higher than the bottom which is also a prarie covered with high grass Plumbs Grape Vine & Hezel—both forming a Bluff to the River, the Lower Prarie is above high water mark at the foot of the riseing ground & below the High Bluff we came to in a grove of timber and formed a Camp raised a flag Pole, and deturmind to waite for the OttuIndians—The white Horse which we found below Died last night, after posting out the Guards &c. & Sent out 4 men to hunt I am ingaged in and Drawing off my courses to accompany the map Drawn at White Catfish Camp, Capt. Lewis and my Self walked in the Prarie on the top of the Bluff and observed the most butifull prospects imagionable, this Prarie is Covered with grass about 10 or 12 Inch high, (Land rich) rises about ½ a mile back Something higher and is a Plain as fur as Can be Seen, under those high Lands next the river is butifull Bottom interspersed with Groves of timber, the River may be Seen for a great Distance both above & below meandering thro: the plains between two ranges of High land which appear to be from 4 to 20 ms. apart, each bend of the river forming a point which Contains tall timber, principally Willow Cotton wood some Mulberry elm Sycamore & ash. the groves Contain walnit coffeenut & Oake in addition & Hickory & Lynn Jo. Fields Killed *Brarow* or as the Ponie call it *Cho car tooch*, this animale burrows in the ground & feeds on Bugs and flesh principally the little Dogs of the Prarie, also Something of Vegetable Kind his Shape & Size is like that of a *Beever*, his head Mouth &c. is like a Dog with its ears Cut off, his tale and hair like that of a Ground *hog* Something longer and lighter, his interals like a Hogs, his Skin thick & loose, white & hair

Short under its belly, of the Species of the *Bear*, and it has a white Streake from its nose to its Sholders, the Toe *nails* of its fore feet which is large is 1 Inch and ¾ qtr. long and those of his hind feet which is much Smaller is ¾ long. We have this animale Skined and Stuffed. Short legs, raseing himself just above the ground when in motion Jo & R. fields Killed Som Deer at a Distance and Came in for a horse to bring them in, they have not returned this evening, a gred number of Swans in a pond above L. S. to our Camp. Serjt. Floyd verry unwell a bad Cold &c. Several men with Boils, great qts. of Catfish G. D.Cought one Small Beever alive. Some Turkey & Gees Killed to day. arms & all things in order. a fair evining, and Cool.

Source: Thwaites, Reuben Gold, ed. *Original Journals of the Lewis and Clark Expedition, 1804–1806.* Volume 2. New York: Dodd, Mead & Company, 1904.

Further Reading

Bergon, Frank, ed. *The Journals of Lewis and Clark.* New York: Penguin Press, 1989.

Blumberg, Rhoda. *The Incredible Journey of Lewis and Clark.* New York: Scholastic, 1993.

Botkin, Daniel. *Our Natural History, The Lessons of Lewis and Clark.* Oxford University Press, 2004.

Brodhead, Micheal. "The Military Naturalist: A Lewis and Clark Heritage." *We Proceeded On,* vol. 9, no. 4 (November 1983).

Burroughs, Raymond Darwin. *The Natural History of the Lewis and Clark Expedition.* East Lansing: Michigan State University Press, 1961.

Holloway, David. *Lewis and Clark and the Crossing of North America.* New York: Saturday Review Press, 1974.

Slaughter, Thomas P. *Exploring Lewis and Clark: Reflections on Men and Wilderness.* Vintage Press, 2004.

Document 36

COUNCIL BLUFF, IOWA (AUGUST 3, 1804)

Introduction: First Meeting between Representatives of the Government of the United States and Native Americans

During the early days of August 1804, the first official meetings between official representatives of the government of the United States and the Native nations took place, when Lewis and Clark met with delegates from the Otoe and Missouri peoples. The system that Lewis and Clark established here—that of giving gifts, making a speech on behalf of the president, explaining how peace as opposed to war would be of great benefit to all—would continue to be used for the rest of the journey. The three journal entries here, from all eastern social and military groups, recognize the importance of this peaceful moment in history.

The Otoe and Missouri, who were part of the south Sioux Nation, were primarily buf-falo hunters and farmers. By the time they met with Lewis and Clark here, their popula-tion had been ravaged by smallpox, and their numbers had dropped to about 250 people.

Mad up a Small preasant for those people in perpotion to their Consiqunce. also a package with a meadile to accompany a Speech for the Grand Chief which we intend to send to him after Brackfast we Collected those Indians under an orning of our Main Sail, in presence of our Party paraded & Delivered a long Speech to them expressive of our journey the wirkes of our Government, Some advice to them and Directions how They were to Conduct themselves, the princapal Chief for the nation being absente we sent him the Speech *flag* Meadel & Some Cloathes. after hering what they had to say Delivered a medal of Second Grade to one for the Ottos & and one for the Missourie present and 4 medals of a third Grade to the inferior Chief two for each tribe. Those two parts of nations, Ottos & Mis-souries now residing together is about 250 men are the Ottoes Composeing ⅔d and Missourie ⅓ part.

The names of the Chiefs we acknowledged Made this day are as follows Viz

	Indian Name		English signf
1st	We ār ruge nor	Ottoe call'ed	Little Thief
2	Shōn gŭ tōn gŭ	" "	Big Horse
	We- the-ā	Miss: "	Hospatality
3	Shon Guss cān.	Ottoe	White Horse
	Wau pe ŭh	M.	
	Āh hō ning gă	M.	
	Baza cou jā	Ottoe	
	Āh hō nē gă	M.	

Those Chiefs all Delivered a Speech acknowledgeing Their approbation to the Speech and promissing to prosue the advice & Derictions given them that they wer happy to find that they had fathers which might be depended on &c.

We gave them a Cannister of Powder and a Bottle of whiskey and delivered a few presents to the whole after giveing a *Br: Cth* Some Pain guartering & a Meadele to those we *made* Cheifs after Capt Lewis's Shooting the air gun a feiw Shots (which astonished those nativs) we Set out and proceeded on five miles on a Direct line passed a point on the S. S. & round a large Sand bar on the L. S. & Camped on the upper point. The Misquitors excessively troublesom this evening Great appearance of wind and rain to the N. W. we prepare to rec've it—The man Liberty whome we Sent for the Ottoes has not Come up he left the Ottoes Town one Day before the Indians. This man has eithered tired his horse or, lost himself in the Plains Some Indians are to hunt for him.

The Situationof our last Camp Councill Bluff or Handssom Prarie appears to be a verry proper place for a Tradeing establishment & fortification The Soil of the Bluff well adapted for Brick, Great deel of timbers above in the two Points. many other advantages of a Small nature. and I am told Senteral to Several nations Viz. one Days march from the OttoeTown, one Day & a half from the great Pania village, 2 days from the Mahar Towns, two ¼ Days from the Loups Village, & Convenient to the Countrey thro: which Bands of the Soux hunt. perhaps no other Situation is as well Calculated for a Tradeing establishment. The air is pure and helthy So far as we can Judge.

Source: Thwaites, Reuben Gold, ed. *Original Journals of the Lewis and Clark Expedition, 1804–1806.* Volume 2. New York: Dodd, Mead & Company, 1904.

Friday august 3dth the Council was held and all partes was agreed the Captens Give them meney presents thes is the ottoeand the Missouries The Missouries is a verry Small nathion the ottoes is a very Large nathion So thay Live in one village on the Plate River after the Council was over we took ouer Leave of them and embarked at 3 oclock P. m under Jentell Brees from the South Est. Sailed made 6 miles Campt on the South Side the Land Low, that on the N. prarie Land—

Source: Journals of Charles Floyd. Worcester, MA: Charles Hamilton Press, 1894.

Friday 3rd. Captain Lewis and Captain Clarke held a council with the Indians, who appeared well pleased with the change of government, and what had been done for them. Six of them were made chiefs, three Otos and three Missouris.

We renewed our voyage at 3 o'clock; went six miles and encamped on the south side; where we had a storm of wind and rain, which lasted two hours.

Source: Journals of Patrick Gass. Chicago: A.C. McClurg, 1904.

Further Reading

Bergon, Frank, ed. *The Journals of Lewis and Clark.* New York: Penguin Press, 1989.

Duffy, John. *Epidemics in Colonial America.* Louisiana State University, 1971.

Holloway, David. *Lewis and Clark and the Crossing of North America.* New York: Saturday Review Press, 1974.

Husner, Verne. *On the River with Lewis and Clark.* Austin, TX: A & M Press, 2004.

Jones, Landon Y. *William Clark and the Shaping of the West.* New York: Hill and Wang, 2004.

Josephy, Alvin M. *Lewis and Clark through Indian Eyes: None Indian Writers on the Legacy of the Expedition.* New York: Vintage Press, 2007.

Merrell, James H. *Into the American Woods: Negotiators on the Pennsylvania Frontier.* New York: W.W. Norton, 1999.

Turner, Erin H. *It Happened on the Lewis and Clark Expedition.* Guilford, CT: Globe Pequot Press, 2003.

Document 37

THE DEATH OF SGT. CHARLES FLOYD. FLOYDS BLUFF, SOUTHERN SIOUX CITY, IOWA (AUGUST 20, 1804)

Introduction: Death by Appendix

Clark had earlier noted that Floyd had a cold and was unwell. The captains of the trip diagnosed his complaint as "bilious colic" or a sick stomach and without doubt treated him with some of Rush's pills, and perhaps even bled him. While this would not have helped and without doubt made Floyd feel worse, the truth is that no doctor at the time could have saved him. It is thought that he died of peritonitis after a ruptured appendix.

In his last hours, Floyd was nursed by York, Clark's African American slave, with kindness and care something that was commented on later by the men. Floyd was buried with full military honors, and a short speech was given by Clark. When the expedition was over, Floyd's family received his wages: Floyd's allotment of land, 320 acres, was the same as everyone's else, and his family also received his half year salary: $86.33.

August 20, 1804

Sergeant Floyd much weaker and no better. Made Mr. Fauforn the interpter a fiew presents, and the Indians a Canister of whisky we Set out under a gentle breeze from the S. E. and proceeded on verry well—Serjeant Floyd as bad as he can be no pulse & nothing will Stay a moment on his Stomach or bowels—

Passed two Islands on the S. S. and at first Bluff on the S S. Serj.' Floyd Died with a great deel of Composure, before his death he Said to me, "I am going away" I want you to write me a letter"—We buried him on the top of the bluff ½ Miles below a Small river to which we Gave his name, he was buried with the Honors of War much lamented; a Seeder post with the (1) Name Sergt. C. Floyd died here 20th of August 1804 was fixed at the head of his grave—This Man at all times gave us proofs of his firmness and Determined resolution to doe Service to his Countrey and honor to himself after paying all the honor to our Decesed brother we Camped in the mouth of floyds river about 30 yards wide, a butifull evening.

Source: Thwaites, Reuben Gold, ed. *Original Journals of the Lewis and Clark Expedition, 1804–1806.* Volume 2. New York: Dodd, Mead & Company, 1904.

Sergeant Floyd continued very ill. We embarked early, and proceeded, having a fair wind and fine weather, till 2 o'clock, when we landed for dinner. Here Sergeant Floyd died, notwithstanding every possible effort was made by the commanding officers, and other persons, to save his life. We went on about a mile to high prairie hills on the north side of the river, and there interred his remains in the most decent manner our circumstances would admit; we then proceeded a mile further to a small river on the same side and encamped. Our commanding officers gave it the name of Floyd's river; to perpetuate the memory of the first man who had fallen in this important expedition.

Source: Journals of Patrick Gass. Chicago: A.C. McClurg, 1904.

August 20, 1804

Pleasant, we Set of under a gentle Breeze from S. E. the Indians chiefs Set out to return to their village. Sgt. Floyd worse than he was yesterday we Sailed on verry well till noon when we came too on S. S. Sergt. Charles Floyd Expired directly after we halted a little past the middle of the day. he was laid out in the Best Manner possable. we proceeded on to the first hills N. S. there we dug the Grave on a handsome Sightly Round knob close to the Bank. we buried him with the honours of war. the usal Serrymony performed as custommary in a Settlement, we put a red ceeder post, hughn & branded his name date &.C—we named those Bluffs Sergeant Charles Floyds Bluff. Distant from the Mouth of the Missouri 949½ miles by water, we then proceeded on a Short distance to a creek which we Call Floyds Creek.

Source: The Journals of Captain Meriwether Lewis and Sergeant John Ordway: Kept on the Expedition of Western Exploration, 1803–1806. Madison, WI: The Society, 1916.

Further Reading

Bergon, Frank, ed. *The Journals of Lewis and Clark.* New York: Penguin Press, 1989.
Chuinard, Eldon G. *Only One Man Died: The Medical Aspects of the Lewis and Clark Expedition.* Glendale, CA: Arthur Clark Company, 1980.
Cutright, Paul Russell. "I Gave Him Barks and Saltpeter." *American Heritage: The Magazine of History,* vol. 15 (December 1963): 58–61, 94–101.
Duffi, Jacalyn. *History of Medicine: A Scandalously Short Introduction.* University of Toronto Press, 1999.
Duffy, John. *Epidemics in Colonial America.* Louisiana State University, 1971.
Fisher, John W. *Medical Appendices of the Lewis and Clark Expedition.* Juliaetta, ID: Fisher, 2006.
Turner, Erin H. *It Happened on the Lewis and Clark Expedition.* Guilford, CT: Globe Pequot Press, 2003.

Document 38

ELECTION. FLOYDS BLUFF, SOUTHERN SIOUX CITY, IOWA (AUGUST 22, 1804)

Introduction: Patrick Gass Promoted to Sergeant

After the death of Floyd, there was an open sergeant's position, and Lewis and Clark surprisingly allowed the men to make the decision. There was a choice of three candidates, and from three—Patrick Gass, William Bratten, and George Gibson—Gass was chosen with 19 votes. The votes for the others have not been recorded. Gass was a career soldier and had carpenter skills, which was to be useful during the expedition.

Set out early wind from the South at three miles we landed at a Bluff where the two men Sent with the horses were waiting with two Deer, by examonation of this (1) Bluff Contained alum, Copperas, Cobalt, Pyrites; a alum rock Soft & Sand Stone. Capt. Lewis in proveing the quality of those minerals was near poisoning himself by the fumes & task of the *Cabalt* which had the appearance of Soft Isonglass—Copperas & alum is verry pure, Above this Bluff a Small Creek Coms in from the L. S. passing under the Clifts for Several miles, this Creek I Call Roloje a name I learned last night in m S. (2) Seven miles above is a Clift of Allom Stone of a Dark Brown Colr. Containing also in crusted in the Crevices & Shelves of the rock great qts. of Cabalt, Semented Shels & a red earth. from this the (3) river bends to the East and is within 3 or 4 miles of the River Soues at the place where that river Coms from the high land into the Low Prarie & passed under the foot of those Hills to its mouth.

Capt Lewis took a Dost of salts to work off the effects of the Arsenic, we Camped on the S. S. Sailed the greater part of this day with a hard wind from the S. E. great deel of Elk Sign, and great appearance of wind from the N.W. ordered a vote for a Serjeant to chuse one of three which may be the highest number the highest numbers are P. Gass had 19 Votes, Bratten & Gibson.

Source: Thwaites, Reuben Gold, ed. *Original Journals of the Lewis and Clark Expedition, 1804–1806.* Volume 1. New York: Dodd, Mead & Company, 1904, 116–117.

Further Reading

Bergon, Frank, ed. *The Journals of Lewis and Clark.* New York: Penguin Press, 1989.

Chuinard, Eldon G. *Only One Man Died: The Medical Aspects of the Lewis and Clark Expedition.* Glendale, CA: Arthur Clark Company, 1980.

Cutright, Paul Russell. "I Gave Him Barks and Saltpeter." *American Heritage: The Magazine of History,* vol. 15 (December 1963): 58–61, 94–101.

Duffi, Jacalyn. *History of Medicine: A Scandalously Short Introduction.* University of Toronto Press, 1999.

Duffy, John. *Epidemics in Colonial America.* Louisiana State University, 1971.

Fisher, John W. *Medical Appendices of the Lewis and Clark Expedition.* Juliaetta, ID: Fisher, 2006.

Turner, Erin H. *It Happened on the Lewis and Clark Expedition.* Guilford, CT: Globe Pequot Press, 2003.

Document 39

NEBRASKA–SOUTH DAKOTA BORDER (AUGUST 30, 1804)

Introduction: Meeting with French Canadian Fur Traders

By the end of August, the expedition had reached the Nebraska–South Dakota border, and they camped on the Nebraska side. The constant diplomatic aspect of this expedition can be seen here again; as Clark notes in the excerpt that follows that they are going to spend some time with the local Native American peoples, here it was the Sioux. In July, Lewis and Clark had hired Pierre Dorion (c. 1750–1810) as an interpreter. Probably born in Quebec, Canada, Dorion was trapper and fur trader who had met George Rogers Clark in the 1790s. In June 1804, the Corps desperately needed an interpreter who could help them communicate with the Sioux, and so Dorion was hired. Dorion already had a reputation as a scammer, and so as was typical for Dorion, who recognized the desperation of Lewis and Clark, he also persuaded them to purchase 300 pounds of buffalo grease from him. Whether Lewis and Clark or anyone on the expedition needed the grease was irrelevant, Dorion wanted it to be bought and got money.

On August 27, Lewis and Clark had discovered that a large group of Sioux were camped nearby, and they were anxious to make contact. Dorion, Nathaniel Pryor, and Pierre Cruzette (dates unknown) were sent to make contact and to invite the Sioux chiefs to meet. Dorion's son, Pierre Dorion Jr., lived with the Sioux and was invaluable as an interpreter of speeches and rituals. Both father and son were typical of the fur trappers and traders who lived in the West, outside of social norms, living between societies, but knowing the language and customs of both. These men were as vital to the success of the expedition as anyone else.

August 30, 1804

30th August Thursday 1804 A Foggeie morning I am much engagd. after Brackfast we sent Mr. Doroun in a Perogue to the other Side i'e' L S. for the Chiefs and arri- ers of the Soues, he returned at 10 oClock with the Chiefs, at 12 oclock I finished and we delivered a Speech to the Indians expressive of the wishes of our govern- ment and explaining of what would be good for themselves, after delivering the Speech we made one grand Chief 1 2d Cheif and three third Chiefs and deliverd. to each a few articles and a Small present to the whole the grand Chief a Parole, Some wampom & a flag in addition to his present, they with Drew and we retired to dinner, Mr. Durions Sun much displeased that he could not dine with Cap Lewis and my Self—the number of Soues present is about 70 men—Dressed in Buffalow roabes a fiew fusees, Bows and arrows, and verry much deckerated with porcupine quills, a Society of which only four remains is present, this Society has made a vow never to giv back let what will happen, out of 22 only 4 remains, those are Stout likely men who Stay by them Selves, fond of mirth and assume a degree of Superiority— [he air gun astonished them verry much after night a circle was forrm around 3 fires and those Indians danced untill late, the Chiefs looked on with great dignity much pleased with what they had, we retired late and went to bead. wind hard from the South.

Source: Thwaites, Reuben Gold, ed. *Original Journals of the Lewis and Clark Expedi- tion, 1804–1806.* Volume 3. New York: Dodd, Mead & Company, 1905.

A foggy morning, and heavy dew. At nine o'clock the Indians came over the river. Four of them, who were musicians, went backwards and forwards, through and round our camp, singing and making a noise. After that ceremony was over they all sat in council. Captain Lewis and Captain Clarke made five of them chiefs, and gave them some small presents. At dark Captain Lewis gave them a grained deer skin to stretch over a half keg for a drum. When that was ready they all assembled round some fires made for the purpose: two of them beat on the drum, and some of the rest had little bags of undressed skins dried, with beads or small pebbles in them, with which they made a noise. These are their instruments of musick. Ten or twelve acted as musicians, while twenty or thirty young men and boys engaged in the dance, which was continued during the night.

Source: Journals of Patrick Gass. Chicago: A.C. McClurg, 1904.

Further Reading

Bergon, Frank, ed. *The Journals of Lewis and Clark.* New York: Penguin Press, 1989.

Dunbar-Ortiz, Roxanne. *An Indigenous Peoples' History of the United States.* Beacon Press, reprint, 2015.

Gass, Patrick. *A Journal of the Voyages and Travels of a Corps of Discovery under the Command of Capt. Lewis and Capt. Clark.* Minneapolis, MN: Ross and Haines, 1958.

Gibbon, Guy. *The Sioux: The Dakota and Lakota Nations.* Wiley-Blackwell, 2002.

Holloway, David. *Lewis and Clark and the Crossing of North America.* New York: Saturday Review Press, 1974.

Jenkinson, Clay. *The Character of Meriwether Lewis in the Wilderness.* The Dakota Institute, 2011.

Turner, Erin H. *It Happened on the Lewis and Clark Expedition.* Guilford, CT: Globe Pequot Press, 2003.

Document 40

SOUTH DAKOTA (SEPTEMBER 11, 1804)

Introduction: George Shannon Is Found

George Shannon was found starving. He had spent 16 days alone and was presumed lost and indeed dead. On August 26, Shannon had been sent out to look for horses and had found them much more quickly than he had thought he would, so he began traveling upriver searching for the Corps. This was his mistake as the Corps were not ahead of him but behind him. Though he had a rifle with him, he had very little ammunition and was soon hungry, with little to eat but grapes. He had managed to shoot and kill one rabbit by using hard sticks as ammunition. He had sat down by the river waiting for a boat to come by, when the Corps caught up with him, and he was saved. Clark in his journal is conscience of Shannon's luck and how fragile life is.

A cloudy morning, Set out verry early, the river wide & Shallow the bottom narrow, & the river Crouded with Sand bars, passed the Island on which we lay at one mile—, pased three Islands one on the L. S. and 2 on the S. S. opposit the Island on the L. S. I Saw a village of Barking Squriel 970 yds. long, and 800 yds. wide Situated on a gentle Slope of a hill, those anamals are noumerous, I killed 4 with a view to have their Skins Stufed.

here the man who left us with the horses 22 days ago and has been a head ever Since joined, us nearly Starved to Death, he had been 12 days without any thing to eate but Grapes & one Rabit, which he Killed by shooting a piece of hard Stick in place of a ball—. This man Supposeing the boat to be a head pushed on as long as he Could, when he became weak and fiable deturmined to lay by and waite for a tradeing boat, which is expected Keeping one horse for the last resorse,—thus a man had like to have Starved to death in a land of Plenty for the want of Bulletes or Something to kill his meat we Camped on the L. S. above the mouth of a run a hard rain all the after noon, & most of the night, with hard wind from the N W. I walked on Shore the fore part of this day over Some broken Country which Continus about 3 miles back & then is leavel & rich all Plains, I saw Several foxes & Killed a Elk & 2 Deer. & Squirels the men with me killed an Elk, 2 Deer & a Pelican.

Source: Thwaites, Reuben Gold, ed. *Original Journals of the Lewis and Clark Expedition, 1804–1806.* Volume 2. New York: Dodd, Mead & Company, 1904.

Further Reading

Blackhawk, Ned. *Violence over Land: Indians and Empires in the Early American West.* Cambridge, MA: Harvard University Press, 1998.

Buckley, Jay H. *William Clark: Indian Diplomat.* University of Oklahoma Press, 2008.

Danisli, Thomas. *Meriwether Lewis.* Prometheus Books, 2009.

Dunbar-Ortiz, Roxanne. *An Indigenous Peoples' History of the United States.* Beacon Press, reprint, 2015.

Fenn, Elizabeth. *Encounters at the Heart of the World: A History of the Mandan People.* Hill and Wang, reprint, 2015.

Jenkinson, Clay. *The Character of Meriwether Lewis in the Wilderness.* The Dakota Institute, 2011.

Richter, Daniel K. *Facing East from Indian Country: A Native History of Early America.* Cambridge, MA: Harvard University Press, 2001.

Document 41

FORT MANDAN, NORTH DAKOTA (NOVEMBER 3, 1804)

Introduction: Building a Fort for the Winter

Due to the keelboat's heavy load, travel upriver had been extremely slow. By November, the expedition had reached a place that they were to call Fort Mandan, in North Dakota, about 12 miles from present-day Washburn. With winter fast approaching, the Corps had to build a fort to keep them safe and warm for the winter. Construction began on November 2, and the buildings were finished on November 27. There was a room for the men, storage rooms for supplies, and another room that was shared by Lewis and Clark.

The fort was named after the Mandan Nation, whose people were interested in forming alliances with Lewis and Clark as well as other nations for the sake of peace. Throughout the winter, the Mandan and the Corps shared food, and when food was scarce, both groups went together and hunted buffalo. This again was exactly what George Clark suggested and Jefferson wanted. Within the context of future American history, these months of cooperation, coexistence, and respect seem unthinkable. The future would bring war, forced resettlement, and accusations of genocide. Indeed, some of the accusations of genocide would be made about William Clark. But right now, this winter of 1804–1805, the cooperation, respect, and willingness to learn about different cultures and each other superseded everything.

A clear day; we continued building, and six men went down the river in a periogue to hunt. They will perhaps have to go 30 or 40 miles before they come to good hunting ground.—The following is the manner in which our huts and fort were built; the huts were in two rows, containing four rooms each, and joined at one end forming an angle. When rasied about 7 feet high a floor of puncheons or split plank were laid, and covered with grass and clay; which made a warm loft. The upper part projected a foot over and the roofs were made shed-fashion, rising from the inner side, and making the outer wall about 18 feet high. The part not inclosed by the huts we intended to picket. In the angle formed by the two rows of huts we built two rooms, for holding our provisions and stores.

Source: Journals of Patrick Gass. Chicago: A.C. McClurg, 1904.

November 3, 1804

A cloudy morning. Capt. Clark went with Some men down the Bottom to look for a place to Build our huts. they Returned Shortly had found a Good place a Short distance down where their was an Indian camp in a Grove of large cottonwood Timber. Sevral Indians at Sd. camp Capt. Lewis & Several of the party went in a pearogue up to the 1st village of the Mandans in order to Git corn. we droped down a Short distance farther to a body & Bottom of large Timber where we commenced falling Timber, and fixing a camp close by the place where we intend for to build. picthed our tents & laid the foundation of one line of our huts, which consisted of 4 Rooms 14 feet Square. the other line will be the Same Capt. Lewis returned. brought us 10 or 12 bushels of Good corn. we find the cottonwood Timber will Split Tollorable well, and as their is no other building timber in this bottom we expect to Split punchin to cover the huts with. one of our french hands is discharged & gone down the river.

Source: The Journals of Captain Meriwether Lewis and Sergeant John Ordway: Kept on the Expedition of Western Exploration, 1803–1806. Madison, WI: The Society, 1916.

Further Reading

Blackhawk, Ned. *Violence over Land: Indians and Empires in the Early American West.* Cambridge, MA: Harvard University Press, 1998.

Buckley, Jay H. *William Clark: Indian Diplomat.* University of Oklahoma Press, 2008.

Danisli, Thomas. *Meriwether Lewis.* Prometheus Books, 2009.

Dunbar-Ortiz, Roxanne. *An Indigenous Peoples' History of the United States*. Beacon Press, reprint, 2015.

Fenn, Elizabeth. *Encounters at the Heart of the World: A History of the Mandan People*. Hill and Wang, reprint, 2015.

Jenkinson, Clay. *The Character of Meriwether Lewis in the Wilderness*. The Dakota Institute, 2011.

Richter, Daniel K. *Facing East from Indian Country: A Native History of Early America*. Cambridge, MA: Harvard University Press, 2001.

Document 42

FORT MANDAN, NORTH DAKOTA (NOVEMBER 4, 1804)

Introduction: Arrival of Toussaint Charbonneau and Sacagawea

While the fort was under construction, in the winter of 1804, Toussaint Charbonneau and his wives arrived. Charbonneau (c. 1759–1843) was born in Quebec, Canada, and was a fur trapper and trader who lived in an area close to the Hidatsa Nation, close to present-day Bismarck, North Dakota. Soon after Sacagawea was brought to North Dakota, Charbonneau bought, won while gambling, or was given two women to be his wives: Sacagawea and another unnamed woman. Sacagawea was a member of the Shoshone Nation who had been kidnapped from her home in modern-day Idaho. When Sacagawea and Charbonneau arrived at Fort Mandan, she was expecting a child. With the language skills that Charbonneau and his wives offered, Lewis and Clark quickly hired him as a translator for the "Gross Vintre" (Hidatsa), knowing how vital these skills would be in the spring when the expedition continued west.

Fort Mandan would prove to be not just a safe place of rest for the winter but also a place of preparation. Here, Lewis and Clark would spend time in conversation, taking notes, and making maps, as they gathered as much information as they could about a possible route west. The Mandans had never traveled as far as the Pacific, but they had certainly traveled farther than Lewis and Clark. Therefore, any information they could provide was crucial to the expedition's next steps.

This winter, while cold and long, was productive and educational and one that passed quickly for all members of the Corps.

November 4, 1804

Fine morning we Continued to Cut Down trees and raise our houses, a Mr. Chaubonée, interpeter for the *Gross Vintre* nation Came to See us, and informed that he came Down with Several Indians from a Hunting expedition up the river, to here what we had told the Indians in Councl this man wished to hire as an interpeter, the wind rose this evining from the East & Clouded up—Great numbers of Indians pass hunting and Some on the return.

Source: Thwaites, Reuben Gold, ed. *Original Journals of the Lewis and Clark Expedition, 1804–1806.* Volume 2. New York: Dodd, Mead & Company, 1904.

Further Reading

Bergon, Frank, ed. *The Journals of Lewis and Clark.* New York: Penguin Press, 1989.

Dunbar-Ortiz, Roxanne. *An Indigenous Peoples' History of the United States.* Beacon Press, reprint, 2015.

Josephy, Alvin M. *Lewis and Clark through Indian Eyes: None Indian Writers on the Legacy of the Expedition.* New York: Vintage Press, 2007.

Merrell, James H. *Into the American Woods: Negotiators on the Pennsylvania Frontier.* New York: W.W. Norton, 1999.

Nelson, W. Dale. *Interpreters with Lewis and Clark: The Story of Sacagawea and Toussaint Charbonneau.* University of North Texas Press, 2004.

Richter, Daniel K. *Facing East from Indian Country: A Native History of Early America.* Cambridge, MA: Harvard University Press, 2001.

Ritter, Michael. *Jean Baptiste Charbonneau, Man of Two Worlds.* Create Space Publishing, 2004.

Document 43

FORT MANDAN, NORTH DAKOTA (DECEMBER 7, 1804)

Introduction: Preparation for the Spring

Up to this point food had been plentiful and shared between the Corps and the Mandans. It was also a particularly cold winter, one where the men of the Corps were experiencing the type of cold they had never experienced before. Lewis and Clark used the time to put the notes together and drew maps of what they had seen up to this point and where they had traveled so far. All of this information would be sent back to Jefferson in the spring. For decades afterward, this map of the West would be the most accurate one available. It would be used for military training as well as for the settlers who began to go west. Lewis's and Clark's map would change American culture and government, as it finally allowed for and encouraged movement between coasts.

Lewis and Clark spent a great deal of time talking to and questioning people, both the Native population and the fur traders, about what lay west. What could they expect? Were there natural markers to help them on their way? Were there people who would help? Lewis and Clark were both aware that as rigorous as the traveling had been up to now, in the spring they were about to embark into a different level of the unknown, where they were fewer people, less fur traders, and even the local Mandans knew relatively little of the geography.

On Friday, December 7, 1804, the Corps went with the Mandans and hunted buffaloes, which would keep everyone in food and clothes throughout the winter. That day, Clark estimated that the Mandans killed between 30 and 40 buffaloes, while the Corps killed 11. Patrick Gass noted in his journal that what struck him most was that the Mandan horses were trained to move extremely close to the buffalos and only move away at the last second, allowing for the Mandan to kill easily. Again the contrast between the beginning and the middle of the nineteenth century could not have been greater: while the Mandans and the Corps of Discovery killed what they needed, in 50 years, buffaloes were killed for the sake of killing. Tens of thousands were killed, and as they were killed, Native American nations were killed off. Winter survival meant an understanding of a fragile ecosystem, one that was respected in 1804 but, by 1864, was ignored.

But in 1804, the biggest threat to Mandans had been diseases. They had been decimated by smallpox and whooping cough epidemics and had been reduced from nine villages to two, but they were still considered a wealthy tribe whose system of spirituality was based on nature and its ability to contact animals.

December 7, 1804

A verry Cold day wind from the N W. the Big White Grand Chief of the 1s Village, Came and informed us that a large Drove of Buffalow was near and his people was wating for us to join them in a Chase Capt. Lewis took 15 men & went out joined the Indians, who were at the time he got up, Killing the Buffalows on Horseback with arrows which they done with great dexterity, his party killed 14 Buffalow, *five* of which we got to the fort by the assistance of a horse in addition to what the men Packed on their backs—one Cow was killed on the ice after drawing her out of a vacancey in the ice in which She had fallen, and Butchered her at the fort—those we did not get in was taken by the indians under a Custon which is established amongst them 'i 'e. any person Seeing a buffalow lying without an arrow Sticking in him, or Some purticular mark takes possesion, many times (as I am told) a hunter who Kills maney Buffalow in a chase only Gets a part of one, all meat which is left out all night falls to the Wolves which are in great numbers, always in the Buffalows—the river Closed opposit the fort last night 1½ inches thick The Thermometer Stood this morning at 1 d. below 0—three men frost bit badly to day.

Source: Thwaites, Reuben Gold, ed. *Original Journals of the Lewis and Clark Expedition, 1804–1806.* Volume 1. New York: Dodd, Mead & Company, 1904, 234–235.

A clear cold morning. At 9 o'clock, the Big-white head chief, of the first village of the Mandans, came to our garrison and told us that the buffaloe were in the prairie coming into the bottom. Captain Lewis and eleven more of us went out immediately, and saw the prairie covered with buffaloe and the Indians on horseback killing them. They killed 30 or 40 and we killed eleven of them. They shoot them with bows and arrows, and have their horses so trained that they will advance very near and suddenly wheel and fly off in case the wounded buffaloe attempt an attack.

Source: Journals of Patrick Gass. Chicago: A.C. McClurg, 1904.

A clear cold frosty morning. 2 or 3 hunters went out early a hunting. about 9 o.C. the head chief of the 1st vill. of the Mandans called the Big White came to our Garrison in Great haste on horse back & Informed us that the Buffalow were comming towards the River in large Gangs and that the praries a little back was covered with Game. Capt. Lewis Immediately Started with 12 men in order to hunt with the natives. they had not been Gone long before we Saw Some buffalow in cite abo. the Garrison near the bank of the River two of our men & Several of the natives were Shooting at them. they Shot three & run one off a Steep bank in to the River which we got out with a chord, and halled it down on the Ice to our landing as the River Shut up last night the Ice had not Got Strong enofe to bear the Buffalow out in the middle of the R. but we dragged Sd. bufo. down near Shore & dressed it. it was a cow with calf our Interpreters Squaws cut the calf. the 2 men who went out this morning came in & Informed us that they had killed Six buffaloe out in the prarie besides those 4 they had killed in part with the natives. the horses were got up & Several men Sent with them out for the meat, but they found that the Savvage had carried off 3 of them. the 4 horses came in loaded with meat also the most of the men they Said that the Savvages had killed upwards of 20 buffalow & our men killed abt. 12 one of them very fat Som of them cows & Some calfs or yearlins. they Saw also large flocks of Goats in the praries & could See the prarie black with buffaloe at a distance aiming to come into the bottoms on the River. the prarie being covered with Snow and extreamly cold 2 of our men Got their feet frost Bitten & one Got his Ear frost bitten this day by being exposed in the praries. a half Gill of Taffee gave to the men by our officers this evening.

Source: The Journals of Captain Meriwether Lewis and Sergeant John Ordway: Kept on the Expedition of Western Exploration, 1803–1806. Madison, WI: The Society, 1916.

Further Reading

Allen, John Logan. *Passage through the Garden: Lewis and Clark and the Image of the American Northwest.* Urbana: University of Illinois Press, 1975.

Ambrose, Stephen. *Undaunted Courage.* Urbana: University of Chicago Press, 1991.

Bergon, Frank, ed. *The Journals of Lewis and Clark.* New York: Penguin Press, 1989.

Blumberg, Rhoda. *The Incredible Journey of Lewis and Clark.* New York: Scholastic, 1993.

Botkin, Daniel. *Our Natural History, The Lessons of Lewis and Clark.* Oxford: Oxford University Press, 2004.

Brodhead, Micheal. "The Military Naturalist: A Lewis and Clark Heritage." *We Proceeded On,* vol. 9, no. 4 (November 1983).

Husner, Verne. *On the River with Lewis and Clark.* Austin, TX: A & M Press, 2004.

Jones, Landon Y. *William Clark and the Shaping of the West.* New York: Hill and Wang, 2004.

Ronda, James P. *Lewis and Clark among the Indians.* Lincoln: University of Nebraska Press, 1984.

Document 44

CHRISTMAS DAY, FORT MANDAN
(DECEMBER 25, 1804)

Introduction: Fun and Games

Christmas Day 1804 was celebrated with cannon fire, a drink for everyone, music, and dance. The relaxed atmosphere; the easy mixing between the Corps, the Mandans, and fur traders; the food, gifts, and drink (taffee) from Lewis and Clark; and fun are all noted in every journal entry. They had every reason to celebrate. While far away from home, they were safe, warm, and well fed.

Military discipline was nevertheless insisted upon by Lewis and Clark. Nine o'clock was the deadline set for the end of all partying. After this, normal security and station duty applied.

December 25, 1804

I was awakened before Day by a discharge of 3 platoons from the Party and the french, the men merrily Disposed, I give them all a little Taffia and permited 3 Cannon fired, at raising Our flag, Some men went out to hunt & the Others to Danceing and Continued untill 9 oClock P, M, when the frolick ended &c.

Source: Thwaites, Reuben Gold, ed. *Original Journals of the Lewis and Clark Expedition, 1804–1806.* Volume 1. New York: Dodd, Mead & Company, 1904, 240.

The morning was ushered in by two discharges of a swivel, and a round of small arms by the whole corps. Captain Clarke then presented to each man a glass of brandy, and we hoisted the American flag in the garrison, and its first waving in fort Mandan was celebrated with another glass.—The men then cleared out one of the rooms and commenced dancing. At 10 o'clock we had another glass of brandy, and at 1 a gun was fired as a signal for dinner. At half past 2, another gun was fired, as a notice to assemble at the dance, which was continued in a jovial manner till 8 at night.

Source: Journals of Patrick Gass. Chicago: A.C. McClurg, 1904.

Cloudy. we fired the Swivels at day break & each man fired one round. our officers Gave the party a drink of Taffee. we had the Best to eat that could be had, & continued firing dancing & frolicking dureing the whole day. the Savages did not Trouble us as we had requested them not to come as it was a Great medician day with us. we enjoyed a merry cristmas dureing the day & evening untill nine oClock—all in peace & quietness.

Source: The Journals of Captain Meriwether Lewis and Sergeant John Ordway: Kept on the Expedition of Western Exploration, 1803–1806. Madison, WI: The Society, 1916.

Further Reading

Allen, John Logan. *Passage through the Garden: Lewis and Clark and the Image of the American Northwest.* Urbana: University of Illinois Press, 1975.

Ambrose, Stephen. *Undaunted Courage.* Urbana: University of Chicago Press, 1991.

Bergon, Frank, ed. *The Journals of Lewis and Clark.* New York: Penguin Press, 1989.

Blumberg, Rhoda. *The Incredible Journey of Lewis and Clark.* New York: Scholastic, 1993.

Botkin, Daniel. *Our Natural History, The Lessons of Lewis and Clark.* Oxford: Oxford University Press, 2004.

Brodhead, Micheal. "The Military Naturalist: A Lewis and Clark Heritage." *We Proceeded On,* vol. 9, no. 4 (November 1983).

Husner, Verne. *On the River with Lewis and Clark.* Austin, TX: A & M Press, 2004.

Jones, Landon Y. *William Clark and the Shaping of the West.* New York: Hill and Wang, 2004.

Ronda, James P. *Lewis and Clark among the Indians.* Lincoln: University of Nebraska Press, 1984.

Document 45

FORT MANDAN, NORTH DAKOTA (FEBRUARY 11, 1805)

Introduction: Birth of Jean Baptiste Charbonneau

On February 11, 1805, at Fort Mandan, North Dakota, Jean Baptiste Charbonneau was born. Once again Lewis was called upon to help, as he had training from Benjamin Rush. Rush, however, had not foreseen childbirth in all the instructions he had given to Lewis, and so Lewis was unsurprisingly unsure of how best to help. He did take advice from a fur trader at the fort, who, to Lewis's horror, suggested that the rattle rings from a rattle-snake given in water would help with the birth. While the baby boy was born very soon after Sacagawea took the medication, even Lewis was unsure this time if this alternative medicine really worked. Jean Baptiste had just become the youngest member of the expedition. William Clark soon gave him the nickname "Pomp," or "Little Pompy," while Sacagawea was soon known as "Janey."

February 11, 1805

The party that were ordered last evening set out early this morning. the weather was fair and could wind N. W. about five oclock this evening one of the wives of Charbono was delivered of a fine boy. it is worthy of remark that this was the first child which this woman had boarn and as is common in such cases her labour was tedious and the pain violent; Mr. Jessome informed me that he had freequently adminstered a small portion of the rattle of the rattle-snake, which he assured me had never failed to produce the desired effect, that of hastening the birth of the child; having the rattle of a snake by me I gave it to him and he administered two rings of it to the woman broken in small pieces with the fingers and added to a small quantity of water. Whether this medicine was truly the cause or not I shall not undertake to determine, but I was informed that she had not taken it more than ten minutes before she brought forth perhaps this remedy may be worthy of future experiments, but I must confess that I want faith as to it's efficacy.—

Source: Thwaites, Reuben Gold, ed. *Original Journals of the Lewis and Clark Expedition, 1804–1806.* Volume 1. New York: Dodd, Mead & Company, 1904, 257–258.

Further Reading

Bergon, Frank, ed. *The Journals of Lewis and Clark.* New York: Penguin Press, 1989.

Dunbar-Ortiz, Roxanne. *An Indigenous Peoples' History of the United States.* Beacon Press, reprint, 2015.

Josephy, Alvin M. *Lewis and Clark through Indian Eyes: None Indian Writers on the Legacy of the Expedition.* New York: Vintage Press, 2007.

Merrell, James H. *Into the American Woods: Negotiators on the Pennsylvania Frontier.* New York: W.W. Norton, 1999.

Nelson, W. Dale. *Interpreters with Lewis and Clark: The Story of Sacagawea and Toussaint Charbonneau.* University of North Texas Press, 2004.

Richter, Daniel K. *Facing East from Indian Country: A Native History of Early America.* Cambridge, MA: Harvard University Press, 2001.

Ritter, Michael. *Jean Baptiste Charbonneau, Man of Two Worlds.* Create Space Publishing, 2004.

Document 46

LETTER FROM MERIWETHER LEWIS TO THOMAS JEFFERSON. FORT MANDAN, NORTH DAKOTA (MARCH 5, 1805)

Introduction: Plants Used as Medicine

During the winter spent at Fort Mandan, Lewis was always interested in medicine and herbal cures, and knowing that Jefferson and the American Philosophical Society had similar interests, he took the time to write Jefferson a letter that was sent to Washington, D.C., when the barge was sent downstream in April.

Here Lewis explains to Jefferson that he is sending him a few pounds of a plant that when pulverized and made into a poultice is used by the native people as a cure from bites from mad dogs and even snakebites. Knowledge about this plant was given to him by Hugh Heney, a Canadian trader from Montreal who worked with the North West Company, a rival of the Hudson Bay Trading Company. Heney was one of the many Canadian traders they met who lived their lives away from so-called civilization and among the Native peoples. Heney visited Fort Mandan twice that winter and had long conversation with Lewis and Clark on a variety of subjects, including herbal cures. Sadly, we do not know what the plant was, and the samples of it have never been found.

16 Nov. 1804–5 Mch. 1805

Fort Mandan March 5. 1805

This specimen of a plant common to the prairies in this quarter was presented to me by Mr. Hugh Heney, a gentleman of respectability and information who has resided many years among the natives of this country, from whom he obtained the knowledge of it's virtues. Mr. Heney informed me that he had used the root of this plant frequently with the most happy effect in cases of the bite of the mad wolf or dog and also for the bite of the rattle snake he assured me that he had made a great number of experiments on various subjects of men horses and dogs particularly in the case of madness, where the symptoms were in some instances far advanced and had never witnessed it's failing to produce the desired effect. the method of using it is by external application, to half an ounce of the root finely pulverized, add as much water as is necessary to reduce it to the consistency of a common poltice and apply it to the bitten part renewing the dressing once in twelve hours, in cases of the bite of the mad dog where the wound has heald before the symptoms of madness appears, the bitten part must be lacerated or scarfyed before the application is made—the application had always better be made as early as possible after the injury has been sustained.—

I have sent herewith a few pounds of this root, in order that experiments may be made by some skilfull person under the direction of the pilosophical society of Philadelphia.

I have the honor to be with much rispect Your Obt. Servt.

MERIWETHER LEWIS

Source: "To Thomas Jefferson from Meriwether Lewis, 5 March 1805." *Founders Online,* National Archives. Available at: http://founders.archives.gov/documents/Jefferson/99-01-02-1308.

Further Reading

Allen, John Logan. *Passage through the Garden: Lewis and Clark and the Image of the American Northwest.* Urbana: University of Illinois Press, 1975.

Botkin, Daniel. *Our Natural History, The Lessons of Lewis and Clark.* Oxford University Press, 2004.

Brodhead, Micheal. "The Military Naturalist: A Lewis and Clark Heritage." *We Proceeded On,* vol. 9, no. 4 (November 1983).

Burroughs, Raymond Darwin. *The Natural History of the Lewis and Clark Expedition.* East Lansing: Michigan State University Press, 1961.

Cutright, Paul Russell. *Lewis and Clark: Pioneering Naturalists.* Urbana: University of Illinois Press, 1969 (reprinted by University of Nebraska, 1989).

Gibbon, Guy. *The Sioux: The Dakota and Lakota Nations.* Wiley-Blackwell, 2002.

Jenkinson, Clay. *The Character of Meriwether Lewis in the Wilderness.* The Dakota Institute, 2011.

Document 47

FORT MANDAN, NORTH DAKOTA (APRIL 3, 1805)

Introduction: Sending the Barge Back to St. Louis

By April 1806, spring had come, the snows were melting rapidly, and the Corps were now ready to continue their journey west. But first the Corps were going to divide, with a small group heading back to St. Louis. This group was going to take with them letters and gifts to family members, but most important of all, they were to return with boxes full of information about their voyage so far. These included maps, letters, as well as some skeletons, plants, skins of various animals, and even some live animals to Thomas Jefferson. Lewis was optimistic about the trip ahead, writing to Jefferson that he expected to meet with him in September 1806 at Monticello.

While it was not noted at the time in the journals, York, Clark's African American slave, also sent gifts home to his wife. York was in fact the only married member of the Corps. William Clark in a letter he sent home at this time noted the gift that York was sending back, but it needs to be noted that Clark did not stop York from doing this and was therefore recognizing York's marriage.

Corporal Richard Warfington (1777–?) would lead a party of four on this return journey, including Moses Reed and John Newman. Reed had been found guilty of desertion and was dismissed from the expedition. Newman had been found guilty of "having uttered repeated expressions of a highly criminal and mutinous nature."

When the keelboat left to return to St. Louis under Warfington's command, the Corps now had the two pirogues and six canoes made from cottonwood logs at Fort Mandan to continue the journey westward. Lewis and Clark had gathered together as many maps and as much information as they could, hired new interpreters, and were ready for the next part of the adventure into the unknown.

April 3, 1805

We are all day ingaged packing up Sundery articles to be Sent to the President of the U. S.

Box No. 1, contains the following articles i e'

In package No. 3 & 4 Male & Female antelope, with their Skelitons.

"No. 7 & 9 the horns of two mule or Black tailed deer. a Mandan bow an quiver of arrows—with some Ricara's tobacco seed.

"No. 11 a Martin Skin, Containing the tail of a Mule Deer, a [white] weasel and three Squirels from the Rockey mountains.

"No. 12. The bones & Skeleton of a Small burrowing wolf of the Praries the Skin being lost by accident.

"No. 99 The Skeliton of the white and Grey *hare*.

Box No. 2, contains 4 Buffalow *Robes*, and a ear of Mandan Corn.

The large Trunk Contains a male & female *Brarow* [ML: *or burrowing dog of the Prarie*] and female's Skeliton.

a Carrote of Ricaras *Tobacco*

a red fox Skin Containing a *Magpie*.

No. 14 Minitarras Buffalow robe Containing Some articles of Indian dress.

No. 15 a Mandan *robe* containing two burrowing Squirels, a white *weasel* and the Skin of a Loucirvea. also

13 red fox Skins.

1 white Hare Skin &.

4 horns of the mountain ram

1 Robe representing a battle between the Sioux & Ricaras, Minetarras and Mandans.

In Box No. 3.

nos. 1 & 2 The Skins of the Male & female Antelope with their Skelitons. & the Skin of a yellow *Bear* which I obtained from the Scious

No. 4. Box Specimens of plants numbered from 1 to 67.

Specimens of Plants numbered frome 1 to 60.

1 Earthen pot Such as the Mandans Manufacture and use for culinary purposes.

Box No 4 Continued

1 Tin box, containing insects mice &c.

a Specimine of the fur of the antelope.

a Specimon of a plant, and a parcel of its roots highly prized by the natives as an efficatious remidy in Cases of the bite of the rattle Snake or Mad Dog.

In a large Trunk

Skins of a Male and female Braro, or burrowing Dog of the Prarie, with the Skeliton of the female.

1 Skin of the red fox Containing a Magpie.

2 Cased Skins of the white hare.

1 Minitarra Buffalow robe Containing Some articles of Indian Dress

1 Mandan Buffalow robe Containing a dressed Lousirva Skin, and 2 Cased Skins of the Burrowing Squirel of the Praries.

13 red fox Skins

4 Horns of the Mountain Ram or big horn.

1 Buffalow robe painted by a mandan man representing a battle fought 8 years Since by the Sioux & Ricaras against the mandans, menitarras & Ah wah har ways (Mandans &c. on horseback

Cage No. 6.

Contains a liveing burrowing Squirel of the praries

Cage No. 7.

Contains 4 liveing magpies

Cage No. 9.

Containing a liveing hen of the Prarie

a large par of Elks horns containing by the frontal bone—

Source: Thwaites, Reuben Gold, ed. *Original Journals of the Lewis and Clark Expedition, 1804–1806.* Volume 3. New York: Dodd, Mead & Company, 1905.

Clear and pleasant. The articles which was to be Sent back to the States in the Big Barge was packed and boxed up ready to go on board.

Source: The Journals of Captain Meriwether Lewis and Sergeant John Ordway: Kept on the Expedition of Western Exploration, 1803–1806. Madison, WI: The Society, 1916.

Further Reading

Bedini, Silvio. *Thomas Jefferson: Statesman of Science.* New York: Macmillan, 1990.

Bergon, Frank, ed. *The Journals of Lewis and Clark.* New York: Penguin Press, 1989.

Betts, Robert. *In Search of York: The Slave Who Went to the Pacific with Lewis and Clark.* Denver: University of Colorado Press, 2002.

Botkin, Daniel. *Our Natural History, The Lessons of Lewis and Clark.* Oxford University Press, 2004.

Duncan, Dayton and Ken Burns. *Lewis and Clark: The Journey of the Corps of Discovery: An Illustrated History.* New York: Alfred A. Knopf, 1997.

Gutzman, Kevin. *Thomas Jefferson—Revolutionary: A Radical's Struggle to Remake America.* New York: St. Martin's Press, 2017.

Saunt, Claudio. *A New Order of Things: Property, Power, and the Transformation of the Creek Indians, 1773–1816.* Cambridge University Press, 1999.

Slaughter, Thomas P. *Exploring Lewis and Clark: Reflections on Men and Wilderness.* New York: Vintage Press, 2004.

Document 48

LETTER FROM WILLIAM CLARK TO THOMAS JEFFERSON (APRIL 3, 1805)

Introduction: Sending the Journals to the President

In the box to Thomas Jefferson were copies of the journals written up to that point by Lewis and Clark in particular. Clark admits in this cover letter to Jefferson that there are mistakes, as much of the journal is in note form. But once again Lewis and Clark were doing exactly what Jefferson wanted: this time sending back the journals in case anything should happen to them on the voyage.

Fort Mandan April the 3rd. 1805.

SIR

It being the wish of Captain Lewis, I take the liberty to send you, for your own perusal the notes which I have taken in the form of a journal in their original state. you will readily perceive in reading over those notes, that many parts are incorrect. owing to the variety of information received at different times,

I most sincerely wish that leasure had permitted me to offer them in a more correct form.

Receive I pray you my unfained acknowledgements for your friendly recollection of me in your letters to my friend and companion Captn. Lewis. and be assured of the sincere regard with which I have the honor to be.

Your most obedient and Humble Servent

WM CLARK

Source: "To Thomas Jefferson from William Clark, 3 April 1805," in Thwaites, Reuben Gold, ed. *Original Journals of the Lewis and Clark Expedition, 1804–1806.* Volume 7. New York: Dodd, Mead & Company, 1905, 313.

Further Reading

Allen, John Logan. *Passage through the Garden: Lewis and Clark and the Image of the American Northwest.* Urbana: University of Illinois Press, 1975.

Botkin, Daniel. *Our Natural History, The Lessons of Lewis and Clark.* Oxford University Press, 2004.

Brodhead, Micheal. "The Military Naturalist: A Lewis and Clark Heritage." *We Proceeded On,* vol. 9, no. 4 (November 1983).

Burroughs, Raymond Darwin. *The Natural History of the Lewis and Clark Expedition.* East Lansing: Michigan State University Press, 1961.

Cutright, Paul Russell. *Lewis and Clark: Pioneering Naturalists.* Urbana: University of Illinois Press, 1969 (reprinted by University of Nebraska, 1989).

Gibbon, Guy. *The Sioux: The Dakota and Lakota Nations.* Wiley-Blackwell, 2002.

Jenkinson, Clay. *The Character of Meriwether Lewis in the Wilderness.* The Dakota Institute, 2011.

Nelson, W. Dale. *Interpreters with Lewis and Clark: The Story of Sacagawea and Toussaint Charbonneau.* University of North Texas Press, 2004.

Document 49

LETTER FROM MERIWETHER LEWIS TO THOMAS JEFFERSON. FORT MANDAN, NORTH DAKOTA (APRIL 7, 1805)

Introduction: A Report on the Trip So Far

Lewis wrote this cheerful and optimistic letter to Jefferson and sent it back to St. Louis with the barge. Here he explains that he is sending a variety of specimens of earth and various minerals as well as 60 different plants. Each of these had been dated as to when and where they were found. Each place they were found can be seen from the map of the Missouri that Lewis had created and had been sent to secretary of war, Henry Dearborn. Lewis also explains in the letter that he has sent Dearborn a full report on each of the Native people he has met. He also tells Jefferson that Captain Clark's journals are going back to D.C. at this time.

Lewis then explains that his group now consists of 33 people, including interpreters, and that they plan to travel in six canoes and two pirogues, about 15 to 20 miles a day. He also explains that they will need horses from the "Snake People" (Hidatsa). He comments that everyone is in good health and optimistic in spirit and that while they will not complete their journey in 1805 but he can expect him in Monticello in 1806.

Fort Mandan, April 7th. 1805.

DEAR SIR

Herewith inclosed you will receive an invoice of certain articles, which I have forwarded to you from this place. among other articles, you will observe by reference to the invoice, 67. specimens of earths, salts and minerals; and 60 specimens of plants: these are accompanyed by their rispective labels expressing the days on which obtained, places where found, and also their virtues and properties when known. by means of these labels, reference may be made to the Chart of the Missouri forwarded to the Secretary at War, on which, the encampment of each day has been carefully marked; thus the places at which these specimens have been obtained may be easily pointed out, or again found, should any of them prove valuable to the community on further investegation. these have been forwarded with a view of their being presented to the Philosophical society of Philadelphia, in order that they may under their direction be examined or analyzed. after examining these specimens yourself, I would thank you to have a copy of their labels made out, and retained untill my return. the other articles are intended particularly for yourself, to be retained, or disposed off as you may think proper.—

You will also receive herewith inclosed a part of Capt. Clark's private journal, the other part you will find inclosed in a seperate tin box. this journal is in it's original state, and of course incorrect, but it will serve to give you the daily detales of our progress, and transactions. Capt. Clark dose not wish this journal exposed in it's present state, but has no objection, that one or more copies of it be made by some confidential person under your direction, correcting it's gramatical errors &c. indeed it is the wish of both of us, that two of those copies should bee made, if convenient, and retained untill our return; in this state there is no objection to your submitting them to the perusal of the heads of the departments, or such others as you may think proper. a copy of this journal will assist me in compiling my own for publication after my return. I shall dispatch a canoe with three, perhaps four persons, from the extreem navigable point of the Missouri, or the portage betwen this river, and the Columbia river, as either may first happen; by the return of this canoe, I shal send you my journal, and some one or two of the best of those kept by my men. I have sent a journal kept by one of the Sergeants to Capt. Stoddard, my agent at St. Louis, in order as much as possible to multiply the chances of saving something. we have encouraged our men to keep journals, and seven of them do so, to whom in this respect we give every assistance in our power.—

I have transmitted to the Secretary at War, every information relative to the geography of the country which we possess, together with a view of the Indian nations, containing information relative to them, on those points with which, I conceived it important that the government should be informed. If it could be done with propriety and convenience, I should feel myself much obliged by your having a copy taken of my dispatches to the Secretary at War, on those subjects, retaining them for me untill my return. By reference to the Musterrolls forwarded to the War Department, you will see the state of the party; in addition to which, we have two Interpreters, one negroe man, servant to Capt. Clark, one Indian woman, wife to one of the interpreters, and a Mandan man, whom we take with a view to restore peace between the Snake Indians, and those in this neighbourhood amounting in total with ourselves to 33 persons. by means of the Interpreters and Indians, we shall be enabled to converse with all the Indians that we shall probably meet with on the Missouri.—

I have forwarded to the Secretary at War, my public Accounts rendered up to the present day. they have been much longer delayed than I had any idea that they would have been, when we departed from the Illinois, but this delay, under the circumstances which I was compelled to act, has been unavoidable. The provision perogue and her crew, could not have been dismissed in time to have returned to St. Louis last fall without evidently in my opinion, hazarding the fate of the enterprise in which I am engaged, and I therefore did not hesitate to prefer the sensure that I may have incurred by the detention of these papers, to that of risking in any degree the success of the expedition. to me, the detention of those papers have formed a serious source of disquiet and anxiety; and the recollection of your particular charge to me on this subject, has made it still more poignant. I am fully aware of the inconvenience which must have arrisen to the War Department, from the want of these vouchers previous to the last session of Congress, but how to divert it was out of my power to devise.—

From this place we shall send the barge and crew early tomorrow morning with orders to proceed as expeditiously as possible to St. Louis, by her we send our dispatches, which I trust will get safe to hand. Her crew consists of ten ablebodied men well armed and provided with a sufficient stock of provisions to last them to St. Louis. I have but little doubt but they will be fired on by the Siouxs; but they have pledged themselves to us that they will not yeald while there is a man of them living.

Our baggage is all embarked on board six small canoes and two perogues; we shall set out at the same moment that we dispatch the barge. one or perhaps both of these perogues we shall leave at the falls of the Missouri, from whence we intend continuing our voyage in the canoes and a perogue of skins, the frame of which was prepared at Harper's ferry. this perogue is now in a situation which will enable us to prepare it in the course of a few hours. as our vessels are now small and the current of the river much more moderate, we calculate on traveling at the rate of 20 or 25 miles per day as far as the falls of the Missouri. beyond this point, or the first range of rocky Mountains situated about 100 miles further, any calculations with rispect to our daily progress, can be little more than bare conjecture. the circumstance of the Snake Indians possessing large quantities of horses, is much in our favour, as by means of horses, the transportation of our baggage will be rendered easy and expeditious over land, from the Missouri, to the Columbia river. should this river not prove navigable where we first meet with it, our present intention is, to continue our march by land down the river untill it becomes so, or to the Pacific Ocean. The map, which has been forwarded to the Secretary at War, will give you the idea we entertain of the connection of these rivers, which has been formed from the corresponding testemony of a number of Indians who have visited that country, and who have been seperately and carefully examined on that subject, and we therefore think it entitled to some degree of confidence. Since our arrival at this place we have subsisted principally on meat, with which our guns have supplyed us amply, and have thus been enabled to reserve the parched meal, portable soup, and a considerable proportion of pork and flour, which we had intended for the more difficult parts of our voyages. if Indian information can be credited, the vast quantity of game with which the country abounds through which we are to pass leaves us but little to apprehend from the want of food.—

We do not calculate on completeing our voyage within the present year, but expect to reach the Pacific Ocean, and return, as far as the head of the Missouri, or perhaps to this place before winter. You may therefore expect me to meet you at Montochello in September 1806.—

On our return we shal probably pass down the yellow stone river, which from Indian informations, waters one of the fairest portions of this continent.

I can foresee no material or probable obstruction to our progress, and entertain therefore the most sanguine hopes of complete success. As to myself individually I never enjoyed a more perfect state of good health, than I have since we commenced our voyage. my inestimable friend and companion Capt. Clark has also enjoyed good health generally. At this moment every individual of the party are in good health, and excellent sperits; zealously attached to the enterprise, and anxious to proceed; not a whisper of discontent or murmur is to be heard among them; but all in unison, act with the most perfect harmony. with such men I have every thing to hope, and but little to fear.

Be so good as to present my most affectionate regard to all my friends, and be assured of the sincere and unalterable attachment of.

Your most Obt. Servt.

MERIWETHER LEWIS CAPT.
1ST. US. REGT. INFTY.

Source: Thwaites, Reuben Gold, ed. *Original Journals of the Lewis and Clark Expedition, 1804–1806.* Volume 7. New York: Dodd, Mead & Company, 1905, 318–321.

Further Reading

Bedini, Silvio. *Thomas Jefferson: Statesman of Science.* New York: Macmillan, 1990.

Bergon, Frank, ed. *The Journals of Lewis and Clark.* New York: Penguin Press, 1989.

Betts, Robert. *In Search of York: The Slave Who Went to the Pacific with Lewis and Clark.* Denver: University of Colorado Press, 2002.

Botkin, Daniel. *Our Natural History, The Lessons of Lewis and Clark.* Oxford University Press, 2004.

Duncan, Dayton and Ken Burns. *Lewis and Clark: The Journey of the Corps of Discovery: An Illustrated History.* New York: Alfred A. Knopf, 1997.

Gutzman, Kevin. *Thomas Jefferson—Revolutionary: A Radical's Struggle to Remake America.* New York: St. Martin's Press, 2017.

Saunt, Claudio. *A New Order of Things: Property, Power, and the Transformation of the Creek Indians, 1773–1816.* Cambridge University Press, 1999.

Slaughter, Thomas P. *Exploring Lewis and Clark: Reflections on Men and Wilderness.* New York: Vintage Press, 2004.

Document 50

THE CORPS LEAVE FORT MANDAN (APRIL 7, 1805)

Introduction: They Proceeded West

On April 7, the keelboat returned to St. Louis under the command of Corporal Richard Warfington. Included in the group who returned to St. Louis were Moses Reed, who had been found guilty of desertion, and John Newman, who had asked to continue on as part of the expedition but had been refused. The trip upstream had taken 173 days, while the return trip took a mere 47.

The same day, the Corps, which were now expanded to include Charbonneau, Sacagawea, and Jean Baptiste, set out west, leaving Fort Mandan behind and beginning to travel through North Dakota and into Montana.

Meriwether Lewis, who writes his journal for the first time since September 17, 1804, describes this day as one of the happiest in his life. He gives a full list of everyone who is leaving Fort Mandan as part of the expedition and explains that they are now traveling using six small canoes and two pirogues, jokingly comparing the fleet to that of Columbus or Captain Cook, suggesting both the optimism and the spirit of adventure he was feeling at this moment. Lewis describes the tent where Lewis, Clark, the two interpreters, Sacagawea, and Jean Baptiste sleep, which is made of buffalo skin, and is erected with a series of poles.

Having on this day at 4 P.M. completed every arrangement necessary for our departure, we dismissed the barge and crew with orders to return without loss of time to S. Louis, a small canoe with two French hunters accompanyed the barge; these men had assended the missouri with us the last year as engages. The barge crew consisted of six soldiers and two Frenchmen; two Frenchmen and a Ricara Indian also take their passage in her as far as the Ricara Vilages, at which place we expect Tiebeau to embark with his peltry who in that case will make an addition of two, perhaps four men to the crew of the barge. We gave Richard Warfington, a discharged Corpl., the charge of the Barge and crew, and confided to his care likewise our dispatches to the government, letters to our private friends, and a number of articles to the President of the United States. One of the Frenchmen by the name of Gravline an honest discrete man and an excellent boat-man is imployed to conduct the barge as a pilot; we have therefore every hope that the barge and with her our dispatches will arrive safe at St. Louis. Mr. Gravlin who speaks the Ricaralanguage extremely well, has been imployed to conduct a few of the Recara Chiefs to the seat of government who have promised us to decend in the barge to St. Liwis with that view.—

At same moment that the Barge departed from Fort Mandan, Capt. Clark embaked with our party and proceeded up the river. as I had used no exercise for several weeks, I determined to talk on shore as far as our encampment of this evening; accordingly I continued my walk on the N. side of the River about six miles, to the upper Village of the Mandans, and called on the Black Cat or Pose cop'se há, the great chief of the Mandans; he was not as home; I rested myself a minutes, and finding that the party had not arrived I returned about 2 miles and joined them at their encampment on the N. side of the river opposite the lower Mandan village. Our party now consisted of the following Individuals. Sergts. John Ordway, Nathaniel Prior, & Patric Gass; Privates, William Bratton, John Colter, Reubin, and Joseph Fields, John Shields, George Gibson, George Shannon, John Potts, John Collins, Joseph Whitehouse, Richard Windsor, Alexander Willard, Hugh Hall, Silas Goodrich, Robert Frazier, Crouzatt, John Baptiest la Page, Francis Labiech, Hue McNeal, William Werner, Thomas P. Howard, Peter Wiser, and John B. Thompson.—

Interpreters, George Drewyer and Tauasant Charbono also a Black man by the name of York, servant to Capt. Clark, an Indian Woman wife to Charbono with a young child, and a Mandan man who had promised us to accompany us as far as the Snake Indians with a view to bring about a good understanding and friendly intercourse between that nation and his own, the Minetares and Ahwahharways.

Our vessels consisted of six small canoes, and two large perogues. This little fleet altho' not quite so rispectable as those of Columbus or Capt. Cook were still viewed by us with as much pleasure as those deservedly famed adventurers ever beheld theirs; and I dare say with quite as much anxiety for their safety and preservation. we were now about to penetrate a country at least two thousand miles in width, on which the foot of civillized man had never trodden; the good or evil it had in store for us was for experiment yet to determine, and these little vessells contained every article by which we were to expect to subsist or defend ourselves. however as this the state of mind in which we are, generally gives the colouring to events, when the immagination is suffered to wander into futurity, the picture which now presented itself to me was a most pleasing one. entertaing as I do, the most confident hope of succeading in a voyage which had formed a daling project of mine for the last ten years, I could but esteem this moment of my departure as among the most happy of my life. The party are in excellent health and sperits, zealously attached to the enterprise, and anxious to proceed; not a whisper of murmur or discontent to be heard among them, but all act in unison, and with the most perfect harmony. I took an early supper this evening and went to bed. Capt. Clark myself the two Interpretters and the woman and child sleep in a tent of dressed skins. this tent is in the Indian stile, formed of a number of dressed Buffaloe skins sewed together with sniues. it is cut in such manner that when foalded double it forms the quarter of a circle, and is left open at one side where it may be attached or loosened at pleasure by strings which are sewed to its sides to the purpose. to erect this tent, a parsel of ten or twelve poles are provided, fore or five of which are attatched together at one end, they are then elivated and their lower extremities are spread in a circular manner to a width proportionate to the demention of the lodge, in the same position orther poles are leant against those, and the leather is then thrown over them forming a conic figure.

Source: Thwaites, Reuben Gold, ed. *Original Journals of the Lewis and Clark Expedition, 1804–1806.* Volume 1. New York: Dodd, Mead & Company, 1904, 283–285.

Sunday 7th. The men returned and four of the Rickarees with them. The commanding officers held a conversation with these Indians; and they concluded that some of them would go down in the boat from their village to St. Louis. About 5 o'clock in the afternoon we left fort Mandans in good spirits. Thirty one men and a woman went up the river and thirteen returned down it in the boat. We had two periogues and six canoes, and proceeded about four miles, and encamped opposite the first Mandan village, on the North side.

Source: Journals of Patrick Gass. Chicago: A.C. McClurg, 1904.

Further Reading

Burroughs, Raymond Darwin. *The Natural History of the Lewis and Clark Expedition.* East Lansing: Michigan State University Press, 1961.

Cutright, Paul Russell. *Lewis and Clark: Pioneering Naturalists.* Urbana: University of Illinois Press, 1969 (reprinted by University of Nebraska, 1989).

Duncan, Dayton and Ken Burns. *Lewis and Clark: The Journey of the Corps of Discovery: An Illustrated History.* New York: Alfred A. Knopf, 1997.

Ostler, Jeffrey. *The Plains Sioux and U.S. Colonialism from Lewis and Clark to Wounded Knee.* Cambridge: Cambridge University Press, 2004.

Saunt, Claudio. *A New Order of Things: Property, Power, and the Transformation of the Creek Indians, 1773–1816.* Cambridge University Press, 1999.

Slaughter, Thomas P. *Exploring Lewis and Clark: Reflections on Men and Wilderness.* New York: Vintage Press, 2004.

Document 51

McCONE COUNTY, MONTANA (MAY 5, 1805)

Introduction: Grizzly Bears

Just about a month after the Corps left Fort Mandan, they were now in what is present-day McCone County, in northeast Montana. It was here on May 5 that the expedition encountered a grizzly bear for the first time. They had been told about such an animal but were skeptical about its existence, believing that the Natives were exaggerating. But now having found one and killed it, they were able to get measurements of the animal and to study it in detail. As well as being of scientific interest, they also used various parts of the animal to eat and to use as clothes on the trip.

Ordway in his journal entry is careful to detail many aspects of the bear—noting its age, based on the bear's claws. But the physical enormity is worth noting here, as it took several men to get the bear into a boat.

May 5, 1805

A fine morning I walked on shore untill 8 A M when we halted for breakfast and in the course of my walk killed a deer which I carried about a mile and a half to the river, it was in good order. soon after seting out the rudder irons of the white perogue were broken by her runing fowl on a sawyer, she was however refitted in a few minutes with some tugs of raw hide and nales. as usual saw a great quantity of game today; Buffaloe Elk and goats or Antelopes feeding in every direction; we kill whatever we wish, the buffaloe furnish us with fine veal and fat beef, we also have venison and beaver tales when we wish them; the flesh of the Elk and goat are less esteemed, and certainly are inferior. we have not been able to take any fish for some time past. The country is as yesterday beatifull in the extreme.—

saw the carcases of many Buffaloe lying dead along the shore partially devoured by the wolves and bear. saw a great number of white brant also the common brown brant, geese of the common kind and a small species of geese which differ considerably from the common canadian goose; their neck head and beak are considerably thicker shorter and larger than the other in proportion to it's size, they are also more than a third smaller, and their note more like that of the brant or a young goose which has not perfectly acquired his notes, in all other rispects they are the same colour habits and the number of feathers in the tale, they frequently also ascociate with the large geese when in flocks, but never saw them pared off with the large or common goose. The white brant ascociate in very large flocks, they do not appear to be mated or pared off as if they intended to raise their young in this quarter, I therefore doubt whether they reside here during the summer for that purpose. this bird is about the size of the common brown brant or two thirds of the common goose, it is not so long by six inches from point to point of the wings when extended as the other; the beak head and neck are also larger and stronger; their beak [and] legs and feet are of a redish or fleshcoloured white. the eye is of moderate size, the puple of a deep sea green incircled with a ring of yellowish brown. it has sixteen feathers of equal length in the tale; their note differs but little from the common brant, their flesh much the same, and in my opinion preferable to the goose, the flesh is dark. they are entirely of a beatifull pure white except the large feathers of the 1st and second joints of the wings which are jut black. form and habits are the same with the other brant; they sometimes ascociate and form one common flock. Capt Clark found a den of young wolves in the course of his walk today and also saw a great number of those anamals; they are very abundant in this quarter, and are of two species the small woolf or burrowing dog of the praries are the inhabitants almost invariably of the open plains; they usually ascociate in bands of ten or twelve sometimes more and burrow near some pass or place much frequented by game; not being able alone to take deer or goat they are rarely ever found alone but hunt in bands; they frequently watch and seize their prey near their burrows; in these burrows they raise their young and to them they also resort when pursued; when a person approaches them they frequently bark, their note being precisely that of the small dog. they are of an intermediate size between that of the fox and dog, very active fleet and delicately formed; the [years] ears large erect and pointed the head long and pointed more like that of the fox; tale long [and bushey]; the hair and fur also resembles the fox tho' is much coarser and inferior. they are of a pale redish brown colour. the eye of a deep sea green colour small and piercing. their tallons are reather longer than those of the ordinary wolf or that common to the atlantic states, none of which are to be found in this quarter, nor I believe above the river Plat.—The large woolf found here is not as large as those of the atlantic states. they were lower and [heaver] thicker made shorter leged. their colour which is not effected by the seasons, is a grey or blackish brown and every intermediate shade from that to a creen [cream] coloured white; these wolves resort the woodlands and are also found in the plains, but never take refuge in the ground or burrow so far as I have been able to inform myself. we scarcely see a gang of buffaloe without observing a parsel of those faithfull shepherds on their skirts in readiness to take care of the mamed & wounded. the large wolf never barks, but howls as those of the atlantic states do. Capt. Clark and Drewyer killed the largest brown bear this evening which we have yet seen. it was a most tremendious looking anamal, and extreemly hard to kill notwithstanding he had five balls through his lungs and five others in various parts he swam more than half the distance across the river to a sandbar & it was at least twenty minutes before he died; he did not attempt to attact, but fled and made the most tremendous roaring from the moment he was shot. We had no means of weighing this monster; Capt. Clark thought he would weigh 500 lbs. for my own part I think the estimate too small by 100 lbs. he measured 8 Feet 7½ Inches from the nose to the extremety of the hind feet, 5 F. 10½ Inch arround the breast, 1 F. 11 I. arround the middle of the arm, & 3 F. 11 I. arround the neck; his tallons which were five in number on each foot were 4⅜ Inches in length. he was in good order, we therefore divided him among the party and made them boil the oil and put it in a cask for future uce; the oil is as hard as hogs lard when cool, much more so than that of the black bear. this bear differs from the common black bear in several respects; it's tallons are much longer and more blont, it's tale shorter, it's hair which is of a redish or bey brown, is longer thicker and finer than that of the black bear; his liver lungs and heart are much larger even in proportion with his size; the heart particularly was as large as that of a large Ox. his maw was also ten times the size of black bear, and was filled with flesh and fish. his testicles were pendant from the belly and placed four inches assunder in seperate bags or pouches.—this animal also feeds on roots and almost every species of wild fruit.

The party killed two Elk and a Buffaloe today, and my dog caught a goat, which he overtook by superior fleetness, the goat it must be understood was with young and extreemly poor. a great number of these goats are devowered by the wolves and bear at this season when they are poor and passing the river from S. W. to

N. E. they are very inactive and easily taken in the water, a man can out swim them with great ease; the Indians take them in great numbers in the river at this season and in autumn when they repass to the S. W.

Source: Thwaites, Reuben Gold, ed. *Original Journals of the Lewis and Clark Expedition, 1804–1806.* Volume 1. New York: Dodd, Mead & Company, 1904, 369–373.

Clear and pleasant. we Set off eairly proceeded on. one hunter who [s]tay on the S. Shore all night came to us at breakfast time. had killed two buffaloe Calfs which we took on board. we proceeded on. passed bottoms of timber on each Side. passed a large handsom plains on the N. S. where we saw a great nomber of buffaloe and white geese. [6] we halted for to dine about 2 o.C. on the S. S. at a bottom of timber where we Saw buffaloe and Goats our officers gave the party a half a Gill of ardent Spirits. Jo. Fields who was taken Sick yesterday is some worse to day. jest as I went Set off with the canoe the bank fell in & all most filled it. we directly took out the Sand & bailed out the water and proceeded on towards evening Capt. Clark and Several more of the party killed a verry large bair which the natives and the french tradors call white but all of the kind that we have seen is of a light brown only owing to the climate as we suppose. we shot him as he was Swimming the River. the place where he dyed was Shallow or perhaps he would have Sunk to the bottom. with the assistance of Several men was got on board a perogue and took him to the Shore on N. S. and dressed it after taking the measure of him. he was verry old the tushes most wore out as well as his claws. the measure of the brown bair is as follows round the head is 3 feet 5 Inches. do the neck 3 feet 11 Inches do the breast 5 feet 10½ Inches. do the middle of the arm 1 foot 11 Inches. the length from the nose to the extremity of the hind toe is 8 feet 7½ Inches. the length of tallons better than four feet [inches]. we found a Cat fish in him which he had Eat. we Camped and rendered out about 6 gallons of the greese of the brown bair. he was judged to weigh about 4 hundred after dressed. one of the party went out and killed an Elk, and Saw another brown bair. we Came 16 miles to day before we killed the brown bair. we Sailed considerable in the course of the day with an East wind.

Source: The Journals of Captain Meriwether Lewis and Sergeant John Ordway: Kept on the Expedition of Western Exploration, 1803–1806. Madison, WI: The Society, 1916.

Further Reading

Allen, John Logan. *Passage through the Garden: Lewis and Clark and the Image of the American Northwest.* Urbana: University of Illinois Press, 1975.

Botkin, Daniel. *Our Natural History, The Lessons of Lewis and Clark.* Oxford University Press, 2004.

Brodhead, Micheal. "The Military Naturalist: A Lewis and Clark Heritage." *We Proceeded On,* vol. 9, no. 4 (November 1983).

Burroughs, Raymond Darwin. *The Natural History of the Lewis and Clark Expedition.* East Lansing: Michigan State University Press, 1961.

Cutright, Paul Russell. *Lewis and Clark: Pioneering Naturalists*. Urbana: University of Illinois Press, 1969 (reprinted by University of Nebraska, 1989).

Gibbon, Guy. *The Sioux: The Dakota and Lakota Nations*. Wiley-Blackwell, 2002.

Jenkinson, Clay. *The Character of Meriwether Lewis in the Wilderness*. The Dakota Institute, 2011.

Nelson, W. Dale. *Interpreters with Lewis and Clark: The Story of Sacagawea and Toussaint Charbonneau*. University of North Texas Press, 2004.

Document 52

MONTANA (MAY 19, 1805)

Introduction: Seaman the Dog

While in Pittsburgh waiting for the boat to be built, Meriwether Lewis bought a New-foundland dog for $20, which was considered a huge amount of money in 1805. The dog was named Seaman, went on the expedition, and seemed to have survived the whole trip, but like all the humans who went on the trip, Seaman suffered because of mosquitoes and had its share of injuries. The dog was used often to fetch the game killed by the men, and it accompanied Lewis on his regular walks on the shoreline.

On Sunday, May 19, 1805, while going through Montana, Seaman went to get a wounded beaver and was instead attacked and bitten by the beaver. Seaman was bitten in the back leg, and an artery was severed. Lewis who had been trained before the trip both by his mother and by Benjamin Rush in basic medical training was now treating his dog. They had brought a tourniquet with them on the trip, so it is probable that this was used on the dog.

Somehow with both Lewis and Clark attending to the dog, they managed to stop the blood flowing, though the risk of infection was high. Yet, Seaman, despite the blood loss, managed to heal without an infection.

Seaman must have healed quickly, as about 10 days after this, everyone in the camp was woken by the dog barking. There was a large buffalo about to come into the camp. Such an animal, usually about 1,400 pounds, could have destroyed the camp and injured and/or killed many of the Corps. With the warning from Seaman, its barking and the noise created by the men, the buffalo changed its path, and the men, camp, and equipment were all safe. Seaman saved the expedition.

May 19, 1805

The last night was disagreeably could; we were unable to set out untill 8 oclock A. M. in consequence of a heavy fogg, which obscured the river in such a manner that we could not see our way; this is the first we have experienced in any thing like so great a degree; there was also a fall of due last evening, which is the second we have experienced since we have entered this extensive open country. at eight we set out and proceeded as yesterday by means of the cord principally, the hills are high and the country similar to that of yesterday. Capt Clark walked on shore with two of the hunters and killed a brown bear; notwithstanding that it was shot through the heart it ran as it's usual pace near a quarter of a mile before it fell. one of the party wounded a beaver, and my dog as usual swam in to catch it; the beaver bit him through the hind leg and cut the artery; it was with great difficulty that I could stop the blood; I fear it will yet prove fatal to him. on Capt. Clark's return he informed me that he had from the top of one of the adjacent hights discovered the entrance of a large stream which discharged itself into the Missouri on the Lard. side distant 6 or seven miles; from the same place he also saw a range of Mountains, bearing W. distant 40 or 50 miles; they appeared to proceed in a S. S. W. direction; the N. N. E. extremity of these mountains appeared abrupt.

Source: Thwaites, Reuben Gold, ed. *Original Journals of the Lewis and Clark Expedition, 1804–1806.* Volume 1. New York: Dodd, Mead & Company, 1904, 47–48.

Further Reading

Cutright, Paul Russell. "Meriwether Lewis's 'Coloring of Events.'" *We Proceeded On,* vol. 11, no. 1 (February 1985).

Danisi, Thomas C. and Robert Moore. *Uncovering the Truth about Meriwether Lewis.* New York: Prometheus Book, 2001.

Dillon, Richard. *Meriwether Lewis: A Biography.* New York: Coward-McCann, 1965.

Jenkinson, Clay. *The Character of Meriwether Lewis in the Wilderness.* The Dakota Institute, 2011.

Ronda, James P. *Lewis and Clark among the Indians.* Lincoln: University of Nebraska Press, 1984.

Slaughter, Thomas P. *Exploring Lewis and Clark: Reflections on Men and Wilderness.* New York: Vintage Press, 2004.

Smith, Ronald. *The Captain's Dog.* New York: HMH Books, 2008.

Stroud, Patricia. *Bitterroot: The Life and Death of Meriwether Lewis.* Philadelphia: University of Pennsylvania Press, 2018.

Document 53

THE JUDITH RIVER (MAY 29, 1805)

Introduction: Naming a River with Thoughts of Home

On May 29, William Clark named a tributary of the Missouri River, the Judith River. Judith was the name of Julia Hancock, whom Clark had met a number of years before, and the person he hoped to marry. Up to now, her father, Colonel George Hancock, a Revolutionary War hero, had refused Clark permission to even court his daughter. One of the reasons that Hancock gave for his refusal was Clark's lack of money, and many historians have wondered if one of the reasons why Clark agreed so readily to go on the *voyage with Lewis was to get money and fame and to persuade Colonel Hancock that Clark was worthy of his daughter.*

Last night we were all allarmed by a large buffaloe Bull, which swam over from the opposite shore and coming along side of the white perogue, climbed over it to land, he then alarmed ran up the bank in full speed directly towards the fires, and was within 18 inches of the heads of some of the men who lay sleeping before the centinel could allarm him or make him change his course, still more alarmed, he now took his direction immediately towards our lodge, passing between 4 fires and within a few inches of the heads of one range of the men as they yet lay sleeping, when he came near the tent, my dog saved us by causing him to change his course a second time, which he did by turning a little to the right, and was quickly out of sight, leaving us by this time all in an uproar with our guns in or hands, enquiring of each other the case of the alarm, which after a few moments was explained by the centinel; we were happy to find no one hirt. The next morning we found that the buffaloe in passing the perogue had trodden on a rifle, which belonged to Capt. Clark's black man, who had negligently left her in the perogue, the rifle was much bent, he had also broken the spindle, pivit, and shattered the stock of one of the bluntderbushes on board, with this damage I felt well content, happey indeed, that we had sustaned no further injury. it appears that the white perogue, which contains our most valuable stores, is attended by some evil gennii. This morning we set out at an early hour and proceded as usual by the Chord. at the distance of 2½ miles passed a handsome river which discharged itself on the Lard. side, I walked on shore and acended this river about a mile and a half in order to examine it. I found this river about 100 yds. wide from bank to bank, the water occupying about 75 yard. the bed was formed of gravel and mud with some sand; it appeared to contain much more water as [NB: than] the Muscle-Shell river, was more rappid but equally navigable; there were no large stone or rocks in it's bed to obstruct the navigation; the banks were low yet appeared seldom to overflow; the water of this River is [NB: clearer much] than any we have met with great abundance of the Argalia or Bighorned animals in the high country through which this river passes Cap. C who assended this R. much higher than I did has call it *Judieths* River.

Source: Thwaites, Reuben Gold, ed. *Original Journals of the Lewis and Clark Expedition, 1804–1806.* Volume 4. New York: Dodd, Mead & Company, 1905.

Further Reading

Buckley, Jay H. *William Clark: Indian Diplomat.* University of Oklahoma Press, 2008.

Foley, William. *Wilderness Journey: The Life of William Clark.* University of Missouri, 2004.

Holmberg, James. *Dear Brother: Letters of William Clark to Jonathan Clark.* New Haven, CT: Yale University Press, 2002.

Jones, Landon. *William Clark and the Shaping of the West.* Bison Books, 2009.

Turner, Erin H. *It Happened on the Lewis and Clark Expedition.* Guilford, CT: Globe Pequot.

Document 54

MARIAS RIVER, MONTANA (JUNE 3, 1805)

Introduction: Which Way to the Great Falls?

From June 2 to June 12, the group stayed at a fork in the Marias River in Montana. The Mandans had made no mention of a fork in the river, and the question was, which of these rivers was the Missouri and therefore the way to the Great Falls?

The doubt was caused by the fact that the south fork seemed to be wider than the north, but the north fork seemed muddy and was like the water they had been traveling on since they left Fort Mandan. While Lewis and Clark favored the south fork, the men preferred the north. In the end, Cark traveled 45 miles on the south fork, while Lewis went nearly 80 miles on the north fork. When Lewis returned, he reported that the north fork went too far north and could not be a route west, while Clark realized the south fork traveled west rather than south.

It was not until they heard the Great Falls that they all realized that the correct decision had been made.

On June 12, they set out south, with Lewis and Clark hoping they had made the correct decision. Complicating any decision is the fact that many of the group, including Sacagawea, were sick. Clark gave her a Thunderbolt Pill, while another person on the trip had a sore tooth. As no one was convinced about the decision, Lewis scouted ahead, and on June 13, 1805, Lewis heard and saw the Great Falls of the Missouri River. It was not the easy trip they had thought; instead, it was a slow, tough 18-mile hike over almost impossible terrain.

June 3, 1805

This morning early we passed over and formed a camp on the point formed by the junction of the two large rivers. here in the course of the day I continued my observations as are above stated. An interesting question was now to be determined; which of these rivers was the Missouri, or that river which the Minnetares call *Amahte Arz zha* or Missouri, and which they had discribed to us as approaching very near to the Columbia river. to mistake the stream at this period of the season, two months of the traveling season having now elapsed, and to ascend such stream to the rocky Mountain or perhaps much further before we could inform ourselves whether it did approach the Columbia or not, and then be obliged to return and take the other stream would not only loose us the whole of this season but would probably so dishearten the party that it might defeat the expedition altogether. convinced we were that the utmost circumspection and caution was necessary in deciding on the stream to be taken. to this end an investigation of both streams was the first thing to be done; to learn their widths, debths, comparitive rappidity of their courants and thence the comparitive bodies of water furnished by each; accordingly we dispatched two light canoes with three men in each up those streams; [we also sent out several small parties by land with instructions to penetrate the country as far as they conveniently can permiting themselves time to return this evening and indeavour if possible to discover the distant bearing of those rivers by ascending the rising grounds. between the time of my A. M. and meridian Capt. C & myself stroled out to the top of the hights in the fork of these rivers from whence we had an extensive and most inchanting view; the country in every derection around us was one vast plain in which innumerable herds of Buffalow were seen attended by their shepperds the wolves; the solatary antelope which now had their young were distributed over it's face; some herds of Elk were also seen; the verdure perfectly cloathed the ground, the weather was pleasent and fair; to the South we saw a range of lofty mountains which we supposed to be a continuation of the S. Mountains, streching themselves from S. E. to N. W. terminating abbrubtly about S. West from us; these were partially covered with snow; behind these Mountains and at a great distance, a second and more lofty range of mountains appeared to strech across the country in the same direction with the others, reaching from West, to the N of N. W., where their snowey tops lost themselves beneath the horizon. this last range was perfectly covered with snow.] the direction of the rivers could be seen but little way, soon loosing the break of their channels, to our view, in the common plain. on our return to camp we boar a little to the left and discovered a handsome little river falling into the N. fork on Lard. side about 1½ ms. above our camp. this little river has as much timber in it's bottoms as either of the larger streams. there are a great number of prickley pears in these plains; the Choke cherry grows here in abundance both in the river bottoms and in the steep ravenes along the river bluffs. saw the yellow and red courants, not yet ripe; also the goosberry which begins to ripen; the wild rose which grows here in great abundance in the bottoms of all these rivers is now in full bloom, and adds not a little to the beaty of the cenery. we took the width of the two rivers, found the left hand or S. fork 372 yards and the N. fork 200. The noth fork is deeper than the other but it's courant not so swift; it's waters run in the same boiling and roling manner which has uniformly characterized the Missouri throughout it's whole course so far; it's waters are of a whitish brown colour very thick and terbid, also characteristic of the Missouri; while the South fork is perfectly transparent runds very rappid but with a smoth unriffled surface it's bottom composed of round and flat smooth stones like most rivers issuing from a mountainous country.

the bed of the N. fork composed of some gravel but principally mud; in short the air & character of this river is so precisely that of the missouri below that the party with very few exceptions have already pronounced the N. fork to be the Missouri; myself and Capt. C. not quite so precipitate have not yet decided but if we were to give our opinions I believe we should be in the minority, certain it is that the North fork gives the colouring matter and character which is retained from hence to the gulph of Mexico. I am confident that this river rises in and passes a great distance through an open plain country I expect that it has some of it's souces on the Eastern side of the rocky mountain South of the Saskashawan, but that it dose not penetrate the first range of these Mountains and that much the greater part of it's sources are in a northwardly direction towards the lower and middle parts of the Saskashawan in the open plains. convinced I am that if it penetrated the Rocky Mountains to any great distance it's waters would be clearer unless it should run an immence distance indeed after leaving those mountains through these level plains in order to acquire it's turbid hue. what astonishes us a little is that the Indians who appeared to be so well acquainted with the geography of this country should not have mentioned this river on wright hand if it be not the Missouri; *the river that scolds at all others,* as they call it if there is in reallity such an one, ought agreeably to their account, to have fallen in a considerable distance below, and on the other hand if this righthand or N. fork be the Missouri I am equally astonished at their not menioning the S. fork which they must have passed in order to get to those large falls which they mention on [that] the Missouri. thus have our cogitating faculties been busily employed all day.

Those who have remained at camp today have been busily engaged in dressing skins for cloathing, notwithstanding that many of them have their feet so mangled and bruised with the stones and rough ground over which they passed barefoot, that they can scarcely walk or stand; at least it is with great pain they do either. for some days past they were unable to wear their mockersons; they have fallen off considerably, but notwithstanding the difficulties past, or those which seem now to mennace us, they still remain perfectly cheerfull. In the evening the parties whom we had sent out returned agreeably to instructions. The parties who had been sent up the rivers in canoes informed that they ascended some disance and had then left their canoes and walked up the rivers a considerable distance further barely leaving themselves time to return; the North fork was not so rappid as the other and afforded the easiest navigation of course; Six [NB: 7] feet appeared to be the shallowest water of the S. Branch and 5 feet that of the N. Their accounts were by no means satisfactory nor did the information we acquired bring us nigher to the decision of our question or determine us which stream to take. Sergt. Pryor hand [had] ascended the N. fork and had taken the following courses and distances.

Sergt Gass Ascended the South Fork

Joseph and Reubin Fields reported that they had been up the South fork about 7 mes. on a streight course somewhat N of W. and that there the little river which discharges itself into the North fork just above us, was within 100 yards of the S. fork; that they came down this little river and found it a boald runing stream of about 40 yds. wide containg much timber in it's bottom, consisting of the narrow and wide leafed cottonwood with some birch and box alder undrgrowth willows rosebushes currents &c. they saw a great number of Elk on this river and some beaver. Those accounts being by no means satisfactory as to the fundamental point; Capt. C. and myself concluded to set out early the next morning with a small party each, and ascend these rivers untill we could perfectly satisfy ourselves of the one, which it would be most expedient for us to take on our main journey to the Pacific. accordingly it was agreed that I should ascend the right hand fork and he the left. I gave orders to Sergt. Pryor Drewyer, Shields, Windsor, Cruzatte and La Pageto hold themselves in readiness to accompany me in the morning. Capt. Clark also selected Reubin & Joseph Fields, Sergt. Gass, Shannon and his black man York, to accompany him. we agreed to go up those rivers one day and a halfs march or further if it should appear necessary to satisfy us more fully of the point in question. the hunters killed 2 Buffaloe, 6 Elk and 4 deer today. the evening proved cloudy. we took a drink of grog this evening and gave the men a dram, and made all matters ready for an early departure in the morning. I had now my sack and blanket happerst in readiness to swing on my back, which is the first time in my life that I had ever prepared a burthen of this kind, and I am fully convinced that it will not be the last. I take my Octant with me also, this I confide La Page.

Source: Thwaites, Reuben Gold, ed. *Original Journals of the Lewis and Clark Expedition, 1804–1806.* Volume 2. New York: Dodd, Mead & Company, 1904, 112–117.

Further Reading

Frank Bergon, ed. *The Journals of Lewis and Clark.* New York: Penguin Press, 1989, 147.

Danisli, Thomas. *Meriwether Lewis.* Prometheus Books, 2009.

Ostler, Jeffrey. *The Plains Sioux and U.S. Colonialism from Lewis and Clark to Wounded Knee.* Cambridge: Cambridge University Press, 2004.

Rogers, Ann. *Lewis and Clark in Missouri.* University of Missouri, 2002.

Ronda, James P. *Lewis and Clark among the Indians.* Lincoln: University of Nebraska Press, 1984.

Slaughter, Thomas P. *Exploring Lewis and Clark: Reflections on Men and Wilderness.* New York: Vintage Press, 2004.

Thwaites, Reuben Gold, ed. *Original Journals of the Lewis and Clark Expedition.* New York: Arno Press reprint, 1969.

Turner, Erin H. *It Happened on the Lewis and Clark Expedition.* Guilford, CT: Globe Pequot Press, 2003.

Document 55

MONTANA (JUNE 29, 1805)

Introduction: A Hailstorm Washes Away Some of the Equipment

Clark, who was exploring the prairies with York (whom he describes here as his servant and not slave), Charbonneau, Sacagawea, and Jean Baptiste, was caught in a furious hailstorm, with nowhere to shelter. The vastness and relative emptiness of the Plains made them defenseless to a storm of this size; they eventually found some shelter at a river bank, but Clark lost an important compass. When the Clark group got back to camp, he notes that the same storm had forced the others to drop everything they had and run back to the camp in an attempt to find shelter. That night there was nothing they could do about lost supplies, as the storm had created another river in the Plains.

A little rain verry early this morning after Clear, finding that the Prarie was So wet as to render it impossible to pass on to the end of the portage, deturmined to Send back to the top of the hill at the Creek for the remaining part of the baggage left at that place yesterday, leaveing one man to take care of the baggage at this place. I deturmined my Self to proceed on to the falls and take the river, according we all Set out, I took my Servent & one man Chabono our Interpreter & his Squar accompanied, Soon after I arrived at the falls, I perceived a Cloud which appeared black and threaten imediate rain, I looked out for a Shelter but Could See no place without being in great danger of being blown into the river if the wind Should prove as turbelant as it is at Some times about ¼ of a mile above the falls I obsd a Deep rivein in which was Shelveing rocks under which we took Shelter near the river and placed our guns the Compass &c. &c. under a Shelveing rock on the upper Side of the Creek, in a place which was verry Secure from rain, the first Shower was moderate accompanied with a violent wind, the effects of which we did not feel, Soon after a torrent of rain and hail fell more violent than ever I Saw before, the rain fell like one voley of water falling from the heavens and gave us time only to get out of the way of a torrent of water which was Poreing down the hill in the rivin with emence force tareing every thing before it takeing with it large rocks & mud, I took my gun & Shot pouch in my left hand, and with the right Scrambled up the hill pushing the Interpreters wife (who had her Child in her arms) before me, the Interpreter himself makeing attempts to pull up his wife by the hand much Scared and nearly without motion—we at length retched the top of the hill Safe where I found my Servent in Serch of us greatly agitated, for our wellfar—. before I got out of the bottom of the revein which was a flat dry rock when I entered it, the water was up to my waste & wet my watch, I Scrcely got out before it raised 10 feet deep with a torrent which turrouble to behold, and by the time I reached the top of the hill, at least 15 feet water, I directed the party to return to the Camp at the run as fast as possible to get to our lode where Clothes Could be got to Cover the Child whose Clothes were all lost, and the woman who was but just recovering from a Severe indispostion, and was wet and Cold, I was fearfull of a relaps I caused her as also the others of the party to take a little Spirits, which my Servent had in a Canteen, which revived verry much. on arrival at the Camp on the willow run—met the party who had returned in great Confusion to the run leaveing their loads in the Plain, the hail & wind being So large and violent in the plains, and them naked, they were much brused, and Some nearly killed one knocked down three times, and others without hats or any thing on their heads bloodey & Complained verry much; I refreshed them with a little grog—Soon after the run began to rise and rose 6 feet in a few minits—. I lost at the river in the torrent the large *Compas*, an eligant fusee, Tomahawk *Humbrallo*, Shot pouh, & horn wih powder & Ball, mockersons, & the woman lost her Childs

Bear & Clothes bedding &c.—[*X: Sah car gah we â*] The Compass is a Serious loss; as we have no other large one. The plains are So wet that we Can do nothing this evining particilarly as two deep reveins are between ourselves & Load.

Source: Thwaites, Reuben Gold, ed. *Original Journals of the Lewis and Clark Expedition, 1804–1806.* Volume 4. New York: Dodd, Mead & Company, 1905.

Further Reading

Ambrose, Stephen. *Undaunted Courage.* Urbana: University of Chicago Press, 1991.

Botkin, Daniel. *Our Natural History, The Lessons of Lewis and Clark.* Oxford University Press, 2004.

Criswell, Elijah. *Lewis and Clark: Linguistic Pioneers.* Columbia: University of Missouri Press, 1940.

Danisli, Thomas. *Meriwether Lewis.* Prometheus Books, 2009.

Dillon, Richard. *Meriwether Lewis: A Biography.* New York: Coward-McCann, 1965.

Holloway, David. *Lewis and Clark and the Crossing of North America.* New York: Saturday Review Press, 1974.

Jones, Landon Y. *William Clark and the Shaping of the West.* New York: Hill and Wang, 2004.

West, Elliot. *The Last Indian War: The Nez Perce Story.* Oxford University Press, 2011.

Document 56

MONTANA (JUNE 30, 1805)

Introduction: The Constant Dangers

Lewis was frustrated. It was three months since they left Fort Mandan, and they still had not reached the Rocky Mountains. He realized that his pledge to President Jefferson that they would meet in Virginia in September was impossible. At this rate, they would not even go back to Fort Mandan by the winter.

Lewis was also always afraid that more members of the Corps might die. Each day brought multiple dangers—from the terrain, from wild animals, and of course from the weather. Given the size of the party, the loss of even one or two people might mean failure for the whole expedition. Lewis was afraid when a group went out and did not come back on time. While Floyd was the only member of the group to die, at this stage no one knew that. So Lewis's last line in his journal entry this night reflects this fear.

On June 30, the group did return, and also on this day, the volume of buffalo was amazing. The Corps saw over 10,000. This constant awareness of the enormity of nature also seems to emphasize their littleness. While preparing and making boats and preparing for when they were to cross the Rockies, the men were constantly given work to do. Part of the reason behind this was the military notion that enlisted men could not be trusted doing nothing, and so they were always worked, always given chores to do. Part of it was also the practical nature of this group; they had to be ready to cross the Rockies when they came to the mountains, as they could not afford any delays.

One of the more interesting aspects of this journal entry is Lewis's detail about the animals he saw, in particular his description of what he referred to as a "goat-sucker" bird or hawk. Lewis's eye for detail and descriptive abilities are shown here, and this detail and writing about nature would fascinate Jefferson, among others, when Lewis returned East.

June 30, 1805

We had a heavy dew this morning which is a remarkable event. Fraizer and Whitehouse still continue their opperation of sewing the skins together. I set Shields and gass to shaving bark and Fields continued to make the cross brases. Drewyer and myself rendered a considerable quantity of tallow and cooked. I begin to be extremely impatient to be off as the season is now waisting a pace nearly three months have now elapsed since we left Fort Mandan and not yet reached the Rocky Mountains I am therefore fully preswaded that we shall not reach Fort Mandan again this season if we even return from the ocean to the Snake Indians. wherever we find timber there is also beaver; Drewyer killed two today. There are a number of large bat or goatsucker here I killed one of them and found that there was no difference between them and those common to the U' States; I have not seen the leather winged bat for some time nor is there any of the small goatsuckers in this quarter of the country. we have not the whip-poor-will either. this last is by many persons in the U' States confounded with the large goat-sucker or night-hawk as it is called in the Eastern States, and are taken for the same bird. it is true that there is a great resemblance but they are distinct species of the goatsucker. here the one exists without the other. the large goat sucker lays it's eggs in these open plains without the preperation of a nest we have found their eggs in several instances they lay only two before they set nor do I beleive that they raise more than one brood in a season; they have now just hatched their young.—This evening the bark was shaved and the leather covering for the sections were also completed and I had them put into the water, in order to toughen the bark, and prepare the leather for sewing on the sections in the morning. it has taken 28 Elk skins and 4 Buffaloe skins to complete her. the cross bars are also finished this evening; we have therefore only the way strips now to obtain in order to complete the wood work, and this I fear will be a difficult task. The party have not returned from the lower camp I am therefore fearfull that some uncommon accedent has happened.

Occurrences with Capt. Clark and Party

This morning Capt. Clark dispatched two men to kill some buffaloe, two others to the falls to surch for the articles lost yesterday, one he retained to cook and sent the others for the baggage left in the plains yesterday. the hunters soon returned loaded with meat those sent for the baggage brought it up in a few hours, he then set four men at work to make axeltrees and repare the carrages; the others he employed in conveying the baggage over the run on their sholders it having now fallent to about 3 feet water. the men complained much today of the bruises and wounds which they had received yesterday from the hail. the two men sent to the falls returned with the compas which they found covered in the mud and sand near the mouth of the rivene the other articles were irrecoverably lost. they found that part of rivene in; which Capt. C. had been seting yesterday, filled with huge rocks. at 11 A. M. Capt. Clark dispatched the party with a load of the baggage as far as the 6 miles stake, with orders to deposit it there and return with the carriages which they did accordingly. they experienced a heavy gust of wind this evening from the S. W. after which it was a fair afternoon. more buffaloe than usual were seen about their camp; Capt. C assured me that he beleives he saw at least ten thousand at one view.

Source: Thwaites, Reuben Gold, ed. *Original Journals of the Lewis and Clark Expedition, 1804–1806.* Volume 2. New York: Dodd, Mead & Company, 1904, 200–201.

Further Reading

Ambrose, Stephen. *Undaunted Courage.* Urbana: University of Chicago Press, 1991.
Botkin, Daniel. *Our Natural History, The Lessons of Lewis and Clark.* Oxford University Press, 2004.
Criswell, Elijah. *Lewis and Clark: Linguistic Pioneers.* Columbia: University of Missouri Press, 1940.
Danisli, Thomas. *Meriwether Lewis.* Prometheus Books, 2009.
Dillon, Richard. *Meriwether Lewis: A Biography.* New York: Coward-McCann, 1965.
Holloway, David. *Lewis and Clark and the Crossing of North America.* New York: Saturday Review Press, 1974.
Jones, Landon Y. *William Clark and the Shaping of the West.* New York: Hill and Wang, 2004.
West, Elliot. *The Last Indian War: The Nez Perce Story.* Oxford University Press, 2011.

Document 57

THE IRON BOAT (JULY 9, 1805)

Introduction: Lewis's Invention

In 1803, Meriwether Lewis had the federal armory in Harpers Ferry, Virginia, in today's West Virginia to work on his invention: a collapsible iron boat. The boat that had been brought along on the trip up to this point as luggage was finally needed as the river had become too shallow, and it had become clear that all their luggage and equipment was to be carried if this iron boat did not work.

Lewis had been convinced that the boat could be put together in hours, but two weeks later, the boat that had finally been put together leaked badly and could not be used. Lewis was frustrated stating that wasting any more time on trying to fix the boat was "madness," while historians have often wondered about the possible irony and perhaps anger in Clark's phrase of "our favourite boat." Was he being cynical? How angry was he with Lewis and the time they had spent on the boat?

Clear worm morning wind from the S W. Lanced the Leather boat, and found that it leaked a little; Corked Lanced & loaded the Canoes, burried our truk wheels, & made a Carsh for a Skin & a fiew papers I intend to leave here.

on trial found the leather boat would not answer without the addition of Tar which we had none of, haveing Substituted *Cole & Tallow* in its place to Stop the Seams &c. which would not answer as it Seperated from the Skins when exposed to the water and left the Skins naked & Seams exposed to the water this falire of our favoure boat was a great disapointment to us, we haveing more baggage than our Canoes would Carry. Concluded to build Canoes for to Carry them; no timber near our Camp. I deturmined to proceed on up the river to a bottom in which our hunters reported was large Trees &c.

Source: Thwaites, Reuben Gold, ed. *Original Journals of the Lewis and Clark Expedition, 1804–1806.* Volume 4. New York: Dodd, Mead & Company, 1905, 371.

The morning was fair and pleant. the Islands seem crouded with blackbirds; the young brude is now completely feathered and flying in common with the others. we corked the canoes and put them in the water and also launched the boat, she lay like a perfect cork on the water. five men would carry her with the greatest ease. I now directed seats to be fixed in her and oars to be fitted. the men loaded the canoes in readiness to depart. just at this moment a violent wind commenced and blew so hard that we were obliged to unload the canoes again; a part of the baggage in several of them got wet before it could be taken out. the wind continued violent untill late in the evening, by which time we discovered that a greater part of the composition had seperated from the skins and left the seams of the boat exposed to the water and she leaked in such manner that she would not answer. I need not add that this circumstance mortifyed me not a little; and to prevent her leaking without pich was impossible with us, and to obtain this article was equally impossible, therefore the evil was irraparable I now found that the section formed of the buffaloe hides on which some hair had been left, answered much the best purpose; this leaked but little and the parts which were well covered with hair about ⅛th of an inch in length retained the composition perfectly and remained sound and dry. from these circumstances I am preswaided, that had I formed her with buffaloe skins singed not quite as close as I had done those I employed, that she would have answered even with this composition. but to make any further experiments in our present situation seemed to me madness; the buffaloe had principally dserted us, and the season was now advancing fast. I therefore relinquished all further hope of my favorite boat and ordered her to be sunk in the water, that the skins might become soft in order the better to take her in peices tomorrow and deposite the iron fraim at this place as it could probably be of no further service to us. had I only singed my Elk skins in stead of shaving them I beleive the composition would have remained and the boat have answered; at least untill we could have reached the pine country which must be in advance of us from the pine which is brought down by the water and which is probably at no great distance where we might have supplyed ourselves with the necessary pich or gum. but it was now too late to introduce a remidy and I bid a dieu to my boat, and her expected services.—The next difficulty which presented itself was how we should convey the stores and baggage which we had purposed carrying in the boat. both Capt. Clark and myself recollected having heard the hunters mention that the bottoms of the river some few miles above us were much better timbered than below and that some of the trees were large. the idea therefore suggested itself of building two other canoes sufficiently large to carry the surplus baggage. on enquiry of the hunters it seemed to be the general opinion that trees sufficiently a large for this purpose might be obtained in a bottom on the opposite side about 8 miles distant by land and reather more than double that distance by water; accordingly Capt. Clark determined to set out early in the morning with ten of the best workmen and proceede by land to that place while the others would in the mean time be employed by myself in taking the Boat in peices and depositing her, toger with the articles which we had previously determined to deposit at this place, and also in trasporting all the baggage up the river to that point in the six small canoes. this plan being settled between us orders were accordingly given to the party, and the ten men who were to accompany Capt. Clark had ground and prepared their axes and adds this evening in order to prepare for an early departure in the morning. we have on this as well as on many former occasions found a small grindstone which I brought with me from Harper's ferry extreemly convenient to us. if we find trees at the place mentioned sufficiently large for our purposes it will be extreemly fortunate; for we have not seen one for many miles below the entrance of musselshell River to this place, which would have answered.—

Source: Thwaites, Reuben Gold, ed. *Original Journals of the Lewis and Clark Expedition, 1804–1806.* Volume 2. New York: Dodd, Mead & Company, 1904, 217–219.

July 9th Tuesday 1805. a beautiful pleasant morning. the Island near the Camp is covered with black birds. we put the Iron boat which we covered with green hides in to the water. Corked Some of the canoes in order to git in readiness to depart from this place in the afternoon we loaded the 6 canoes but did not load the Iron boat as it leaked considerable Soo[n] after we got the canoes loaded Thunder and high wind came on So that we had to unload again. our officers concludes for to leave & burry the Iron boat, as we cannot git tar or pitch to pay the over the out Side of the Skins. the coal Tallow & bease wax would not stick to the hides as they were Shaved the time is So far expended that they did not think proper to try any more experiments with it. So we Sank hir in the water So that She might be the easier took to peaces tomorrow. our officers conclude to build 2 canoes more So that we can carry all our baggage without the Iron boat. about 10 men got ready to up the river to build 2 canoes.

Source: The Journals of Captain Meriwether Lewis and Sergeant John Ordway: Kept on the Expedition of Western Exploration, 1803–1806. Madison, WI: The Society, 1916.

Further Reading

Ambrose, Stephen. *Undaunted Courage.* Urbana: University of Chicago Press, 1991.
Danisli, Thomas. *Meriwether Lewis.* Prometheus Books, 2009.

Dillon, Richard. *Meriwether Lewis: A Biography.* New York: Coward-McCann, 1965.

Holloway, David. *Lewis and Clark and the Crossing of North America.* New York: Saturday Review Press, 1974.

Jones, Landon Y. *William Clark and the Shaping of the West.* New York: Hill and Wang, 2004.

Slaughter, Thomas P. *Exploring Lewis and Clark: Reflections on Men and Wilderness.* New York: Vintage Press, 2004.

Document 58

THREE FORKS RIVER, MONTANA (JULY 28, 1805)

Introduction: Naming the Rivers

On July 25, 1805, the Lewis and Clark expedition reached Three Forks River in Montana. Clark, who was ill with a high fever, refused to stop as he and the Corps were searching for the Shoshone Nation in the hope of getting horses from them. Lewis was convinced that this was a place of huge geographic importance, and so took his time mapping and noting the place. When Lewis and Clark discussed the rivers, they decided to name them after Thomas Jefferson, James Madison, and Albert Gallitin.

At the same time, as Lewis and Clark were noting the rivers on the map, the men were making clothes and shoes, as the toil of travel had worn their clothes.

My friend Capt. Clark was very sick all last night but feels himself somewhat better this morning since his medicine has opperated. I dispatched two men early this morning up the S. E. Fork to examine the river; and permitted sundry others to hunt in the neighbourhood of this place. Both Capt. C. and myself corrisponded in opinion with rispect to the impropriety of calling either of these streams the Missouri and accordingly agreed to name them after the President of the United States and the Secretaries of the Treasury and state having previously named one river in honour of the Secretaries of War and Navy. In pursuance of this resolution we called the S. W. fork, that which we meant to ascend, Jefferson's River in honor of Thomas Jefferson. the Middle fork we called Madison's River in honor of James Madison, and the S. E. Fork we called Gallitin's River in honor of Albert Gallitin. the two first are 90 yards wide and the last is 70 yards. all of them run with great valocity and thow out large bodies of water. Gallitin's River is reather more rapid than either of the others, is not quite as deep but from all appearances may be navigated to a considerable distance. Capt. C. who came down Madison's river yesterday and has also seen Jefferson's some distance thinks Madison's reather the most rapid, but it is not as much so by any means as Gallitan's. the beds of all these streams are formed of smooth pebble and gravel, and their waters perfectly transparent; in short they are three noble streams. there is timber enough here to support an establishment, provided it be erected with brick or stone either of which would be much cheaper than wood as all the materials for such a work are immediately at the spot. there are several small sand-bars along the shores at no great distance of very pure sand and the earth appears as if it would make good brick. I had all our baggage spread out to dry this morning; and the day proving warm, I had a small bower or booth erected for the comfort of Capt. C. our leather lodge when exposed to the sun is excessively hot. I observe large quantities of the sand rush in these bottoms which grow in many places as high as a man's breast and stand as thick as the stalks of wheat usually do. this affords one of the best winter pastures on earth for horses or cows, and of course will be much in favour of an establishment should it ever be thought necessary to fix one at this place. the grass is also luxouriant and would afford a fine swarth of hay at this time in parsels of ma[n]y acres together. all those who are not hunting altho' much fatieued are busily engaged in dressing their skins, making mockersons lexing [leggings] &c to make themselves comfortable. the Musquetoes are more than usually trouble-some, the knats are not as much so. in the evening about 4 O'Ck the wind blew hard from South West and after some little time brought on a Cloud attended with thunder and Lightning from which we had a fine refreshing shower which cooled the air considerably; the showers continued with short intervals untill after dark. in the evening the hunters all returned they had killed 8 deer and 2 Elk. some of the deer wer[e] in excellent order. those whome I had sent up Gallitin's river reported that after it passed the point to which I had seen it yesterday that it turned more to the East to a considerable distance or as far as they could discover the opening of the Mountains formed by it's valley which was many miles. the bot-toms were tolerably wide but not as much so as at or near it's mouth. it's current is rappid and the stream much divided with islands but is sufficiently deep for canoe navigation. Our present camp is precisely on the spot that the Snake Indians were encamped at the time the Minnetares of the Knife R. first came in sight of them five years since. from hence they retreated about three miles up Jeffersons river and concealed themselves in the woods, the Minnetares pursued, attacked them, killed 4 men 4 women a number of boys, and mad[e] prisoners of all the females and four boys, Sah-cah-gar-we-ah o[u]r Indian woman was one of the female prisoners taken at that time; tho' I cannot discover that she shews any immotion of sorrow in recollecting this events, or of joy in being again restored to her native country; if she has enough to eat and a few trinkets to wear I believe she would be perfectly content anywhere.—

Source: Thwaites, Reuben Gold, ed. *Original Journals of the Lewis and Clark Expedition, 1804–1806.* Volume 2. New York: Dodd, Mead & Company, 1904, 281–283.

Further Reading

Criswell, Elijah. *Lewis and Clark: Linguistic Pioneers.* Columbia: University of Missouri Press, 1940.

Danisli, Thomas. *Meriwether Lewis.* Prometheus Books, 2009.

Dillon, Richard. *Meriwether Lewis: A Biography.* New York: Coward-McCann, 1965.

Holloway, David. *Lewis and Clark and the Crossing of North America.* New York: Saturday Review Press, 1974.

Jones, Landon Y. *William Clark and the Shaping of the West*. New York: Hill and Wang, 2004.
Slaughter, Thomas P. *Exploring Lewis and Clark: Reflections on Men and Wilderness*. New York: Vintage Press, 2004.

Document 59
MONTANA (AUGUST 12, 1805)

Introduction: The Continental Divide

In late July, as the Corps continued to travel toward the Rockies, Sacagawea had begun to remember the area as being close to her home from where she had been kidnapped by the Hidatsas five years before. On August 8, she recognized Beaverhead Rock, north of present-day Dillon, Montana. She told Lewis and Clark that they were getting near to her home and family. Anxious to try to get horses from the Shoshones so that they could begin to cross the Rockies, Lewis with three others—George Drouillard, John Shields, and Hugh McNeal—went ahead of the main party in the hope that they could find the Shoshone village.

On August 11, Lewis saw a Shoshone woman, and he attempted to contact her, but the woman was petrified of a white person, and she quickly rode away. The following day, Lewis, still searching for the Shoshones, climbed to the top of Lehmi Pass, where Lewis and Hugh McNeal reached the source of the Missouri River. While Lewis drank from the river, Hugh McNeal stood with a foot each side of the river, amazed at what he had just achieved. Lewis then proceeded to climb to the top of the mountain ridge where he expected to see a river flowing down into a huge plain, and instead he saw "an immense ranges of high mountains still to the west of us." At that moment, the dream of the Northwest Passage died. There was no river route that crossed the American continent.

So the Lewis and Clark expedition continued west but now with a similar but different goal—to reach the Pacific Ocean, report what was not there, and then return home.

They still had to find a route west, but it was not going to be as easy as Jefferson and others had thought.

August 12, 1805

This morning I sent Drewyer out as soon as it was light, to try and discover what rout the Indians had taken. he followed the track of the horse we had pursued yesterday to the mountain wher it had ascended, and returned to me in about an hour and a half. I now determined to pursue the base of the mountains which form this cove to the S. W. in the expectation of finding some Indian road which lead over the Mountains, accordingly I sent Drewyer to my right and Shields to my left with orders to look out for a road or the fresh tracks of horses either of which we should first meet with I had determined to pursue. at the distance of about 4 miles we passed 4 small rivulets near each other on which we saw som resent bowers or small conic lodges formed with willow brush. near them the indians had geathered a number of roots from the manner in which they had toarn up the ground; but I could not discover the root which they seemed to be in surch of. I several large hawks that were nearly black. near this place we fell in with a large and plain Indian road which came into the cove from the N. E. and led along the foot of the mountains to the S. W. oliquely approaching the main stream which we had left yesterday. this road we now pursued to the S. W. at 5 miles it passed a stout stream which is a principal fork of the man stream and falls into it just above the narrow pass between the two clifts before mentioned and which we now saw below us. here we halted and breakfasted on the last of our venison, having yet a small peice of pork in reseve. after eating we continued our rout through the low bottom of the main stream along the foot of the mountains on our right the valley for 5 mes. further in a S. W. direction was from 2 to 3 miles wide the main stream now after discarding two stream on the left in this valley turns abruptly to the West through a narrow bottom betwen the mountains. the road was still plain, I therefore did not dispair of shortly finding a passage over the mountains and of taisting the waters of the great Columbia this evening. we saw an animal which we took to be of the fox kind as large or reather larger than the small wolf of the plains. it's colours were a curious mixture of black, redis-brown and yellow. Drewyer shot at him about 130 yards and knocked him dow bet he recovered and got out of our reach. it is certainly a different animal from any that we have yet seen. we also saw several of the heath cock with a long pointed tail and an uniform dark brown colour but could not kill one of them. they are much larger than the common dunghill fowls, and in their [h]abits and manner of flying resemble the growse or pra-rie hen. at the distance of 4 miles further the road took us to the most distant fountain of the waters of the mighty Missouri in surch of which we have spent so many toilsome days and wristless nights. thus far I had accomplished one of those great objects on which my mind has been unalterably fixed for many years, judge then of the pleasure I felt in allying my thirst with this pure and ice cold water which issues from the base of a low mountain or hill of a gentle ascent for ½ a mile. the mountains are high on either hand leave this gap at the head of this rivulet through which the road passes. here I halted a few minutes and rested myself. two miles below McNeal had exultingly stood with a foot on each side of this little rivulet and thanked his god that he had lived to bestride the mighty & heretofore deemed endless Missouri. after refreshing ourselves we proceeded on to the top of the dividing ridge from which I discovered immence ranges of high mountains still to the West of us with their tops partially covered with snow. I now decended the mountain about ¾ of a mile which I found much steeper than on the opposite side, to a handsome bold running Creek of cold Clear water. here I first tasted the water of the great Columbia river. after a short halt of a few minutes we continued our march along the Indian road which lead us over steep hills and deep hollows to a spring on the side of a mountain where we found a sufficient quantity of dry willow brush for fuel, here we encamped for the night having traveled about 20 Miles. as we had killed nothing during the day we now boiled and eat the remainder of our pork, having yet a little flour and parched meal. at the creek on this side of the mountain I observed a species of deep perple currant lower in its growth, the stem more branched and leaf doubly as large as that of the Missouri. the leaf is covered on it's under disk with a hairy pubersence. the fruit is of the ordinary size and shape of the currant and is supported in the usual manner, but is ascid & very inferior in point of flavor.

Source: Thwaites, Reuben Gold, ed. *Original Journals of the Lewis and Clark Expedition, 1804–1806.* Volume 2. New York: Dodd, Mead & Company, 1904, 333–336.

Further Reading

Bergon, Frank, ed. *The Journals of Lewis and Clark.* New York: Penguin Press, 1989.

Josephy, Alvin M. *Lewis and Clark through Indian Eyes: None Indian Writers on the Legacy of the Expedition.* New York: Vintage Press, 2007.

Nelson, W. Dale. *Interpreters with Lewis and Clark: The Story of Sacagawea and Toussaint Charbonneau.* University of North Texas Press, 2004.

Richter, Daniel K. *Facing East from Indian Country: A Native History of Early America.* Cambridge, MA: Harvard University Press, 2001.

Ronda, James P. *Lewis and Clark among the Indians.* Lincoln: University of Nebraska Press, 1984.

Slaughter, Thomas P. *Exploring Lewis and Clark: Reflections on Men and Wilderness.* New York: Vintage Press, 2004.

Smith, Ronald. *The Captain's Dog.* New York: HMH Books, 2008.

West, Elliot. *The Last Indian War: The Nez Perce Story.* Oxford University Press, 2011.

Document 60

SHOSHONE VILLAGE (AUGUST 17, 1805)

Introduction: Sacagawea Comes Home

After crossing the Continental Divide, Lewis, who was still a few days ahead of the main party, had successfully met with the chief of the Shoshones, Cameahwait. Lewis was still trying to explain him that he wanted to buy horse from him when the remainder of the party arrived.

As Sacagawea was needed urgently to translate and communicate, she was rushed inside in the tent. She had no time to take in her surroundings or to notice the people. But when she went into the tent, she looked up and realized that Chief Cameahwait was her brother. Lewis seemed overcome by the scene as the brother and sister met after so many years, having had their family violently torn apart years earlier.

Amazingly Sacagawea also met another Shoshone woman who had been kidnapped at the same time she was but who had managed to escape.

After this safe return of his sister, unsurprisingly Sacagawea's brother, Caeahwait, agreed to give them the horses they needed to cross the mountains and also agreed to send a guide with them.

August 17, 1805

This morning I arrose very early and dispatched Drewyer and the Indian down the river. sent Shields to hunt. I made McNealcook the remainder of our meat which afforded a slight breakfast for ourselves and the Cheif. Drewyer had been gone about 2 hours when an Indian who had straggled some little distance down the river returned and reported that the whitemen were coming, that he had seen them just below. they all appeared transported with joy, & the chef repeated his fraturnal hug. I felt quite as much gratified at this information as the Indians appeared to be. Shortly after Capt. Clark arrived with the Interpreter Charbono, and the Indian woman, who proved to be a sister of the Chif Cameahwait. the meeting of those people was really affecting, particularly between Sah cah-gar-we-ah and an Indian woman, who had been taken prisoner at the same time with her, and who had afterwards escaped from the Minnetares and rejoined her nation. At noon the Canoes arrived, and we had the satisfaction once more to find our-selves all together, with a flattering prospect of being able to obtain as many horses shortly as would enable us to prosicute our voyage by land should that by water be deemed unadvisable.

Source: Thwaites, Reuben Gold, ed. *Original Journals of the Lewis and Clark Expedition, 1804–1806.* Volume 2. New York: Dodd, Mead & Company, 1904, 361.

Further Reading

Bergon, Frank, ed. *The Journals of Lewis and Clark.* New York: Penguin Press, 1989.

Dunbar-Ortiz, Roxanne. *An Indigenous Peoples' History of the United States.* Beacon Press, reprint, 2015.

Josephy, Alvin M. *Lewis and Clark through Indian Eyes: None Indian Writers on the Legacy of the Expedition.* New York: Vintage Press, 2007.

Merrell, James H. *Into the American Woods: Negotiators on the Pennsylvania Frontier.* New York: W.W. Norton, 1999.

Nelson, W. Dale. *Interpreters with Lewis and Clark: The Story of Sacagawea and Toussaint Charbonneau.* University of North Texas Press, 2004.

Richter, Daniel K. *Facing East from Indian Country: A Native History of Early America.* Cambridge, MA: Harvard University Press, 2001.

Ritter, Michael. *Jean Baptiste Charbonneau, Man of Two Worlds.* Create Space Publishing, 2004.

Document 61

NEAR TENDOY, IDAHO (AUGUST 18, 1805)

Introduction: Meriwether Lewis Turns 31

On August 18, 1805, Meriwether Lewis was 31 years old. His journal entry for that day is notably philosophical, as he expresses his regret at the time he had previously wasted and promises to use his time and talents for better purposes in the future.

This morning while Capt Clark was busily engaged in preparing for his rout, I exposed some articles to barter with the Indians for horses as I wished a few at this moment to releive the men who were going with Capt Clark from the labour of carrying their baggage and also one to keep here in order to pack the meat to camp which the hunters might kill. I soon obtained three very good horses for which I gave an uniform coat, a pair of legings, a few handkerchiefs, three knives and some other small articles the whole of which did not cost more than about 20$ in the U' States. the Indians seemed quite as well pleased with their bargin as I was. the men also purchased one for an old checked shirt a pair of old legings and a knife. two of those I purchased Capt. C. took on with him. at 10 A. M. Capt. Clark departed with his detatchment and all the Indians except 2 men and 2 women who remained with us. Two of the inferior chiefs were a little displeased at not having received a present equivolent to that given the first Chief. to releive this difficulty Capt. Clark bestoed a couple of his old coats on them and I promised that if they wer active in assisting me over the mountains with horses that I would give them an additional present; this seemed perfectly to satisfy them and they all set out in a good humour. Capt. Clark encamped this evening near the narrow pass between the hills on Jefferson's river in the Shoshone Cove. his hunters killed one deer which the party with the aid of the Indians readily consumed in the course of the evening.—after there departure this morning I had all the stores and baggage of every discription opened and aired. and began the operation of forming the packages in proper parsels for the purpose of transporting them on horseback. the rain in the evening compelled me to desist from my operations. I had the raw hides put in the water in order to cut them in throngs proper for lashing the packages and forming the necessary geer for pack horses, a business which I fortunately had not to learn on this occasion. Drewyer Killed one deer this evening. a beaver was also caught by one of the party. I had the net arranged and set this evening to catch some trout which we could see in great abundance at the bottom of the river. This day I completed my thirty first year, and conceived that I had in all human probability now existed about half the period which I am to remain in this Sublunary world. I reflected that I had as yet done but little, very little indeed, to further the hapiness of the human race, or to advance the information of the succeeding generation. I viewed with regret the many hours I have spent in indolence, and now soarly feel the want of that information which those hours would have given me had they been judiciously expended. but since they are past and cannot be recalled, I dash from me the gloomy thought and resolved in future, to redouble my exertions and at least indeavour to promote those two primary objects of human existence, by giving them the aid of that portion of talents which nature and fortune have bestoed on me; or in future, to live for *mankind,* as I have heretofore lived for myself.—

Source: Thwaites, Reuben Gold, ed. *Original Journals of the Lewis and Clark Expedition, 1804–1806.* Volume 2. New York: Dodd, Mead & Company, 1904, 367–368.

Further Reading

Danisli, Thomas. *Meriwether Lewis.* Prometheus Books, 2009.

Hine, Robert V. and John Mack Faragher. *The American West: A New Interpretive History.* New Haven, CT: Yale University Press, 2000.

Holloway, David. *Lewis and Clark and the Crossing of North America.* New York: Saturday Review Press, 1974.

Richter, Daniel K. *Facing East from Indian Country: A Native History of Early America.* Cambridge, MA: Harvard University Press, 2001.

Document 62

BITTERROOT MOUNTAINS (SEPTEMBER 16, 1805)

Introduction: Starving and Cold

The crossing of the Bitterroot Mountains in the winter of 1805 was one of the toughest parts of the whole journey. It was freezing, and the snow on the ground was 6 to 8 feet deep, making it almost impossible for the Corps and horses to travel. As well as this, their food ran out, and there were tress across the route, all of which for an almost impossible situation. Gass, who wrote on September 18 that the Bitterroot were "the most terrible mountains I ever beheld," expressed the exhaustion, hunger, and frustration that the whole party experienced at this time.

Last night about 12 o'clock it began to snow. We renewed our march early, though the morning was very disagreeable, and proceeded over the most terrible mountains I ever beheld. It continued snowing until 3 o'clock P. M. when we halted, took some more soup, and went on till we came to a small stream where we encamped for the night. Here we killed another colt and supped on it. The snow fell so thick, and the day was so dark, that a person could not see to a distance of 200 yards. In the night and during the day the snow fell about 10 inches deep.

Source: Journals of Patrick Gass. Chicago: A.C. McClurg, 1904.

Further Reading

Ambrose, Stephen. *Undaunted Courage.* Urbana: University of Chicago Press, 1991.

THE VOYAGE WEST 133

Hine, Robert V. and John Mack Faragher. *The American West: A New Interpretive History.* New Haven, CT: Yale University Press, 2000.

Holloway, David. *Lewis and Clark and the Crossing of North America.* New York: Saturday Review Press, 1974.

Richter, Daniel K. *Facing East from Indian Country: A Native History of Early America.* Cambridge, MA: Harvard University Press, 2001.

Document 63

FROM THE JOURNAL OF WILLIAM CLARK (SEPTEMBER 18, 1805)

Introduction: Eating Tallow Candles

One of the lowest moments on the voyage occurred on September 18, 1805, when starving and freezing cold made the Corps eat soup mix that was made up primarily of tallow candles. William Clark set out with six of the hunters searching for food, but there was none to be found.

At the end of the day, they made a soup, out of snow, bear oil, and candles.

Cap Clark set out this morning to go a head with six hunters. there being no game in these mountains we concluded it would be better for one of us to take the hunters and hurry on to the leavel country a head and there hunt and provide some provision [for] while the other remained with and brought on the party the latter of these was my part; accordingly I directed the horses to be gotten up early being determined to force my march as much as the abilities of our horses would permit. the negligence of one of the party Willard who had a spare horse [in] not attending to him and bringing him up last evening was the cause of our detention this morning untill ½ after 8 A M when we set out. I sent Willard back to serch for his horse, and proceeded on with the party at four in the evening he overtook us without the horse, we marched 18 miles this day and encamped on the side of a steep mountain; we suffered for water this day passing one rivulet only; we wer fortunate in finding water in a steep raviene about ½ maile from our camp. this morning we finished the remainder of our last coult. we dined & suped on a skant proportion of portable soupe, a few canesters of which, a little bears oil and about 20 lbs. of candles form our stock of provision, the only resources being our guns & packhorses. the first is but a poor dependance in our present situation where there is nothing upon earth exept ourselves and a few small pheasants, small grey Squirrels, and a blue bird of the vulter kind about the size of a turtle dove or jay bird. our rout lay along the ridge of a high mountain course S. 20 W. 18 m. used the snow for cooking.—

Source: Thwaites, Reuben Gold, ed. *Original Journals of the Lewis and Clark Expedition, 1804–1806.* Volume 3. New York: Dodd, Mead & Company, 1905, 71.

Further Reading

Hine, Robert V. and John Mack Faragher. *The American West: A New Interpretive History.* New Haven, CT: Yale University Press, 2000.

Holloway, David. *Lewis and Clark and the Crossing of North America.* New York: Saturday Review Press, 1974.

Josephy, Alvin M. *Lewis and Clark through Indian Eyes: None Indian Writers on the Legacy of the Expedition.* New York: Vintage Press, 2007.

Ostler, Jeffrey. *The Plains Sioux and U.S. Colonialism from Lewis and Clark to Wounded Knee.* Cambridge: Cambridge University Press, 2004.

Richter, Daniel K. *Facing East from Indian Country: A Native History of Early America.* Cambridge, MA: Harvard University Press, 2001.

Ronda, James P. *Lewis and Clark among the Indians.* Lincoln: University of Nebraska Press, 1984.

Document 64

CLEARWATER COUNTY, IDAHO (SEPTEMBER 20, 1805)

Introduction: Meeting the Nez Perce

When the Corps had finally gotten through the Rockies and arrived at Weippe Prairie, in modern-day Clearwater County, Idaho, they arrived hungry and tired. The group they met on the western side of the Rockies were the Nez Perce, and the Lewis and Clark expedition were the first white people they had ever seen. The Nez Perce known to live in the Rockies were known for their horse skills, in particular their breeding of the appaloosa horses. The Nez Perce welcomed the Corps, sharing food and showing them various skills, including how to build canoes from trees through burning. In return for their help, the Corps gave the Nez Perce gifts and established such a strong relationship with them that they left their horses with them for the winter as the Corps traveled down the Columbia River to the Pacific.

Even at this moment, Clark noted the beauty of the quawmash, a flower that became part of the constant scientific journal.

September 20, 1805

I Set out early and proceeded on through a Countrey as ruged as usial passed over a low mountain into the forks of a large Creek which I kept down 2 miles and assended a Steep mountain leaveing the Creek to our left hand passed the head of Several dreans on a divideing ridge, and at 12 miles decended the mountain to a leavel pine Countrey proceeded on through a butifull Countrey for three miles to a Small Plain in which I found maney Indian lodges, at the distance of 1 mile from the lodges I met 3 boys, when they Saw me ran and *hid* themselves searched found gave them Small pieces of ribin & Sent them forward to the village a man Came out to meet me with great Caution & Conducted [me] us to a lage Spacious Lodge which he told me (by Signs) was the Lodge of his great Chief who had Set out 3 days previous with all the Warriers of the nation to war on a South West derection & would return in 15 or 18 days. the fiew men that were left in the Village aged, great numbers of women geathered around me with much apparent Signs of fear, and apr. pleased they [those people] gave us a Small piece of Buffalow meat, Some dried Salmon beries & roots in different States, Some round and much like an onion which they call [*Pas she co*] quamash the Bread or Cake is called Passhe-co Sweet, of this they make bread & Super they also gave us the bread made of this root all of which we eate hartily, I gave them a fiew Small articles as preasents, and proceeded on with a Chief to this Village 2 miles in the Same Plain, where we were treated kindly in their way and continued with them all night Those two Villages consist of about 30 double lodges, but fiew men a number of women & children; They call themselves Cho pun-nish or Pierced Noses; their dialect appears verry different from the Tushapaws altho origneally the Same people They are darker than the Tushapaws Their dress Similar, with more beads white & blue principally, brass & Copper in different forms, Shells and ware their haire in the Same way. they are large Portley men Small women & handsom fetued Emence quantity of the quawmash or *Pas-shi-co* root gathered & in piles about the plains, those roots grow much an onion in marshey places the seed are in triangular Shell on the Stalk. they Sweat them in the following manner i. e. dig a large hole 3 feet deep Cover the bottom with Split wood on the top of which they lay Small Stones of about 3 or 4 Inches thick, a Second layer of Splited wood & Set the whole on fire which heats the Stones, after the fire is extinguished they lay grass & mud mixed on the Stones, on that dry grass which Supports the Pâsh-Shi-co root a thin Coat of the Same grass is laid on the top, a Small fire is kept when necessary in the Center of the kile &c.

I find myself verry unwell all the evening from eateing the fish & roots too freely. Sent out the hunters they killed nothing Saw Some Signs of deer.

Source: Thwaites, Reuben Gold, ed. *Original Journals of the Lewis and Clark Expedition, 1804–1806.* Volume 5. New York: Dodd, Mead & Company, 1905.

Further Reading

Hine, Robert V. and John Mack Faragher. *The American West: A New Interpretive History.* New Haven, CT: Yale University Press, 2000.

Holloway, David. *Lewis and Clark and the Crossing of North America.* New York: Saturday Review Press, 1974.

Josephy, Alvin M. *Lewis and Clark through Indian Eyes: None Indian Writers on the Legacy of the Expedition.* Vintage Press, 2007.

Ostler, Jeffrey. *The Plains Sioux and U.S. Colonialism from Lewis and Clark to Wounded Knee.* Cambridge: Cambridge University Press, 2004.

Richter, Daniel K. *Facing East from Indian Country: A Native History of Early America.* Cambridge, MA: Harvard University Press, 2001.

Ronda, James P. *Lewis and Clark among the Indians.* Lincoln: University of Nebraska Press, 1984.

Document 65

CLEARWATER COUNTY, IDAHO (SEPTEMBER 26, 1805)

Introduction: Making Canoes with the Nez Perce

There was plenty of salmon available for the Corps while they were with the Nez Perce. However, as Clark notes, they were all sick. It would turn out that the fish was making them sick. Regardless of this, Clark organized a group to begin building canoes out of the wood in the area to prepare for the river journey.

Set out early and proceeded on down the river to a bottom opposit the forks of the river on the South Side and formed a Camp. Soon after our arrival a raft Came down the N. fork on which was two men, they came too, I had the axes distributed and handled and men apotned. ready to commence building canoes on tomorrow, our axes are Small & badly Calculated to build Canoes of the large Pine, Capt Lewis Still very unwell, Several men taken Sick on the way down, I administered *Salts* Pils Galip, Tarter emetic &c. I feel unwell this evening, two Chiefs & their families follow us and encamp near us, they have great numbers of horses. This day proved verry hot, we purchase fresh Salmon of the Indians.

Source: Thwaites, Reuben Gold, ed. *Original Journals of the Lewis and Clark Expedition, 1804–1806.* Volume 3. New York: Dodd, Mead & Company, 1905, 88–89.

Further Reading

Hine, Robert V. and John Mack Faragher. *The American West: A New Interpretive History.* New Haven, CT: Yale University Press, 2000.

Holloway, David. *Lewis and Clark and the Crossing of North America.* New York: Saturday Review Press, 1974.

Josephy, Alvin M. *Lewis and Clark through Indian Eyes: None Indian Writers on the Legacy of the Expedition.* New York: Vintage Press, 2007.

Ostler, Jeffrey. *The Plains Sioux and U.S. Colonialism from Lewis and Clark to Wounded Knee.* Cambridge: Cambridge University Press, 2004.

Richter, Daniel K. *Facing East from Indian Country: A Native History of Early America.* Cambridge, MA: Harvard University Press, 2001.

Ronda, James P. *Lewis and Clark among the Indians.* Lincoln: University of Nebraska Press, 1984.

Document 66

NORTHWEST OF MODERN STARBUCK, WASHINGTON, AT LYONS FERRY STATE PARK (OCTOBER 13, 1805)

Introduction: Sacagawea Was Noted as a Token of Peace

The canoes they now had, thanks to the Nez Perce showing them how to build canoes, were making this part of the journey quicker. The expedition was finally making progress downstream. In a moment of introspection, Clark notes that Sacagawea has been seen by the Native populations as a sign of peace, as she is a woman in a party of men.

Rained a little before day, and all the morning, a hard wind from the S West untill 9 oClock, the rained Seased & wind luled, and Capt Lewis with two Canoes Set out & [Crossed] passed down the rapid The others Soon followed and we passed over this bad rapid Safe. We Should make more portages if the Season was not So far advanced and time precious with us.

The wife of Shabono our interpetr we find reconsiles all the Indians, as to our friendly intentions a woman with a party of men is a token of peace.

Source: Thwaites, Reuben Gold, ed. *Original Journals of the Lewis and Clark Expedition, 1804–1806.* Volume 3. New York: Dodd, Mead & Company, 1905, 111–112.

Further Reading

Hine, Robert V. and John Mack Faragher. *The American West: A New Interpretive History.* New Haven, CT: Yale University Press, 2000.

Holloway, David. *Lewis and Clark and the Crossing of North America.* New York: Saturday Review Press, 1974.

Josephy, Alvin M. *Lewis and Clark through Indian Eyes: None Indian Writers on the Legacy of the Expedition.* New York: Vintage Press, 2007.

Ostler, Jeffrey. *The Plains Sioux and U.S. Colonialism from Lewis and Clark to Wounded Knee.* Cambridge: Cambridge University Press, 2004.

Richter, Daniel K. *Facing East from Indian Country: A Native History of Early America.* Cambridge, MA: Harvard University Press, 2001.

Ronda, James P. *Lewis and Clark among the Indians.* Lincoln: University of Nebraska Press, 1984.

Document 67

ESTUARY OF THE COLUMBIA RIVER (NOVEMBER 7, 1805)

Introduction: The Pacific Ocean

On November 7, Clark wrote as he stared from the distance "Ocian in view! O! the joy." He was too early. What he saw was an inlet, and as bad weather set in, the group was stuck between November 10 and November 15, wet, tried, and frustrated, as they waited for the weather to clear so that they could finally see the ocean. Finally they were able to move closer to the shore line, and on November 27, Clark wrote having finally seen the Pacific: "this great Pacific Octean which we been so long anxious to see." Nevertheless, they were to finally achieve the goal and reach the Pacific.

But it was November, and there was no way back east until the spring, so they had to build another fort and stay for the winter.

November 7, 1805

Great joy in camp we are in *View* of the *Ocian*, [*NB: in the morning when fog cleared off just below last village just on leaving the village of Warkiacum*], this great Pacific Octean which we been So long anxious to See. and the roreing or noise made by the waves brakeing on the rockey Shores (as I Suppose) may be heard distinctly.

we made 34 miles to day as Computed

Miles to a point on the Stard Side passg. under a high mountanious Countrey and Encamped on the rocks Stard. Side oposit a rock Situated ½ a mile in the river 50 feet high & 20

Diamuter Some high mountains to the S W. on the top of oneis Snow. *Ocian in view! O! the joy.*

Source: Thwaites, Reuben Gold, ed. *Original Journals of the Lewis and Clark Expedition, 1804–1806.* Volume 3. New York: Dodd, Mead & Company, 1905, 209–210.

Further Reading

Allen, John Logan. *Passage through the Garden: Lewis and Clark and the Image of the American Northwest.* Urbana: University of Illinois Press, 1975.

Ambrose, Stephen. *Undaunted Courage.* Urbana: University of Chicago Press, 1991.

Danisli, Thomas. *Meriwether Lewis.* Prometheus Books, 2009.

Duncan, Dayton and Ken Burns. *Lewis and Clark: The Journey of the Corps of Discovery: An Illustrated History.* New York: Alfred A. Knopf, 1997.

Gass, Patrick. *A Journal of the Voyages and Travels of a Corps of Discovery under the Command of Capt. Lewis and Capt. Clark.* Minneapolis, MN: Ross and Haines, 1958.

Holloway, David. *Lewis and Clark and the Crossing of North America.* New York: Saturday Review Press, 1974.

Slaughter, Thomas P. *Exploring Lewis and Clark: Reflections on Men and Wilderness.* New York: Vintage Press, 2004.

Document 68

THE VOTE (NOVEMBER 24, 1805)

Introduction: Everyone Had an Equal Vote

On November 24, each member of the party was allowed to vote to decide where they should spend the winter. Every decision up to this moment had been made by Lewis and Clark; they were the commanding officers, and questioning of their decisions had led to severe punishments. Previously Lewis and Clark had allowed the group to give an opinion about which route they should take, but Lewis and Clark had made the final decision. They had also allowed the soldiers to vote for a sergeant after the death of Charles Floyd, but this vote did not include everyone. But here in the Pacific Northwest, everyone's opinion was sought. And the vote was not overturned by Lewis and/or Clark.

There were a variety of opinions, and a vote was taken. The options were to stay where they were, to return inland, or to move to the more southern shore. The majority voted to move to the south side of the Columbia River, to what is Astoria, Oregon, today, and built Fort Clatsop. Recorded here as having a vote, and an equal vote, were York, the African American slave, and Sacagawea, the Native American woman. Each vote is recorded in the journal, with Sacagawea being recorded as "Janey" the name Clark had given her in Fort Mandan. She voted to go where there was plenty of food.

November 24, 1805

Sergt J. Ordway	Cross & examine	S
Serjt. N. Pryor	do do	S
Sgt. P. Gass	do do	S
Jo. Shields	proceed to Sandy R.	
Go. Shannon	Examn. Cross	falls
T. P. Howard	do do	falls
P. Wiser	do do	S. R
J. Collins	do do	S. R
Jo Fields	do do	up
Al. Willard	do do	up
R Willard [4]	do do	up
J. Potts	do do	falls
R. Frasure	do do	up
Wm. Bratten	do do	up
R. Fields	do do	falls
J: B: Thompson	do do	up
J. Colter	do do	up
H. Hall	do do	S. R.
Labeech	do do	S R
Peter Crusatte	do do	S R
J. B. Depage	do do	up
Shabono	——	—
S. Guterich	do do	falls
W. Werner	do do	up
Go: Gibson	do do	up
Jos. Whitehouse	do do	up
Geo Drewyer	Examn other side	falls
McNeal	do do	up
York	" "	lookout
falls	Sandy River	lookout up
6	10	12

Janey in favour of a place where there is plenty of Potas.

Source: Thwaites, Reuben Gold, ed. *Original Journals of the Lewis and Clark Expedition, 1804–1806.* Volume 3. New York: Dodd, Mead & Company, 1905, 246–247.

Further Reading

Allen, John Logan. *Passage through the Garden: Lewis and Clark and the Image of the American Northwest.* Urbana: University of Illinois Press, 1975.

Ambrose, Stephen. *Undaunted Courage.* Urbana: University of Chicago Press, 1991.

Danisli, Thomas. *Meriwether Lewis.* Prometheus Books, 2009.

Gass, Patrick. *A Journal of the Voyages and Travels of a Corps of Discovery under the Command of Capt. Lewis and Capt. Clark.* Minneapolis, MN: Ross and Haines, 1958.

Jenkinson, Clay. *The Character of Meriwether Lewis in the Wilderness.* The Dakota Institute, 2011.

Ronda, James P. *Lewis and Clark among the Indians.* Lincoln: University of Nebraska Press, 1984.

Chapter 4

Return Journey

Introduction

The Corps had one more mission: to survive this last winter and then return to St. Louis with the expedition's findings. The winter of 1805–1806, from December 5 to March 23, was spent at what became known as Fort Clatsop, near the mouth of the Columbia River, in modern-day Oregon, and was named after one of the local Native American nations, the Clatsops, which means "dried salmon people." The Clatsops and the Chinooks were the two main Native nations in the area, and both were peaceful nations who traded furs and were hunters in an area where fish and deer were plentiful.

It took only three weeks to build the fort—just two buildings, surrounded by a protective wall. One building was divided into four rooms, one shared by Lewis and Clark, the other by Sacagawea, Toussaint Charbonneau, and Jean Baptiste. The other two were a meat room and an orderly room. The rest of the men were all housed in the second building.

Of the 106 days they spent in the Pacific Northwest, it rained for 94 days. The rain and wind frustrated the Corps, as the damp days led to boredom. Their clothing quickly fell into disrepair, as the moisture rotted their shoes and clothes. This constant rain and humidity overrode everything that winter. On December 10, 1805, Clark noted in his journal, "rained all last night." On December 12, he wrote, "rained at intervals." The entry for December 13 notes, "some Showers of rain last night, and to day Several very [sic] hard Showers." December 24, Christmas Eve was no different, "hard rain at Different times last night and all this day without intermission."

On top of the endless rain, everyone was sick that winter. Colds, aches, and pains were all common. Some of the few moments of distraction that winter included going to see a beached whale and Hugh McNeal's experience nearly getting killed by a member of the Tillamoo Nation who wanted his blanket. After this last incident, Lewis and Clark ordered that the fort doors be shut each night, and that no one other than members of the Corps was allowed to remain inside. The orders demanded that even the sight of an Indian coming toward the fort should be reported. Despite these orders, there was still some interaction between the Corps and the Clatsops and Chinookans.

These Native peoples of the Pacific Northwest proved more difficult to deal with than those the expedition had hitherto encountered on the voyage west. Lewis and Clark noted in their journals that the locals asked for higher prices from them than they did from the fur traders. Consequently, the Corps quickly expended many of the gifts that they planned to use on the return journey. Part of the reason behind this change in attitude was that Europeans were more common to the area, with ships regularly plying to and from Canada. The Chinookan and other nations simply had much more practice at making deals and demands and were seldom interested in the simpler gifts such as beads, which Lewis and Clark had successfully offered when they crossed the continent.

The most important business that winter was to prepare for the return journey. To this end, Lewis and Clark looked at the journals, rewrote, added notes, and prepared all the scientific information they had gathered. The men had to make and sew clothes and shoes out of the deer and elk, which were plentiful in the area and which they hunted successfully for food as well as for hide. In the meantime, Lewis and Clark continued their observation of the flora and fauna in the surrounding area.

The initial plan had been to leave Fort Clatsop on April 1 to begin the journey east. However, depressed with the weather and anxious to go home, Lewis and Clark decided to begin the return journey on March 20, 1806. But the wet, stormy weather of the winter of 1805–1806 was such that their start was delayed until March 23. Lewis and Clark had a plan for this return journey, which, if successful, would mean they would reach St. Louis by the summer. It was a matter of timing, luck, and supplies. First, they had to get back up the Columbia River in order to retrieve their horses at the Nez Perce village. The timing here was particularly tricky, as this had to be achieved before the Nez Perce left for their summer encampment.

Traveling up the Columbia River against the current was difficult. It was also complicated by miserable relations they had with some of the Native Americans, who stole from the Corps. These local nations were not afraid of the Corps, nor were they impressed by the gifts offered to them by Lewis and Clark. Lewis at one stage threatened to burn a village if anything else was stolen, and after someone stole his dog Seaman, he ordered the men to kill the next person who tried to steal the dog.

With the current being so strong to paddle against and with all the problems they were having with the Native population, Lewis and Clark decided to stop traveling by river and instead chose to buy horses from the Eneshers and Skillutes and to continue by land. Both Native nations bargained hard, as they were used to dealing with traders, and while Lewis eventually managed to buy 13 horses, he paid a high price and ended up with unruly animals. Nevertheless, on May 14, the party arrived at Camp Chopunnish, in Idaho, on the north bank of the Clearwater River. Here they gathered 65 horses ready to cross the Bitterroot Mountains. But here again, they had to wait, as the mountain snows had not yet melted, and the Lolo Trail at the start of Lemhi Pass was impassable.

On June 24, with the help of three Nez Perce guides, they eventually crossed the Lolo Trail in only six days and arrived at Traveler's Rest on June 30.

On July 3, the group set out again, but split into two: Clark and his group went down the Yellowstone River, while Lewis took a small group to explore the Marias River. By July 25, Clark and his group had once again found their way back to the Great Plains, while Lewis and his small group were 300 miles away in what is present-day Cut Bank, Montana, close to the Canadian border.

On August 12, both groups met up again. Lewis, however, had been accidently shot by one of his own men the day before, when the extremely shortsighted Pierre Cruzatte mistook him for an elk. The same day they all arrived back at the Mandan villages, and here the group began to disband: John Colter was given permission to leave the group early, as he already wanted to return to the West, working as a guide and a fur trapper. Toussaint Charbonneau, Sacagawea, and Jean Baptiste also left the group. Charbonneau was paid for his work during the expedition, but Sacagawea got nothing.

Everyone else then sailed quickly downstream and headed for St. Louis and home. They arrived in St. Louis on September 23, 1806.

Document 69

FORT CLATSOP, ASTORIA, OREGON (DECEMBER 29, 1805)

Introduction: A Whale

On December 29, Clark and the rest of the Corps got word that a whale had beached near what is today called Canon Beach, Tillamook, Oregon. They were all anxious to see the animal, but as was usual, that winter the weather was proving difficult. While this was not the first time that whales had been spotted or named, they were still unusual, and as Clark uses the term "monster" to describe the animal, obviously they were nervous as well as excited.

Rained all the last night as usial, this morning Cloudy without rain, a hard wind from the S. E I gave the Cheif a razor, and himself and party left us after begging us for maney articles none of which they recvied as we Could not Spare the articles they were most in want of. Peter Crusat Sick with a violent Cold, Y. better. all hands employed about the Pickets & gates of the fort. we were informed day before yesterday that a whale had foundered on the coast to the S. W. near the Kil a mox N. and that the greater part of the Clat Sops were gorn for the oile & blubber, the wind proves too high for us to proceed by water to See this monster, Capt Lewis has been in readiness Since we first heard of the whale to go and see it and collect Some of its Oil, the wind has proved too high as yet for him to proceed—

Source: Thwaites, Reuben Gold, ed. *Original Journals of the Lewis and Clark Expedition, 1804–1806.* Volume 3. New York: Dodd, Mead & Company, 1905, 296.

Further Reading

Allen, John Logan. *Passage through the Garden: Lewis and Clark and the Image of the American Northwest.* Urbana: University of Illinois Press, 1975.

Blackhawk, Ned. *Violence over Land: Indians and Empires in the Early American West.* Cambridge, MA: Harvard University Press, 1998.

Blumberg, Rhoda. *The Incredible Journey of Lewis and Clark.* New York: Scholastic, 1993.

Botkin, Daniel. *Our Natural History, The Lessons of Lewis and Clark.* Oxford University Press, 2004.

Brodhead, Micheal. "The Military Naturalist: A Lewis and Clark Heritage." *We Proceeded On,* vol. 9, no. 4 (November 1983).

Calloway, Colin G. *One Vast Winter Count: The Native American West before Lewis and Clark.* Lincoln: University of Nebraska Press, 2003.

Document 70

FORT CLATSOP, ASTORIA, OREGON (JANUARY 1, 1806)

Introduction: New Year, New Hope

The new year began, and celebrations were muted: with just one volley fired from the guns. Lewis was looking forward to January 1, 1807, when he hoped to be back with his family and friends. Everything was about the future. The Corps continued to have plenty to eat and drink, but they were waiting impatiently for the weather to improve so they could travel home.

This morning I was awoke at an early hour by the discharge of a volley of small arms, which were fired by our party in front of our quarters to usher in the new year; this was the only mark of rispect which we had it in our power to pay this celebrated day. our repast of this day tho' better than that of Christmass, consisted principally in the anticipation of the 1st day of January 1807, when in the bosom of our friends we hope to participate in the mirth and hilarity of the day, and when the zest given by the recollection of the present, we shall completely, both mentally and corporally, enjoy the repast which the hand of civilization has prepared for us. at present we were content with eating our boiled Elk and wappetoe, and solacing our thirst with our only beverage *pure water.* two of our hunters who set out this morning reterned in the evening having killed two bucks elk.

Source: Thwaites, Reuben Gold, ed. *Original Journals of the Lewis and Clark Expedition, 1804–1806.* Volume 3. New York: Dodd, Mead & Company, 1905, 305.

Further Reading

Allen, John Logan. *Passage through the Garden: Lewis and Clark and the Image of the American Northwest.* Urbana: University of Illinois Press, 1975.

Ambrose, Stephen. *Undaunted Courage.* Urbana: University of Chicago Press, 1991.

Blackhawk, Ned. *Violence over Land: Indians and Empires in the Early American West.* Cambridge, MA: Harvard University Press, 1998.

Blumberg, Rhoda. *The Incredible Journey of Lewis and Clark.* New York: Scholastic, 1993.

Botkin, Daniel. *Our Natural History, The Lessons of Lewis and Clark*. Oxford: Oxford University Press, 2004.

Brodhead, Micheal. "The Military Naturalist: A Lewis and Clark Heritage." *We Proceeded On*, vol. 9, no. 4 (November 1983).

Calloway, Colin G. *One Vast Winter Count: The Native American West before Lewis and Clark*. Lincoln: University of Nebraska Press, 2003.

Husner, Verne. *On the River with Lewis and Clark*. Austin, TX: A & M Press, 2004.

Document 71

FORT CLATSOP, ASTORIA, OREGON (JANUARY 2, 1806)

Introduction: Flea Problems

The food was plentiful and easy to obtain near Fort Clatsop, but the issue was wetness, from the constant rain, and the bugs, in particular the fleas. If the Corps were just waiting for winter to end so that they could travel, part of their anxiety was based on the fleas. The Corps were covered in them, and they were frustrated by the constant swarms.

A Cloudy rainey morning after a wet night. Dispatched 12 Men for the two Elk Killed yesterday which they brought in at 11 oClock. the day proved Cloudy and wet, the Indians left us at 1 oClock P. M, Drewyer visited his traps which had one otter in one of them. The flees are verry troublesom, our huts have already Sworms of those disagreeable insects in them, and I fear we Shall not get rid of them dureing our delay at this place.

Source: Thwaites, Reuben Gold, ed. *Original Journals of the Lewis and Clark Expedition, 1804–1806*. Volume 3. New York: Dodd, Mead & Company, 1905, 307–308.

Further Reading

Allen, John Logan. *Passage through the Garden: Lewis and Clark and the Image of the American Northwest*. Urbana: University of Illinois Press, 1975

Ambrose, Stephen. *Undaunted Courage*. Urbana: University of Chicago Press, 1991.

Blackhawk, Ned. *Violence over Land: Indians and Empires in the Early American West*. Cambridge, MA: Harvard University Press, 1998.

Blumberg, Rhoda. *The Incredible Journey of Lewis and Clark*. New York: Scholastic, 1993

Botkin, Daniel. *Our Natural History, The Lessons of Lewis and Clark*. Oxford University Press, 2004.

Brodhead, Micheal. "The Military Naturalist: A Lewis and Clark Heritage." *We Proceeded On*, vol. 9, no. 4 (November 1983).

Calloway, Colin G. *One Vast Winter Count: The Native American West before Lewis and Clark*. Lincoln: University of Nebraska Press, 2003.

Husner, Verne. *On the River with Lewis and Clark*. Austin, TX: A & M Press, 2004.

Document 72

FORT CLATSOP (JANUARY 3, 1806)

Introduction: Eating Dogs

With the exception of William Clark, dog meat was one of the favorite foods on the voyage. The men were tired of fish and traded with the local Native nations for dogs, which would be cooked and eaten. Here Lewis comments that he prefers dog meat to venison or elk. He also notes that the whole Corps are actually healthier when they are eating dogs.

Always the observer of nature, Lewis points to the birds he can see on a daily basis: Wrens, sparrows, a grey jay.

At 11 A. M. we were visited by our near neighbours, Chief or Tiá, Co-mo-wool; alias Conia and six Clatsops. the brought for sale some roots buries and three dogs also a small quantity of fresh blubber. this blubber they informed us they had obtained from their neighbours the Callamucks who inhabit the coast to the S. E. near whose vilage a whale had recently perished. this blubber the Indians eat and esteeme is excellent food. our party from necessaty have been obliged to subsist some length of time on dogs have now become extreemly fond of their flesh; it is worthy of remark that while we lived principally on the flesh of this anamal we were much more healthy strong and more fleshey than we had been since we left the Buffaloe country. for my own part I have become so perfectly reconciled to the dog that I think it an agreeable food and would prefer it vastly to lean Venison or Elk. a small Crow, the blue crested Corvus and the smaller corvus with a white brest, the little brown ren, a large brown sparrow, the bald Eagle and the beatifull Buzzard of the columbia still continue with us.—Sent Sergt. Gass and George shannon to the saltmakers who are somewhere on the coast to the S. W. of us, to enquire after Willard and Wiser who have not yet returned. Reubin Fields Collins and Pots the hunters who set out on the 26th Ulto. returned this evening after dark. they reported that they had been about 15 Miles up the river at the head of the bay just below us and had hunted the country from thence down on the East side of the river, even to a considerable distance from it and had proved unsuccessful having killed one deer and a few fowls, barely as much as subsisted them. this reminded us of the necessity of taking time by the forelock, and keep out several parties while we have yet a little meat beforehand.—I gave the Chief a pare of sattin breechies with which he appeared much pleased.—

Source: Thwaites, Reuben Gold, ed. *Original Journals of the Lewis and Clark Expedition, 1804–1806.* Volume 3. New York: Dodd, Mead & Company, 1905, 308–309.

Further Reading

Allen, John Logan. *Passage through the Garden: Lewis and Clark and the Image of the American Northwest.* Urbana: University of Illinois Press, 1975.

Ambrose, Stephen. *Undaunted Courage.* Urbana: University of Chicago Press, 1991.

Blackhawk, Ned. *Violence over Land: Indians and Empires in the Early American West.* Cambridge, MA: Harvard University Press, 1998.

Blumberg, Rhoda. *The Incredible Journey of Lewis and Clark.* New York: Scholastic, 1993.

Botkin, Daniel. *Our Natural History, The Lessons of Lewis and Clark.* Oxford University Press, 2004.

Brodhead, Micheal. "The Military Naturalist: A Lewis and Clark Heritage." *We Proceeded On,* vol. 9, no. 4 (November 1983).

Calloway, Colin G. *One Vast Winter Count: The Native American West before Lewis and Clark.* Lincoln: University of Nebraska Press, 2003.

Husner, Verne. *On the River with Lewis and Clark.* Austin, TX: A & M Press, 2004.

Document 73

FORT CLATSOP, ASTORIA, OREGON (JANUARY 5, 1806)

Introduction: Tasting Whale

A week after having being told that a whale had beached nearby, Lewis finally got to taste the whale. He notes that it tasted like dog, or indeed beaver, but was spongier than pork. While the weather and bugs of the Pacific Northwest were dire, food was in plentiful supply that winter.

At 5 P. M. Willard and Wiser returned, they had not been lost as we apprehended. they informed us that it was not untill the fifth day after leaving the Fort that they could find a convenient place for making salt; that they had at length established themselves on the coast about 15 Miles S. W. from this, near the lodge of some Killamuck families; that the Indians were very friendly and had given them a considerable quantity of the blubber of a whale which perished on the coast some distance S. E. of them; part of this blubber they brought with them, it was white & not unlike the fat of Poark, tho' the texture was more spongey and somewhat coarser. I had a part of it cooked and found it very pallitable and tender, it resembled the beaver or the dog in flavour.

Source: Thwaites, Reuben Gold, ed. *Original Journals of the Lewis and Clark Expedition, 1804–1806.* Volume 3. New York: Dodd, Mead & Company, 1905, 312–313.

Further Reading

Allen, John Logan. *Passage through the Garden: Lewis and Clark and the Image of the American Northwest.* Urbana: University of Illinois Press, 1975.

Blackhawk, Ned. *Violence over Land: Indians and Empires in the Early American West.* Cambridge, MA: Harvard University Press, 1998.

Blumberg, Rhoda. *The Incredible Journey of Lewis and Clark.* New York: Scholastic, 1993.

Botkin, Daniel. *Our Natural History, The Lessons of Lewis and Clark.* Oxford University Press, 2004.

Brodhead, Micheal. "The Military Naturalist: A Lewis and Clark Heritage." *We Proceeded On,* vol. 9, no. 4 (November 1983).

Calloway, Colin G. *One Vast Winter Count: The Native American West before Lewis and Clark.* Lincoln: University of Nebraska Press, 2003.

Document 74

FORT CLATSOP, ASTORIA, OREGON (JANUARY 6, 1806)

Introduction: Sacagawea Insists on Seeing the Pacific

Though Sacagawea had been allowed to vote when the Corps were deciding where to spend the winter, by January she had to push both Lewis and Clark to let her see the Pacific Ocean. Both record in their journals that she demanded to be allowed. Clark in particular seems annoyed describing her as "impatient." Yet on January 6, 1806, Sacagawea, along with Toussaint Charbonneau—there is no mention of Jean Baptiste—traveled with the group, and she saw the Pacific Ocean.

January 6, 1806

Capt Clark set out after an early breakfast with the party in two canoes as had been concerted the last evening; Charbono and his Indian woman were also of the party; the Indian woman was very impotunate to be permited to go, and was therefore indulged; she observed that she had traveled a long way with us to see the great waters, and that now that monstrous fish was also to be seen, she thought it very hard she could not be permitted to see either (she had never yet been to the Ocean).

Source: Thwaites, Reuben Gold, ed. *Original Journals of the Lewis and Clark Expedition, 1804–1806.* Volume 6. New York: Dodd, Mead & Company, 1905, 168.

The last evening Shabono and his Indian woman was very impatient to be permitted to go with me, and was therefore indulged; She observed that She had traveled a long way with us to See the great waters, and that now that monstrous fish was also to be Seen, She thought it verry hard that She Could not be permitted to See either (She had never yet been to the Ocian).

Source: Thwaites, Reuben Gold, ed. *Original Journals of the Lewis and Clark Expedition, 1804–1806.* Volume 6. New York: Dodd, Mead & Company, 1905, 171.

Further Reading

Bergon, Frank, ed. *The Journals of Lewis and Clark.* New York: Penguin Press, 1989.

Dunbar-Ortiz, Roxanne. *An Indigenous Peoples' History of the United States.* Beacon Press, reprint, 2015.

Josephy, Alvin M. *Lewis and Clark through Indian Eyes: None Indian Writers on the Legacy of the Expedition.* New York: Vintage Press, 2007.

Merrell, James H. *Into the American Woods: Negotiators on the Pennsylvania Frontier.* New York: W.W. Norton, 1999.

Nelson, W. Dale. *Interpreters with Lewis and Clark: The Story of Sacagawea and Toussaint Charbonneau.* University of North Texas Press, 2004.

Richter, Daniel K. *Facing East from Indian Country: A Native History of Early America.* Cambridge, MA: Harvard University Press, 2001.

Ritter, Michael. *Jean Baptiste Charbonneau, Man of Two Worlds.* Create Space Publishing, 2004.

Document *75*

FORT CLATSOP, ASTORIA, OREGON (MARCH 17, 1806)

Introduction: Preparing for the Return

There had been many frustrating aspects of the winter of 1805–1806: bugs, in particular fleas, wetness, and dampness, the number of people who were ill, and the difficult relations the Corps had with the Native population. This population was in fairly constant contact with people from outside their community, sailors on boats and fur trappers, so they knew how to make a bargain. As Lewis and Clark were preparing the return journey, they realized they needed another canoe; Lewis was frustrated with the price being asked for and decided to steal a canoe, arguing that Native population had stolen six elk from them that winter.

We have had our perogues prepared for our departer, and shal set out as soon as the weather will permit. the weather is so precarious that we fear by waiting untill the first of April that we might be detained several days longer before we could get from this to the Cathlahmahs as it must be calm or we cannot accomplish that part of our rout. Drewyer returned late this evening from the Cathlahmahs with our canoe which Sergt. Pryor had left some days since, and also a canoe which he had purchased from those people. for this canoe he gave my uniform laced coat and nearly half a carrot of tobacco. it seems that nothing excep this coat would induce them to dispose of a canoe which in their mode of traffic is an article of the greatest val[u]e except a wife, with whom it is equal, and is generally given in exchange to the father for his daughter. I think the U' States are indebted to me another Uniform coat, for that of which I have disposed on this occasion was but little woarn.—we yet want another canoe, and as the Clatsops will not sell us one at a price which we can afford to give we will take one from them in lue of the six Elk which they stole from us in the winter.

Source: Thwaites, Reuben Gold, ed. Original Journals of the Lewis and Clark Expedition, 1804–1806. Volume 6. New York: Dodd, Mead & Company, 1905.

Further Reading

Allen, John Logan. *Passage through the Garden: Lewis and Clark and the Image of the American Northwest.* Urbana: University of Illinois Press, 1975.

Ambrose, Stephen. *Undaunted Courage.* Urbana: University of Chicago Press, 1991.

Blackhawk, Ned. *Violence over Land: Indians and Empires in the Early American West.* Cambridge, MA: Harvard University Press, 1998.

Blumberg, Rhoda. *The Incredible Journey of Lewis and Clark.* New York: Scholastic, 1993.

Botkin, Daniel. *Our Natural History, The Lessons of Lewis and Clark.* Oxford University Press, 2004.

Brodhead, Micheal. "The Military Naturalist: A Lewis and Clark Heritage." *We Proceeded On,* vol. 9, no. 4 (November 1983).

Calloway, Colin G. *One Vast Winter Count: The Native American West before Lewis and Clark.* Lincoln: University of Nebraska Press, 2003.

Daniels, Jonathan. *Devil's Backbone: The Story of the Natchez Trace.* Pelican Press, 1985.

Husner, Verne. *On the River with Lewis and Clark.* Austin, TX: A & M Press, 2004.

Document 76

LEAVING FORT CLATSOP (MARCH 23, 1806)

Introduction: The Wet Weather Continues

By the end of March, all the members of the Corps of Discovery were ready to set off. It had rained all winter, and their shoes and clothes had literally rotted away. The excitement of seeing the Pacific Ocean had faded quickly. If the first winter at Fort Mandan had been an adventure, the following winter at Fort Clatsop seemed in comparison to be only a source of annoyance and frustration as everyone was anxious to return home.

Initially, the group was meant to leave in April, but in March, the decision was made to begin the journey home a few weeks earlier. On March 23, 1806, the Corps of Discovery left Fort Clatsop and at last began their journey home.

When leaving Fort Clatsop, Clark tried to find the silver lining in their prolonged stay, noting that they had at least eaten three meals a day since they arrived.

March 23, 1806

The rained Seased and it became fair about Meridean, at which time we loaded our Canoes & at 1 P. M. left Fort Clatsop on our homeward bound journey.

at this place we had wintered and remained from the 7th of Decr. 1805 to this day and have lived as well as we had any right to expect, and we can Say that we were never one day without 3 meals of Some kind a day either pore Elk meat or roots, not withstanding the repeeted fall of rain which has fallen almost Constantly Since we passed the long narrows . . . Novr. last . . . Soon after we had Set out from Fort Clatsop we were met by De lash el wilt & 8 men of the Chinnooks, and Delashelwilts wife the old boud and his Six Girls, they had, a Canoe, a Sea

otter Skin, Dried fish and hats for Sale, we purchased a Sea otter Skin, and proceeded on, thro' Meriwethers Bay, there was a Stiff breese from the S. W. which
raised Considerable Swells around Meriwethers point which was as much as our
Canoes Could ride.

Source: Thwaites, Reuben Gold, ed. *Original Journals of the Lewis and Clark Expedition, 1804–1806.* Volume 4. New York: Dodd, Mead & Company, 1905, 197.

Further Reading

Allen, John Logan. *Passage through the Garden: Lewis and Clark and the Image of the American Northwest.* Urbana: University of Illinois Press, 1975.

Ambrose, Stephen. *Undaunted Courage.* Urbana: University of Chicago Press, 1991.

Blackhawk, Ned. *Violence over Land: Indians and Empires in the Early American West.* Cambridge, MA: Harvard University Press, 1998.

Blumberg, Rhoda. *The Incredible Journey of Lewis and Clark.* New York: Scholastic, 1993.

Botkin, Daniel. *Our Natural History, The Lessons of Lewis and Clark.* Oxford University Press, 2004.

Brodhead, Micheal. "The Military Naturalist: A Lewis and Clark Heritage." *We Proceeded On,* vol. 9, no. 4 (November 1983).

Calloway, Colin G. *One Vast Winter Count: The Native American West before Lewis and Clark.* Lincoln: University of Nebraska Press, 2003.

Daniels, Jonathan. *Devil's Backbone: The Story of the Natchez Trace.* Pelican Press, 1985.

Husner, Verne. *On the River with Lewis and Clark.* Austin, TX: A & M Press, 2004.

Document 77

AT MODERN-DAY CASCADES-BONNEVILLE DAM, COLUMBIA RIVER, OREGON (APRIL 11, 1806)

Introduction: Horse-Buying Difficulties and the Theft of Seaman

April 11 was a tough day with a narrow, slippery trail that had to be walked. At the end of the day, everyone was exhausted. The local Native nations, the Watlala and Clahclellar, both fishing and hunting nations, crowded into the camp and tried to steal from the Corps. Knives were drawn as the Corps defended their property and themselves.

Lewis got particularly angry when Seaman was stolen. The dog was returned quickly, but Lewis posted sentries with orders to kill anyone who tried to steal anything from the Corps.

As the tents and skins which covered both our men and baggage were wet with the rain which fell last evening, and as it continued still raining this morning we concluded to take our canoes first to the head of the rapids, hoping that by evening the rain would cease and afford us a fair afternoon to take our baggage over the portage. this portage is two thousand eight hundred yards along a narrow rough and slipery road. the duty of getting the canoes above the rapid was by mutual consent confided to my friend Capt. C. who took with him for that purpose all the party except Bratton who is yet so weak he is unable to work, three others who were lamed by various accedents and one other to cook for the party. a few men were absolutely necessary at any rate to guard our baggage from the War-clel-lars who crouded about our camp in considerable numbers. these are the greates theives and scoundrels we have met with. by the evening Capt. C. took 4 of our canoes above the rapids tho' with much difficulty and labour. the canoes were much damaged by being driven against the rocks in dispite of every precaution which could be taken to prevent it. the men complained of being so much fatiegued in the evening that we posponed taking up our 5th canoe untill tomorrow. these rapids are much worse than they were fall when we passed them, at that time there were only three difficult points within seven miles, at present the whole distance is extreemly difficult of ascent, and it would be impracticable to decend except by leting down the empty vessels by a cord and then even the wrisk would be greater than in taking them up by the same means. the water appears to be upwards of 20 feet higher than when we decended the river. the distance by way of the river between the points of the portage is 3 Ms—many of the natives crouded abot the bank of the river where the men were engaged in taking up the canoes; one of them had the insolence to cast stones down the bank at two of the men who happened to be a little detatched from the party at the time. on the return of the party in the evening from the head of the rapids they met with many of the natives on the road, who seemed but illy disposed; two of these fellows met with John Sheilds who had delayed some time in purchasing a dog and was a considerable distance behind the party on their return with Capt. C. they attempted to take the dog from him and pushed him out of the road. he had nothing to defend himself with except a large knife which he drew with an intention of puting one or both of them to death before they could get themselves in readiness to use their arrows, but discovering his design they declined the combat and instantly fled through the woods. three of this same tribe of villains the Wah-clel-lars, stole my dog this evening, and took him towards their village; I was shortly afterwards informed of this transaction by an indian who spoke the Clatsop language, and sent three men in pursuit of the theives with orders if they made the least resistence or difficulty in surrendering the dog to fire on them; they overtook these fellows or reather came within sight of them at the distance of about 2 miles; the indians discovering the party in pursuit of them left the dog and fled. they also stole an ax from us, but scarcely had it in their possession before Thompson detected them and wrest it from them. we ordered the centinel to keep them out of camp, and informed them by signs that if they made any further attempts to steal our property or insulted our men we should put them to instant death.

Source: Thwaites, Reuben Gold, ed. *Original Journals of the Lewis and Clark Expedition, 1804–1806.* Volume 4. New York: Dodd, Mead & Company, 1905, 266–267.

Further Reading

Allen, John Logan. *Passage through the Garden: Lewis and Clark and the Image of the American Northwest*. Urbana: University of Illinois Press, 1975.

Blackhawk, Ned. *Violence over Land: Indians and Empires in the Early American West*. Cambridge, MA: Harvard University Press, 1998.

Jenkinson, Clay. *The Character of Meriwether Lewis in the Wilderness*. The Dakota Institute, 2011.

Josephy, Alvin M. *Lewis and Clark through Indian Eyes: None Indian Writers on the Legacy of the Expedition*. New York: Vintage Press, 2007.

Ronda, James P. *Lewis and Clark among the Indians*. Lincoln: University of Nebraska Press, 1984.

Slaughter, Thomas P. *Exploring Lewis and Clark: Reflections on Men and Wilderness*. New York: Vintage Press, 2004.

Smith, Ronald. *The Captain's Dog*. New York: HMH Books, 2008.

Document 78

COLUMBIA RIVER, BENTON COUNTY, OREGON (APRIL 27, 1806)

Introduction: Food, Rest, and a Map

On April 27, they once again reached the Walla Walla village, where they were invited to have dinner with Chief Yelleppit. The chief supplied them with food and horses and gave them detailed information about the area where they were about to travel. The chief, who also had influence with the surrounding villages, persuaded others to give the Corps supplies of food. Yelleppit also confirmed that there was a way to shorten their journey by 80 miles, and as they were determined to get back east as quickly as possible, every mile counted. So they moved on, rested, well fed, and had enough supplies for the next part of their journey. In return for his help, Lewis and Clark gave Chief Yelleppit a Jefferson Peace Medal.

This morning we were detained untill 9 A. M. in consequence of the absence of one of Charbono's horses. the horse at length being recovered we set out and at the distance of fifteen miles passed through a country similar to that of yesterday; the hills at the extremity of this distance again approach the river and are rocky abrupt and 300 feet high. we ascended the hill and marched through a high plain for 9 miles when we again returned to the river, I now thought it best to halt as the horses and men were much fatiegued altho had not reached the Wallah wollah village as we had been led to beleive by our guide who informed us that the village was at the place we should next return to the river, and the consideration of our having but little provision had been our inducement to make the march we had made this morning. we collected some of the dry stalks of weeds and the stems of a shrub which resembles the southern wood; made a small fire and boiled a small quantity of our jerked meat on which we dined; while here the principal Cheif of the Wallahwallahs joined us with six men of his nation. this Cheif by name *Yel-lept'* had visited us on the morning of the 19 of October at our encampment a little below this place; we gave him at that time a small medal, and promised him a larger one on our return. he appeared much gratifyed at seeng us return, invited us to remain at his village three or four days and assured us that we should be furnished with a plenty of such food as they had themselves; and some horses to assist us on our journey. after our scanty repast we continued our march accompanyed by Yellept and his party to the village which we found at the distance of six miles situated on the N. side of the river at the lower side of the low country about 12 ms. below the entrance of Lewis's river. This Cheif is a man of much influence not only in his own nation but also among the neighbouring tribes and nations.—This Village consists of 15 large mat lodges. at present they seem to subsist principally on a speceis of mullet which weigh from one to three lbs. and roots of various discriptions which these plains furnish them in great abundance. they also take a few salmon trout of the white kind.—Yellept haranged his village in our favour intreated them to furnish us with fuel and provision and set the example himself by bringing us an armfull of wood and a platter of 3 roasted mullets. the others soon followed his example with rispect to fuel and we soon found ourselves in possession of an ample stock. they birn the stems of the shrubs in the plains there being no timber in their neighbourhood of any discription. we purchased four dogs of these people on which the party suped heartily having been on short allowance for near two days. the indians retired when we requested them this evening and behaved themselves in every rispect extreemly well. the indians informed us that there was a good road which passed from the columbia opposite to this village to the entrance of the Kooskooske on the S. side of Lewis's river; they also informed us, that there were a plenty of deer and Antelopes on the road, with good water and grass. we knew that a road in that direction if the country would permit would shorten our rout at least 80 miles. the indians also informed us that the country was level and the road good, under these circumstances we did not hesitate in pursuing the rout recommended by our guide whos information was corroberated by Yellept & others. we concluded to pass our horses over early in the morning.—

Source: Thwaites, Reuben Gold, ed. *Original Journals of the Lewis and Clark Expedition, 1804–1806.* Volume 4. New York: Dodd, Mead & Company, 1905, 327–330.

Further Reading

Blackhawk, Ned. *Violence over Land: Indians and Empires in the Early American West.* Cambridge, MA: Harvard University Press, 1998.

Jenkinson, Clay. *The Character of Meriwether Lewis in the Wilderness.* The Dakota Institute, 2011.

Josephy, Alvin M. *Lewis and Clark through Indian Eyes: None Indian Writers on the Legacy of the Expedition.* New York: Vintage Press, 2007.

Ronda, James P. *Lewis and Clark among the Indians.* Lincoln: University of Nebraska Press, 1984.

Slaughter, Thomas P. *Exploring Lewis and Clark: Reflections on Men and Wilderness.* New York: Vintage Press, 2004.

Document 79

KAMIAH, IDAHO (MAY 11, 1806)

Introduction: With the Nez Perce

By May 11, 1806, the expedition had reached the Nez Perce village, but they had not gotten this far without incident. The Columbia River was tough to paddle against, and along the way, many Native groups had stolen from them.

Exhausted and frustrated, Lewis and Clark changed their plans: they decided that instead of traveling by river, they would travel by horse. Lewis successfully bought 13 horses, but he was forced to buy them at a higher price than he wanted. He ended up with some wild stallions, and some of the horses he bought were quickly stolen back. Regardless, the Corps made it to Nez Perce territory but were then forced to wait again by the weather. This time, they had to wait for the snow to melt on the Lolo Pass. The Lolo Pass, at 5,233 feet above sea level, is in the Bitterroot Mountains, at the northern part of the Rockies, between Montana and Idaho.

Relieved to be with the Nez Perce, the Corps also discovered that the winter of 1805–1806 had been tough for them too, and that they had been forced to make a stew from the bark of a tree to survive. Unsurprisingly then many Nez were in need of medical attention, which Lewis and Clark dispensed. Once again Rush's medical education was put to use as they handed out his "Thunderbolt Pills."

The relationship between the Nez Perce and the Corps was noticeably different from the relationship they had with the Native population in the Pacific Northwest. Here gifts were exchanged, and in his journal, Clark compares one of the chiefs, named Five Big Hearts, to Jefferson. In turn, the Nez Perce were glad to see the Corps and gave them horses as a gift. The Nez Perce were famous for their horses. On February 15, 1806, Clark had noted in his journal that

> their horses appear to be of an excellent race; they are lofty eligantly formed active and durable; in short many of them look like the fine English coarsers and would make a figure in any country. some of those horses are pided [pied] with large spots of white irregularly scattered and intermixed with the black brown bey or some other dark colour, but much the larger portion are of an uniform colour with stars snips and white feet, or in this rispect marked much like our best blooded horses in Virginia, which they resemble as well in fleetness and bottom as in form and colours.

So a gift of a horse of this type and quality was a sign of respect.

At night, the contrast in relationship was obvious as here they played music and danced, whereas in Fort Clatsop, Lewis and Clark banned anyone other than the Corps to be in the fort at night. The Corps were finally able to rest and relax.

Sunday 11th of May 1806.

A fair morning. a number of the natives who were diseased came to our officers to be healed Capt. Clark applyed meddison and done all possable for them. one of the Indians gave Capt. Clark a fine horse. George DrewyerCame in from hunting. had killed two Deer. the Indians brought us Several more of our horses &C. in the evening we fiddled and danced a while. the natives assembled to See us.

Source: The Journals of Captain Meriwether Lewis and Sergeant John Ordway: Kept on the Expedition of Western Exploration, 1803–1806. Madison, WI: The Society, 1916.

This was a fine clear morning; and we lay here all day. The natives treat us very well; the officers practise as physicians among their sick, and they gave them a very handsome mare and colt. About 12 o'clock our hunter came in and brought two deer with him. We now find a great many more men among the Indians than when we went down last fall; and several chiefs, which had them been out at war. In the evening the natives brought in six more of our horses.

Source: Journals of Patrick Gass. Chicago: A.C. McClurg, 1904.

Further Reading

Allen, John Logan. *Passage through the Garden: Lewis and Clark and the Image of the American Northwest.* Urbana: University of Illinois Press, 1975.

Chuinard, Eldon G. *Only One Man Died: The Medical Aspects of the Lewis and Clark Expedition.* Glendale, CA: Arthur Clark Company, 1980.

Duffy, John. *Epidemics in Colonial America.* Louisiana State University, 1971.

Jenkinson, Clay. *The Character of Meriwether Lewis in the Wilderness.* The Dakota Institute, 2011.

Josephy, Alvin M. *Lewis and Clark through Indian Eyes: None Indian Writers on the Legacy of the Expedition.* New York: Vintage Press, 2007.

Ronda, James P. *Lewis and Clark among the Indians.* Lincoln: University of Nebraska Press, 1984.

Slaughter, Thomas P. *Exploring Lewis and Clark: Reflections on Men and Wilderness.* New York: Vintage Press, 2004.

Document 80

KAMIAH, IDAHO (MAY 16, 1806)

Introduction: Crossing the Rockies Again

The Corps of Discovery had survived and succeeded thus far in their trip largely because of the skills of the Native Americans, particularly their companion. Knowledge of the trails and rivers was only one aspect of survival; another was the knowledge of which wild plants and animals were safe to eat. On May 16, 1806, Sacagawea gathered roots as food. At a time when the whole group was still physically recovering from winter illnesses, Clark noted that this food quickly helped them feel better.

The group was anxious to continue their trip homeward, and despite warnings from the Nez Perce that it was still too early to attempt to recross the mountains, on June 10 they started to trek east. But with the snow still so deep by June 17 they were forced to give up and return to the village. On June 24, 1806, they began again. This time, they had the help of three guides from the Nez Perce, who brought them on specific trails, including some where the horses were able to walk on the deep snow. With the help of the Nez Perce, six days later, on June 30, they arrived at Traveler's Rest, Montana.

Drewyer's horse left his camp last night and was brought to us this morning by an indian who informed us he had found him a considerable distance towards the mountains. Hohâstillpilp and all the natives left us about noon and informed us that they were going up the river some distance to a place at which they expected to fine a canoe, we gave them the head and neck of a bear, a part of which they eat and took the balance with them. these people sometimes kill the variegated bear when they can get them in the open plain where they can pursue them on horseback and shoot them with their arrows. the black bear they more frequently kill as they are less ferocious. our sick men are much better today. Sahcargarmeah gathered a quantity of the roots of a speceis of fennel which we found very agreeable food, the flavor of this root is not unlike annis seed, and they dispell the wind which the roots called Cows and quawmash are apt to create particularly the latter. we also boil a small onion which we find in great abundance, with other roots and find them also an antidote to the effects of the others. the mush of roots we find adds much to the comfort of our diet.—we sent out several hunters this morning but they returned about 11 A. M. without success; they killed a few pheasants only. at 5 P. M. Drewyer and Cruzatte returned having killed one deer only. Drewyer had wounded three bear which he said were as white as sheep but had obtained neither of them. they informed us that the hunting was but bad in the quarter they had been, the Country was broken and thickly covered in most parts with underbrush. a little after dark Shannon and Labuish returned with one deer; they informed us that game was wild and scarce, that a large creek ran parallel with the river at the distance of about 5 or 6 miles which they found impracticable to pass with their horses in consequence of the debth and rapidity of it's current. beyond this creek the Indians inform us that there is great abundance of game. Sergt. Pryor and Collins who set out this morning on a hunting excurtion did not return this evening.—I killed a snake near our camp, it is 3 feet 11 Inches in length, is much the colour of the rattlesnake common to the middle atlantic states, it has no poisonous teeth. it has 218 scutae on the abdomen and fifty nine squamae or half formed scutae on the tail. the eye is of moderate size, the iris of a dark yellowish brown and puple black. there is nothing remarkable in the form of the head which is not so wide across the jaws as those of the poisonous class of snakes usually are.—I preserved the skin of this snake.

Source: Thwaites, Reuben Gold, ed. *Original Journals of the Lewis and Clark Expedition, 1804–1806.* Volume 5. New York: Dodd, Mead & Company, 1905, 41–42.

Further Reading

Botkin, Daniel. *Our Natural History, The Lessons of Lewis and Clark.* Oxford University Press, 2004.

Buckley, Jay H. *William Clark: Indian Diplomat*. University of Oklahoma Press, 2008.

Burroughs, Raymond Darwin. *The Natural History of the Lewis and Clark Expedition*. East Lansing: Michigan State University Press, 1961.

Calloway, Colin G. *One Vast Winter Count: The Native American West before Lewis and Clark*. Lincoln: University of Nebraska Press, 2003.

Coates, Robert. *Outlaw Years: The History of the Land Pirates of the Natchez Trace*. Pelican Press, 2002.

Daniels, Jonathan. *Devil's Backbone: The Story of the Natchez Trace*. Pelican Press, 1985.

Dunbar-Ortiz, Roxanne. *An Indigenous Peoples' History of the United States*. Beacon Press, reprint, 2015.

Gibbon, Guy. *The Sioux: The Dakota and Lakota Nations*. Wiley-Blackwell, 2002.

Document 81

KAMIAH, IDAHO (JUNE 2, 1806)

Introduction: York as a Part of the Corps

One of the most amazing aspects of the Lewis and Clark expedition was the fact that the social norms, constraints, biases, and pervasive racism of the day were ignored during the trip. The only rule on this trip was military law and discipline, and though that had been imposed harshly through a series of courts-martial early in the trip, there had been no major disciplinary issues since.

York was a slave, owned by William Clark. He is thought to have been born the same year as Clark. York's job was to be playmate when they were both children and then to attend to Clark as his personal slave as they got older. York's parents, Old York and Rosa, had also been owed by the Clark family, as were his siblings and his wife. It is not known if York had any real choice about going on the expedition. But while on the trip, he was not treated as a slave. He was treated as one of the other men. He bunked with them, worked with them, and was given various jobs to do just like anyone else in the Corps. When Sergeant Charles Floyd was dying, York attended to him and showed particular kindness and care. There were other occasions when it was York who negotiated with the Native groups. Many of them had never before seen an African American.

On June 2, York was sent out to find food along with Hugh McNeal. York, like McNeal, was given a gun. In their journals, neither Lewis nor Clark mentions any reservations they harbored about York's not returning.

The freedom York experienced during the expedition was in sharp contrast not just with the previous life he had endured, but with the life he was forced back into upon his return to "civilization." Once back home, Clark immediately reverted into the role of slave owner and expected York to acquiesce to slavery. When York objected, Clark got angry and had him flogged. But on this day, June 2, 1806, York was living as an equal to all around him.

McNeal and york were sent on a trading voyage over the river this morning. having exhausted all our merchandize we are obliged to have recourse to every subterfuge in order to prepare in the most ample manner in our power to meet that wretched portion of our journy, the Rocky Mountain, where hungar and cold in their most rigorous forms assail the waried traveller; not any of us have yet forgotten our sufferings in those mountains in September last, and I think it probable we never shall. Our traders McNeal and York were furnished with the buttons which Capt. C. and myself cut off our coats, some eye water and Basilicon which we made for that purpose and some Phials and small tin boxes which I had brought out with Phosphorus. in the evening they returned with about 3 bushels of roots and some bread having made a successfull voyage, not much less pleasing to us than the return of a good cargo to an East India Merchant.—Collins, Sheilds, R & J. Feilds and Shannon set out on a hunting excurtion to the Quawmash grounds on the lower side of Collins's Creek. our horses many of them have become so wild that we cannot take them without the assistance of the Indians who are extreemly dextrous in throwing a rope and taking them with a noose about the neck; as we frequently want the use of our horses when we cannot get the assistance of the indians to take them, we had a strong pound formed today in order to take them at pleasure. Drewyer arrived this evening with Neeshneparkkeeook and Hohâstillpilp who had accompanyed him to the lodges of the persons who had our tomahawks. he obtained both the tomahawks principally by the influence of the former of these Cheifs. the one which had been stolen we prized most as it was the private property of the late Sergt. Floyd and Capt. C. was desireous of returning it to his friends. the man who had this tomahawk had purchased it from the Indian that had stolen it, and was himself at the moment of their arrival just expiring. his relations were unwilling to give up the tomehawk as they intended to bury it with the disceased owner, but were at length induced to do so for the consideration of a hadkerchief, two strands of beads, which Drewyer gave them and two horses given by the cheifs to be killed agreeably to their custom at the grave of the disceased. The bands of the Chopunnish who reside above the junction of Lewis's river and the Kooskooske bury their dead in the earth and place stones on the grave. they also stick little splinters of wood in betwen the interstices of the irregular mass of stone piled on the grave and afterwards cover the whole with a roof of board or split timber. the custom of sacreficing horses to the disceased appears to be common to all the nations of the plains of Columbia. a wife of Neeshneeparkkeeook died some short time since, himself and hir relations saceficed 28 horses to her. The Indians inform us that there are a plenty of Moos to the S. E. of them on the East branch of Lewis's river which they call Tommanamah R. about Noon Sergt. Ordway Frazier and Wizer returned with 17 salmon and some roots of cows; the distance was so great from which they had brought the fish that most of them were nearly spoiled. these fish were as fat as any I ever saw; sufficiently so to cook themselves without the addition of grease; those which were sound were extreemly delicious; their flesh is of a fine rose colour with a small admixture of yellow. these men set out on the 27th ult. and in stead of finding the fishing shore at the distance of half a days ride as we had been informed, they did not reach the place at which they obtained their fish untill the evening of the 29th having travelled by their estimate near 70 miles. the rout they had taken however was not a direct one; the Indians conducted them in the first instance to the East branch of Lewis's river about 20 miles above it's junction with the South branch, a distance of about 50 Ms. where they informed them they might obtain fish; but on their arrival at that place finding that the salmon had not yet arrived or were not taken, they were conducted down that river to a fishery a few miles below the junction of the forks of Lewis's river about 20 ms. further, here with some difficulty and remaining one day they purchased the salmon which they brought with them. the first 20 Ms. of their rout was up Commeâp Creek and through a plain open country, the hills of the creek continued high and broken with some timber near it's borders. the ballance of their rout was though a high broken mountanous country generally well timbered with pine the soil fertile in this quarter they met with an abundance of deer and some bighorned animals. the East fork of Lewis's river they discribe as one continued rapid about 150 Yds. wide it's banks are in most places solid and perpendicular rocks, which rise to a great hight; it's hills are mountains high. on the tops of some of those hills over which they passed, the snow had not entirely disappeared, and the grass was just springing up. at the fishery on Lewis's riverbelow the forks there is a very considerable rapid nearly as great from the information of Segt. Ordway as the great falls of the Columbia the river 200 Yds. wide. their common house at this fishery is built of split timber 150 feet long and 35 feet wide flat at top. The general course from hence to the forks of Lewis's river is a little to the West of south about 45 Ms.—The men at this season resort their fisheries while the women are employed in collecting roots. both forks of Lewis's river above their junction appear to enter a high Mountainous country.—my sick horse being much reduced and apearing to be in such an agoni of pain that there was no hope of his recovery I ordered him shot this evening. the other horses which we casterated are all nearly recovered, and I have no hesitation in declaring my beleif that the indian method of gelding is preferable to that practiced by ourselves.

Source: Thwaites, Reuben Gold, ed. *Original Journals of the Lewis and Clark Expedition, 1804–1806.* Volume 5. New York: Dodd, Mead & Company, 1905, 98–100.

Further Reading

Betts, Robert. *In Search of York: The Slave Who Went to the Pacific with Lewis and Clark.* Denver: University of Colorado Press, 2002.

Buckley, Jay H. *William Clark: Indian Diplomat.* University of Oklahoma Press, 2008.

Danisi, Thomas C. and John C. Jackson. "Homeward Bound." *We Proceeded On* 33, no. 2 (May 2007): 16–19.

Dunbar-Ortiz, Roxanne. *An Indigenous Peoples' History of the United States.* Beacon Press, reprint, 2015.

Gibbon, Guy. *The Sioux: The Dakota and Lakota Nations.* Wiley-Blackwell, 2002.

Holloway, David. *Lewis and Clark and the Crossing of North America.* New York: Saturday Review Press, 1974.

Holmberg, James. *Dear Brother: Letters of William Clark to Jonathan Clark.* New Haven, CT: Yale University Press, 2002.

Husner, Verne. *On the River with Lewis and Clark.* Austin, TX: A & M Press, 2004.

Slaughter, Thomas P. *Exploring Lewis and Clark: Reflections on Men and Wilderness.* New York: Vintage Press, 2004.

Document 82

THROUGH MONTANA (JULY 3, 1806)

Introduction: Still Exploring

On July 3, 1806, the Corps were divided into two groups: Lewis took nine of the men and went north to explore the Marias River, and Clark and his group stayed on the southern route. The plan was that they would all meet up again in about a month where the Missouri and Yellowstone Rivers met. Lewis's party had Gass, Drouillard, Joseph and Reubin Field, Werner, Frazer, Thompson, McNeal, and Goodrich, while Ordway, Sacagawea, and Jean Baptiste were part of the group who went with Clark.

We got up our horses and boath parties Set out about one time. Capts. Lewis & Clark parted here with their parties & proceed. on I with Capt. Clark up the flat head River. we kept up the west Side as it is too high at this time to cross. we are now on our way to the head of the Missourie. we wrode fast & Crossed a number of large creeks in which is beaver dams &C. about noon we halted to dine at a branch and bottom of fine feed white clover &C. proceeded on the plains partly covd. with pitch pine timber. Saw a number of deer. in the evening we Camped at a bottom having made 35 miles in 10 hours this day. one of the hunters killed a deer this evening.

Source: The Journals of Captain Meriwether Lewis and Sergeant John Ordway: Kept on the Expedition of Western Exploration, 1803–1806. Madison, WI: The Society, 1916.

We had again a fine morning; collected our horses and set out. Captain Lewis and his party went down Clarke's river, and Captain Clarke with the rest of the party went up it. All the natives accompanied Captain Lewis. We proceeded on down Clarke's river about 12 miles, when we came to the forks; and made three rafts to carry ourselves and baggage over. The river here is about 150 yards wide, and very beautiful. We had to make three trips with our rafts, and in the evening got all over safe; when we moved on up the north branch, which is our way over to the falls of the Missouri, and, after travelling a mile and a half encamped for the night. Two hunters went out and killed three deer. The musketoes are worse here than I have known them at any place, since we left the old Maha village on the Missouri. This north branch of the river is called by the natives Isquet-co-qual-la, which means the road to the buffaloe.

Source: Journals of Patrick Gass. Chicago: A.C. McClurg, 1904.

Further Reading

Cutright, Paul Russell. "Meriwether Lewis's 'Coloring of Events.'" *We Proceeded On*, vol. 11, no. 1 (February 1985).

Danisi, Thomas C. and Robert Moore. *Uncovering the Truth about Meriwether Lewis*. New York: Prometheus Book, 2001.

Dillon, Richard. *Meriwether Lewis: A Biography*. New York: Coward-McCann, 1965.

Jenkinson, Clay. *The Character of Meriwether Lewis in the Wilderness*. The Dakota Institute, 2011.

Dunbar-Ortiz, Roxanne. *An Indigenous Peoples' History of the United States*. Beacon Press, reprint, 2015.

Gibbon, Guy. *The Sioux: The Dakota and Lakota Nations*. Wiley-Blackwell, 2002

Ronda, James P. *Lewis and Clark among the Indians*. Lincoln: University of Nebraska Press, 1984.

Slaughter, Thomas P. *Exploring Lewis and Clark: Reflections on Men and Wilderness*. New York: Vintage Press, 2004.

Document 83

LOGAN, MONTANA (JULY 13, 1806)

Introduction: Further Divisions in the Corps

Guided by Sacagawea, whom he trusted totally, William Clark broke the group up again: Clark sent Ordway, Collins, Colter, Cruzatte, Howard, Lepage, Potts, Weiser, White-house, and Willard down the Missouri in canoes, while he, along with Pryor, Shields, Shannon, Bratton, Labiche, Windsor, Hall, Gibson, Sacagawea, Charbonneau, baby Pomp, and York, set out on foot. His plan was to reach the Yellowstone River that they would use to travel until the river intertwined with the Missouri River. With 49 horses and Sacagawea, Clark felt confident that this could be achieved.

Set out early this morning and proceeded on very well to the enterance of Madi-cines river at our old Encampment of the 27th July last at 12 where I found Sergt. Pryor and party with the horses, they had arived at this place one hour before us. his party had killed 6 deer & a white bear I had all the horses driven across Madi-cine & gallitines rivers and halted to dine and let the horses feed imediately below the enterance of Gallitine. had all the baggage of the land party taken out of the Canoes and after dinner the 6 Canoes and the party of 10 men under the direc-tion of Sergt. Ordway Set out. previous to their departur I gave instructions how they were to proceed &c. I also wrote to Capt Lewis by Sergt. Ordway—. my party now Consists of the following persons Viz: Serjeant N. Pryor, Jo. Shields, G. Shannon William Bratton, Labiech, Windsor, H. Hall, Gibson, Interpreter Sha-bono his wife & Childand my man york; with 49 horses and a colt. the horses feet are very sore and Several of them can Scercely proceed on. at 5. P. M I Set out from the head of Missouri at the 3 forks, and proceded on nearly East 4 miles and Encamped on the bank of Gallitines Riverwhich is a butifull navigable Stream. Saw a large Gange of Elk in the plains and Deer in the river bottoms. I also observe beaver and Several otter in galletines river as I passed along. Gibson killed an otter the fur of which was much longer and whiter than any which I had Seen. Wil-lard killed 2 deer this morning. all the meat I had put into the Canoes except a Sufficiency for Supper. The Country in the forks between Gallitins & Madisens riv-ers is a butifull leavel plain Covered with low grass.—on the lower or N E. Side of Gallitins river the Country rises gradually to the foot of a mountain which runs nearly parrelal. those plains are indefferant or the Soil of which is not very rich they are Stoney & Contain Several Stratas of white rock. the Current of the river is rapid and near the mouth contains Several islands, it is navigable for Canoes. I saw Several Antelope Common Deer, wolves, beaver, Otter, Eagles, hawks, Crows, wild gees both old and young, does &c. &c. I observe Several leading roads which appear to pass to a gap of the mountain in a E. N E. direction about 18 or 20 miles distant. The indian woman who has been of great Service to me as a pilot through this Country recommends a gap in the mountain more South which I shall cross.

Source: Thwaites, Reuben Gold, ed. *Original Journals of the Lewis and Clark Expedition, 1804–1806.* Volume 5. New York: Dodd, Mead & Company, 1905, 259–260.

Further Reading

Burroughs, Raymond Darwin. *The Natural History of the Lewis and Clark Expedition.* East Lansing: Michigan State University Press, 1961.

Kukla, Jon. *A Wilderness So immense: The Louisiana Purchase and the Destiny of America.* Anchor Books, 2004.

Morris, Larry E. *The Fate of the Corps: What Became of the Lewis and Clark Explorers after the Expedition.* New Haven, CT: Yale University Press, 2005.

Ostler, Jeffrey. *The Plains Sioux and U.S. Colonialism from Lewis and Clark to Wounded Knee.* Cambridge: Cambridge University Press, 2004.

Ronda, James P. *Lewis and Clark among the Indians.* Lincoln: University of Nebraska Press, 1984.

Slaughter, Thomas P. *Exploring Lewis and Clark: Reflections on Men and Wilderness.* New York: Vintage Press, 2004.

Stroud, Patricia. *Bitterroot: The Life and Death of Meriwether Lewis.* Philadelphia: University of Pennsylvania Press 2018.

Turner, Erin H. *It Happened on the Lewis and Clark Expedition.* Guilford, CT: Globe Pequot Press, 2003.

Document 84

GREAT FALLS, MONTANA (JULY 15, 1806)

Introduction: The Last Mention of Seaman

While exploring, mapping, and making notes about nature were among the vital scientific aspects of this trip, the practical everyday issue was often just coping with the animals and insects. Two of the creatures that proved most troublesome for them throughout their journey were bears and mosquitoes. Large and dangerous, bears earned the expedition's utmost respect. There was no guarantee even with a gun and all the firepower they could muster that any encounter with a bear would end with the human surviving. Luck always played a part. Here McNeal was attacked by a bear and broke his musket over the grizzly bear's head, and then climbed a tree to get away.

Throughout the journals, there are constant descriptions of the mosquitoes and the pain inflicted by them on the men. On July 15, Lewis's faithful dog Seaman was howling out with what Lewis describes as torture.

This July 15, 1806, entry is the last time that Seaman is mentioned in the journals. Just as there was a creek, river, or mountain named after every person who went on the expedition, Seaman had a creek named after him—Monture Creek in Montana was originally named Seaman's Creek on July 5, 1806.

July 15, 1806

Dispatched McNeal early this morning to the lower part of portage in order to learn whether the Cash and white perogue remained untouched or in what state they were. the men employed in drying the meat, dressing deerskins and preparing for the reception of the canoes. at 1 P. M. Drewyer returned without the horses and reported that after a diligent surch of 2 days he had discovered where the horses had passed Dearborn's river at which place there were 15 lodges that had been abandoned about the time our horses were taken; he pursued the tracks of a number of horses from these lodges to the road which we had traveled over the mountains which they struck about 3 ms. South of our encampment of the 7th inst. and had pursued this road Westwardly; I have no doubt but they are a party of the Tushapahs who have been on a buffaloe hunt. Drewyer informed that there camp was in a small bottom on the river of about 5 acres inclosed by the steep and rocky and lofty clifts of the river and that so closely had they kept themselves and horses within this little spot that there was not a track to be seen of them within a quarter of a mile of that place. every spire of grass was eaten up by their horses near their camp which had the appearance of their having remained here some time. his horse being much fatiegued with the ride he had given him and finding that the indians had at least 2 days the start of him thought it best to return. his safe return has releived me from great anxiety. I had already settled it in my mind that a whitebear had killed him and should have set out tomorrow in surch of him, and if I could not find him to continue my rout to Maria's river. I knew that if he met with a bear in the plains even he would attack him. and that if any accedent should happen to seperate him from his horse in that situation the chances in favour of his being killed would be as 9 to 10. I felt so perfectly satisfyed that he had returned in safety that I thought but little of the horses although they were seven of the best I had. this loss great as it is, is not intirely irreparable, or at least dose not defeat my design of exploring Maria's river. I have yet 10 horses remaining, two of the best and two of the worst of which I leave to assist the party in taking the canoes and baggage over the portage and take the remaining 6 with me; these are but indifferent horses most of them but I hope they may answer our purposes. I shall leave three of my intended party, Gass, Frazier and Werner, and take the two Feildses and Drewyer. by having two spare horses we can releive

those we ride. having made this arrangement I gave orders for an early departure in the morning, indeed I should have set out instantly but McNeal road
one of the horses which I intend to take and has not yet returned. a little before
dark McNeal returned with his musquet broken off at the breech, and informed
me that on his arrival at willow run he had approached a white bear within ten
feet without discover him the bear being in the thick brush, the horse took the
allarm and turning short threw him immediately under the bear; this animal
raised himself on his hinder feet for battle, and gave him time to recover from
his fall which he did in an instant and with his clubbed musquet he struck the
bear over the head and cut him with the guard of the gun and broke off the
breech, the bear stunned with the stroke fell to the ground and began to scratch
his head with his feet; this gave McNeal time to climb a willow tree which was
near at hand and thus fortunately made his escape. the bear waited at the foot
of the tree untill late in the evening before he left him, when McNeal ventured
down and caught his horse which had by this time strayed off to the distance of
2 ms. and returned to camp. these bear are a most tremenduous animal; it seems
that the hand of providence has been most wonderfully in our favor with rispect
to them, or some of us would long since have fallen a sacrifice to their farosity.
there seems to be a sertain fatality attatched to the neighbourhood of these falls,
for there is always a chapter of accedents prepared for us during our residence at
them. the musquetoes continue to infest us in such manner that we can scarcely
exist; for my own part I am confined by them to my bier at least ¾ths of my
time. my dog even howls with the torture he experiences from them, they are
always most insupportable, they are so numerous that we frequently get them
in our thrats as we breath.

Source: Thwaites, Reuben Gold, ed. *Original Journals of the Lewis and Clark Expedition, 1804–1806.* Volume 5. New York: Dodd, Mead & Company, 1905, 202–204.

Further Reading

Cutright, Paul Russell. "Meriwether Lewis's 'Coloring of Events.'" *We Proceeded On,* vol.
    11, no. 1 (February 1985).
Danisi, Thomas C. and Robert Moore. *Uncovering the Truth about Meriwether Lewis.* New
    York: Prometheus Book, 2001.
Dillon, Richard. *Meriwether Lewis: A Biography.* New York: Coward-McCann, 1965.
Jenkinson, Clay. *The Character of Meriwether Lewis in the Wilderness.* The Dakota
    Institute, 2011.
Ronda, James P. *Lewis and Clark among the Indians.* Lincoln: University of Nebraska
    Press, 1984.
Slaughter, Thomas P. *Exploring Lewis and Clark: Reflections on Men and Wilderness.* New
    York: Vintage Press, 2004.
Smith, Ronald. *The Captain's Dog.* New York: HMH Books, 2008.
Stroud, Patricia. *Bitterroot: The Life and Death of Meriwether Lewis.* Philadelphia: University
    of Pennsylvania Press 2018.

Document 85

POMPEY'S TOWER, BILLINGS, MONTANA (JULY 25, 1806)

Introduction: Clark Makes His Mark

After the Corps split, Clark and his group, which included Sacagawea and Jean Baptiste, continued on the Yellowstone River. On July 25, 1806, they came across a rock formation in present-day Nibbe, Montana, that Clark called, after Jean Baptiste, Pompey's Tower.

In the rock formation, Clark carved his name and date "Wm Clark July 25 1806," and this remains today, the only physical evidence on the expedition anywhere on the route today. It was designated a national monument, on January 17, 2001.

At 4 P M arived at a remarkable rock Situated in an extensive bottom on the Stard. Side of the river & 250 paces from it. this rock I ascended and from it's top had a most extensive view in every direction. This rock which I shall Call Pompy's Tower is 200 feet high and 400 paces in secumphrance and only axcessable on one Side which is from the N. E the other parts of it being a perpendicular Clift of light-ish Coloured gritty rock on the top there is a tolerable Soil of about 5 or 6 feet thick Covered with Short grass. The Indians have made 2 piles of Stone on the top of this Tower. The nativs have ingraved on the face of this rock the figures of animals &c. near which I marked my name and the day of the month & year. From the top of this Tower I Could discover two low Mountains & the Rocky Mts. covered with Snow S W. one of them appeard to be extencive and bore S. 15° E. about 40 miles.

Source: Thwaites, Reuben Gold, ed. *Original Journals of the Lewis and Clark Expedition, 1804–1806.* Volume 5. New York: Dodd, Mead & Company, 1905, 292–293.

Further Reading

Burroughs, Raymond Darwin. *The Natural History of the Lewis and Clark Expedition.* East Lansing: Michigan State University Press, 1961.

Kukla, Jon. *A Wilderness So immense: The Louisiana Purchase and the Destiny of America.* Anchor Books, 2004.

Morris, Larry E. *The Fate of the Corps: What Became of the Lewis and Clark Explorers after the Expedition.* New Haven, CT: Yale University Press, 2005.

Ostler, Jeffrey. *The Plains Sioux and U.S. Colonialism from Lewis and Clark to Wounded Knee.* Cambridge: Cambridge University Press, 2004.

Ronda, James P. *Lewis and Clark among the Indians.* Lincoln: University of Nebraska Press, 1984.

Slaughter, Thomas P. *Exploring Lewis and Clark: Reflections on Men and Wilderness.* New York: Vintage Press, 2004.

Stroud, Patricia. *Bitterroot: The Life and Death of Meriwether Lewis.* Philadelphia: University of Pennsylvania Press 2018.

Turner, Erin H. *It Happened on the Lewis and Clark Expedition.* Guilford, CT: Globe Pequot Press, 2003.

Document 86

MARIAS ROVER, THE GREAT PLAINS (JULY 27, 1806)

Introduction: Lewis and the Blackfeet

Lewis had taken a group to explore the Marias River and the Great Plains, but he also hoped to meet some of the Blackfeet Nation. Native to Montana, Blackfeet were given this name in the 1730s by French explorers who noted the color of their shoes. The Blackfeet Nation were primarily traders who regularly exchanged animal skins for guns and other supplies. Eight warriors met Lewis in July, and after exchanging pleasantries, the warriors decided to camp with the Corps.

That night, Lewis explained to them that Thomas Jefferson intended to bring peace to the Native nations and that the Shoshones and Nez Perce had already agreed terms and would therefore receive guns and ammunition. The Blackfeet and other Native nations were enemies, and Lewis therefore seemed to be siding with them and against the Blackfoot. That night, the Blackfoot warriors who tried to steal guns from the Corps were caught, and two Blackfoot warriors were killed. Frightened that the Blackfeet would kill them, Lewis ordered his men to break camp as quickly as possible and they rode south.

This morning at day light the indians got up and crouded around the fire, J. Fields who was on post had carelessly laid his gun down behind him near where his brother was sleeping, one of the indians the fellow to whom I had given the medal last evening sliped behind him and took his gun and that of his brothers unperceived by him, at the same instant two others advanced and seized the guns of Drewyer and myself, J. Fields seing this turned about to look for his gun and saw the fellow just runing off with her and his brothers he called to his brother who instantly jumped up and pursued the indian with him whom they overtook at the distance of 50 or 60 paces from the camp sized their guns and rested them from him and R Fields as he seized his gun stabed the indian to the heart with his knife the fellow ran about 15 steps and fell dead; [1] of this I did not know untill afterwards, having recovered their guns they ran back instantly to the camp; Drewyer who was awake saw the indian take hold of his gun and instantly jumped up and sized her and rested her from him but the indian still retained his pouch, his jumping up and crying damn you let go my gun awakened me I jumped up and asked what was the matter which I quickly learned when I saw drewyer in a scuffle with the indian for his gun. I reached to seize my gun but found her gone, I then drew a pistol from my holster and terning myself about saw the indian making off with my gun I ran at him with my pistol and bid him lay down my gun [at the instant] which he was in the act of doing when the Fieldses returned and drew up their guns to shoot him which I forbid as he did not appear to be about to make any resistance or commit any offensive act, he droped the gun and walked slowly off, I picked her up instantly, Drewyer having about this time recovered his gun and pouch asked me if he might not kill the fellow which I also forbid as the indian did not appear to wish to kill us, as soon as they found us all in possession of our arms they ran and indeavored to drive off all the horses I now hollowed to the men and told them to fire on them if they attempted to drive off our horses, they accordingly pursued the main party who were drving the horses up the river and I pursued the man who had taken my gun who with another was driving off a part of the horses which were to the left of the camp, I pursued them so closely that they could not take twelve of their own horses but continued to drive one of mine with some others; at the distance of three hundred paces they entered one of those steep nitches in the bluff with the horses before them being nearly out of breath I could pursue no further, I called to them as I had done several times before that I would shoot them if they did not give me my horse and raised my gun, one of them jumped behind a rock and spoke to the other who turned around and stoped at the distance of 30 steps from me and I shot him through the belly, he fell to his knees and on his wright elbow from which position he partly raised himself up and fired at me, and turning himself about crawled in behind a rock which was a few feet from him. he overshot me, being bearheaded I felt the wind of his bullet very distinctly. not having my shotpouch I could not reload my peice and as there were two of them behind good shelters from me I did not think it prudent to rush on them with my pistol which had I discharged I had not the means of reloading untill I reached camp; I therefore returned leasurely towards camp, on my way I met with Drewyer who having heared the report of the guns had returned in surch of me and left the Fieldes to pursue the indians, I desired him to haisten to the camp with me and assist in catching as many of the indian horses as were necessary and to call to the Fieldes if he could make them hear to come back that we still had a sufficient number of horses, this he did but they were too far to hear him. we reached the camp and began to catch the horses and saddle them and put on the packs. the reason I had not my pouch with me was that I had not time to return about 50 yards to camp after geting my gun before I was obliged to pursue the indians or suffer them to collect and drive off all the horses. we had caught and saddled the horses and began to arrange the packs when the Fieldses returned with four of our horses; we left one of our horses and took four of the best of those of the indian's; while the men were preparing the horses I put four sheilds and two bows and quivers of arrows which had been left on the fire, with sundry other articles; they left all their baggage at our mercy. they had but 2 guns and one of them they left the others were armed with bows and arrows and eyedaggs. the gun we took with us. I also retook the flagg but left the medal about the neck of the dead man that they might be informed who we were. we took some of their buffaloe meat and set out ascending the bluffs by the same rout we had decended last evening leaving the ballance of nine of their horses which we did not want. the Feildses told me that three of the indians whom they pursued swam the river one of them on my horse. and that two others ascended the hill and escaped from them with a part of their horses, two I had pursued into the nitch one lay dead near the camp and the eighth we could not account for but suppose that he ran off early in the contest. having ascended the hill we took our course through a beatiful level plain a little to the S of East. my design was to hasten to the entrance of Maria's river as quick as possible in the hope of meeting with the canoes and party at that place having no doubt but that they would pursue us with a large party and as there was a band near the broken mountains or probably between them and the mouth of that river we might expect them to receive inteligence from us and arrive at that place nearly as soon as we could, no time was therefore to be lost and we pushed our horses as hard as they would bear. at 8 miles we passed a large branch 40 yds. wide which I called battle river. at 3 P. M. we arrived at rose river about 5 miles above where we had passed it as we went out, having traveled by my estimate compared with our former distances and couses about 63 ms. here we halted an hour and a half took some refreshment and suffered our horses to graize; the day proved warm but the late rains had supplyed the little reservors in the plains with water and had put them in fine order for traveling, our whole rout so far was as level as a bowling green with but little stone and few prickly pears. after dinner we pursued the bottoms of rose river but finding inconvenient to pass the river so often we again ascended the hills on the S. W. side and took the open plains; by dark we had traveled about 17 miles further, we now halted to rest ourselves and horses about 2 hours, we killed a buffaloe cow and took a small quantity of the meat. after refreshing ourselves we again set out by moon light and traveled leasurely, heavy thunderclouds lowered arround us on every quarter but that from which the moon gave us light. we contineud to pass immence herds of buffaloe all night as we had done in the latter part of the day. we traveled untill 2 OCk in the morning having come by my estimate after dark about 20 ms. we now turned out our horses and laid ourselves down to rest in the plain very much fatiegued as may be readily conceived. my indian horse carried me very well in short much better than my own would have done and leaves me with but little reason to complain of the robery.

Source: Thwaites, Reuben Gold, ed. *Original Journals of the Lewis and Clark Expedition, 1804–1806.* Volume 5. New York: Dodd, Mead & Company, 1905, 227–334.

Further Reading

Blackhawk, Ned. *Violence over Land: Indians and Empires in the Early American West.* Cambridge, MA: Harvard University Press, 1998.

Blumberg, Rhoda. *The Incredible Journey of Lewis and Clark.* New York: Scholastic, 1993.

Botkin, Daniel. *Our Natural History, The Lessons of Lewis and Clark.* Oxford University Press, 2004.

Brodhead, Micheal. "The Military Naturalist: A Lewis and Clark Heritage." *We Proceeded On,* vol. 9, no. 4 (November 1983).

Calloway, Colin G. *One Vast Winter Count: The Native American West before Lewis and Clark.* Lincoln: University of Nebraska Press, 2003.

Ronda, James P. *Lewis and Clark among the Indians.* Lincoln: University of Nebraska Press, 1984.

Slaughter, Thomas P. *Exploring Lewis and Clark: Reflections on Men and Wilderness.* New York: Vintage Press, 2004.

Stroud, Patricia. *Bitterroot: The Life and Death of Meriwether Lewis.* Philadelphia: University of Pennsylvania Press 2018.

Document 87

MOUNTRAIL COUNTY, NORTH DAKOTA (AUGUST 11, 1806)

Introduction: Lewis Is Shot

One of the most amazing facts about the expedition is that only one member of the Corps died: Sergeant Charles Floyd. But everyone in the group had been severely ill at some point.

Of the two captains, Lewis was far more accident prone: he had fallen off a cliff on one occasion, and on another he managed to poison himself. On August 11, 1806, near what would later become Fort Union Trading Post, in North Dakota, Lewis saw some elk and decided to go hunting. His mistake was that he took along Pierre Cruzatte. Cruzette had been hired to be part of the expedition as he spoke a number of languages. However, he was blind in one eye and severely shortsighted in the other. While hunting elk, Cruzette accidentally shot Lewis in the buttocks. When Lewis cried out for help, Cruzette remained silent, so Lewis assumed they were under attack. Bleeding and in agony, Lewis stumbled back toward the boat, crying out for help. Thinking that Cruzette's life was in danger, Lewis instructed those with the other members of the Corps to go and help Cruzette.

Later, when everyone arrived back to the boat with Cruzette, they reported that there was no one else in sight! In the meantime, Lewis had examined the bullet that had gone through him and lodged in his trousers. He discovered that it was a .54 caliber slug from a U.S. Army Model 1803—the exact gun that Cruzette was still carrying. Perhaps remembering the courts-martial that had taken place in the first nine months of the expedition, Cruzette denied that it was he who shot Lewis.

Lewis, with Gass's help, treated his wound as best he could that day, but when Lewis and his group met up with Clark and his group the next day, Clark attended to Lewis's wound. When the whole Corps began to travel again by boat, Lewis embarrassingly was forced to travel face down in a pirogue. This was one of the times when Lewis (understandably) did not write in his journal. Cruztte was not disciplined either for shooting Lewis or for lying.

Monday 11th, August 1806

A fair morning we Set out as usal and procd. on verry well we killed a buffaloe in the river. about 12 oClock Capt. Lewis halted at a bottom on S. Side to kill Some Elk Peter Cruzatte a frenchman went out with Capt. Lewis they Soon found a gangue of Elk in a thicket. Capt. Lewis killed one and cruzatte killed two, and as he Still kept firing one of his balls hit Capt. Lewis in his back side and the ball passed through one Side of his buttock and the ball went out of the other Side of the other buttock and lodged at his overalls which wounded him bad. he instantly called to peter but Peter not answering he Supposd. it to be Indians and run to the canoes and ordered the men to their armes. they were in readiness in a moment and Capt. Lewis attempd. to go back for battle but being faint the men purswaded him not to go himself but the party run out found Cruzatte and he had Seen no Indians then peter knew that it must have been him tho an exidant. we dressed the wound prepared a place for him to lay in the white perogue Jo. Fields killed one Elk. we then took the best of the meat on board and proced. on about 4 P. M. we passd. a Camp of Capt. Clark where we found a note or line informing us that Sergt. pryor & party had joined them here as the Indians had Stole all the horses & they came down in leather canoes. they had left here to day. we procd. on untill about Sunset and Camped on a Sand beach on Ld Side high winds.—

Source: The Journals of Captain Meriwether Lewis and Sergeant John Ordway: Kept on the Expedition of Western Exploration, 1803–1806. Madison, WI: The Society, 1916.

Further Reading

Cutright, Paul Russell. "Meriwether Lewis's 'Coloring of Events.'" *We Proceeded On*, vol. 11, no. 1 (February 1985).

Danisi, Thomas C. and Robert Moore. *Uncovering the Truth about Meriwether Lewis.* New York: Prometheus Book, 2001.

Dillon, Richard. *Meriwether Lewis: A Biography.* New York: Coward-McCann, 1965.

Jenkinson, Clay. *The Character of Meriwether Lewis in the Wilderness.* The Dakota Institute, 2011.

Ronda, James P. *Lewis and Clark among the Indians.* Lincoln: University of Nebraska Press, 1984.

Slaughter, Thomas P. *Exploring Lewis and Clark: Reflections on Men and Wilderness.* New York: Vintage Press, 2004.

Smith, Ronald. *The Captain's Dog.* New York: HMH Books, 2008.

Stroud, Patricia. *Bitterroot: The Life and Death of Meriwether Lewis.* Philadelphia: University of Pennsylvania Press 2018.

Document 88

THE MANDAN VILLAGE (AUGUST 14, 1806)

Introduction: Back with the Mandans

The Corps were once again reunited and had now all reached the Mandan village, where they had previously spent a winter. Here, Clark tended to Lewis's wound to try and ensure it would not get infected. He applied some poultices made of Peruvian bark, a plant known at the time as a cure for fevers, including malaria. Lewis had ordered 15 pounds of the bark for the trip.

Thursday 14th, August 1806

A fair morning we Set out eairly and procd. on about 9 A. M. we arived at our old neighbours the Grousevauntaus and Mandans. we Saluted them by firing our Swivvel and blunderbusses a number of times they answered us with a blunderbuss and Small arms and were verry glad to See us we halted a Short time at the Grousevauntaus village then mooved down convenient to boath the Grousevauntaus and Mandans and Campd. in order to Stay 2 or 3 days to try to git Some of these chiefs to do down with us to Show them the power of the united States &C. they gave us corn & beans &C. &C. Capt. Lewisfainted as Capt. Clark was dressing his wound, but Soon came too again.

Source: The Journals of Captain Meriwether Lewis and Sergeant John Ordway: Kept on the Expedition of Western Exploration, 1803–1806. Madison, WI: The Society, 1916.

Further Reading

Danisi, Thomas C. and John C. Jackson. "Homeward Bound." *We Proceeded On* 33, no. 2 (May 2007): 16–19.

Dillon, Richard. *Meriwether Lewis: A Biography.* New York: Coward-McCann, 1965.

Duncan, Dayton and Ken Burns. *Lewis and Clark: The Journey of the Corps of Discovery: An Illustrated History.* New York: Alfred A. Knopf, 1997.

Lentz, Gary. "Meriwether Lewis's Medicine Chests." *We Proceeded On* 26, no. 2 (May 2000): 10–17.

Slaughter, Thomas P. *Exploring Lewis and Clark: Reflections on Men and Wilderness.* New York: Vintage Press, 2004.

Stroud, Patricia. *Bitterroot: The Life and Death of Meriwether Lewis.* Philadelphia: University of Pennsylvania Press 2018.

Turner, Erin H. *It Happened on the Lewis and Clark Expedition.* Guilford, CT: Globe Pequot Press, 2003.

Document 89

THE MANDAN VILLAGE (AUGUST 16, 1806)

Introduction: John Colter Leaves

When the Corps returned to the Mandan village, it began to break up. The first person to leave was John Colter (c. 1774–1812). As he was a soldier bound by military law, he requested permission to leave early. Formally, the mission would not end until they reached St. Louis. Colter was born in Virginia, but he moved to Kentucky with his family as a child. He was an expert hunter and trapper, and during the expedition, he had an important role often serving as a scout.

When Colter arrived at the Mandan village with everyone else, he met two fur trappers, Forrest Hancock and Joseph Dickenson, who were headed to the Yellowstone River. Colter, who seems not to have been that interested in returning to "civilization," wanted to head back west and perhaps make some money as he knew the geography that few others did at this point. Permission was granted, and Colter returned west, where he lived the rest of his life.

Colter one of our men expressed a desire to join Some trappers who offered to become Shearers with and furnish traps &c. the offer a very advantagious one, to him, his Services Could be dispenced with from this down and as we were disposed to be of Service to any one of our party who had performed their duty as well as Colter had done, we agreed to allow him the prvilage provided no one of the party would ask or expect a Similar permission to which they all agreeed that they wished Colter every Suckcess and that as we did not wish any of them to Seperate untill we Should arive at St. Louis they would not apply or expect it &c.

Source: Thwaites, Reuben Gold, ed. *Original Journals of the Lewis and Clark Expedition, 1804–1806.* Volume 5. New York: Dodd, Mead & Company, 1905, 341.

Further Reading

Blackhawk, Ned. *Violence over Land: Indians and Empires in the Early American West.* Cambridge, MA: Harvard University Press, 1998.

Blumberg, Rhoda. *The Incredible Journey of Lewis and Clark.* New York: Scholastic, 1993.

Buckley, Jay H. *William Clark: Indian Diplomat.* University of Oklahoma Press, 2008.

Morris, Larry E. *The Fate of the Corps: What Became of the Lewis and Clark Explorers after the Expedition.* New Haven, CT: Yale University Press, 2005.

Nelson, W. Dale. *Interpreters with Lewis and Clark: The Story of Sacagawea and Toussaint Charbonneau.* University of North Texas Press, 2004.

Slaughter, Thomas P. *Exploring Lewis and Clark: Reflections on Men and Wilderness.* New York: Vintage Press, 2004.

Document 90

NORTH DAKOTA (AUGUST 17, 1806)

Introduction: Charbonneau, Sacagawea, and Jean Baptiste Leave

It was here in North Dakota Mandan that Charbonneau, Sacagawea, and little Jean Baptiste also left the Corps. Charbonneau was paid $500 for his work on the trip. He offered to stay with the group in case they needed him to continue translating. But they did not. In turn, Clark offered for him to come further south with them, but Charbonneau refused saying that his life was there. Despite her work, Sacagawea got nothing. The agreement initially reached between Charbonneau and Lewis, and Clark had included her as she was Charbonneau's wife. The freedom of the trip and the lack of bias and racism were about to come to a dramatic halt. Charbonneau the man was paid, while Sacagawea the woman was not. William Clark had grown very fond of Jean Baptiste, even giving him the nicknames

"Pompy" or "Little Pomp" and wanted to adopt him. He offered at this stage to raise him and was refused, but he soon wrote again to Charbonneau offering to raise the boy as his own. Again Sacagawea seemed to have no say in what was happening around her, even when it came to her child.

Clark would eventually adopt Jean Baptiste and Sacagawea's daughter Lizette, who was born in 1812.

August 17, 1806

Settled with Touisant Chabono for his Services as an enterpreter the pric of a horse and Lodge purchased of him for public Service in all amounting to 500$ 33⅓ cents. derected two of the largest of the Canoes be fastened together with poles tied across them So as to make them Study for the purpose of Conveying the Indians and enterpreter and their families.

we were visited by all the principal Chiefs of the Menetarras to take their leave of us at 2 oClock we left our encampment after takeing leave of Colter who also Set out up the river in Company with Messrs. Dickson & Handcock. we also took our leave of T. Chabono, his Snake Indian wife and their Son Child who had accompanied us on our rout to the pacific Ocean in the Capacity of interpreter and interpretes. T. Chabono wished much to accompany us in the Said Capacity if [he] we could have provailed the Menetarre Chiefs to dcend the river with us to the U. States, but as none of those chiefs of whoes [set out] language he was Conversant would accompany us, his Services were no longer of use to the U' States and he was therefore discharged and paid up. we offered to convey him down to the Illinois if he Chose to go, he declined proceeding on at present, observing that he had no acquaintance or prospects of makeing a liveing below, and must continue to live in the way that he had done. I offered to take his little Son a butifull promising Child who is 19 months old to which they both himself & wife wer willing provided the Child had been weened. they observed that in one year the boy would be Sufficiently old to leave his mother & he would then take him to me if I would be so freindly as to raise the Child for him in Such a manner as I thought proper, to which I agreeed &c.—we droped down to the Big white *Cheifs* Mandan Village ½ a mile below on the South Side, all the Indians proceeded on down by land. and I walked to the lodge of the Chief whome I found Sorounded by his friends the men were Setting in a circle Smokeing and the womin Crying. he Sent his bagage with his wife & Son, with the Interpreter Jessomme & his wife and 2 children to the Canoes provided for them. after Smoking one pipe, and distributing Some powder & lead which we had given him, he informed me that he was ready and we were accompd to the Canoes by all the village Maney of them Cried out aloud. as I was about to Shake with the Grand Cheifs of all the Villages there assembled they requested me to Set one minit longer with them which I readily agreed to and directed a pipe to be lit. the Cheifs informed that when we first came to their Country they did not beleive all we Said we then told them. but they were now Convinced that every thing we had told them were true, that they Should keep in memory every thing which he had Said to them, and Strictly attend to our advice, that their young men Should Stay at home and Should no go again to war against any nation, that if any atacted them they Should defend themselves, that we might depend on what they Said, and requested us to inform their great father. the also requested me to tell the Ricaras to Come and See them, not to be afraid that no harm Should be done them, that they were anxious to be in peace with them.

The Seeoux they Said they had no dependance in and Should kill them whenever they Came into their Country to do them harm &c. I told them that we had always told them to defend themselves, but not to Strike those nations we had taken by the hand, the Sieoux with whome they were at war we had never Seen on our return we Should inform their great fathe of their conduct towards his faithfull red Children and he would take Such Steps as will bring about a lasting peace between them and his faithfull red children. I informed them that we should inform the ricaras what they had requested &c. The Grand Chief of the Mineterres Said that the great Cheif who was going down with to see their great father was a well as if he went also, and on his return he would be fully informed of the words of his great father, and requested us to take care of this Gt. Chief. we then Saluted them with a gun and Set out and proceeded on to Fort Mandan where I landed and went to view the old works the houses except one in the rear bastion was burnt by accident, Some pickets were Standing in front next to the river. we proceeded on to the old Ricara village.

Source: Thwaites, Reuben Gold, ed. *Original Journals of the Lewis and Clark Expedition, 1804–1806.* Volume 5. New York: Dodd, Mead & Company, 1905, 91, 346.

Further Reading

Blackhawk, Ned. *Violence over Land: Indians and Empires in the Early American West.* Cambridge, MA: Harvard University Press, 1998.

Blumberg, Rhoda. *The Incredible Journey of Lewis and Clark.* New York: Scholastic, 1993.

Buckley, Jay H. *William Clark: Indian Diplomat.* University of Oklahoma Press, 2008.

Morris, Larry E. *The Fate of the Corps: What Became of the Lewis and Clark Explorers after the Expedition.* New Haven, CT: Yale University Press, 2005.

Nelson, W. Dale. *Interpreters with Lewis and Clark: The Story of Sacagawea and Toussaint Charbonneau.* University of North Texas Press, 2004.

Slaughter, Thomas P. *Exploring Lewis and Clark: Reflections on Men and Wilderness.* New York: Vintage Press, 2004.

Document 91

LETTER FROM WILLIAM CLARK TO TOUSSAINT CHARBONNEAU (AUGUST 20, 1806)

Introduction: Clark Offers to Adopt Jean Baptiste

In this letter written to Touissant Charbonneau on August 20, 1806, Clark renews his request to raise the child. He is concerned about the safety of all of them, and he offers to help

Charbonneau and Sacagawea no matter where they want to live, whether that was in Canada, the West, or St. Louis. He offers horses, land, and advice on selling and dealing furs.

Jean Baptiste did eventually go to live with William Clark and his family. In 1809, Toussaint Charbonneau, Sacagawea, and Jean Baptiste attempted to live on farm land near St. Louis. Two years later, Charbonneau and Sacagawea left the area and returned to the West; it seems that Charbonneau could not settle in one place or cope with farming. In 1811, they sold the land to William Clark and left Jean Baptiste with him to be educated and raised by Clark and his family.

As an adult, Jean Baptiste also liked to travel, and as soon as his formal education was over, he traveled west, trading and leading expeditions. He also traveled to Europe and had a skill for languages, becoming fluent in many European languages. After his return to America in 1829, he continued his travels in the West. In 1846–1847, he even scouted a way west for the Mormon Battalion fighting in Mexican-American War. After this, he served as a magistrate of the San Luis Rey Mission in Southern California. He later attempted and failed to get rich during the gold rush in California in 1848.

August 20, 1806

Charbono
SIR

   Your present situation with the Indians givs me some concern. I wish now that I had advised you to come on with me to the Illinois where it most probably would be in my power to put you in some way todo something for your self. I was so engaged after the Big White had concluded to go down with Jessomme as his Interpreter, that I had not time to talk with you as much as I intended to have done. You have been a long time with me and have conducted your Self in Such a manner as to gain my friendship, your woman who accompanied you that long dangerous and fatigueing rout to the Pacific Ocian and back diserved a greater reward for her attention and services on that rout than we had in our power to give her at the Mandans. As to your little Son (my boy Pomp) you know well my fondness for him and my anxiety to take and raise him as my own child. I once more tell you if you will bring your son Baptiste to me I will educate him and treat him as my own child. I do not forgit the promis which I made to you and shall now repeat them that you may be certain. Charbono, if you wish to live with the white people, and will come to me I will give you a piece of land and furnish you with horses cows & hogs. If you wish to visit your friends in Montrall I will let you have a horse, and your family shall be taken care of untill your return. If you wish to return as an Interpreter for the Menetarras when the troops come up to form the establishment, you will be with me ready and I will precure you the place—or if you wish to return to trade with the indians and will leave your little Son Pomp with me, I will assist you with merchendize for that purpose from time [to time] and become my self conserned with you in trade on a Small scale that is to say not exceeding a perogue load at one time. If you are desposed to accept either of my offers to you and will bring down your Son your famn Janey had best come along with you to take care of the boy untill I get him. Let me advise you to keep your Bill of exchange and what furs and pelteries you have in possession, and get as much more as you can—and get as maney robes, and big horn and Cabbra Skins as you can collect in the course of this winter and take them down to St. Louis as early as possible in the Spring. When you get to St. Louis enquire of the Govorner of that place for a letter which I shall leave with him for you. In the letter which I shall leave with the governer I shall inform you what you had best do with your firs pelteries and robes &c. and derect you where to find me. If you should meet with any misfortune on the river &c. when you get to St. Louis write a letter to me by the post and let me know your situation. If you do not intend to go down either this fall or in the Spring, write a letter to me by the first oppirtunity and inform me what you intend to do that I may know if I may expect you or not. If you ever intend to come down this fall or the next Spring will be the best time. This fall would be best if you could get down before the winter. I shall be found either in St. Louis or in Clarksville at the Falls of the Ohio.

Wishing you and your family great suckcess & with anxious expectations of seeing my little danceing boy Baptiest I shall remain your Friend.

WILLIAM CLARK

Source: *The Century Illustrated Monthly Magazine*, Volume 68. New York: The Century Co., 1904, 867.

Further Reading

Buckley, Jay H. *William Clark: Indian Diplomat.* University of Oklahoma Press, 2008.
Foley, William. *Wilderness Journey: The Life of William Clark.* University of Missouri, 2004.
Holmberg, James. *Dear Brother: Letters of William Clark to Jonathan Clark.* New Haven, CT: Yale University Press, 2002.
Jones, Landon. *William Clark and the Shaping of the West.* Bison Books, 2009.
Nelson, W. Dale. *Interpreters with Lewis and Clark: The Story of Sacagawea and Toussaint Charbonneau.* University of North Texas Press, 2004.
Ritter, Michael. *Jean Baptiste Charbonneau, Man of Two Worlds.* Create Space Publishing, 2004.

Document 92

ON THE MISSOURI RIVER (SEPTEMBER 19, 1806)

Introduction: Going Home

It was time for the remainder of the Corps to finally return to St. Louis. Heading homeward, travel on the Missouri would be different: there was no keelboat to haul upstream, as the 3,500 pounds of supplies was used up. What mattered at this stage was speed.

They had spent enough time away, and home was in sight. Sometimes on the way back down to St. Louis, they met various people who were surprised at who they were, as just about everyone thought them dead.

The 19th, was a fine day, and at day light we continued our voyage; passed the mouth of Mine river; saw several turkeys on the shores, but did not delay a moment to hunt:

being so anxious to reach St. Louis, where, without any important occurrence, we arrived on the 23rd, and were received with great kindness and marks of friendship by the inhabitants, after an absence of two years, four months and ten days.

Source: Gass's Journal of the Lewis and Clark Expedition. Chicago: A.C. McClurg, 1904.

Further Reading

Blumberg, Rhoda. *The Incredible Journey of Lewis and Clark.* New York: Scholastic, 1993.

Gass, Patrick. *A Journal of the Voyages and Travels of a Corps of Discovery under the Command of Capt. Lewis and Capt. Clark.* Minneapolis, MN: Ross and Haines, 1958.

Jenkinson, Clay. *The Character of Meriwether Lewis in the Wilderness.* The Dakota Institute, 2011.

Jones, Landon Y. *William Clark and the Shaping of the West.* New York: Hill and Wang, 2004.

Morris, Larry E. *The Fate of the Corps: What Became of the Lewis and Clark Explorers after the Expedition.* New Haven, CT: Yale University Press, 2005.

Slaughter, Thomas P. *Exploring Lewis and Clark: Reflections on Men and Wilderness.* New York: Vintage Press, 2004.

Turner, Erin H. *It Happened on the Lewis and Clark Expedition.* Guilford, CT: Globe Pequot Press, 2003.

Document 93

NEAR CHARRETTE TOWNSHIP, MISSOURI (SEPTEMBER 20, 1806)

Introduction: Cows!

The Corps wanted to get back home as quickly as possible. After two years in the wilderness, none of them was healthy, and some were decidedly sick: three people were having problems with their sight, and to help ensure that everyone would get back to St. Louis, they abandoned two canoes and continued on downriver.

They had reached Charrette Township, in Warren County, Missouri, at the time a small French Village that Clark refers to as "Charriton." As they got closer to civilization, it was no longer the sight of any of the exotic, strange, or unknown animals that excited them. It was instead the cow. Cows meant people, and people meant home. They were getting closer and closer to St. Louis.

September 20, 1806

As three of the party was unabled to row from the State of their eyes we found it necessary to leave one of our Crafts and divide the men into the other Canoes, we left the two Canoes lashed together which I had made high up the River Roche-jhone, those Canoes we Set a drift and a little after day light we Set out and proceeded on very well. The Osage river very low and discharges but a Small quantity of water at this time for so large a river. at meridian we passed the enterance of the Gasconnade river below which we met a perogue with 5 french men bound to the Osarge Gd. village. the party being extreemly anxious to get down ply their ores very well, we Saw Some cows on the bank which was a joyfull Sight to the party and Caused a Shout to be raised for joy at P M we Came in Sight of the little french Village called Charriton the men raised a Shout and Sprung upon their ores and we soon landed opposit to the Village. our party requested to be permited to fire off their Guns which was alowed & they discharged 3 rounds with a harty Cheer, which was returned from five tradeing boats which lay opposit the village. we landed and were very politely received by two young Scotch men from Canada one in the employ of Mr. Aird a Mr. and the other Mr. Reed, two other boats the property of Mr. Lacomb & Mr. all of those boats were bound to the Os/age and Ottoes. those two young Scotch gentlemen furnished us with Beef flower and Some pork for our men, and gave us a very agreeable supper. as it was like to rain we accepted of a bed in one of their tents. we purchased of a Citizen two gallons of Whiskey for our party for which we were obliged to give Eight dollars in Cash, an imposition on the part of the Citizen. every person, both French and americans Seem to express great pleasure at our return, and acknowledged them selves much astonished in Seeing us return. they informed us that we were Supposed to have been lost long Since, and were entirely given out by every person &c.

Source: Thwaites, Reuben Gold, ed. *Original Journals of the Lewis and Clark Expedition, 1804–1806.* Volume 5. New York: Dodd, Mead & Company, 1905, 389–390.

Further Reading

Blumberg, Rhoda. *The Incredible Journey of Lewis and Clark.* New York: Scholastic, 1993.

Gass, Patrick. *A Journal of the Voyages and Travels of a Corps of Discovery under the Command of Capt. Lewis and Capt. Clark.* Minneapolis, MN: Ross and Haines, 1958.

Jenkinson, Clay. *The Character of Meriwether Lewis in the Wilderness.* The Dakota Institute, 2011.

Jones, Landon Y. *William Clark and the Shaping of the West.* New York: Hill and Wang, 2004.

Morris, Larry E. *The Fate of the Corps: What Became of the Lewis and Clark Explorers after the Expedition.* New Haven, CT: Yale University Press, 2005.

Slaughter, Thomas P. *Exploring Lewis and Clark: Reflections on Men and Wilderness.* New York: Vintage Press, 2004.

Turner, Erin H. *It Happened on the Lewis and Clark Expedition.* Guilford, CT: Globe Pequot Press, 2003.

Document 94

LETTER FROM MERIWETHER LEWIS TO THOMAS JEFFERSON (SEPTEMBER 23, 1806)

Introduction: Home and (Almost) Successful

On September 23, 1806, the Lewis and Clark expedition arrived back in St. Louis. They had been gone so long with no communication that most people thought them dead.

Lewis's first job as commanding officer was to write to Thomas Jefferson and tell him that he and the whole group who had left Fort Mandan were alive.

Lewis explained to Jefferson that he had found a route across the American continent, and one that would help expand the fur trade, one of the most important parts of the early nineteenth-century economy. Lewis explained in the letter when the Rockies could be crossed: between April and August, and how this short time slot could be most effectively used.

Lewis mentioned the successful relationship between the Corps and the Mandan Nation, and how the chief of the Mandans would be coming to Washington, D.C., to talk to Jefferson. Lewis also explained to Jefferson the value of William Clark on the trip and how he should get equal credit for the success of the expedition.

Lewis also apologizes to Jefferson for not sending back letters and reports, but Lewis explained that the number of people in the expedition was small and that they could not afford to send back anyone.

Finally, Lewis explains to Jefferson that he was anxious to go and see his mother to find out if she was still alive.

September 23, 1806

SIR

It is with pleasure that I anounce to you the safe arrival of myself and party at 12 Obtr. today at this place with our papers and baggage. In obedience to your orders we have penitrated the Continent of North America to the Pacific Ocean, and sufficiently explored the interior of the country to affirm with confidence that we have discovered the most practicable rout which dose exist across the continent by means of the navigable branches of the Missouri and Columbia Rivers. such is that by way of the Missouri to the foot of the rapids, five miles below the great falls of that river a distance of 2575 miles, thence by land passing the Rocky Mountains to a navigable part of the Kooskooske 340; with the Kooskooske 73 mls. a South Easterly branch of the Columbia 154 miles and the latter river 413 mls. to the Pacific Ocean; making the total distance from the confluence of the Missouri and Mississippi to the discharge of the Columbia into the Pacific Ocean 3555 miles. the navigation of the Missouri may be deemed safe and good; it's difficulties arrise from it's falling banks, timber imbeded in the mud of it's channels, it's sand bars and steady rapidity of it's current, all which may be overcome with a great degree of certainty by taking the necessary precautions. the passage by land of 340 miles from the Missouri to the Kooskooske is the most formidable part of the tract proposed across the Continent; of this distance 200 miles is along a good road, and 140 over tremendious mountains which for 60 mls. are covered with eternal snows; however a passage over these mountains is practicable from the latter part of June to the last of September, and the cheep rate at which horses are to be obtained from the Indians of the Rocky Mountains and West of them, reduces the expences of transportation over this portage to a mere trifle. The navigation of the Kooskooske, the South East branch of the Columbia itself is safe and good from the 1st. of April to the middle of August, by making three portages on the latter; the first of which in descending is that of 1200 paces at the great falls of the Columbia, 261 mls.

from the Ocean, the second of two miles at the long narrows, six miles below the falls, and the 3rd. also of 2 miles at the great rapids 65 miles still lower down. the tides flow up the Columbia 183 miles, or within seven miles of the great rapids, thus far large sloops might ascend in safety, and vessels of 300 tons burthen could with equal safety reach the entrance of the river Multnomah, a large Southern branch of the Columbia, which taking it's rise on the confines of Mexico with the Callarado and Apostles rivers, discharges itself into the Columbia 125 miles from it's mouth.—from the head of tide water to the foot of the long narrow the Columbia could be most advantageously navigated with large batteaux and from thence upwards by perogues. the Missouri possesses sufficient debth of water as far as is specifyed for boats of 15 tons burthen, but those of smaller capacity are to be prefered.—

We view this passage across the Continent as affording immense advantages to the fur trade, but fear that the advantages which it offers as a communication for the productions of the East Indies to the United States and thence to Europe will never be found equal on an extensive scale to that by way of the Cape of Good-hope; still we beleive that many articles not bulky brittle nor of a very perishable nature may be conveyed to the United States by this rout with more facility and at less expence than by that at present practiced.

The Missouri and all it's branches from the Chyenne upwards abound more in beaver and Common Otter, than any other streams on earth, particularly that proportion of them lying within the Rocky Mountains. The furs of all this immence tract of country including such as may be collected on the upper portion of the River St. Peters Red river and the Assenniboin with the immence country watered by the Columbia, may be conveyed to the mouth of the Columbia by the 1st of August in each year and from thence be shiped to, and arrive in Canton earlier than the furs at present shiped from Montreal annually arrive in London. The British N. West Company of Canada were they permitted by the United States might also convey their furs collected in the Athabaske, on the Saskashawan, and South and West of Lake Winnipie by that rout within the period before mentioned. thus the productions nine tenths of the most valuable fur country of America could be conveyed by the rout proposed to the East Indies.—

In the infancy of the trade across the continent, or during the period that the trading establishments shall be confined to the Missouri and it's branches, the men employed in this trade will be compelled to convey the furs collected in that quarter as low on the Columbia as tide water, in which case they could not return to the falls of the Missouri untill about the 1st. of October, which would be so late in the season that there would be considerable danger of the river being obstructed by ice before they could reach this place and consequently that the comodites brought from the East indies would be detained untill the following spring; but this difficulty will at once vanish when establishments are also made on the Columbia, and a sufficient number of men employed at them to convey annually the productions of the East indies to the upper establishment on the Kooskooske, and there exchange them with the men of the Missouri for their furs, in the begining of July. by this means the furs not only of the Missouri but those also of the Columbia may be shiped to the East indies by the season before mentioned, and the comodities of the East indies arrive at St. Louis or the mouth of the Ohio, by the last of September in each year.

Although the Columbia dose not as much as the Missouri abound in beaver and Otter, yet it is by no means despicable in this rispect, and would furnish a valuable fur trade distinct from any other consideration. in addition to the otter and beaver which it could furnish, there might be collected considerable quantities of the skins of three speceis of bear affording a great variety of colours and of superior delicacy, those also of the tyger cat, several species of fox, Martin and several others of an inferior class of furs, besides the valuable sea Otter of the coast.

If the government will only aid, even in a very limited manner, the enterprize of her Citizens I am fully convinced that we shall shortly derive the benifits of a most lucrative trade from this source, and that in the course of ten or twelve years a tour across the Continent by the rout mentioned will be undertaken by individuals with as little concern as a voyage across the Atlantic is at present.—

The British N. West Company of Canada has for several years, carried on a partial trade with the Minnetares Ahwayhaways and Mandans on the Missouri from their establishments on the Assinniboin at the entrance of Mouse river; at present I have good reason for beleiving that they intend shortly to form an establishment near those nations with a view to engroce the fur trade of the Missouri. the known enterprize and resources of this Company, latterly strengthened by an union with their powerfull rival the X.Y. Company renders them formidable in that distant part of the continent to all other traders; and in my opinion if we are to regard the trade of the Missouri as an object of importance to the United States; the strides of this Company towards the Missouri cannot be too vigilantly watched nor too firmly and speedily opposed by our government. The embarrasments under which the navigation of the Missouri at present labours from the unfriendly dispositions of the Kancez, the several bands of Tetons, Assinniboins and those tribes that resort to the British establishments on the Saskashawan is also a subject which requires the earliest attention of our government. As I shall shortly be with you I have deemed it unnecessary here to detail the several ideas which have presented themselves to my mind on those subjects, more especially when I consider that a thorough knowledge of the geography of the country is absolutely necessary to their being undestood, and leasure has not yet permited us to make but one general map of the country which I am unwilling to wrisk by the Mail.—

As a sketch of the most prominent features of our perigrination since we left the Mandans may not be uninteresting, I shall indevour to give it to you by way of letter from this place, where I shall necessarily be detained several days in order to settle with and discharge the men who accompanyed me on the voyage as well as to prepare for my rout to the City of Washington.

We left Fort Clatsop where we wintered near the entrance of the Columbia on the 27th. of March last, and arrived at the foot of the Rocky mountains on the 10th. of May where we were detained untill the 24th. of June in consequence of the snow which rendered a passage over the those Mountains impracticable untill that moment; had it not been for this detention I should ere this have joined you at Monticello. In my last communication to you from the Mandans I mentioned my intention of sending back a canoe with a small party from the Rocky Mountains;

but on our arrival at the great falls of the Missouri on the 14th. of June 1805, in view of that formidable snowey barrier, the discourageing difficulties which we had to encounter in making a portage of eighteen miles of our canoes and baggage around those falls were such that my friend Capt. Clark and myself conceived it inexpedient to reduce the party, lest by doing so we should lessen the ardor of those who remained and thus hazard the fate of the expedition, and therefore declined that measure, thinking it better that the government as well as our friends should for a moment feel some anxiety for our fate than to wish so much; experience has since proved the justice of our dicision, for we have more than once owed our lives and the fate of the expedition to our number which consisted of 31 men.

I have brought with me several skins of the Sea Otter, two skins of the native sheep of America, five skins and skelitons complete of the Bighorn or mountain ram, and a skin of the Mule deer beside the skins of several other quadrupeds and birds natives of the countries through which we have passed. I have also preserved a pretty extensive collection of plants, and collected nine other vocabularies.

I have prevailed on the great Cheif of the Mandan nation to accompany me to Washington; he is now with my frind and colligue Capt. Clark at this place, in good health and sperits, and very anxious to proceede.—

With rispect to the exertions and services rendered by that esteemable man Capt. William Clark in the course of late voyage I cannot say too much; if Sir any credit be due for the success of that arduous enterprize in which we have been mututally engaged, he is equally with myself entitled to your consideration and that of our common country.

The anxiety which I feel in returning once more to the bosom of my friends is a sufficient guarantee that no time will be unnecessarily expended in this quarter.—

I have detained the post several hours for the purpose of making you this haisty communication. I hope that while I am pardoned for this detention of the mail, the situation in which I have been compelled to write will sufficiently apologize for having been this laconic.

The rout by which I purpose traveling from hence to Washington is by way of Cahokia, Vincennes, Louisville Ky, the Craborchard, Abington, Fincastle, Stanton and Charlottsville. any letters directed to me at louisville ten days after the receipt of this will most probably meet me at that place. I am very anxious to learn the state of my friends in Albemarle particularly whether my mother is yet living. I am with every sentiment of esteem Your Obt. and very Humble servent.

MERIWETHER LEWIS CAPT.

1ST. US REGT. INFTY.
N.B. the whole of the party who accompanyed me from the Mandans have returned in good health, which is not, I assure you, to me one of the least pleasing considerations of the Voyage.

M.L.

Source: Library of Congress, Manuscript Division.

Further Reading

Blackhawk, Ned. *Violence over Land: Indians and Empires in the Early American West*. Cambridge, MA: Harvard University Press, 1998.

Blumberg, Rhoda. *The Incredible Journey of Lewis and Clark*. New York: Scholastic, 1993.

Buckley, Jay H. *William Clark: Indian Diplomat*. University of Oklahoma Press, 2008.

Calloway, Colin G. *One Vast Winter Count: The Native American West before Lewis and Clark*. Lincoln: University of Nebraska Press, 2003.

Carlson, Paul. *The Plains Indians*. Austin, TX: A & M University, 1998.

Dowd, Gregory Evans. *A Spirited Resistance: The North American Indian Struggle for Unity, 1745–1815*. Baltimore, MD: Johns Hopkins University Press, 1992.

Gibbon, Guy. *The Sioux: The Dakota and Lakota Nations*. Wiley-Blackwell, 2002.

Holloway, David. *Lewis and Clark and the Crossing of North America*. New York: Saturday Review Press, 1974.

Nelson, W. Dale. *Interpreters with Lewis and Clark: The Story of Sacagawea and Toussaint Charbonneau*. University of North Texas Press, 2004.

Document 95

THE LAST JOURNAL ENTRY (SEPTEMBER 26, 1806)

Introduction: The Final Entry

The final entry in the journal of William Clark marks the beginning of organizing the various collections of animals, fossils, and notes from the trip to get to Jefferson and to others. At this stage, the journals and papers as well as animals, skins, bones, and fossils were all being organized. But the most important thing they had to do was write. This was the only real method of communication, and Jefferson as well as family and friends needed to be told that they were alive and home. It was indeed a fine morning!

A fine morning we commenced wrighting &c

Source: Thwaites, Reuben Gold, ed. *Original Journals of the Lewis and Clark Expedition, 1804–1806*. Volume 8. New York: Dodd, Mead & Company, 1905.

Further Reading

Bedini, Silvio. *Thomas Jefferson: Statesman of Science*. New York: Macmillan, 1990.

Bernstein, R. B. *Thomas Jefferson*. Oxford: Oxford University Press, 2005.

Cerami, Charles. *Jefferson's Great Gamble: The Remarkable Story of Jefferson, Napoleon and the Men behind the Louisiana Purchase*. New York: Source Books, 2004.

Chuinard, Eldon G. *Only One Man Died: The Medical Aspects of the Lewis and Clark Expedition*. Glendale, CA: Arthur Clark Company, 1980.

Ellis, Joseph. *American Sphinx: The Character of Thomas Jefferson*. New York: Vintage Books, 1998.

Ellis, Joseph. *Founding Brothers: The Revolutionary Generation.* New York: Vintage Books, 2002.

Fenster, Julie. *Jefferson's America: The President, the Purchase, and the Explorers Who Transformed a Nation.* New York: Crown, 2016.

Kukla, Jon. *A Wilderness So immense: The Louisiana Purchase and the Destiny of America.* Anchor Books, 2004.

Ostler, Jeffrey. *The Plains Sioux and U.S. Colonialism from Lewis and Clark to Wounded Knee.* Cambridge: Cambridge University Press, 2004.

Peterson, Larry. *American Trinity: Jefferson, Custer and the Spirit of the West.* Sweetgrass Books, 2017.

Document 96

KENTUCKY (OCTOBER 2, 1806)

Introduction: First Newspaper Account Published

The first report of the successful return of Meriwether Lewis and William Clark and their party was published on October 2, 1806, in the Kentucky newspaper The Palladium *written in a letter from John Mullanphy. The newspaper published a longer story two days later, and both stories were soon picked up by newspapers all over the country. Lewis and Clark were headline news.*

ST LOUIS
September 23, 1806

DEAR SIR

Captain Lewis and Clark are just arrived, all in very good health. They had left the Pacific Ocean on 23d March last—they wintered there—they arrived there last November: there was some American vessels there just before their arrival. They had to pack one hundred and sixty miles from the head of the Missouri to the Columbia River. One of the hands, and intelligent man, tells me the Indians are as numerous on the Columbia as the whites are in any part of the United States. They brought one family of Indians, of the Mandan nation. They have brought several curiosities with them from the Ocean. The Indians are being represented as being very peaceful! The winter was very mild on the Pacific.

I am yours &c

JOHN MULLANPHY

PS They left St. Charles May 20th 1804 and returned there September 21, 1806

Source: Palladium Newspaper, October 2, 1806.

Further Reading

Bedini, Silvio. *Thomas Jefferson: Statesman of Science*. New York: Macmillan, 1990.

Bernstein, R. B. *Thomas Jefferson*. Oxford: Oxford University Press, 2005.

Cerami, Charles. *Jefferson's Great Gamble: The Remarkable Story of Jefferson, Napoleon and the Men behind the Louisiana Purchase*. New York: Source Books, 2004.

Chuinard, Eldon G. *Only One Man Died: The Medical Aspects of the Lewis and Clark Expedition*. Glendale, CA: Arthur Clark Company, 1980.

Ellis, Joseph. *American Sphinx: The Character of Thomas Jefferson*. New York: Vintage Books, 1998.

Ellis, Joseph. *Founding Brothers: The Revolutionary Generation*. New York: Vintage Books, 2002.

Fenster, Julie. *Jefferson's America: The President, the Purchase, and the Explorers Who Transformed a Nation*. New York: Crown, 2016.

Kukla, Jon. *A Wilderness So immense: The Louisiana Purchase and the Destiny of America*, Anchor Books, 2004.

Ostler, Jeffrey. *The Plains Sioux and U.S. Colonialism from Lewis and Clark to Wounded Knee*. Cambridge: Cambridge University Press, 2004.

Peterson, Larry. *American Trinity: Jefferson, Custer and the Spirit of the West*. Sweetgrass Books, 2017.

Document 97

FROM THOMAS JEFFERSON TO MERIWETHER LEWIS (OCTOBER 20, 1806)

Introduction: "Unspeakable Joy"

Meriwether Lewis wrote to Jefferson on September 23, 1804, and just under a month later, Jefferson received the news that Lewis and the whole expedition were alive and had successfully reached the Pacific Ocean. Jefferson's reaction was what he described as "unspeakable joy." He had no words, but his delight and relief were obvious, as he had long given them for dead.

Jefferson assured Lewis that his hard work of creating friendship between the government of the United States and the Native American population was already paying off, as Jefferson was creating a place where the gifts exchanged can be seen. Jefferson also specifically refers to the Mandans as "friends," remembering probably how the Mandans had helped and supported the expedition during that first winter.

I recieved, my dear Sir, with unspeakable joy your letter of Sep. 23 announcing the return of yourself, Capt Clarke & your party in good health to St. Louis. the unknown scenes in which you were engaged, & the length of time without hearing of you had begun to be felt awfully. your letter having been 31. days coming, this cannot find you at Louisville, & I therefore think it safest to lodge it at Charlottesville. it's only object is to assure you of what you already known, my constant affection for you & the joy with which all your friends here will recieve you. tell my friend of Mandane also that I have already opened my arms to recieve him. perhaps, while in our neighborhood, it may be gratifying to him, & not otherwise to yourself to take a ride to Monticello and see in what manner I have arranged the tokens of friendship I have recieved from his country particularly as well as from other Indian friends: that I am in fact preparing a kind of Indian hall. mr Dinsmore, my principal workman will shew you every thing there. had you not better bring him by Richmond, Fredericksburg, & Alexandria? he will thus see what none of the others have visited, & the convenience of the public stages will facilitate your taking that route. I salute you with sincere affection.

TH: JEFFERSON

Source: Library of Congress, Manuscript Division.

Further Reading

Bedini, Silvio. *Thomas Jefferson: Statesman of Science.* New York: Macmillan, 1990.

Bernstein, R. B. *Thomas Jefferson.* Oxford: Oxford University Press, 2005.

Cerami, Charles. *Jefferson's Great Gamble: The Remarkable Story of Jefferson, Napoleon and the Men behind the Louisiana Purchase.* New York: Source Books, 2004.

Chuinard, Eldon G. *Only One Man Died: The Medical Aspects of the Lewis and Clark Expedition.* Glendale, CA: Arthur Clark Company, 1980.

Ellis, Joseph. *American Sphinx: The Character of Thomas Jefferson.* New York: Vintage Books, 1998.

Ellis, Joseph. *Founding Brothers: The Revolutionary Generation.* New York: Vintage Books, 2002.

Fenster, Julie. *Jefferson's America: The President, the Purchase, and the Explorers Who Transformed a Nation.* New York: Crown, 2016.

Kukla, Jon. *A Wilderness So immense: The Louisiana Purchase and the Destiny of America.* Anchor Books, 2004.

Ostler, Jeffrey. *The Plains Sioux and U.S. Colonialism from Lewis and Clark to Wounded Knee.* Cambridge: Cambridge University Press, 2004.

Peterson, Larry. *American Trinity: Jefferson, Custer and the Spirit of the West.* Sweetgrass Books, 2017.

Document 98

JEFFERSON WRITES TO CONGRESS ABOUT THE ACHIEVEMENTS OF LEWIS AND CLARK (DECEMBER 2, 1802)

Introduction: A Successful Voyage

The Lewis and Clark expedition had been paid for by Congress, so Jefferson was obliged to return to Congress to give a report to assure it that its money was well spent. On December 2, 1806, he announced that Lewis and Clark had achieved what Congress asked of them: they reached the Pacific Ocean from the East Coast, they noted the geography along the way, and they established relations with various people on the way. Lewis and Clark served their country well.

Jefferson was probably also aware that the Federalists were not in favor of western expansion, one change that was now guaranteed by their return and their maps. This Republican-Federalist debate was evident even in how people responded to the return of Lewis and Clark: while Republicans celebrated, Federalists' opposition to expansion increased to even making fun of the successful of the scientific discoveries seeing them as a waste of money.

The expedition of Messrs. Lewis & Clarke, for exploring the river Missouri, & the best communication from that to the Pacific Ocean, has had all the success which could have been expected. They have traced the Missouri nearly to it's Source, descended the Columbia to the Pacific Ocean, ascertained with accuracy the geography of that interesting communication across our continent, learnt the Character of the Country, of it's commerce & Inhabitants, & it is but justice to say that Messrs. Lewis & Clarke, & their brave Companions, have, by this arduous service, deserved well of their Country.

Source: A Compilation of the Messages and Papers of the Presidents, Volume 1. New York: Bureau of National Literature, Inc., 1897, 396.

Further Reading

Allen, John Logan. *Passage through the Garden: Lewis and Clark and the Image of the American Northwest.* Urbana: University of Illinois Press, 1975.
Ambrose, Stephen. *Undaunted Courage.* Urbana: University of Chicago Press, 1991.
Blumberg, Rhoda. *The Incredible Journey of Lewis and Clark.* New York: Scholastic, 1993.
Buckley, Jay H. *William Clark: Indian Diplomat.* University of Oklahoma Press, 2008.
Danisli, Thomas. *Meriwether Lewis.* Prometheus Books, 2009.
Ellis, Joseph. *Founding Brothers: The Revolutionary Generation.* New York: Vintage Books, 2002.
Jenkinson, Clay. *The Character of Meriwether Lewis in the Wilderness.* The Dakota Institute, 2011.
Jones, Landon Y. *William Clark and the Shaping of the West.* New York: Hill and Wang, 2004.
Morris, Larry E. *The Fate of the Corps: What Became of the Lewis and Clark Explorers after the Expedition.* New Haven, CT: Yale University Press, 2005.
Slaughter, Thomas P. *Exploring Lewis and Clark: Reflections on Men and Wilderness.* New York: Vintage Press, 2004.

Document 99

JAMES MADISON APPOINTS FREDERICK BATES AS SECRETARY OF LOUISIANA (JANUARY 31, 1807)

Introduction: Frederick Bates Is Appointed Secretary of Louisiana

While Lewis was being toasted in Washington, he was unaware that the appointment of Frederick Bates (1777–1825) as secretary of Louisiana would soon complicate his life and make him miserable. Bates and Lewis would openly fight in Louisiana in the coming years, and Bates's attitude toward Lewis would later be seen as one of the biggest reasons as to why Lewis committed suicide.

Bates was born in Goochland County, Virginia, and after being initially educated at home, he went to college and studied law. He worked in the army in the Department of the Quartermaster General, from 1795 to 1802, after which he became postmaster in Detroit. While in Detroit, Bates changed his party allegiance from Federalist to Republican.

On February 4, 1807, Jefferson, a family friend, appointed him as secretary to Louisiana Territory and recorder of lands. While Bates and Lewis were both appointed to these new positions at about the same time, Lewis did not actually get to St. Louis for a year, and during this time, Bates took over the role as acting governor. When Lewis did finally arrive, he found Bates difficult to manage. It was not uncommon for the two to have public arguments, with Bates jealous of Lewis's fame and frustrated by Lewis's inability to govern. This tense relationship and the fact that Lewis discovered that Bates was going to complain to the president about him were the factors that led Lewis to making that last trip to Washington, D.C.

February 4, 1807

THOMAS JEFFERSON, President of the United States of America,

To all who shall see these presents, Greeting:

Know Ye, That reposing special Trust and Confidence in the Integrity, Diligence and Abilities of FREDERICK BATES, of the Michigan Territory, I have nominated, and by and with the advice and consent of the Senate do appoint him Secretary in and for the Territory of Louisiana; and do authorize and empower him to execute and fulfil the duties of that office according to Law; and to Have and to Hold the said office with all the powers, privileges and Emoluments to the same of right appertaining for the term of four years from the day of the date hereof, unless the President of the United States for the time being should be pleased sooner to revoke and determine this Commission.

LS   In Testimony whereof, I have caused these Letters to be made patent and the Seal of the United States to be hereunto affixed.

Given under my hand at the City of Washington the Fourth day of February in the year of our Lord One thousand Eight hundred and Seven; and of the Independence of the United States of America the Thirty first.

TH: JEFFERSON
BY THE PRESIDENT
JAMES MADISON SECRETARY OF STATE

Source: Carter, Clarence Edwin, ed. *The Territorial Papers of the United States: The Territory of Louisiana-Missouri, 1806–1814.* Volume 14. Washington, DC: Government Printing Office, 1949, 117.

Further Reading

Fisher, Vardis. *Suicide or Murder? The Strange Death of Governor Meriwether Lewis*. Chicago, IL: Swallow Press, 1962.

Guice, John D. W. and Jay H. Buckley. *By His Own Hand?: The Mysterious Death of Meriwether Lewis*. University of Oklahoma Press, 2006.

Jenkinson, Clay. *The Character of Meriwether Lewis in the Wilderness*. The Dakota Institute, 2011.

Morris, Larry E. *The Fate of the Corps: What Became of the Lewis and Clark Explorers after the Expedition*. New Haven, CT: Yale University Press, 2005.

Peterson, Merrill. *Thomas Jefferson and the New Nation: A Biography*. Oxford University Press, 2013.

Stroud, Patricia. *Bitterroot: The Life and Death of Meriwether Lewis*. Philadelphia: University of Pennsylvania Press, 2018.

Document 100

FEDERALIST POETRY (MARCH 1807)

Introduction: Poetry Slam

One of the more politically amusing incidents that happened after the return of the Lewis and Clark was the "Poetry Slam," which took place between Joel Barlow (1758–1812) and John Quincy Adams (1767–1848). Barlow, a poet best known for his The Vision of Columbus: A Poem in Nine Books, *wrote a poem celebrating Meriwether Lewis for a dinner given in Lewis's honor in Washington, D.C., on January, 14, 1807. The metaphor behind the poem is that Christopher Columbus is looking down and praising Lewis, with the last line of the poem suggesting that the Columbia River be renamed the Lewis River.*

Two months later, a poem was published in the Monthly Anthology *and* Boston Review, *thought to be the work of John Quincy Adams. While Adams never officially claimed to be the author of the poem, the society's February minutes included the note that "an excellent poetical communication from J.Q. Adams at Washington was approved." It is also worth noting that Adams never denied authorship.*

Set to the tune of "Yankee Doodle," the poem, as its footnote indicates, is a response to Barlow and that the author appreciates Lewis. Nevertheless, Jefferson's political rival is scathing of the scientific achievements and notes what Lewis did not discover. The poem also makes reference to Thomas Jefferson's well-known relationship with Sally Hemings, an African American Slave, with whom he had six children.

> Let the Nile cloak his head in the clouds, and defy
> The researches of science and time;
> Let the Niger escape the keen traveller's eye,
> By plunging or changing his clime.
> Columbus! not so shall thy boundless domain

Defraud thy brave sons of their right;
Streams, midlands, and shorelands elude us in vain.
We shall drag their dark regions to light.
Look down, sainted sage, from thy synod of Gods;
See, inspired by thy venturous soul,
Mackenzie roll northward his earth-draining floods,
And surge the broad waves to the pole.
With the same soaring genius thy Lewis ascends,
And, seizing the car of the sun,
O'er the sky-propping hills and high waters he bends,
And gives the proud earth a new zone.
Potowmak, Ohio, Missouri had felt
Half her globe in their cincture comprest;
His long curving course has completed the belt,
And tamed the last tide of the west.
Then hear the loud voice of the nation proclaim,
And all ages resound the decree:
Let our occident stream bear the young hero's name,
Who taught him his path to the sea.
These four brother floods, like a garland of flowers,
Shall entwine all our states in a band
Conform and confederate their wide-spreading powers,
And their wealth and their wisdom expand.
From Darien to Davis one garden shall bloom,
Where war's weary banners are furl'd,
And the far scenting breezes that waft its perfume,
Shall settle the storms of the world.
Then hear the loud voice of the nation proclaim
And all ages resound the decree:
Let our occident stream bear the young hero's name,
Who taught him his path to the sea.

Source: Barlow, Joel. "On the Discoveries of Captain Lewis." *American Register*, Volume 1. Philadelphia, PA: C. & A. Conrad & Co., 1807, 198–199.

Good people listen to my tale, 'Tis nothing but what true is;
I'll tell you of the mighty deed Atchiev'd by Captain Lewis—
How starting from the Atlantick shore By fair and easy motion,
He journied, all the way by land, Until he met the ocean.
Heroick, sure, the toil must be To travel through the woods, sir;
And never meet a foe, yet save His person and his goods, sir!
What marvels on the way he found He'll tell you, if inclin'd, sir—
But I shall only now disclose The things he did not find, sir.
He never with a Mammoth met, However you may wonder;
Not even with a Mammoth's bone, Above the ground or under—
And, spite of all the pains he took The animal to track, sir,
He never could o'ertake the hog With navel on his back, sir.

And from this day his course began, Till even it was ended,
He never found an Indian tribe From Welchmen straight descended:
Nor, much as of Philosophers The fancies it might tickle;
To season his adventures, met A Mountain, sous'd in pickle.
He never left this nether world, For still he had his reason
Nor once the wagon of the sun Attempted he to seize on
To bind a Zone about the earth he was not able
They say he did but ask himself, He'll tell you 'tis a fable
He never dreamt of taming *tides*, Like monkeys or like bears, sir—
A school, for teaching floods to flow, Was not among his cares, sir—
Had rivers ask'd of him their path, They had but mov'd his laughter-
They knew their courses, all, as well Before he came as after.
And must we then resign the hope These Elements of changing?
And must we still, alas! be told That after all his ranging,
The Captain could discover nought But Water in the Fountains?
Must Forests still be form'd of Trees? Of rugged Rocks the Mountains?
We never will be so fubb'd off, As sure as I'm a sinner!
Come-let us all subscribe, and ask The HERO to a Dinner—
And Barlow stanzas shall indite—A Bard, the tide who tames, sir—
And if we cannot alter things, By G—, we'll change their names, sir!
Let old Columbus be once more Degraded from his glory;
And not a river by his name Remember him in story—
For what is *old* Discovery Compar'd to that which new is?
Strike-strike *Columbia* river out, And put in— *river Lewis!*
Let dusky Sally henceforth bear The name of Isabella;
And let the mountain, all of salt, Be christen'd Monticella—
The hog with navel on his back Tom Pain may be when drunk, sir—
And Joel call the Prairie-dog, Which once was call'd a Skunk, sir.
And when the wilderness shall yield To bumpers, bravely brimming,
A nobler victory then men;—While all our head are swimming
We'll dash the bottle on the wall And name (the thing's agreed on)
Our first-rate-ship United States, The flying frigate *Fredon*.
True—Tom and Joel now, no more Can overturn a nation;
And work, by butchery and blood, A great regeneration;—
Yet, still we can turn inside out Old Nature's Constitution,
And bring a Babel back of names—Huzzah! for REVOLUTION

Footnote: There are some understandings, graduated on such a scale that it may be necessary to inform them that our intention is not to depreciate the merits of Captain Lewis's publick services. We think highly of the spirit and judgement with which he has executed the duty undertaken by him, and we rejoice at the awards bestowed by congress upon him and his companions.

Source: "On the Discoveries of Captain Lewis." *Monthly Anthology and Boston Review.* Boston: Munroe & Francis, 1807, 143–144.

Further Reading

Bedini, Silvio. *Thomas Jefferson: Statesman of Science*. New York: Macmillan, 1990.

Gordon-Reed, Annette. *The Hemingses of Monticello*. New York: W.W. Norton, 2009.

Morris, Larry E. *The Fate of the Corps: What Became of the Lewis and Clark Explorers after the Expedition*. New Haven, CT: Yale University Press, 2005.

Slaughter, Thomas P. *Exploring Lewis and Clark: Reflections on Men and Wilderness*. New York: Vintage Press, 2004.

Stroud, Patricia. *Bitterroot: The Life and Death of Meriwether Lewis*. Philadelphia: University of Pennsylvania Press, 2018.

Unger, Harlow Giles. *John Quincy Adams*. New York: Da Capo Press, reprint, 2013.

Document 101

LETTER TO THOMAS JEFFERSON FROM HENRY DEARBORN (MARCH 12, 1807)

Introduction: Rewards for William Clark

Lewis and Clark were heroes. Their safe return was front-page news. Everyone thought they were dead; the fact that they were alive, had successfully got to the Pacific Ocean, and had returned was miraculous. Jefferson was determined to reward them handsomely. Both Lewis and Clark had received double pay and land for the adventure, and Jefferson had appointed Lewis as governor of the territory of Louisiana and appointed Clark to be in charge of the militia of the territory. Jefferson would also appoint him U.S. agent for Indian affairs, where he would report directly to Governor Lewis.

Clark's successful interactions with various Native peoples during the expedition made him an ideal candidate for the job. He understood, like his brother, that there were different cultures, history, and languages. The difference here in this new position was that the West he had helped explore, which would not begin to be populated by immigrants from the East and from Europe, would become a place of colonization. There would be bloody wars and serious consequences for the Native people. Clark had seen what a smallpox epidemic had done to the Native peoples, and he would soon see what expansion through Manifest Destiny would do.

War Department March 12. 1807

Sir,

I have the honor of proposing for your approbation William Clark to be appointed Brigadier General of the Militia of the Territory of Louisiana.

Accept Sir, assurances of my high respect & consideration

H Dearborn

Source: Carter, Clarence Edwin, ed. *The Territorial Papers of the United States: The Territory of Louisiana-Missouri, 1806–1814.* Volume 14. Washington, DC: Government Printing Office, 1949, 436.

Further Reading

Bedini, Silvio. *Thomas Jefferson: Statesman of Science.* New York: Macmillan, 1990.

Betts, Robert. *In Search of York: The Slave Who Went to the Pacific with Lewis and Clark.* Denver: University of Colorado Press, 2002.

Buckley, Jay H. *William Clark: Indian Diplomat.* University of Oklahoma Press, 2008.

Holmberg, James. *Dear Brother: Letters of William Clark to Jonathan Clark.* New Haven, CT: Yale University Press, 2002.

Morris, Larry E. *The Fate of the Corps: What Became of the Lewis and Clark Explorers after the Expedition.* New Haven, CT: Yale University Press, 2005.

Slaughter, Thomas P. *Exploring Lewis and Clark: Reflections on Men and Wilderness.* New York: Vintage Press, 2004.

Chapter 5

The Trouble with Home

Introduction

On October 11, 1809, three years after his return from the Pacific, Meriwether Lewis was dead.

While the full circumstances surrounding his death will probably never be known, they have been complicated by a changing story, facts difficult to pin down, rumors, the tabloid press, and a known highly dangerous route that Lewis used for his last journey from St. Louis to Washington, D.C.

On September 3, 1809, Meriwether Lewis left St. Louis on another journey, this time for Washington, D.C. His time as governor of the Territory of Louisiana had been frustrating and problematic: there was a need for cash to pay the bills of the federal government, and little was forthcoming. As well as that, Lewis openly fought with some of the long-time officials in the area, in particular Frederick Bates, who complicated his life at every turn, making accusations that Lewis was using government money improperly, and who threatened to report him to the president. Lewis also wanted to go east to try to get his journals published, something Jefferson was anxious to happen. This became increasingly important as Patrick Gass, one of the sergeants on the voyage, had in 1807 published his journals, in which he first coined the phrase, "The Corps of Discovery." Each time Lewis had previously attempted to go to Washington, a crisis broke out, and he was forced to stay. Constantly accused of being dishonest, he was unhappy, perhaps even depressed, and on top of everything else, he was sick much of the time, probably with malaria, which had most likely been picked up while on the expedition.

On September 3, 1809, Lewis set out on what would prove to be his last journey. The trip was unusually slow, and the weather was especially hot and humid. On top of these trying conditions, Lewis was once again sick. He medicated himself by using opium pills daily. He was also drinking heavily.

On September 11, 1809, Lewis arrived at New Madrid, Missouri, where he sent his servant, John Pernier, ashore to look for a legal witness. Lewis wrote his will, leaving everything to his mother, and he needed a legal witness to recognize its validity. It is worth noting that this same night Lewis also wrote a letter to William Clark. The letter has since been lost, but Clark would later refer to its description of how low Lewis was feeling.

The original plan was for Lewis to travel to Washington, D.C., by boat via New Orleans. However, Lewis changed his mind en route. In a letter written on September 6 to James Madison, who had succeeded Jefferson as president on March 4,

1809, Lewis explained his change of travel plans, first as he was concerned about the heat in the South. He also mentioned to Madison that he had what could be described as "security concerns" regarding the papers he was carrying: the maps and journals from the expedition. He did not want to take the chance that the maps in particular might end up in the hands of the British, whose ships were in the Gulf Coast at the time. The year 1809 was only three years after Aaron Burr (1756–1836) and James Wilkinson (1757–1825) had unsuccessfully tried to establish a new nation in the Mississippi area.

By the time Lewis arrived at Fort Pickering, he was once again ill and had to stay there two weeks under medical care, while he regained his strength. He then continued the journey this time by land via the Natchez Trace, a 440-mile trade route that linked Natchez, Mississippi, to Nashville, Tennessee. Lewis was accompanied on this journey by three people: Major James Neely, a Chickasaw Indian agent who had volunteered to help Lewis get to Washington, D.C.; Lewis's servant John Pernier, a freed African American man; and a hired horse packer.

The second part of the journey slowed down when Lewis once again got sick, and the group was forced to stop for another two days. On October 10, two horses strayed from the group, so Major Neely stayed behind to search for them, while Lewis and the two servants went ahead. That night, Lewis and the two servants stopped at Grinder's Stand, a small inn, about 75 miles southwest of Nashville. Mrs. Pricilla Grinder was there, but her husband, Robert, was away. She prepared Lewis a meal, but he ate very little, and went to his room, refusing her offer to get a bed ready for him, insisting that he was going to sleep on the floor. The servants went to sleep in the barn, while Mrs. Grinder slept in the kitchen. Mrs. Grinder later stated that during the night she saw Lewis agitated, pacing the floor, and talking to himself, when she looked at him through a hole in the bedroom door.

Early in the morning of October 11, Mrs. Grinder heard shots and ran to the room to find that Lewis had shot himself in the head and side. A few hours later he died. Major Neely arrived the next day and, according to his account, buried Lewis there. The same day Neely and the two servants left Grinder's Inn and traveled to Nashville. They arrived on October 18, where Neely reported to Captain John Brahan what had happened. Brahan, in turn, wrote to both Jefferson and the secretary of war, William Eustis, to inform them of Lewis's death.

When told of Lewis's death via suicide, neither Clark nor Jefferson was surprised. They both accepted it. They had both been aware of Lewis's physical and emotional struggles, as well as his heavy drinking. They also knew that he had been deeply unhappy since his return and that he was frustrated professionally as governor and personally as he had not gotten married.

The suspicion that Lewis had been murdered seems to have come initially from differing accounts given by Mrs. Grinder: in one account she claimed Lewis was agitated all night in his room, in another she changed the story that there had been a duel, and later she claimed that she had seen Lewis stagger out of the nearby woods, wounded. Others have blamed Major Neely for Lewis's death, as despite the fact he was meant to help or even protect Lewis as he tried to get to Washington, D.C., Neely was not there when Lewis died. Lucy Meriwether Lewis, on the other hand, always claimed that her son was killed by James Pernia, in order to steal Lewis's watch.

A final issue has always been the Natchez Trace, the 400-mile road from Natchez, Mississippi, to Nashville, Tennessee. In 1809, the road, sometimes known as the Old Natchez Trace, Chickasaw Trace, or the Columbian Highway, was about a three-week journey, by wagon. It was considered a highly dangerous road that was, in 1809, in the process of being built. It was known to be a place where highway men, murderers, and groups of marauding Native groups would attack anyone on the route, robbing and killing. So it has been suggested that what Mrs. Grinder saw were highway robbers attacking and killing Lewis.

By 1909, on the 100th anniversary of the death of Meriwether Lewis, all of these complications began news as "Yellow Journalism" or the tabloid press had become popular, and a series of stories were run in various newspapers speculating as to the causes of Lewis's death. All these theories and many more were published.

When trying to consider what happened to Lewis, most historians return to the two people who were closest to him: William Clark and Thomas Jefferson. Their acceptance of his suicide seems to override all other theories. At the time, only one person really did not believe he had committed suicide—his mother. Yet as time has passed, there have been more who see issues with the acceptance of suicide as the cause of Lewis's death. People point out that he was after all positive in his letter to Madison, determined to clear his name and protect the journals, and while it seems that Lewis may have been short of cash, he was not poor by any means, as he still owned large tracts of land. Others wonder what was in the letter he wrote to Clark. It remains missing. We will probably never know for sure what happened that night, except that Lewis died as the result of gunshots.

William Clark's life after the expedition was more successful. He was appointed brigadier general of the militia and superintendent of Indian affairs for the Territory of Louisiana. Later in 1813, he was appointed governor of the Missouri Territory. When Missouri became a state, he ran for election for governor but was defeated. Clark, unlike Lewis, married on his return. In 1808, he married Julia Hancock, after whom he had named a river while on the expedition, and the couple moved to St. Louis. They had five children, and the eldest, a boy, was named Meriwether Lewis Clark. In 1820, Julia became extremely ill, probably of breast cancer. She returned to Virginia hoping to recuperate but died there the same year. Clark then married Harriet Kennerly Radford, a widow, in 1821. She died 10 years later, on Christmas Day, 1831, of unknown causes.

After the expedition, Clark maintained influence over the lives of some of those who had been west with him. He still owned York, and after they returned, Clark insisted that York return to his role as slave. York's resistance and frustration to this was met by severe punishments by Clark, as he had York flogged on a number of different occasions and even hired him out to work to another man where York was treated particularly harshly. Clark even sold York's wife to another slave owner and refused to sell York to the same person. Eventually in 1816, Clark freed York, and York opened a small drainage business. Clark in an exchange with Washington Irving, the American writer, insisted that York was lazy and that the business failed, and that York even wanted a return to slavery; however, he died of cholera before it happened.

While Clark's relationship with York was harsh, Clark did adopt Sacagawea's son Jean Baptiste Charbonneau and her daughter Lizette, born probably in 1812. While Jean Baptiste seems to have gone to live with Clark prior to 1812 in order to get an education, both children were legally adopted by him in 1813. Sacagawea seems to have died the year before. While there are no records of Lizette as an adult, we can only presume that she died very young. Touissant Charbonneau is thought to have died in 1843, as Jean Baptiste legally settled his estate that year. Jean Baptiste was given the promised education by Clark, resulting in him traveling to Europe, being a fur trader, elected to office of San Luis Rey in California. He died aged 61.

The last member of the Corps of Discovery to die was Patrick Gass on April 2, 1870, at 98 years old. Gass stayed in the army after the expedition, fighting in the War of 1812, where he lost an eye. He was given a pension in 1815. It was Gass who first published his journals in 1807, titled "A Journal of the Voyages and Travels of a Corps of Discovery."

Document 102

PATRICK GASS PUBLISHED HIS JOURNALS (1807)

Introduction: The Term "Corps of Discovery" Is Created

When Gass returned in 1806, his friends encouraged him to publish his journals. Gass realized he did not have the skills to prepare his journals for publishing, so he hired David McKeehan, a school teacher, to help. The first copies were published in Pittsburgh and sold for $1. Gass's journals had many printings in the United States and England and were translated into French and German.

JOURNAL
OF THE
VOYAGES AND TRAVELS
OF A CORPS OF DISCOVERY
Under the Command of Capt. Lewis and Capt. Clarke of the army of the United Staes,
FROM THE MOUTH OF THE MISSOURI THROUGH
THE INTERIOR PARTS OF NORTH AMERICA
TO THE PACIFIC OCEAN
DURING THE YEARS 1804, 1805, 1806.
CONTAINING
An authentic relation of the most interesting transitions
During the expedition; a description of the country

And an account of its inhabitants, soil, climate
Curiosities, and vegetable
And animal production
BY PATRICK GASS
One of the persons employed in the expedition

Source: Gass's Journal of the Lewis and Clark Expedition. Chicago: A.C. McClurg, 1904.

Further Reading

Danisi, Thomas and John Danisi. "Uncovering Jefferson's Account of Lewis's 18 Mysterious Death." *We Proceeded On* (November 2012).

Dillon, Richard. *Meriwether Lewis: A Biography.* New York: Coward-McCann, 1965.

Harris, Matthew and Jay H. Buckley. *Zebulon Pike, Thomas Jefferson and the Opening of the American West.* University of Oklahoma Press, 2012.

Meacham, John. *Thomas Jefferson and the Art of Power.* Random House, 2013.

Peterson, Larry. *American Trinity: Jefferson, Custer and the Spirit of the West.* Sweetgrass Books, 2017.

Randall, William Sterne. *Thomas Jefferson: A Life.* Harper Classics, 2014.

Stroud, Patricia. *Bitterroot: The Life and Death of Meriwether Lewis.* Philadelphia: University of Pennsylvania Press 2018.

Turner, Erin H. *It Happened on the Lewis and Clark Expedition.* Guilford, CT: Globe Pequot Press, 2003.

Document 103

LETTER FROM FREDERICK BATES TO RICHARD BATES (APRIL 15, 1809)

Introduction: Bates and Lewis Clash

After the expedition, Lewis returned home to Albemarle County, Virginia, to spend Christmas with his family. Lewis's concerns about his mother were unfounded: she was very much alive and in good health. After Christmas, he went to Washington, D.C., where he was rewarded for the expedition with double pay, 1,600 acres of land, and the governorship of the Territory of Upper Louisiana. But his work in Louisiana proved to be the toughest battle that Meriwether Lewis had ever faced.

Lewis had been an obvious choice for this job. He was, after all, the person who had led the expedition west as a result of the Louisiana Purchase. Lewis understood the independent spirit of the traders and guides in the area. He also had military experience. Jefferson thought he could not have chosen a better person to govern this new territory.

But in fact, Lewis was not at all familiar with the day-to-day workings of federal government in St. Louis, and he could not find anyone willing to teach or guide him.

One of the people with whom Lewis had most trouble was Frederick Bates (1777–1825). Bates had been appointed as secretary to the Louisiana Territory, by Jefferson, but was serving as acting governor pending Lewis's arrival. When Lewis did finally arrive, Bates was one of his most outspoken critics. Here in a letter to his brother Richard Bates, Frederick explains that Lewis is extremely unpopular, but that the blame for this lies totally with Lewis. Bates was ambitious and was building a political base for himself, hoping at some stage in the near future to become governor of the area. Bates here refers to an argument he and Lewis had in public at a ball. The two met in private soon afterward but did not resolve their differences. Bates here asks his brother to destroy the letter, but his brother for unknown reasons did not do it.

April 15, 1809.

DEAR RICHARD

I have spoken my wrongs with extreme freedom the Governor.—it was my intention to have appealed to his superiors and mine; but the altercation was brought about by a circumstance which aroused my indignation, and the overflowings of a heated resentment burst the barriers which Prudence and Principle had prescribed. We now understand each other much better. We differ in everything; but we will be honest and frank in out intercourse.

I lament the unpopularity of the Governor; but he has brought it on himself by harsh and mistaken measures. He is inflexible in error, and the irresistible Fiat of the People, has, I am fearful, already sealed his condemnation. Burn this, and do not speak of it.

Source: The Life and Papers of Frederick Bates. St. Louis, MI: Missouri Historical Society, 1926.

Further Reading

Danisli, Thomas. *Meriwether Lewis.* Prometheus Books, 2009.

Danisli, Thomas. *Uncovering the Truth about Meriwether Lewis.* Prometheus Books, 2012.

Dillon, Richard. *Meriwether Lewis: A Biography.* New York: Coward-McCann, 1965.

Dillon, Richard. *Meriwether Lewis.* Great West Books, 2003.

Fisher, Vardis. *Suicide or Murder? The Strange Death of Governor Meriwether Lewis.* Chicago, IL: Swallow Press, 1962.

Foley, William. *The Genesis of Missouri: From Outpost to Statehood.* University of Missouri, 1989.

Guice, John D. W., ed. *By His Own Hand? The Mysterious Death of Meriwether Lewis.* Norman: Oklahoma University Press, 2006.

Morris, Larry E. *The Fate of the Corps: What Became of the Lewis and Clark Explorers after the Expedition.* New Haven, CT: Yale University Press, 2005.

Stroud, Patricia. *Bitterroot: The Life and Death of Meriwether Lewis.* University of Pennsylvania Press, 2018.

Document 104

LETTER FROM FREDERICK BATES TO RICHARD BATES (JULY 14, 1809)

Introduction: Frederick Bates Tells His Brother That Lewis Is Going to Washington, D.C.

Frederick Bates constantly wrote to his brother, filling him in about the happenings in the political world of St. Louis. This series of letters provides insight into the constant difficulties Lewis faced with Bates. Lewis was not keeping a journal of his life, so historians' primary source of information about Lewis's life during this period are the letters from Bates.

On July 14, 1809, Frederick Bates wrote to his brother again, explaining that Lewis was finally going to Washington, D.C. By this point, Bates had stopped even pretending he had any respect for Lewis. He notes that Lewis had gone from being unpopular to being disliked.

This trip that Lewis finally began was to be his last. This description from Bates of his attitude toward Lewis, how Lewis felt, and how Lewis had to deal with so much day-to-day strife lends credence to the probability that Lewis committed suicide.

July 14, 1809
FREDERICK BATES TO RICHARD BATES

Gov Lewis this in a few days for Phila. Washingn &c He has fallen from the Public esteem & almost into public contempt. He is well aware of my increasing popularity (for one scale sinks as the other rises, without an increase of gravity except comparative and has for some time feared that I was at the head of a Party whose object would be to denounce him to the President and procure his dismission. The Gov: is greatly mistaken in these suspicions; and I have accordingly employed every frank and open explanation which might have a tendency to remove that veil with which a few worthless fellows have endeavoured to exclude from him the sunshine. He called at my Office & personally demanded this explanation. It was made with that independence which I am determined shall mark my conduct on all occasions; and accompanied with an assurance that the path of life which I had long since prescribed to myself did not admit the prevarication. As a Citizen I told him I entertained opinions very different from his, on the subject of civil government and that those opinions had, on various occasions been expressed with emphasis; but that they had been unmixed with personal malice or hostility. I made him sensible that it would be the extreme of folly in me to aspire above my present standing; that in point of Honor my present Offices were nearly equal to the government and greatly superior in emolument—and that the latter could not from any motives of prudence be accepted by me, if offered by the President. "Well" said he "do not suffer yourself to be separated from me in the public opinion; When we meet in public, let us, at least address each other with cordial-ity." My very humanity yielded a prompt assent to thus Request and for this I am resolved to take every opportunity of convincing the People that however I may have disapproved & continue to disapprove the measure of the Governor, that as a man I entertain good opinions of him. He used me badly, but as Pope says "Twas when he knew no better"—In one particular case he had determined to go to Washington (Tho he did not go) he left certain Executive Business to be performed by Genl. Clark; tho the Laws have expressly provided for his absence. I waited in his Excellency& demanded that eh General should be called in. The Gentlemen were then told I would I would suffer no interferences. How unfortunate for this man that he resigned his commission in the army: His habits are altogether military and he never can succeed I think in any other profession."

Source: The Life and Papers of Frederick Bates. St. Louis, MI: Missouri Historical Society, 1926.

Further Reading

Foley, William. *The Genesis of Missouri: From Outpost to Statehood.* University of Missouri, 1989.

Dillon, Richard. *Meriwether Lewis.* Great West Books, 2003.

Danisli, Thomas. *Meriwether Lewis.* Prometheus Books, 2009.

Danisli, Thomas. *Uncovering the Truth about Meriwether Lewis.* Prometheus Books, 2012.

Jenkinson, Clay. *The Character of Meriwether Lewis in the Wilderness.* The Dakota Institute, 2011.

Kukla, Jon. *A Wilderness So immense: The Louisiana Purchase and the Destiny of America.* Anchor Books, 2004.

Morris, Larry E. *The Fate of the Corps: What Became of the Lewis and Clark Explorers after the Expedition.* New Haven, CT: Yale University Press, 2005.

Stroud, Patricia. *Bitterroot: The Life and Death of Meriwether Lewis.* University of Pennsylva-nia Press 2018.

Document 105

LETTER FROM THOMAS JEFFERSON TO MERIWETHER LEWIS (AUGUST 16, 1809)

Introduction: Jefferson Wonders When the Journals Will Be Published

On March 4, 1809, James Madison became the fourth president of the United States, and Jefferson returned to Monticello. In August 1809, Jefferson wrote to Lewis explain-ing how much he was enjoying the work being done in his gardens by William Roscoe (1733–1851), a botanist, but he also commented that he was concerned that Patrick Gass published his journals in 1809, and that there was no sign of the journals of Lewis and Clark being published. Jefferson was getting anxious, as he had promised copies to friends, both at home and in France. Jefferson uses the word "impatient," to describe his frustration.

Monticello Aug. 16. 09.

DEAR SIR

This will be handed you mr Bradbury, an English botanist, who proposes to take St Louis in his botanising tour. he came recommended to me by mr Roscoe of Liverpool, so well known by his histories of Lorenzo of Medicis & Leo X. & who is president of the Botanical society of Liverpool. mr Bradbury comes out in their employ, & having kept him here about ten days, I have had an opportunity of knowing that besides being a botanist of the first order, he is a man of entire worth & correct conduct. as such I recommend him to your notice, advice & patronage, while within your government or it's confines. perhaps you can consult no abler hand on your Western botanical observations. I am very often applied to know when your work will begin to appear; and I have so long promised copies to my literary correspondents in France, that I am almost bankrupt in their eyes. I shall be very happy to recieve from yourself information of your expectations on this subject. every body is impatient for it.

Th: Jefferson

Source: Thwaites, Reuben Gold, ed. *Original Journals of the Lewis and Clark Expedition, 1804–1806.* Volume 7. New York: Dodd, Mead & Company, 1905, 367.

Further Reading

Danisi, Thomas C., and John C. Jackson. *Meriwether Lewis.* Prometheus Books, 2009.

Danisi, Thomas C., and Robert Moore. *Uncovering the Truth about Meriwether Lewis.* New York: Prometheus Book, 2001.

Ellis, Joseph. *American Sphinx: The Character of Thomas Jefferson.* New York: Vintage Books, 1998.

Meacham, John. *Thomas Jefferson: The Art of Power.* New York: Random House, 2013.

Morris, Larry E. *The Fate of the Corps: What Became of the Lewis and Clark Explorers after the Expedition.* New Haven, CT: Yale University Press, 2005.

Stroud, Patricia. *Bitterroot: The Life and Death of Meriwether Lewis.* University of Pennsylvania Press, 2018.

Document 106

FROM MERIWETHER LEWIS TO JAMES MADISON (SEPTEMBER 16, 1809)

Introduction: Lewis Writes That He Has Changed His Plans about How He Will Get to Washington, D.C.

On September 16, 1809, Meriwether Lewis wrote to James Madison, who was now president. Lewis had finally left St. Louis by ship, with the intention of traveling to Washington,

D.C. There was no direct route to Washington at the time, so Lewis's plan was to travel from St. Louis to New Orleans by boat, to board another ship up the East Coast, to Baltimore, and finally to undertake the last, relatively short, part of the journey by land.

Lewis changed this plan when he arrived at Fort Pickering, in Memphis, Tennessee, once again ill from malaria. He was forced to stay there for a few days to recover. In this letter to Madison, Lewis also explains his change of plan: he no longer planned to continue to New Orleans, for he found the heat unbearable. As the following letter illustrates, he was also concerned that his journals might fall in to the hands of the British, should he and his party get attacked. It is important to remember that the journals included maps of the West and detailed information that could be considered matters of national security.

From Meriwether Lewis

CHICKASAW BLUFFS, September 16th. 09

DEAR SIR

I arrived here yesterday about 1 P.M. very much exhausted from the heat of the climate, but having taken medicine feel much better this morning. My appreh[en]sion from the heat of the lower country and my fear of the original papers relative to my voyage to the Pacific ocean falling into the hands of the British has induced me to change my rout and proceed by land through the state of Tennesee to the City of washington. I bring with me duplicates of my vouchers for public expenditures &c which when fully explained, or reather the general view of the circumstances under which they were made I flatter myself they will recieve both sanction & approbation.

Provided my health permits no time shall be lost in reaching Washington. My anxiety to pursue and to fullfill the duties incident to the internal arrangements incident to the government of Louisiana has prevented my writing you more frequently. Inclosed I herewith transmit you a copy of the laws of the territory of Louisiana. I have the honour to be with the most sincere esteem Your Obt. and very humble Servt.

MERIWETHER LEWIS.

Source: "To James Madison from Meriwether Lewis, 16 September 1809," *Founders Online.* National Archives. Available at: http://founders.archives.gov/documents/Madison/03-01-02-0420.

Further Reading

Danisi, Thomas C. and John C. Jackson. *Meriwether Lewis.* Prometheus Books, 2009.

Danisi, Thomas C. and Robert Moore. *Uncovering the Truth about Meriwether Lewis.* New York: Prometheus Book, 2001.

Dillon, Richard. *Meriwether Lewis: A Biography.* New York: Coward-McCann, 1965.

Guice, John D. W. and Jay H. Buckley. *By His Own Hand?: The Mysterious Death of Meriwether Lewis.* University of Oklahoma Press, 2006.

Jenkinson, Clay S. *The Character of Meriwether Lewis: Explorer in the Wilderness.* The Dakota Institute, 2011.

Kukla, Jon. *A Wilderness So immense: The Louisiana Purchase and the Destiny of America.* Anchor Books, 2004.

Rhoda, James P. *Lewis and Clark among the Indians.* Bison Books, 2004.

Saughter, Thomas P. *Exploring Lewis and Clark: Reflections on Men and Wilderness.* New York: Vintage Press, 2004.

Stroud, Patricia. *Bitterroot: The Life and Death of Meriwether Lewis.* University of Pennsylvania Press 2018.

Document 107

LETTER FROM JAMES NEELY TO THOMAS JEFFERSON (OCTOBER 18, 1809)

Introduction: Neely Informs Jefferson of Lewis's Death

Meriwether Lewis died on October 11, 1809, in Grinder's Tavern along the Natchez Trace in Tennessee. On October 18, 1809, Major James Neely arrived in Nashville, Tennessee, about 350 miles away. There, he wrote to Thomas Jefferson, informing him of Lewis's death. Neely is clear in the first sentence that Lewis committed suicide.

Neely recounts to Jefferson the last month of Lewis's life, from September 18, when Neely met him at Chickasaw Bluffs to Grinder's Tavern. While Lewis recovered enough to continue to travel, Neely stayed behind to look for two horses that had gotten loose, and when Neely arrived at the Tavern, Lewis was dead.

Neely here also notes that he is in possession of two trunks belonging to Lewis, as well as some personal items, including his rifle and watch. The trunk, Neely supposes, includes Lewis's papers and diary from his expedition west, as well as governmental papers from Louisiana.

From James Neely

Nashville Tennessee 18th Octr 1809

SIR,

It is with extreme pain that I have to inform you of the death of His Excellency Meriwether Lewis, Governor of upper Louisiana who died on the Morning of the 11th Instant and I am Sorry to Say by Suicide;

I arrived at the Chickasaw Bluffs on or about the 18th of September, where I found the Governor (who had reached there two days before me from St Louis) in Very bad health—It appears that his first intention was to go around by Water to the City of Washington; but his thinking a War with England probable, & that his Valuable papers might be in dainger of falling into the hands of the British, he was thereby induced to Change his route, and to come through the Chickasaw nation by land; I furnished him with a horse to pack his trunks & on, and a man to attend to them; having recovered his health in Some digree at the Chickasaw Bluffs, we Set out together. And on our arrival at the Chickasaw nation I discovered that he appeared at times deranged in mind, we rested there two days & came on. one days Journey after crossing Tennessee River & where we encamped we lost two of our horses, I remained behind to hunt them & the Governor proceeded on, with a promise to wait for me at the first houses he Came to that was inhabited by White people; he reached the house of a Mr Grinder about Sun Set, the man of the house being from home, and no person there but a woman who discovering the governor to be deranged gave him up the house & slept herself in one near it, his Servant and mine Slept in the Stable loft some distance from the other houses, the woman reports that about three OClock She heard two pistols fire off in the Governors Room: the Servants being awakined by her, came in but too late to save him. he had shot himself in the head with one pistol & a little below the Breast with the other—when his Servant came in he Says; I have done the business my good Servant give me Some water. he gave him water, he Survived but a short time, I came up Some time after, & had him as decently Buried as I could in that place—if there is any thing wished by his friends to be done to his grave I will attend to their Instructions.

I have got in my possession his two trunks of papers (amongst which is said to be his travels to the pacific Ocean) and probably some Vouchers for expenditures of Public Money for a Bill which he Said had been protested by the Sec of war; and of which act to his death, he repeatedly complained. I have also in my Care his Rifle, Silver watch, Brace of Pistols, dirk & tomahawk: one of the Governors horses was lost in the wilderness which I will endeavour to regain, the other I have Sent on by his Servant who expressed a desire to go to the governors mothers & to Monticello: I have furnished him with fifteen Dollars to Defray his expences to Charlottsville; Some days preveous to the Governors death he requested of me in Case any Accident happened to him, to Send his trunks with the papers therein to the President, but I think it Very probable he meant to You—I wish to be informed what arrangements may be considered best in Sending on his trunks &c—I have the honor to be

With Great respect Y Ob Ser

James Neelly

U.S. agent to the Chickasaw nation

the governor left two of his trunks at the Chickasaw Bluffs in the Care of Capt Gilbert C. Russell. Commanding officer, & was to write to him from Nashville what to do with them.

Source: Carter, Clarence Edwin, ed. *The Territorial Papers of the United States: The Territory of Louisiana-Missouri, 1806–1814*, Volume 14. Washington, DC: Government Printing Office, 1949, 332–333.

Further Reading

Ambrose, Stephen. *Undaunted Courage*. Urbana: University of Chicago Press, 1991.
Bernstein, R. B. *Thomas Jefferson*. Oxford: Oxford University Press, 2005.
Coates, Robert. *Outlaw Years: The History of the Land Pirates of the Natchez Trace*. Pelican Press, 2002.

Daniels, Jonathan. *Devil's Backbone: The Story of the Natchez Trace.* Pelican Press, 1985.

Danisi, Thomas C. and John Danisi. "Uncovering Jefferson's Account of Lewis's 18 Mysterious Death." *We Proceeded On* (November 2012).

Danisi, Thomas C. and Robert Moore. *Uncovering the Truth about Meriwether Lewis.* New York: Prometheus Book, 2001.

Ellis, Joseph. *American Sphinx: The Character of Thomas Jefferson.* New York: Vintage Books, 1998.

Gordon-Reed, Annette. *The Hemingses of Monticello: An American Family.* New York: W.W. Norton, 2009.

Meacham, John. *Thomas Jefferson: The Art of Power.* New York: Random House, 2013.

Document 108

LETTER FROM RICHARD BATES TO CLEMENT B. PENROSE (OCTOBER 20, 1809)

Introduction: Bates Sends Penrose a Warning

Richard Bates continued to create problems for Lewis even when he was away. Charles Penrose, a land commissioner in the territory, had confronted Bates about his treatment of Lewis, at a meeting. Penrose accused Bates of being responsible for "the mental derangement of the Governor," due to Bates's "barbarous conduct." After the meeting, Bates challenged Penrose that if Penrose ever spoke to him or about him like that again, Bates would "spurn (him) like a puppy."

Not content with a verbal warning, Bates wrote to Penrose to make this warning even more clear: inisting that what Penrose accused him of was false, and that all Penrose was doing was lying.

During this time, Bates fought with a number of officials—not just Lewis and Penrose but many others. It is interesting that the only person with whom he did not fight was William Clark, more because Clark was known not to fight.

Lewis was dead by this time, but this was not known yet in St. Louis. Lewis had died on October 11; Neely arrived the next day, buried him, and then traveled to Nashville, where he arrived on October 18, when he wrote to Jefferson and others informing them of Lewis's death. So all of this drama that was taking place in St. Louis was done presuming not that Lewis was dead but that the many accusations and charges against him would mean that Lewis would be removed from office. Bates wanted to be governor and at this stage was making sure that no one would dare say anything negative about him.

From Richard Bates

SIR

I our conversations this morning I charged you with having said, in the presence of certain gentlemen, that the motives of my misunderstandings with Governor Lewis, were the hopes of acquiring the Executive Office on his removal; and not an honest difference in opinion, in the transaction of the territorial business—This, I think you denied—And indeed, if you have common sense or a very ordinary portion of consistence, you must deny it, since you have on many occasions, been quiet as noisy on the imputed irregularities of the Governor, as any other person.—

I have spoken with the gentlemen—and understood from them, that they may, possibly, have made some inferences from your remarks on these subjects and that they cannot recollect the precise works in which your ideas were conveyed. Here, then, I drop this part of the subject.—But you still say, that I have been and am the enemy of the Governor,—and that I would be very willing to fill that office myself.—And I told you this morning that it was false—and I repeat that it is impudent stupidity in you to persist in the assertion. How is it possible that you should know my wishes, except from declarations of mine, or what part of my conduct justifies you, in the repetition of falsehood like these?

In return for the personal allusions with which you have honored me, I tender to you my most hearty contempt.

Source: The Life and Papers of Frederick Bates. St. Louis, MI: Missouri Historical Society, 1926, 99–100.

Further Reading

Danisli, Thomas. *Meriwether Lewis*. Prometheus Books, 2009.

Danisli, Thomas. *Uncovering the Truth about Meriwether Lewis*. Prometheus Books, 2012.

Dillon, Richard. *Meriwether Lewis*. Great West Books, 2003.

Dillon, Richard. *Meriwether Lewis: A Biography*. New York: Coward-McCann, 1965.

Fisher, Vardis. *Suicide or Murder? The Strange Death of Governor Meriwether Lewis*. Chicago, IL: Swallow Press, 1962.

Foley, William. *The Genesis of Missouri: From Outpost to Statehood*. University of Missouri, 1989.

Guice, John D. W., ed. *By His Own Hand? The Mysterious Death of Meriwether Lewis*. Norman: Oklahoma University Press, 2006.

Morris, Larry E. *The Fate of the Corps: What Became of the Lewis and Clark Explorers after the Expedition*. New Haven, CT: Yale University Press, 2005.

Stroud, Patricia. *Bitterroot. The Life and Death of Meriwether Lewis*. University of Pennsylvania Press 2018.

Document 109

LETTER FROM FREDERICK BATES TO RICHARD BATES (NOVEMBER 9, 1809)

Introduction: Bates's Reaction to the Death of Meriwether Lewis

Frederick Bates continued his communication with his brother on November 9, 1809. The news of Lewis's death a month earlier was at this stage well known, and his suicide was no secret. In his letter that follows, Bates expresses horror at the manner in which Lewis died, but his dislike of the late governor remains intact.

Here, Bates recounts the incident where Lewis and Bates confronted each other publicly. Bates insists that he had taken the moral high road and that it was Lewis who had embarrassed himself and was not capable—politically or personally—of handling the job. Bates also points out that while others were deceived by Lewis, he was not. He specifically refers to the praise given to him by Dr. Samuel Latham Mitchell, one of the leading scientists of the day, and by Joel Barlow, whose poem was read in Washington, D.C., at a dinner, and finally "the high and mighty" probably referred to Thomas Jefferson.

Ironically, Bates cites the old maxim "De mortuis nil nisi bouum" (of the dead speak only good). But Bates cannot abide by those words, as his own character has been maligned. He then goes on to itemize to his brother the many times that he was slighted by Lewis.

November 9, 1809

FREDERICK BATES TO RICHARD BATES

You have heard no doubt of the premature and tragical death of Gov: Lewis. Indeed I had no personal regard for him and a great deal of political contempt; Yet I cannot but lament that after all his toils and dangers he should die in such a manner.

At the first, in Washington he made to me so many friendly assurances that I then imagined our mutual friendship would plant itself on rocky foundations. But a very short acquaintance with the man was sufficient to undeceive me. He had been spoiled by the elegant praises of Mitchell & Barlow, and over whelmed by so many flattering caresses of the high and mighty that, like an over grown baby, he began to think that everybody about the house must regulate their conduct by his caprices.

'De mortuis nil nisi boum' is a good old maxim; but my character has been assailed, as respects our late Governor, and I owe to those I love some little account of myself.

I never saw, after his arrival in this country, anything in his conduct towards me, but alienation and unmerited distrust. I had acquired and shall retain a good portion of the public confidence, and he had not generosity of soul to forgive me for it. I was scarcely myself conscious of my good fortune; for the still voice of approbation with which I was favored by the People, was, as yet drowned in the clamors of my enemies. As soon as I was seen in conflict with my associates in business, my friends came forward with a generous and unexpected support.—I bore in silence the supercilious air of the Governor for a long time; until last summer he took it into his head to disavow certain statements which I had made by order from the Secretary's Office. That was too much—I wasted on him—told him my wrongs—that I could not bear to be treated in such a manner—that he had given me the orders& as truth is always eloquent, the Public would believe it on my assurances. He told me to take my own course—I shall Sir, said I, and I shall come in future to the Executive Office when I have business at it.

Some time after this, there was a ball in St. Louis, I attended early, and was seated in conversation with some Gentlemen when the Governor entered. He drew his chair close to mine—there was a pause in the conversation—I availed myself of it—arose and walked to the opposite side of the room. The dances were now commencing.—He also rose—evidently in passion, retired into an adjoining room and sent a servant for General Clark, who refused to ask me out as he foresaw that a Battle must have been the consequence of our meeting. He complained to the general that I had treated him with contempt & insult in the Ball-Room and that he could not suffer it to pass. He knew my resolutions not to speak to him except on business and he ought not to have thrust himself in my way. The thing did pass nevertheless for some weeks when General Clark waited on me for the purpose of inducing me to make advances. I replied to him, 'NO," the Governor has told me to take my own course and I shall step a high and a proud Path. He has injured me, and he must undo that injury r I shall succeed in fixing the stigma where it ought to rest. You come I added as my friend but I cannot separate you from Gov. Lewis—you have trodden the Ups and Downs of life with him and it appears to me that these proposals are made solely for his convenience.

Source: The Life and Papers of Frederick Bates. St. Louis, MI: Missouri Historical Society, 1926.

Further Reading

Ambrose, Stephen. *Undaunted Courage.* Urbana: University of Chicago Press, 1991.
Danisi, Thomas C. and John Danisi. "Uncovering Jefferson's Account of Lewis's 18 Mysterious Death." *We Proceeded On* (November 2012).
Danisi, Thomas C. and Robert Moore. *Uncovering the Truth about Meriwether Lewis.* New York: Prometheus Book, 2001.
Dillon, Richard. *Meriwether Lewis: A Biography.* New York: Coward-McCann, 1965.
Fisher, Vardis. *Suicide or Murder? The Strange Death of Governor Meriwether Lewis.* Chicago, IL: Swallow Press, 1962.
Guice, John D.W. and Jay H. Buckley. *By His Own Hand?: The Mysterious Death of Meriwether Lewis.* University of Oklahoma Press, 2006.
Morris, Larry E. *The Fate of the Corps: What Became of the Lewis and Clark Explorers after the Expedition.* New Haven, CT: Yale University Press, 2005.
Stroud, Patricia. *Bitterroot: The Life and Death of Meriwether Lewis.* University of Pennsylvania Press 2018.

Document 110

LETTER FROM THOMAS JEFFERSON TO JAMES MADISON (NOVEMBER 26, 1809)

Introduction: The Belongings of Meriwether Lewis

In this letter to James Madison, Jefferson asks if Madison, as president, should be the person to whom all of Lewis's documents should be sent. Another issue that Jefferson writes about is John Pernier's claim that he was owed $240 by Lewis. Jefferson doubts this and writes that he gave Pernier $10 to cover the expenses of the trip from Monticello to Washington, D.C.

John Pernier has become a controversial figure in the death of Meriwether Lewis. He was, after all, present when Lewis died. After leaving Jefferson and Monticello, Pernier went to Lewis's grieving mother, Lucy, and demanded the pay he was owed from her. She refused. Pernier then went to Washington, where he did indeed deliver this letter to the president. On April 28, 1810, John Perner committed suicide, an act that Lucy Marks always suggested was proof that Pernier was involved in the murder of Meriwether Lewis.

Pernier's requests, and later death, have cast a long shadow and added a complication over the death of Lewis. Lucy Marks always forwarded the notion that Pernier had murdered her son, a position that must be seen in a racial historical context. Pernier was black, and Lucy was a slave owner. One of the biggest fears for all slave owners at the time was that they would be murdered in their beds by the slaves. It is more than possible that Lucy firmly believed this and Pernier murdered her son.

November 26, 1809

To James Madison from Thomas Jefferson

I inclose you a letter from Majr. Neely, Chickasaw agent, stating that he is in possession of 2. trunks of the unfortunate Governor Lewis, containing public vouchers, the manuscripts of his Western journey, & probably some private papers. As he desired they should be sent *to the president*, as the public vouchers render it interesting to the public that they should be safely recieved, and they would probably come most safely if addressed to you, would it not be advisable that Major Neely should recieve an order on your part to forward them to Washington addressed to you, by the stage, & if possible under the care of some person coming on? When at Washington, I presume, the papers may be opened & distributed, that is to say, the Vouchers to the proper offices where they are cognisable; the Manuscript voyage Etc to Genl. Clarke who is interested in it, and is believed to be now on his way to Washington; and his private papers if any to his administrator, who is John Marks, his half brother. It is impossible you should have time to examine & distribute them; but if mr. Coles could find time to do it the family would have entire confidence in his distribution. The other two trunks which are in the care of Capt Russel at the Chickasaw bluffs, & which Pernier (Govr. Lewis's servt.) says contain his private property, I write to Capt Russel, at the request of mr. Marks, to forward to mr. Brown at N. Orleans to be sent on to Richmond under my address. Pernier says that Governor Lewis owes him 240. D. for his wages. He has reci[e]ved money from Neely to bring him on here, & I furnish him to Washington, where he will arrive pennyless, and will ask for some money to be placed to the Governor's account. He rides a horse of the Governor's, which with the approbation of the Administrator I tell him to dispose of & give credit for the amount in his account against the Governor. He is the bearer of this letter and of my assurances of constant & affectionate esteem.

TH: JEFFERSON

Source: Washington, H. A., ed. *The Works of Thomas Jefferson,* Volume V. New York: Townsend Mac Coun., 1884, 480–481.

Further Reading

Danisi, Thomas C. and John Danisi. "Uncovering Jefferson's Account of Lewis's 18 Mysterious Death." *We Proceeded On* (November 2012).

Danisi, Thomas C. and Robert Moore. *Uncovering the Truth about Meriwether Lewis.* New York: Prometheus Book, 2001.

Feldman, Noah. *The Three Lives of James Madison: Genius, Partisan, President.* New York: Random House, 2017.

Guice, John D. W. and Jay H. Buckley. *By His Own Hand?: The Mysterious Death of Meriwether Lewis.* University of Oklahoma Press, 2006.

Morris, Larry E. *The Fate of the Corps: What Became of the Lewis and Clark Explorers after the Expedition.* New Haven, CT: Yale University Press, 2005.

Stroud, Patricia. *Bitterroot: The Life and Death of Meriwether Lewis.* University of Pennsylvania Press 2018.

Document 111

LETTER FROM THOMAS JEFFERSON TO PAUL ALLEN (AUGUST 18, 1813)

Introduction: Courage Undaunted

After Lewis's death, the journals of Lewis and Clark had still to be published. Patrick Gass had published his journals in 1807, which had annoyed and even embarrassed Lewis and Clark. Gass had also been the one who used the phrase "Corps of Discovery" for the first time. Clark had initially wanted Thomas Jefferson to edit and prepare the journals, but Jefferson refused, employing Nicholas Biddle (1786–1844) to do the job. Biddle was 17 years old when he edited the journals. He had gone to the University of Pennsylvania when he was just 10 years old, and graduated from Princeton, at 13. He would later become president of the Bank of the United States. Finally, in 1814, 1,417 copies of the journals of Lewis and Clark were published for the first time.

In this letter to Paul Allen, who was helping to prepare the journals for publication, Jefferson provides a brief biography of Lewis. Its importance is that Jefferson was the first person to write Lewis's biography and to attempt to place Lewis's life and work within the context of the history of the United States. Jefferson places Lewis and his family among the greatest patriotic and founding families in America. Jefferson also explains in this letter each of the expeditions west that Jefferson had attempted and the failure of each.

Jefferson explains that with the purchase of Louisiana from France, Lewis and Clark were given specific instructions to explore the new territory. Their journey was not just a trip west, but an event that galvanized the nation. Lewis and Clark's expedition, according to Jefferson, was the first major American success story.

In the latter part of the letter, Jefferson then explains Lewis's death. Jefferson was not there, but he takes the time in this letter to explain the Lewis he knew, how Lewis was emotionally and physically, and how according to all reports Lewis died. Jefferson also recounts that life after the trip was not easy for him and that the bickering in his new position as governor had caused him some stress. The account of Lewis's death is a sum-mary of the letter Neely sent to him previously. Nowhere in this account does Jefferson even hint that Lewis's death is anything but a suicide. Jefferson is anxious, however, that Lewis would not be remembered for the way he died and instead for the life he lived. The publications of the journals would help achieve that.

Monticello. Aug. 18. 1813.

Sir

In compliance with the request conveyed in your letter of May 25. I have en-deavored to obtain, from the relations & friends of the late Governor Lewis, infor-mation of such incidents of his life as might be not unacceptable to those who may read the Narrative of his Western discoveries. the ordinary occurrences of a private life, and those also while acting in a subordinate sphere in the army, in a time of peace, are not deemed sufficiently interesting to occupy the public attention; but a general account of his parentage, with such smaller incidents as marked early character are briefly noted; and to these are added, as being peculiarly within my own knolege, whatever related to the public mission, of which an account is now to be published. the result of my enquiries & recollections, shall now be offered, to be enlarged or abridged as you may think best; or otherwise to be used with the materials you may have collected from other sources.

Meriwether Lewis, late Governor of Louisiana, was born on the 18th of Aug. 1774. near the town of Charlottesville, in the county of Albemarle, in Virginia, of one of the distinguished families of that state. John Lewis, one of his father's uncles, was a member of the king's council, before the revolution. another of them, Fielding Lewis, married a sister of Gen Washington. his father William Lewis, was the young-est of five sons of Col Robert Lewis of Albemarle, the fourth of whom, Charles, was one of the early patriots who stepped forward in the commencement of the revolu-tion, and commanded one of the regiments first raised in Virginia, and placed on Continental establishment. happily situated at home, with a wife and young family, and a fortune placing him at ease, he left all, to aid in the liberation of his country, from foreign usurpations, then first unmasking their ultimate end & aim. his good sense, integrity, bravery, enterprize and remarkable bodily powers, marked him as an officer of great promise. but he unfortunately died early in the revolution. Nicho-las Lewis, the second of his father's brothers, commanded a regiment of militia in the succesful expedition of 1776. against the Cherokee Indians; who, seduced by the agents of the British government, to take up the hatchet against us, had com-mitted great havoc on our Southern frontier, by murdering and scalping helpless women and children, according to their cruel and cowardly principles of warfare. the chastisement they then recieved closed the history of their wars, prepared them for recieving the elements of civilisation, which, zealously inculcated by the present government of the United States, have rendered them an industrious, peaceable and happy people. this member of the family of Lewises, whose bravery was so usefully proved on this occasion, was endeared to all who knew him by his inflexible probity, courteous disposition, benevolent heart, & engaging modesty & manners. he was the Umpire of all the private differences of his county, selected always by both parties. he was also the guardian of Meriwether Lewis, of whom we are now to speak, and who had lost his father at an early age. he continued some years under the fostering care of a tender mother, of the respectable family of Meriwethers of the same county; and was remarkable even in infancy for enterprise, boldness & discretion. when only eight years of age, he habitually went out, in the dead of night, alone with his dogs, into the forest to hunt the raccoon & opossum, which, seeking their food in the night, can then only be taken. in this exercise, no season or circumstance could obstruct his purpose, plunging thro' the winter's snows and frozen streams, in pursuit of his object. at thirteen he was put to the Latin school, and continued at that until eighteen, when he returned to his mother, and entered on the cares of his farm, having, as well as a younger brother, been left by his father with a competency for all the correct and comfortable purposes of temperate life. his talent for observation, which had led him to an accurate knoledge of the plants & animals of his own country, would have distinguished him as a farmer; but at the age of twenty, yielding to the ardor of youth, & a passion for more dazzling pursuits, he engaged as a volunteer in the body of militia which were called out by Gen Washington on occasion of the discontents produced by the Excise-taxes in the Western parts of the United States; and from that situation he was removed to the regular service as a lieutenant in the line. at twenty three he was promoted to a Captaincy; and, always attracting the first attention, where punctuality & fidelity were requisite, he was appointed paymaster to his regiment. about this time a circumstance occurred which, leading to the transaction which is the subject of this book, will justify a recurrence to it's original idea. while I resided in Paris, John Ledyard of Connecticut arrived there, well known in the United States for energy of body & mind. he had accompanied Capt Cook on his voyage to the Pacific ocean, and distinguished himself on that voyage by his intrepidity. being of a roaming disposition, he was now panting for some new enterprize. his immediate object at Paris was to engage a mercantile company in the fur-trade of the Western coast of America, in which however he failed. I then proposed to him to go by land to Kamschatka, cross in some of the Russian vessels to Nootka sound, fall down into the latitude of the Missouri, and penetrate to, and thro', that, to the United States. he eagerly siesed the idea, & only asked to be assured of the permission of the Russian government. I interested, in obtaining that, M. de Simoulin M.P. of the Empress at Paris, but more especially the Baron de Grimm, M.P. of Saxe-Gotha, her more special agent, & correspondent there, in matters not immediately diplomatic. her permission was obtained, & an assurance of protection, while the course of the voyage should be thro' her territories. Ledyard set out from Paris, & arrived at St Petersburg after the Empress had left that place, to pass the winter, I think, at Moscow. his finances not permitting him to make unnecessary stay at St Petersburg, he left it with a passport from one of the ministers; and, at 200. miles from Kamschatka, was obliged to take up his winter quarters. he was preparing, in the spring, to resume his journey, when he was arrested by an officer of the Empress, who by this time had changed her mind, and forbidden his proceeding. he was put into a closecarriage, & conveyed day & night, without ever stopping, till they reached Poland, where he was set down, &

left to himself. the fatigue of this journey broke down his constitution, and when he returned to Paris, his bodily strength was much impaired.31 his mind however remained firm, & he after this undertook the journey to Egypt. I recieved a letter from him, full of sanguine hopes, dated at Cairo, the 15th of Nov. 1788. the day before he was to set out for the head of the Nile, on which day however he ended his career and life. and thus failed the first attempt to explore the Western part of our Northern continent.

In 1792. I proposed to the American Philosophical Society that we should set on foot a subscription to engage some competent person to explore that region in the opposite direction, that is, by ascending the Missouri, crossing the Stony mountains, and descending the nearest river to the Pacific. Capt Lewis being then stationed at Charlottesville, on the recruiting service, warmly sollicited me to obtain for him the execution of that object. I told him it was proposed that the person engaged should be attended by a single companion only, to avoid exciting alarm among the Indians. this did not deter him. but mr André Michaux, a professed botanist, author of the *Flora Boreali-Americana*, and of the *Histoire des chesnes d'Amerique*, offering his services, they were accepted. he recieved his instructions, and when he had reached Kentucky in the prosecution of his journey, he was overtaken by an order from the Minister of France, then at Philadelphia, to relinquish the expedition, and to pursue elsewhere the Botanical enquiries on which he was employed by that government. and thus failed the 2d attempt for exploring that region.

In 1803. the act for establishing trading houses with the Indian tribes being about to expire, some modifications of it were recommended to Congress by a confidential message of Jan. 18. and an extension of it's views to the Indians on the Missouri. in order to prepare the way, the Message proposed the sending an exploring party to trace the Missouri to it's source, to cross the Highlands, and follow the best water-communication which offered itself from thence to the Pacific ocean. Congress approved the proposition, and voted a sum of money for carrying it into execution. Capt Lewis, who had then been near two years with me as private Secretary, immediately renewed his sollicitations to have the direction of the party. I had now had opportunities of knowing him intimately. of courage undaunted, possessing a firmness & perseverance of purpose which nothing but impossibilities could divert from it's direction, careful as a father of those committed to his charge, yet steady in the maintenance of order & discipline, intimate with the Indian character, customs & principles, habituated to the hunting life, guarded, by exact observation of the vegetables and animals of his own country, against losing time in the description of objects already possesd, honest, disinterested, liberal, of sound understanding, and a fidelity to truth so scrupulous that whatever he should report would be as certain as if seen by ourselves; with all these qualifications, as if selected & implanted by nature in one body, for this express purpose, I could have no hesitation in confiding the enterprize to him. to fill up the measure desired, he wanted nothing but a greater familiarity with the technical language of the natural sciences, and readiness in the Astronomical observations necessary for the geography of his route. to acquire these he repaired immediately to Philadelphia, and placed himself under the tutorage of the distinguished Professors of that place, who with a zeal & emulation, enkindled by an ardent devotion to science, communicated to him freely the information requisite for the purposes of the journey. while attending too, at Lancaster, the fabrication of the arms with which he chose that his men should be provided, he had the benefit of daily communication with mr Andrew Ellicot, whose experience in Astronomical observation, and practice of it in the woods, enabled him to apprise Capt Lewis of the wants & difficulties he would encounter, and of the substitutes & resources offered by a woodland and uninhabited country.

Deeming it necessary he should have some person with him, of known competence to the direction of the enterprise, in the event of accident to himself, he proposed William Clarke, brother of General George Rogers Clarke, who was approved, and, with that view recieved a commission of Captain.

In April 1803. a draught of his instructions was sent to Capt Lewis, and on the 20th of June they were signed in the following form.

While these things were going on here, the country of Louisiana, lately ceded by Spain to France, had been the subject of negociation at Paris between us and this last power; and had actually been transferred to us by treaties executed at Paris, on the 30th of April. this information, recieved about the 1st day of July, increased infinitely the interest we felt in the expedition, & lessened the apprehensions of interruption from other powers. every thing in this quarter being now prepared, Capt Lewis left Washington on the 5th of July 1803. and proceeded to Pittsburgh, where other articles had been ordered to be provided for him. the men too were to be selected from the military stations on the Ohio. delays of preparation, difficulties of navigation down the Ohio, & other untoward obstructions, retarded his arrival at Cahokia until the season was so far advanced as to render it prudent to suspend his entering the Missouri before the ice should break up in the succeeding spring.

From this time his journal, now published, will give the history of his journey to and from the Pacific ocean, until his return to St Louis on the 23d of Sep. 1806. never did a similar event excite more joy thro' the United States. the humblest of it's citizens had taken a lively interest in the issue of this journey, & looked forward with impatience for the information it would furnish—their anxieties too for the safety of the corps had been kept in a state of excitement by lugubrious rumors, circulated from time to time, on uncertain authorities, and uncontradicted by letters, or other direct information from the time they had left the Mandan towns, on their ascent up the river, in April of the preceding year 1805. until their actual return to St Louis.

It was the middle of Feb. 1807. before Capt Lewis, with his companion Clarke, reached the city of Washington, where Congress was then in session. that body granted to the two Chiefs and their followers the donation of lands which they had been encoraged to expect in reward of their toil & dangers. Capt Lewis was soon after appointed Governor of Louisiana, and Capt Clarke a General of it's militia, and Agent of the US. for Indian affairs in that department.

A considerable time intervened before the Governor's arrival at St Louis. he found the territory distracted by feuds & contentions among the officers of the government, & the people themselves divided by these into factions & parties. he determined at once to take no side with either; but to use every endeavor to conciliate and harmonise them. the even-handed justice he administered to all soon established a respect for his person & authority; and perseverance and time wore down animosities, & reunited the citizens again into one family.

Governor Lewis had, from early life, been subject to hypocondriac affections. it was a constitutional disposition in all the nearer branches of the family of his name, and was more immediately inherited by him from his father. they had not however been so strong as to give uneasiness to his family. while he lived with me in Washington, I observed at times sensible depressions of mind; but knowing their constitutional source, I estimated their course by what I had seen in the family. during his Western expedition the constant exertion, which that required, of all the faculties of body & mind, suspended these distressing affections; but after his establishment at St Louis in sedentary occupations, they returned upon him with redoubled vigor, & began seriously to alarm his friends. he was in a paroxysm of one of these, when his affairs rendered it necessary for him to go to Washington. he proceeded to the Chickasaw bluffs, where he arrived on the 16th of Sep. 1809. with a view of continuing his journey thence by water. mr Neely, agent of the US. with the Chickasaw Indians, arriving there two days after, found him extremely indisposed, and betraying, at times, some symptoms of a derangement of mind. the rumors of a war with England, & apprehensions that he might lose the papers he was bringing on, among which were the vouchers of his public accounts, & the journals & papers of his Western expedition, induced him here to change his mind, and to take his course by land thro' the Chickasaw country. altho' he appeared somewhat relieved, mr Neely kindly determined to accompany & watch over him. unfortunately, at their encampment, after having passed the Tennisee one day's journey, they lost two horses; which obliging mr Neely to halt for their recovery, the Governor proceeded, under a promise to wait for him at the house of the first white inhabitant on his road. he stopped at the house of a mr Grinder, who not being at home, his wife, alarmed at the symptoms of derangement she discovered, gave him up the house, & retired to rest herself in an outhouse, the Governor's and Neely's servants lodging in another. about three aclock in the night, he did the deed which plunged his friends into affliction, and deprived his country of one of her most valued citizens, whose valour and intelligence would have been now employed in avenging the wrongs of his country, and in emulating by land the splendid deeds which have honored her arms on the ocean. it lost too to the nation the benefit of recieving from his own hand the Narrative now offered them of his sufferings & successes, in endeavoring to extend for them the boundaries of science, and to present to their knolege that vast & fertile country, which their sons are destined to fill with arts, with science, with freedom & happiness.

To this melancholy close of the life of one, whom posterity will declare not to have lived in vain, I have only to add that all the facts I have stated are either known to myself, or communicated by his family or others, for whose truth I have no hesitation to make myself responsible; and I conclude with tendering you the assurances of my respect & consideration.

TH: JEFFERSON

Source: Harper's Encyclopaedia of United States History. Volume V. New York: Harper & Brothers Publishers, 1905, 361–369.

Further Reading

Danisi, Thomas C. and John Danisi. "Uncovering Jefferson's Account of Lewis's 18 Mysterious Death." *We Proceeded On* (November 2012).

Danisi, Thomas C. and Robert Moore. *Uncovering the Truth about Meriwether Lewis.* New York: Prometheus Book, 2001.

Harris, Matthew and Jay H. Buckley. *Zebulon Pike, Thomas Jefferson and the Opening of the American West.* University of Oklahoma Press, 2012.

Meacham, John. *Thomas Jefferson and the Art of Power.* Random House, 2013.

Peterson, Larry. *American Trinity: Jefferson, Custer and the Spirit of the West.* Sweetgrass Books, 2017.

Randall, William Sterne. *Thomas Jefferson: A Life.* Harper Classics, 2014.

Stroud, Patricia. *Bitterroot: The Life and Death of Meriwether Lewis.* Philadelphia: University of Pennsylvania Press, 2018.

Turner, Erin H. *It Happened on the Lewis and Clark Expedition.* Guilford, CT: Globe Pequot Press, 2003.

Document 112

LETTER FROM THOMAS JEFFERSON TO WILLIAM CLARK (SEPTEMBER 8, 1816)

Introduction: The Journals of Lewis and Clark

If Lewis's life after the expedition had been politically difficult and socially awkward, by contrast William Clark seemed to succeed in every aspect of his life. Promoted to lieutenant colonel, he was given two appointments immediately afterward: he was made brigadier general of the militia and superintendent of Indian affairs of the Territory of Upper Louisiana.

After Lewis's death, Clark was given control of all the papers and journals and had Nicholas Biddle edit and prepare them for publication. When they were published, the journals did not sell well, as the American love affair with their adventure was already over.

Even Thomas Jefferson, who had been pushing for the journals of Lewis and Clark to be published, was here asking for more to be done with the information they had gathered during the expedition. Jefferson reminds Clark that one of the more important aspects of the journey was that information about the West would be made available to a broad audience as quickly as possible. This collection and distribution of geographical and scientific data was one of the primary goals of the expedition. Jefferson asked José Corrêa da Serra (1750–1823), a philosopher and scientist, described in this letter as "my friend," to get the papers and to deliver them to the National Philosophical Society, but Corrêa da Serra was turned down by Nicholas Biddle, who said he needed Clark's permission to hand them over, so Jefferson is asking for the necessary permission.

Monticello Sep. 8. 16

Dear Sir

The travelling journal of Govr Lewis and yourself having been published some time ago, I had hoped to hear that something was doing with the astronomical observations, the Geographical chart, the Indian vocabularies, and other papers not comprehended in the journal published. with a view to have these given to the public according to the original intention, I got a friend to apply for them to mr Biddle, in whose hands I understood them to be, referring him for authority to the instructions inserted in the life of Govr Lewis prefixed to the journal. he said he could not deliver them even to the War-office, without an order from you. it is to sollicit this order that I now trouble you, and it may be given in favor either of the war office or of myself. if the latter, I should deliver the Astronomical observations to the Secretary at War, who would employ some one to make the calculations, to correct the longitudes of the map, and to have it published thus corrected; and I should deliver the papers of Natural history & the Vocabularies to the Philos. society at Philadelphia, who would have them properly edited, and I should deposit with them also for safekeeping the travelling pocket journals as originals to be recurred to on all interesting questions arising out of the published journal. I should recieve them only in trust for the War office to which they belong, and take their orders relating to them. I have recieved from DrBarton's exrs 4. vols of the travelling pocket journals, but I think there were 11. or 12. the rest I suppose mr Biddle has. I hope the part I have had in this important voyage, will excuse the interest I take in securing to the world all the beneficial results we were entitled to expect from it, and which would so fully justify the expences of the expedition incurred by the United states in that expedition. I salute you with constant friendship and respect.

Th: Jefferson

Source: Manuscript Division, Library of Congress.

Further Reading

Buckley, Jay H. *William Clark: Indian Diplomat.* University of Oklahoma Press, 2008.

Cerami, Charles. *Jefferson's Great Gamble: The Remarkable Story of Jefferson, Napoleon and the Men behind the Louisiana Purchase.* New York: Source Books, 2004.

Foley, William. *Wilderness Journey: The Life of William Clark.* University of Missouri, 2004.

Holmberg, James. *Dear Brother: Letters of William Clark to Jonathan Clark.* New Haven, CT: Yale University Press, 2002.

Jones, Landon. *William Clark and the Shaping of the West.* Bison Books, 2009.

Turner, Erin H. *It Happened on the Lewis and Clark Expedition.* Guilford, CT: Globe Pequot Press, 2003.

Unger, Harlow. *The Last Founding Father: James Monroe and a Nations Call to Greatness.* De Capo Press, reprint, 2010.

Document 113

LOUISIANA (1814)

Introduction: Death of Sacagawea

Without Sacagawea, there can be no doubt that the Lewis and Clark expedition would have failed. At the end of the expedition, she, Charbonneau, and Jean Baptiste stayed in the West, leaving the group at Fort Mandan. William Clark wanted to raise Jean Baptiste and encouraged Charbonneau and Sacagawea to try life as farmers in St Louis. In 1811, they moved to St. Louis but did not last long as farmers. Within two years, Charbonneau and Sacagawea returned to the West, leaving Jean Baptiste with Clark.

Sacagawea had been an important member of the Corps of Discovery. Her language skills and her local knowledge of the area around the Rocky Mountains saved the expedition. It was her brother who supplied horses that allowed them to cross the mountains, and he even provided them with a guide to help them. She was brave, physically strong, and emotionally tough, when she insisted that she get to see the Pacific Ocean as she had after all traveled like everyone else. She knew about edible plants and fed the group on occasion.

But her life had been tough: she had been kidnapped as a young girl and brought 600 miles from her home, where she became the wife of Touissant Charbonneau. Even when she reached her home with the Corps, there was no option for her to stay there. Clark wanted to adopt her son, Jean Baptiste, and though they had tried farming life in St. Louis, Charbonneau had decided to move back west, and her son was left with Clark. Sacaagawea had a daughter, Lizette, who was born in 1812, but she too was adopted by Clark. It is thought the Lizette died as an infant, as there are no surviving records about her.

In 1811, Henry Brackenridge (1748–1816), a journalist, met Sacagawea and Charbonneau at the Fort Manuel Lisa Trading Fort or, as it was earlier called, Fort Mandan in North Dakota. He noted that she was ill and really wanted to return to be with her family. Sacagawea died on December 20, 1812, a year after this sighting, probably of typhus, a highly contiguous disease spread by fleas. At the end of her life, Sacagawea wanted only to go home to be with her family.

On January 17, 2001, President Bill Clinton bestowed the title of honorary sergeant, regular army to Sacagawea, in recognition for her works, skills, and bravery in the Lewis and Clark expedition.

From Views of Louisiana

We had on board a Frenchman named Charbonet, with his wife, an Indian woman of the Snake nation, both of whom had accompanied Lewis and Clark to the Pacific, and were of great service. The woman, a good creature, of a mild and gentle disposition, greatly attached to the whites, whose manners and dress she tries to imitate, but she had become sickly, and longed to revisit her native country; her husband, also, who had spent many years amongst the Indians, was become weary of civilized life. So true it is, that the attachment to the savage state, or the state of nature, (with which the appellation it has commonly been dignified,) is much stronger that to that of civilization, with all its comforts, its refinements, and its security.

Source: Brackenridge, Henry Marie. *Views of Louisiana.* Pittsburgh: Printed and published by Cramer, Spear and Eichbaum, Franklin Head Office 1814, 212.

Further Reading

Blumberg, Rhoda. *The Incredible Journey of Lewis and Clark.* New York: Scholastic, 1993.

Buckley, Jay H. *William Clark: Indian Diplomat.* University of Oklahoma Press, 2008.

Fenn, Elizabeth. *Encounters at the Heart of the World: A History of the Mandan People.* Hill and Wang, 2015.

Gibbon, Guy. *The Sioux: The Dakota and Lakota Nations.* Wiley-Blackwell, 2002.

Nelson, W. Dale. *Interpreters with Lewis and Clark: The Story of Sacagawea and Toussaint Charbonneau.* University of North Texas Press, 2004.

Ostler, Jeffrey. *The Plains Sioux and US Colonialism from Lewis and Clark to Wounded Knee.* Cambridge University Press, 2004.

Ritter, Michael. *Jean Baptiste Charbonneau, Man of Two Worlds.* Create Space Publishing, 2004.

Document 114

THE DEATH OF YORK (1832)

Introduction: The Life of a Slave

The story of York is one of the most important on this trip. Life for York changed drastically when he returned to Virginia after the expedition was over. Clark demanded from him that he return to the life of a slave. While the other members of the expedition received 320 acres of land, York did not.

In the 1990s, a series of letters were discovered between William Clark and his brother, Jonathan. These letters contained for the first time some details of York's life after the expedition and also provided insights into William Clark's attitude toward slavery. Clark's treatment of York upon their return was cruel. In what can only be described as an act of sheer cruelty, Clark sold York's wife to another slave owner, and then refused to sell York to the same person. Clark instead hired York out to another slave owner for work that was known to be particularly harsh.

Finally, Clark seems to have relented and freed York, but not probably until at least 1815. By the time, Washington Irving (1783–1859), writer and diplomat, met with William Clark on his travels through the West. Irving claimed that Clark had told him that York had been freed, but was miserable in his freedom and wanted to return to Clark and to his life with him. As York was returning to Clark, York fell ill and died of cholera. Another, though less likely, story about York is that he returned to the West, where he had been with the expedition, lived with the Crow Nation, and died there.

York Freed and Died of Cholera

Gov. Clarke fine healthy robust man—tall—about fifty—perhaps more—his hair, originally light now grey—falling on his shoulders—frank intelligent—his son a cadet of W.P. now in the army—aide de camp to Gen(era)l Athinson.

Dinner—plentiful—good—hut rustic—fried chicken, bacon and grouse, roast beef, baked potatoes, tomatoes, excellent cakes, bread, butter, etc. etc.

Gov. C. gives much excellent information concerning Indians.

His slaves—set them free—one he placed at a ferry—another on a farm, giving him land, horses, etc.—a third he gave a large waggon and team of six horses to ply between Nashville and Richmond. They all repented and wanted to come back.

The waggoner was York, the hero of the Missouri expedition and adviser of the Indians. He could not get up early enough in the morn'g—his horses were ill kept—two died—the others grew poor. He sold them and was cheated—entered into service—fared ill. "Damn this freedom," said York, "I have never had a happy day since I got it." He determined to go back to his old master—set off for St. Louis, but was taken with the cholera in Tennessee and died. Some of the traders think they have met traces of York's crowd, on the Missouri.

Source: Trent, William P. and George S. Hellman, eds. *The Journals of Washington Irving.* Boston: Bibliophile Society, 1919.

Further Reading

Betts, Robert. *In Search Of York: The Slave Who Went to the Pacific with Lewis and Clark.* University Press of Colorado, 2002.

Blumberg, Rhoda. *The Incredible Journey of Lewis and Clark.* New York: Scholastic, 1993.

Buckley, Jay H. *William Clark: Indian Diplomat.* University of Oklahoma Press, 2008.

Foley, William. *Wilderness Journey: The Life of William Clark.* University of Missouri, 2004.

Holmberg, James. *Dear Brother: Letters of William Clark to Jonathan Clark.* New Haven, CT: Yale University Press, 2002.

Kastor, Peter. *William Clark's World: Describing American in an Age of Unknowns.* New Haven, CT: Yale University Press 2011.

Morris, Larry E. *The Fate of the Corps: What Became of the Lewis and Clark Explorers after the Expedition.* New Haven, CT: Yale University Press, 2005.

Nelson, W. Dale. *Interpreters with Lewis and Clark: The Story of Sacagawea and Toussaint Charbonneau.* University of North Texas Press, 2004.

Philips, Brad. York: *A Slaves' Journeys with Lewis and Clark.* Apricot Press, 2006.

Appendix

List of the Lewis and Clark Expedition Members

Group A

The following people (and dog) left Fort Mandan in April 1805 and arrived at the Pacific Ocean in November 1805. This group also returned to Fort Mandan the following year. At Fort Mandan, Toussaint Charbonneau, Sacagawea, Jean Baptiste, and John Colter left the group, to remain in the West. The remainder of the group went back to St. Louis.

- Capt. Meriwether Lewis (1774–1809)
- Capt. William Clark (1770–1838)
- Sgt. Patrick Gass (1771–1870)
- Sgt. John Ordway (c.1775–1817)
- Sgt. Nathaniel Hale Pryor (1772–1831)
- Cpl. Richard Warfington (1777–unknown)
- Pvt. John Boley (unknown)
- Pvt. William E. Bratton (1778–1841)
- Pvt. John Collins (unknown–1823)
- Pvt. John Colter (c. 1775–1812)
- Pvt. Pierre Cruzatte (unknown–1828)
- Pvt. John Dame (1784–unknown)
- Pvt. Joseph Field (1775–1823)
- Pvt. Robert Frazer (1775–1837)
- Pvt. George Gibson (c. 1781–1801)
- Pvt. Silas Goodrich (unknown–1825)
- Pvt. Hugh Hall (c. 1772–1828)
- Pvt. Thomas Proctor Howard (1779–1818)
- Pvt. Francois (William) Labiche (unknown–1828)
- Pvt. Jean Baptiste Lepage (unknown–1809)
- Pvt. Hugh McNeal (unknown–1828)
- Pvt. John Potts (1776–1808)

- Pvt. George Shannon (1785–1838)
- Pvt. John Shields (1769–1809)
- Pvt. John B. Thompson (unknown–1828)
- Pvt. Peter M. Weiser (1781–1828)
- Pvt. William Werner (unknown–1828)
- Pvt. Joseph Whitehouse (1775–unknown)
- Pvt. Alexander Hamilton Willard (1778–1865)
- Pvt. Richard Windsor (unknown–1829)

Nonmilitary Members

- Toussaint Charbonneau (1767–unknown)
- Sacagawea (c. 1786–1812)
- Jean Baptiste Charbonneau (1805–1866)
- Pierre Dorion (1782–1814)
- George Drouillard (1773–1810)
- York (1770–unknown)

Nonhuman Member

- Seaman (unknown)

Those Who Returned to St. Louis from Fort Mandan in April 1805

- Cpl. Richard Warfington (1777–unknown) led the group who returned to St. Louis. He was in charge of getting the keelboat back with journals, papers, animals, skins, and gifts, which were sent to Thomas Jefferson as well as family members.
- Pvt. Moses Reed (unknown) was expelled from Corps after being found guilty of desertion and so returned to St. Louis with Warfington.
- Pvt. John Newman (ca. 1785–1838) was found guilty of mutinous acts and was expelled. Newman seemed to have repented and tried to persuade Lewis to let him stay on. Lewis refused, as he thought it necessary to seem strong in imposing discipline. Newman was later given land and money for the time he spent in the Corps.
- Baptiste Dechamps (unknown) was a French Canadian boatman who had been recruited into the army as a private at Fort Kaskaskia, Illinois.

Those Who Returned to St. Louis in June 1804

White and probably Tuttle and Robertson were sent back to St. Louis with fur traders in June 1804. The reasons are not clear, but it is possible that it was related to behavior. At one stage, Robertson's rank is given as corporal, and later he is referred to as a private, so he was probably demoted for some reason.

- Pvt. Ebenezer Tuttle (1773–unknown)
- Pvt. John Robertson (c 1780–unknown)
- Pvt. Issac White (1785–1838)

One Person Died on August 20, 1804

Floyd's appendix seems to have burst while he was on the trip, and he died soon afterward.

- Sgt. Charles Floyd (1782–1809)

List of Native Nations Met by Lewis and Clark

- Alsea
- Amahami
- Arikara
- Assiniboine
- Bannock
- Blackfeet
- Cathlamet
- Cayuse
- Chehalis
- Cheyenne
- Chinook
- Clackamas
- Clatskanie
- Clatsop
- Cowlitz
- Crow
- Flathead
- Gros Ventre
- Hidatsa
- Kickapoo
- Klickitat
- Mandan
- Minitari
- Missouri
- Multnomah

- Nez Perce
- Omaha
- Otoe
- Palouse
- Pawnee
- Quinault
- Shoshone
- Siletz
- Siuslaw
- Skilloot
- Tenino
- Teton Sioux
- Tillamook
- Umatilla
- Umpqua
- Wahkiakum
- Walla Walla
- Wanapum
- Wasco
- Wishram
- Yakima
- Yankton Sioux

Bibliography

Aberbach, Alan David. *In Search of an American Identity: Samuel Latham Mitchell, Jeffersonian Nationalist.* New York: Peter Lang, 1988.

Allen, John Logan. *Passage through the Garden: Lewis and Clark and the Image of the American Northwest.* Urbana: University of Illinois Press, 1975.

Ambrose, Stephen. *Undaunted Courage.* Urbana: University of Chicago Press, 1991.

Aron, Stephen. *The American West: A Very Short Introduction.* Oxford: Oxford University Press, 2015.

Bachleda, Lynne F. *Guide to the Natchez Trace Parkway,* 2nd ed. Birmingham, AL: Menasha Ridge, 2011.

Bedini, Silvio. *Thomas Jefferson: Statesman of Science.* 1990. New York: Macmillan, 1990.

Bergon, Frank, ed. *The Journals of Lewis and Clark.* New York: Penguin Press, 1989.

Bernstein, R. B. *Thomas Jefferson.* Oxford: Oxford University Press, 2005.

Bernier, Oliver. *Lafayette: Hero of Two Worlds.* New York: Dutton Adult, 1993.

Betts, Robert. *In Search of York: The Slave Who Went to the Pacific with Lewis and Clark.* Denver: University of Colorado Press, 2002.

Blackhawk, Ned. *Violence over Land: Indians and Empires in the Early American West.* Cambridge, MA: Harvard University Press, 1998.

Blumberg, Rhoda. *The Incredible Journey of Lewis and Clark.* New York: Scholastic, 1993.

Bober, Natalie. *Thomas Jefferson: Draftsman of a Nation.* Charlottesville: University of Virginia Press, 2008.

Boss, Richard C. "Keelboat, Pirogue, and Canoe: Vessels Used by the Lewis and Clark Corps of Discovery." *Nautical Research Journal* 38, no. 2 (June 1993): 68–87.

Botkin, Daniel. *Our Natural History. The Lessons of Lewis and Clark.* Oxford University Press, 2004.

Brecher, Frank. *Negotiating the Louisiana Purchase: Robert Livingston's Mission to France, 1801–1804.* New York: McFarland and Company, 2006.

Brodhead, Micheal. "The Military Naturalist: A Lewis and Clark Heritage." *We Proceeded On* 9, no. 4 (November 1983): 6.

Brodie, Fawn M. *Thomas Jefferson: An Intimate History.* New York: W.W. Norton, 1974.

Brown, Dee. *The American West.* New York: Touchstone, 1995.

Buckley, Jay H. *William Clark: Indian Diplomat.* University of Oklahoma Press, 2008.

Burroughs, Raymond Darwin. *The Natural History of the Lewis and Clark Expedition.* East Lansing: Michigan State University Press, 1961.

Bursell, Susan. *The Lewis and Clark Expedition.* Nankato, MN: Capstone Press, 2002.

Calloway, Colin G. *One Vast Winter Count: The Native American West before Lewis and Clark.* Lincoln: University of Nebraska Press, 2003.

Carlson, Paul. *The Plains Indians.* Austin, TX: A & M University, 1998.

Cerami, Charles. *Jefferson's Great Gamble: The Remarkable Story of Jefferson, Napoleon and the Men behind the Louisiana Purchase.* New York: Source Books, 2004.

Chandler, David Leon. *The Jefferson Conspiracies: A President's Role in the Assassination of Meriwether Lewis*. New York: William Morrow, 1994.

Chernow, Ron. *Washington: A Life*. New York: Penguin Books, 2011.

Chuinard, Eldon G. "The Court-Martial of Ensign Meriwether Lewis." *We Proceeded On* 8, no.4 (November 1982): 12–15.

Chuinard, Eldon G. "How Did Meriwether Lewis Die? It Was Murder." *We Proceeded On* 18, nos. 1 and 2 (January and May 1992): 4.

Chuinard, Eldon G. "Lewis and Clark, Master Masons." *We Proceeded On* 15, no. 1 February 1989, 12.

Chuinard, Eldon G. *Only One Man Died: The Medical Aspects of the Lewis and Clark Expedition*. Glendale, CA: Arthur Clark Company, 1980.

Chuinard, Eldon G. "Thomas Jefferson and the Corps of Discovery: Could He Have Done More?" *American West* 12, no. 6 (1975): 4–13.

Clary, David. *Adopted Son: Washington, Lafayette and the Friendship That Saved the Revolution*. New York: Bantam, 2007.

Coates, Robert. *Outlaw Years: The History of the Land Pirates of the Natchez Trace*. Pelican Press, 2002.

Colter-Fick, L. Ruth. *Courageous Colter and Companions*. Washington, MO: Colter-Fick, 1997.

Colter-Fick, L. Ruth. "Meriwether Lewis's Personal Finances." *We Proceeded On* 28, no.1 (February 2002): 16–20.

Criswell, Elijah. *Lewis and Clark: Linguistic Pioneers*. Columbia: University of Missouri Press, 1940.

Cutright, Paul Russell. "Contributions of Philadelphia to Lewis and Clark History." *We Proceeded On,* special issue, July 1982.

Cutright, Paul Russell. "I Gave Him Barks and Saltpeter." *American Heritage: The Magazine of History* 15 (December 1963): 58–61, 94–101.

Cutright, Paul Russell. "The Journal of Captain Meriwether Lewis: Some Observations Concerning the Journal Hiatuses of Captain Lewis." *We Proceeded On* 10, no. 1 (February 1984): 8.

Cutright, Paul Russell. *Lewis and Clark: Pioneering Naturalists*. Urbana: University of Illinois Press, 1969 (reprinted by University of Nebraska, 1989).

Cutright, Paul Russell. "Meriwether Lewis's 'Coloring of Events.'" *We Proceeded On* 11, no. 1 (February 1985): 10.

Dangerfield, George. *Chancellor Robert R. Livingston of New York, 1746–1813*. New York: Harcourt Brace and Company, 1960.

Daniels, Jonathan. *Devil's Backbone: The Story of the Natchez Trace*. New York: Pelican Press, 1985.

Danisli, Thomas. *Meriwether Lewis*. New York: Prometheus Books, 2009.

Danisi, Thomas C. and John C. Jackson. "Homeward Bound." *We Proceeded On* 33, no. 2 (May 2007): 16–19.

Danisi, Thomas C., and Robert Moore. *Uncovering the Truth about Meriwether Lewis*. New York: Prometheus Book, 2001.

Dillon, Richard. *Meriwether Lewis: A Biography*. New York: Coward-McCann, 1965.

Dowd, Gregory Evans. *A Spirited Resistance: The North American Indian Struggle for Unity, 1745–1815*. Baltimore, MD: Johns Hopkins University Press, 1992.

Duffi, Jacalyn. *History of Medicine: A Scandalously Short Introduction*. University of Toronto Press, 1999.

Duffy, John. *Epidemics in Colonial America*. Louisiana State University, 1971.

Dunbar-Ortiz, Roxanne. *An Indigenous Peoples' History of the United States*. Beacon Press, reprint, 2015.

Duncan, Dayton, and Ken Burns. *Lewis and Clark: The Journey of the Corps of Discovery: An Illustrated History*. New York: Alfred A. Knopf, 1997.

Ellis, Joseph. *American Sphinx: The Character of Thomas Jefferson*. New York: Vintage Books, 1998.

Ellis, Joseph. *Founding Brothers: The Revolutionary Generation*. New York: Vintage Books, 2002.

Ellis, Joseph. *The Quartet: Orchestrating the Second American Revolution, 1783–1789*. New York: Vintage Reprint, 2016.

Feldman, Noah. *The Three Lives of James Madison: Genius, Partisan, President*. New York: Random House, 2017.

Fenn, Elizabeth. *Encounters at the Heart of the World: A History of the Mandan People*. Hill and Wang, reprint, 2015.

Fenster, Julie. *Jefferson's America: The President, the Purchase, and the Explorers Who Transformed a Nation*. New York: Crown, 2016.

Fisher, John W. *Medical Appendices of the Lewis and Clark Expedition*. Juliaetta, ID: Fisher, 2006.

Fisher, Vardis. *Suicide or Murder? The Strange Death of Governor Meriwether Lewis*. Chicago, IL: Swallow Press, 1962.

Foley, William. *The Genesis of Missouri: From Outpost to Statehood*. University of Missouri, 1989.

Gaines, James. *For Liberty and Glory: Washington, Lafayette, and Their Revolutions*. New York: Norton, 2007.

Gass, Patrick. *A Journal of the Voyages and Travels of a Corps of Discovery under the Command of Capt. Lewis and Capt. Clark*. Minneapolis, MN: Ross and Haines, 1958.

Gibbon, Guy. *The Sioux: The Dakota and Lakota Nations*. New York: Wiley-Blackwell, 2002.

Gifford, Bill. *In Search of the First American Explorer*. New York: Harcourt, 2007.

Gilman, Carol. *Lewis and Clark; Across the Divide*. Washington DC: Smithsonian Books, 2003.

Gray, Edward. *The Making of John Ledyard: Empire and Ambition in the Life of an Early American Traveler*. New Haven, CT: Yale University Press, 2017.

Guice, John D. W., and Jay H. Buckley. *By His Own Hand: The Mysterious Death of Meriwether Lewis*. University of Oklahoma Press, 2006.

Gutzman, Kevin. *Thomas Jefferson—Revolutionary: A Radical's Struggle to Remake America*. New York: St Martin's Press, 2017.

Harris, Matthew, and Jay H. Buckley, eds. *Zebulon Pike, Thomas Jefferson and the Opening of the American West*. Norman: University of Oklahoma Press, 2012.

Harrison, Lowell. *George Roger Clark and the War in the West*. Lexington: University of Kentucky Press, 2001.

Hine, Robert V., and John Mack Faragher. *The American West: A New Interpretive History*. New Haven, CT: Yale University Press, 2000.

Holbrook, Sabra. *Lafayette: Man in the Middle*. New York: Atheneum Books, 1977.

Holloway, David. *Lewis and Clark and the Crossing of North America*. New York: Saturday Review Press, 1974.

Holmberg, James. *Dear Brother: Letters of William Clark to Jonathan Clark*. New Haven, CT: Yale University Press, 2002.

Husner, Verne. *On the River with Lewis and Clark*. Austin, TX: A & M Press, 2004.

Issacson, Walter. *Benjamin Franklin: An American Life*. New York: Simon and Schuster, 2004.

Jenkinson, Clay. *The Character of Meriwether Lewis: Explorer in the Wilderness*. Washburn: Dakota Institute Press, 2010.

Jones, Landon Y., ed. *The Essential Lewis and Clark*. New York: HarperCollins, 2002.

Jones, Landon Y. *William Clark and the Shaping of the West*. New York: Hill and Wang, 2004.

Josephy, Alvin M. *Lewis and Clark through Indian Eyes: None Indian Writers on the Legacy of the Expedition*. New York: Vintage Press, 2007.

Kramer, Lloyd. *Lafayette in Two Worlds: Public Cultures and Personal Identities in an Age of Revolution*. Chapel Hill: North Carolina Press, 1996.

Kukla, Jon. *A Wilderness So Immense: The Louisiana Purchase and the Destiny of America*. Anchor Books, 2004.

Leepson, Marc. *Lafayette: Lessons in Leadership from an Idealist General*. New York: St. Martin's Press, 2011.

Lentz, Gary. "Meriwether Lewis's Medicine Chests." *We Proceeded On* 26, no. 2 (May 2000): 10–17.

Marshall, Thomas Maitland. *The Life and Papers of Frederick Bates*. 2 vols. St. Louis: Missouri Historical Society, 1926.

Meacham, John. *Thomas Jefferson: The Art of Power*. New York: Random House, 2013.

Merrell, James H. *Into the American Woods: Negotiators on the Pennsylvania Frontier*. New York : W.W. Norton, 1999.

Morris, Larry E. *The Fate of the Corps: What Became of the Lewis and Clark Explorers after the Expedition*. New Haven, CT: Yale University Press, 2005.

Nelson, W. Dale. *Interpreters with Lewis and Clark: The Story of Sacagawea and Toussaint Charbonneau*. University of North Texas Press, 2004.

Nester, William. *George Clark: I Glory in War*. University of Oklahoma Press, 2012.

Ostler, Jeffrey. *The Plains Sioux and U.S. Colonialism from Lewis and Clark to Wounded Knee*. Cambridge: Cambridge University Press, 2004.

Peck, David J. "The Death of Meriwether Lewis." *We Proceeded On* 35, no. 4 (November 2009): 16–25.

Peck, David J. *Or Perish in the Attempt: Wilderness Medicine in the Lewis & Clark Expedition*. Helena, MT: Farcountry Press, 2002.

Peterson, Larry. *American Trinity: Jefferson, Custer and the Spirit of the West*. Sweetgrass Books, 2017.

Peterson, Merrill. *Thomas Jefferson and the New Nation: A Biography*. Oxford: Oxford University Press, 2013.

Randall, William Sterne. *Thomas Jefferson: A Life*. Harper Classics, 2014.

Ray, Verne F. "Lewis and Clark and the Nez Perce Indians." *The Great Western Series*. No. 10. Washington, DC: Westerners.

Rhodehamel, John. *George Washington: The Wonder of the Age*. New Haven, CT: Yale University Press, 2017.

Richter, Daniel K. *Facing East from Indian Country: A Native History of Early America*. Cambridge, MA: Harvard University Press, 2001.

Ritter, Michael. *Jean Baptiste Charbonneau, Man of Two Worlds*. New York: Create Space Publishing, 2004.

Rogers, Ann. *Lewis and Clark in Missouri*. Columbia: University of Missouri, 2002.

Ronda, James P. *Lewis and Clark among the Indians*. Lincoln: University of Nebraska Press, 1984.

Russel, Carl. "The Guns of the Lewis and Clark Expedition." *North Dakota History* 27 (Winter 1960): 25–34.

Rutkow, Ira M. *Bleeding Blue and Gray: Civil War Surgery and the Evolution of Medicine*. New York: Random House, 2005.

Saunt, Claudio. A New Order of Things: Property, Power, and the Transformation of the Creek Indians, 1773–1816. Cambridge University Press, 1999.

Savage, Henry, and Elizabeth Savage. *Andre and Francois Michaux*. Charlottesville: University of Virginia Press, 1996.

Slaughter, Thomas P. *Exploring Lewis and Clark: Reflections on Men and Wilderness*. New York: Vintage Press, 2004.

Smith, Ronald. *The Captain's Dog*. New York: HMH Books, 2008.

Stark, Peter. *Young Washington: How Wilderness and War Forged America's Founding Father*. New York: Ecco Press, 2018.

Stroud, Patricia. *Bitterroot: The Life and Death of Meriwether Lewis*. Philadelphia: University of Pennsylvania Press 2018.

Thwaites, Reuben Gold, ed. *Original Journals of the Lewis and Clark Expedition*. New York: Arno Press, reprint, 1969.

Turner, Erin H. *It Happened on the Lewis and Clark Expedition*. Guilford, CT: Globe Pequot Press, 2003.

Unger, Harlow. *Lafette,* Hoboken: Wiley, 2003.

Unger, Harlow. *The Last Founding Father: James Monroe and a Nations Call to Greatness*. De Capo Press, reprint, 2010.

Wernsdorfer, Walther H., and Ian McGregor. *Malaria: Principles and Practice of Malariology*. 2 vols. New York: Churchill Livingstone, 1988.

West, Elliot. *The Last Indian War: The Nez Perce Story*. Oxford: Oxford University Press, 2011.

Wills, Gary. *James Madison*. New York: Henry Holt, 2002.

Zingman, Barry S., and Brant L, Viner. "Splenic Complications in Malaria: Case Report and Review." *Clinical Infectious Diseases* 16 (February 1993): 223–231.

Zug, James. *American Traveler: The Life and Adventures of John Ledyard, The Man Who Dreamed of Walking the World*. New York: Basic Books, 2004.

Index

About the Author

C. Bríd Nicholson is associate professor of history at Kean University, in Union, New Jersey. She is author of *Emma Goldman: Still Dangerous* and has edited *Conflicts in the Early American Republic*. A recipient of the Presidential Excellence Award for Distinguished Scholarship at Kean in 2010, she was inducted into the Kean Chapter of Phi Kappa Phi; in 2011, she was appointed a fellow of the Kean University Center for History, Politics and Policy. She has also produced a number of historical documentaries, including *The Black Eagle of Harlem* and *George Washington: The Farewell Address*.